BOYS WILL BE BOYS

Boys Will Be Boys

Breaking the Link between Masculinity and Violence

MYRIAM MIEDZIAN

Lantern Books • New York
A Division of Booklight Inc

2002

Lantern Books

One Union Square West, Suite 201

New York, NY 10003

Printed in the United States of America

Permission to quote from their song lyrics was given by the following music publishers:

"GANGSTA GANGSTA" (Dr. Dre/Ice Cube/M.C. Ren/Eazy-E) © 1988, Ruthless Attack Muzick (ASCAP).

"Violent Love" by Ted Nugent. Madhouse Management for Magicland Music.

"Suicide's an Alternative/You'll Be Sorry" by Suicidal Tendencies, Bug Music Inc.

"Freedom of Speech" by Ice T, permission granted by E. R. Greenspan.

In Memory of Golda, Balche, Jakob, Julius, Lazer, Moishe, Rifke, and All My Other Aunts, Uncles, and Cousins Killed in Their Prime and in Childhood, Victims of the Holocaust, One of the Endless Waves of Senseless Violence which Have Sullied Human History

For my husband Gary,
and my daughters Nadia and Alisa

Acknowledgments

I am grateful to the teachers (and in some cases liaison teachers) who let me sit in on their classes: at the Germantown Friends Lower School, John B. Kelly Elementary School, and Clarence E. Pickett Middle School in Philadelphia; at P.S. 261 and the Brooklyn Friends School in Brooklyn; at the High School for the Humanities and West Side High School in Manhattan; at Roxbury High School in Succasunna, New Jersey; and at Whitman High School in Bethesda, Maryland. Administrators, principals, and students at these schools were often helpful as well. I appreciate being permitted to examine textbooks at the New York City Board of Education's Social Studies Library.

A number of people, many of whom I have never met—some of them friends of friends, others complete strangers—helped in a variety of ways. I want to thank Kathy Agnon, Jay Coakley, Rody Colon, Gerald Ente, Julie Gilligan, James Levine, Peter Mathiessen, Wilfredo Medina, Don Ross, Steve Sternberg, and the staff at the National Coalition on Television Violence.

I have spent close to four years researching and writing this book. During this time, my husband Gary Ferdman's unbounded enthusiasm and encouragement have sustained me. I can never thank him enough. He has read and commented on numerous drafts of each chapter. His comments, criticisms, and insights have immeasurably improved the text.

My daughters Nadia and Alisa have helped simply by being there. Besides this, their critical comments have led me to make several important changes in the text. I also want to thank them for enduring four years of dinner conversations focused heavily on violence, violence, and more violence.

Right from our first phone conversation, Eric Ashworth, who became my literary agent, fully understood the book and was enthusiastic about it. His suggestions have considerably improved parts of the text. My editor Paul Bresnick's comments have led to a much more focused and readable book. His assistant Mark Garofalo has also been very helpful.

The vast amount of library research required in preparing the book was greatly facilitated by research assistants who found books and articles, photocopied them, and sometimes screened material to assess its relevance to my work. Foremost among them is Cynthia Wiest, who in spite of her graduate work in psychology and her involvement in the world of theater still managed to help me for over two years. While I never found anyone to replace Cynthia fully, my daughter Nadia Malinovich assisted me during her vacations from college. My daughter Alisa Malinovich, David Bosser, Kimberly Reynolds, Jean Heller, and Sandy Levinson helped out for short periods of time.

Friends, relatives, and acquaintances have helped in a variety of ways. Some kept a stream of relevant newspaper and magazine articles coming my way; some sent articles from professional journals in their fields; some directed me toward or put me in touch with professionals and experts who helped me; some shared relevant personal experiences and knowledge. One came up with the title for Chapter 4. Thank you to Jason Ablin, Susan Anderson, Eliane Baumfelder, Devri Byrom, Paula Crandall, Mae Ferdman, Josh Fierer, Allen Fisher, Suzanne Goldberg, Elena Lesser, Sharon Josepho, Mike McCally, Betty Mego, Joe Mego, Mike Oppenheimer, Jean Orsinger, Odette Orsinger, Alex Papachristou, Diane Shainberg, Bill Solomon, Marty Spindel, Ned Schnurman, Ariana Speyer, and Barbara Warch.

I am indebted to Forrester Church, Suzanne Goldberg, Debbie Mego, and Phyllis La Farge, who read and commented on one or more chapters. Special thanks go to Bob Holt, Joan Holt, Bobbie Josepho, and Bea Mego, who read and commented on the entire manuscript. I am especially fortunate in counting among my friends an eminent clinical psychologist and Freud scholar such as Bob Holt. His reading and rereading of the section on psychoanalysis in Chapter 3 led to major changes which have greatly improved the text. I alone am of course responsible for the final product.

Now that the book is completed, my attention has shifted to working for the implementation of its recommendations. I am very grateful to the Ploughshares Foundation for a generous grant intended to help me in this endeavor.

Interviews

The material covered in this book encompasses the fields of psychology, sociology, anthropology, political science, endocrinology, sociobiology, communications, First Amendment law, and public administration. It would have been impossible to cover such a broad terrain without the help of experts within each of these disciplines. In the course of my research I interviewed over 130 people, many of them among the most respected in their fields. I am deeply indebted to those listed below who so generously shared their expertise with me, often referring me to others in their field or guiding me toward further relevant library research. I also want to thank those who shared pertinent life experiences with me. Their stories have deeply enriched the text.

So many people have helped over such an extended period of time that I must apologize in advance to anyone I may have inadvertently forgotten.

CHAPTER 1 David Rothenberg, writer, founder and former director of the Fortune Society

CHAPTER 2   Carol Cohn, research fellow, Center for Psychological Studies in the Nuclear Age; William Colby, former CIA director; Norman Cousins, UCLA School of Medicine; author, editor; James Driscoll, Vietnam War veteran; David Evans, Marine lieutenant colonel (retired); military correspondent, *Chicago Tribune*; John (Randy) Floyd, Vietnam War veteran; Steven Kull, Social Science Research Council MacArthur Fellow, Department of Political Science, Stanford University; Admiral Gene LaRoque, director, Center for Defense Information; Vice-Admiral John Lee (retired); Barbara Levin, Center for Defense Information; Robert McNamara, former Secretary of Defense; Robert L. Rothstein, professor of political science, Colgate University; Robert C. Tucker, professor emeritus of political science, Princeton University; Paul Warnke, former Assistant Secretary of Defense for International Security Affairs and Salt II negotiator; Tom Wicker, *New York Times* columnist

CHAPTERS 3–5   Sandra Bem, professor of psychology, Cornell University; Dr. Phyllis Berman, National Institute of Child Health and Human Development, National Institutes of Health; Dr. Arthur Caplan, director, Biomedical Ethics Center, University of Minnesota; Dr. Stanley Deutsch, attending biochemist, Long Island Jewish Hospital; Marion Diamond, professor, Department of Integrated Biology, University of California at Berkeley; Anke Ehrhardt, professor of psychiatry, College of Physicians and Surgeons, Columbia University; Carol Ember, professor of anthropology, Hunter College, CUNY; Anne Fausto-Sterling, professor of biology, Brown University Medical School; Seymour Feshbach, professor of psychology, UCLA; Dr. David Finkelhor, director, Family Research Laboratory, University of New Hampshire; Dr. Arnold Goldstein, director, Center for Research on Aggression, Syracuse University; Megan Gunnar, professor, Institute of Child Development, University of

Minnesota; Martin Hoffman, professor of psychology, New York University; Robert R. Holt, professor emeritus of clinical psychology, New York University; Dr. James Kavanagh, associate director, Center for Research for Mothers and Children, National Institute of Child Health and Human Development, NIH; coeditor, *Learning Disabilities: Proceedings of the National Conference;* Eleanor Maccoby, professor emeritus of psychology, Stanford University; Judith Martin, professor of social work, University of Pittsburgh; "Mrs. Maxell" (fictitious name), mother of boy suffering from ADDH; Dr. Gerald Obermeyer, Peabody Museum, Harvard University; Joseph Pleck, professor of sociology, Wheaton College; Dr. Wendy Stone, J. F. Kennedy Center for Research in Education and Human Development, Vanderbilt University

CHAPTERS 6–9 Peter Abeles, social studies teacher, Roxbury High School, Succasunna, NJ; Charles Blank, teacher, Friends School, New York, NY; Marie Bronshvag, teacher, West Side High School, New York, NY; Abigail Canfield, Baby Care Program, Collegiate Preparatory School, New York, NY; Joan Chipman, teacher, Warwick Junior High School, Warwick, RI; Ann Cook, codirector, Urban Academy, New York, NY; Chuck Fowler, teacher, West Side High School, New York, NY; Lawrence Gibson, director of social studies and teacher, the Brooklyn Friends School, Brooklyn, NY; Leon Hellerman, teacher, Hewlett School, Long Island; Lou Howort, hygiene and physical education teacher, High School of the Humanities, New York, NY; coauthor, Teaching Child-rearing curriculum; Moorehead Kennedy, Executive Director, Moorehead Kennedy Institute, The American Forum for Global Education; Sally Kennedy, Education for Parenting, Philadelphia, PA; Margaret Kind, M.D., Metropolitan Hospital, New York, NY; coauthor, Teaching Child-rearing curriculum; Phyllis La Farge, author, editor; Linda Lantieri, New

York City Board of Education; cofounder, Resolving Conflict Creatively Program; Colman McCarthy, columnist, the *Washington Post*, teacher; Robert Magnuson, social studies teacher, Roxbury High School, Succasunna, NJ; Sandra Meyers, Education for Parenting, Philadelphia, PA: Linda Nathan, teacher, Fenway Program, Boston English High School, Boston, MA; Virginia Ordway, teacher, South Boston High School, Boston, MA; Adrian Plavin, teacher, the Bronx High School of Science, Bronx, NY; Edward Reynolds, principal, West Side High School, New York, NY; Nancy Rizzo, teacher, Roxbury High School, Succasunna, NJ; Tom Roderick, executive president, Educators for Social Responsibility; cofounder, Resolving Conflict Creatively Program; Sister Elizabeth Saaro, teacher, Good Council Academy, White Plains, NY; Sally Scattergood, founder and former director, Education for Parenting, Philadelphia, PA; Alan Shapiro, Educators for Social Responsibility, U.S.-Soviet Education Collaboration Project; Mark Skvirsky, director, the Facing History and Ourselves National Foundation, Brookline, MA; Jeffrey Solomon, member, City Kids Foundation, New York, NY; Jerold M. Starr, professor of sociology, West Virginia University, creator and contributor, the Lessons of the Vietnam War curriculum; Sheila Sussman, Parenting Education Project, Roosevelt and Freeport, NY; Gene Thompson, codirector, Educators for Social Responsibility; Sarah West, teacher, Germantown Friends Lower School, Philadelphia, PA; Dr. Burton L. White, director, Center for Parent Education, Newton, MA; Gregory Whyte, physical education teacher, Evander Childs High School, Bronx, NY; Christopher W. Wilkens, social studies teacher, Roxbury High School, Succasunna, NJ; Les Willis, director, Teen Father/Young Family Program, Medical College of Pennsylvania

CHAPTER 11 David Blankenhorn, director, Institute for American

Values; Jeffrey Goldstein, professor of sociology, Temple University; Richard Lapchick, director, Center for the Study of Sport in Society, Northeastern University; Keith Lee, former Patriots football player, now associate director, Center for the Study of Sport in Society, Northeastern University; Robert Lipsyte, sportswriter, TV host; Dr. Wilbert McClure, former boxer and former associate director, Center for the Study of Sport in Society, Northeastern University; Dave Meggyesy, former Cardinals football player, now Western Director, National Football League Players Association; Michael Messner, professor of sociology, University of Southern California; Todd Otis, Minnesota State Senator; Allen Sack, former Notre Dame football player, now professor of sociology, University of New Haven; Jeffrey T. Sammons, professor of history, New York University; Vernal Seefeldt, professor, Department of Education, Michigan State University; Michael D. Smith, professor of sociology, York University; Manny Toonkel, former athletic director, Brooklyn Friends School, Brooklyn, NY

CHAPTERS 12–16 Leonard Berkowitz, professor of psychology, University of Wisconsin-Madison; Mary McInnis Boies, attorney, formerly with the Federal Aviation Administration; Peggy Charren, founder and president of Action for Children's Television (ACT); Ronald Collins, visiting professor of law, Catholic University; George Comstock, professor of public communication, Syracuse University; Joan De Neu, executive secretary, Canadians Concerned About Violence in Entertainment; Diane Ensko, director, Buckle My Shoe nursery school, New York, NY; Leonard D. Eron, professor of psychology, University of Illinois-Chicago Circle; Mark Franklin, professor, Stanford University Law School; Rick Gaumer, War Resisters League, Norwich, CT; George Gerbner, dean, Annenberg School of Communication, University of Pennsylvania; Philip J. Harter, attorney, formerly served on Administrative Conference of United States; David H. Horowitz, attorney, former president and chief executive officer of MTV Networks Inc.; Nicholas Johnson, former FCC commissioner; Evelyn Kaye, writer, former president of Action for Children's Television; Captain Joseph La Chance, Greenfield, MA, Police Department; Diane Levin, professor of education, Wheelock College; Catherine MacKinnon, professor, Osgood Hall Law School, York University; Leonard Marks, entertainment attorney; Jennifer Norwood, executive director, Parents Music Resource Center; Rev. Everett Parker, former head of the United Church of Christ's Communication Office; Monroe Price, dean, Cardozo Law School, Yeshiva University; Thomas Radecki, M.D., founder and director, National Coalition on Television Violence (NCTV); John Richard, attorney, Center for the Study of Responsive Law, Washington, D.C.; Alan Rosenbloom, professor of public administration, Syracuse University; Jay Schafritz, professor of public administration, University of Pittsburgh; Jerome L. Singer, professor of psychology, Yale University; Harvey Solomon, cable TV consultant, writer; Arthur Taylor, former president, CBS; Fred Thayer, professor of public administration, University of Pittsburgh, Charles Turner, professor of psychology, University of Utah, Ellen Wartella, professor, Institute of Communications search, University of Illinois-Urbana

CONCLUSION   Robert B. Costello, former Undersecretary of Defense for Acquisitions, Pentagon; Janet and Jakob Gneitung, the Hutterian Brethren; Juliana Winter and Ian Winter (school principal), the Hutterian Brethren; Benjamin Zablocki, professor of sociology, Rutgers University

Contents

II. School Programs That Work

III. Our Children: Commercial Market or Precious National Resource?

CONCLUSION: BEYOND THE MASCULINE MYSTIQUE

Preface

It can be helpful in understanding a book to be aware of the personal perspective that the author brings to it. When I first embarked on this project I gave little thought to how my personal history might have contributed to my interest in the topic of what caused many men to embrace violence—in warfare, in criminal acts, in the family—and how that behavior could be changed. It was only after several people responded to the topic by wondering whether it had grown out of my personal experience—had I been battered, assaulted, raped?—that I started to reflect on the question. I found myself remembering a letter that my father—who was born in Poland in 1901—had written to my older daughter when she was three months old:

Los Angeles, July 12, 1968

My Dear Nadia,

I hope that this letter will find you in good health. Dear Nadia I miss you very much, when you left our house every room was empty . . . I was dreaming of you. Maybe in a short time I will see you . . . I hope that peace will be in this crazy world. All my life I have seen only wars: 1905 even I was a child it was

Russian Japanese war; 1911–12 Balkan war; 1914–18 World War One; 1919–20 Polish Russian war; 1939–45 World War Two; 1950–53 Korean war, and the Vietnam war, and a few smaller wars. 1 hope when you will grow up you will not have terrible times like those your Pépé [French term for "grandpa"] went through and I wish you lots of happiness.

With great love, your
Pépé

As I reread this letter I realized that long before my daughter was born, my father had conveyed to me a deep sense of the insanity, the absurdity, the cruelty of people killing each other because of racial or religious hatred, or over economic or political issues that a few years later are forgotten. My father conveyed verbally and emotionally what I must have experienced as a child but could not integrate or conceptualize. For at the age of three I was suddenly wrenched from my quiet, comfortable home in Brussels, where my father had settled in 1929. When the Germans invaded in 1940 we fled. "I want my bed," I cried all the way through France, Spain, and Morocco, as we ran from bombs, slept in school yards and rat-infested cheap hotels, and sweltered in the 110-degree heat of southern Morocco. After fifteen months as refugees we arrived in the United States. Perhaps even more importantly, my father provided a role model that had nothing to do with toughness, dominance, emotional detachment, callousness toward women, or eagerness to seek out danger and to fight. To him these qualities, which make up the core of what I call the masculine mystique, evoked images of Cossacks ransacking his family's home in Poland, stealing their food and valuables, leaving them penniless and starving. They evoked fears of his mother and sisters being raped. To my father "macho" meant Nazis in lacquered boots dragging his brothers and sisters and their young children to their deaths in concentration camps. At the age of eighty my father sat down and made a list of the relatives he had lost during the Second World War. The final count was 135.

And so when people asked me if my interest in this topic grew out of my personal experience, I began to realize that it did, but not in the way that they had in mind.

True, I had experienced male violence firsthand in the form of war. But on a personal level, in terms of those values, attitudes, and role models which we learn as children and which mold our psyche on the deepest level, masculinity to me had nothing to do with violence, toughness, or emotional detachment. I became intensely aware of and troubled by a male archetype that led so many men down a path of violence not because I had experienced violence in my private life, but rather because I had not. Because I had grown up with a father—and an older brother—who neither fit the macho mold nor valued it, I never took for granted that masculinity was embodied in that archetype. I knew that there was a world of difference between the very positive traits of initiative, independence, curiosity, courage, and abstract thinking, which have traditionally been connected with masculinity, and the mindless aberrations that make up the masculine mystique.

Because of the male role models I experienced as a child, as an adult I sought out men who did not conform to the masculine mystique. Not that I sought them out consciously. But, after hearing other women talk about being battered, assaulted, or raped by boyfriends or husbands, it occurred to me that it was no accident that I had never had any of these experiences and could not share the deep personal rage that some women feel against men.

From my experience I know that there are many gentle, sensitive, caring men in this world, and they are not "wimps" as popular prejudice would have it. Their sensitivity is often joined with unusual courage, curiosity, sense of adventure, and independence from societal pressures. I think of one man who enjoyed parachute jumping but would agonize over killing a cockroach. I think of another who left a lucrative position heading a business to become a high school teacher; he wanted less pressure, more time for himself and his family; he wanted to do more meaningful work. I think of a man who gave up a high-paying, secure job to work full-time for nuclear disarmament at a fraction of his previous salary. These are the kinds of men I know, admire, and find attractive. Because I have never identified masculinity with the characteristics embodied in the masculine mystique, because I have known so many men who have rejected it, I think I have been able to see that there is nothing intrinsically manly or sexually attractive about these characteristics. I have been able to see that men do not have to be the victims of dysfunctional, destructive, atavistic male archetypes.

In the past young men were the primary victims of these archetypes. The values of the masculine mystique were designed to make them good soldiers ready to sacrifice their lives at the altar of their leaders' power and prestige. But technology has changed this. Increasingly in the twentieth century, it is civilians who are the casualties. Today close to sixty thousand nuclear warheads threaten all of us with annihilation.

Domestically we are menaced by an escalation of violence which left us with over 1.8 million reported violent crimes in 1990. We have averaged about twenty thousand murders a year for the last fifteen years.

There is a new urgency to the need to give up destructive modes of thought and behavior fashioned by ancient, outmoded values, and begin to develop a blueprint for a different kind of man.

Introduction to the 1991 Edition

In recent years we have grown more and more aware of and concerned with violence in our streets and in our homes. The women's movement has focused our attention on wife-battering, child-battering, sexual abuse of children, and rape. In some urban centers the evening news begins with a tally of the dead and wounded in local "war zones." The young Brooklyn boy set on fire by a thirteen-year-old and the Central Park jogger raped and beaten by a group of boys out "wilding" have become symbols of nightmarish urban violence.

Our suburbs and small towns, too, are often settings for outbursts of rageful, gruesome acts. The late 1980s brought us machine-gunnings of schoolchildren and coworkers, massacres of parents by their sons, endless vengeful killings of ex-wives, and increases in racist and anti-Semitic acts of violence. We hear increasingly about crimes committed "for fun" or out of curiosity—like the boys in a small Missouri town who wanted to see what it would feel like to kill someone, so they bludgeoned one of their schoolmates to death. Homicide rates have gone up by 100 percent between 1960 and 1990.[1]

It is a major thesis of this book that many of the values of the masculine mystique, such as toughness, dominance, repression of empathy, extreme competitiveness, play a major role in criminal and domestic violence and underlie the thinking and policy decisions of many of our political leaders.

The masculine mystique manifests itself differently in different environments but the end result is the same. For a poor ghetto youth, proving that he is a man might involve a willingness to rob, assault, or kill someone. (Homicide is the major cause of death among young African-American males.) For a group of middle- or upper-class boys, it might mean participating in a gang rape, or going on a hundred-mile-an-hour joy ride. (Automobile accidents are the major cause of death among young white males.) For the men in our National Security Council, proving manhood might mean showing how tough they are by going along with a military intervention that is not really necessary for our national security. (In the case of Vietnam this led to the death of at least fifty-eight thousand Americans and well over one million Vietnamese.) For the men in our nuclear think tanks, it might mean making sure we have at least as many nuclear warheads as "they" do, regardless of whether we need them or not. (We have enough of them now to destroy the Soviet Union hundreds of times over.)

Men are still the most frequent victims of violence. From 1980 to 1987 about three times as many men as women were murdered per year. More men than women continue to be killed in wars.

It is far beyond the scope of this book to analyze how the masculine mystique manifests itself in other cultures. Suffice it to say that it will tend to take somewhat different forms and different degrees of intensity in different societies. For example, in England and Italy some young men prove their toughness, express their desire for dominance, through "soccer hooligan-ism." In the United States gang warfare is more common.

In the United States adherence to the values of the masculine mystique makes intimate, self-revealing, deep friendships between men unusual. In the Soviet Union such friendships seem to be quite common, although Soviet men's preoccupation with dominance and toughness is apparent in other areas.

The role that obsolete male modes of thought and behavior have played and continue to play in perpetuating the nuclear arms race has been recognized by an increasing number of people of differing ethical, political, and religious views.

Such disparate figures as retired Vice Admiral John Lee, a forty-two-year veteran of the U.S. Navy, and Cornell University astronomer Carl Sagan tell us that our nation can no longer relate to foreign powers the way boys relate to each other in the school yard. Whether it be Admiral Lee reminiscing about how the biggest and strongest boy in the yard was always able to dictate to the other boys which games would be played and how, or Carl Sagan describing boyhood snowball fights in which the winner was invariably the one who could make the most snowballs the fastest, the conclusion is the same. In Admiral Lee's words, "We have an obsolete psychology swirling through our system . . . if the Soviets had half as much or double the amount of nuclear weapons they have now it would make no difference."[2] But while the calls for a new way of thinking in international relations are numerous, little attention has been given to how that new way of thinking can be brought about.

Analogously, while there is a growing clamor that something be done about violence in our streets and homes, there has been very little systematic analysis of what it is that reinforces violent, reckless, self-destructive behavior in boys and what can be done to change it.

This book represents a first attempt at both understanding this psychology and making concrete recommendations as to how the socialization of boys might be changed in order to decrease violence.

The question of change can only be dealt with effectively if we achieve some understanding of the psychological resistance and the intellectual objections to it. These are dealt with in Part One.

The first chapter examines the resistance to change that results from the sociocultural assumption, often unconscious, that male behavior is the norm and constitutes a paradigm for human behavior, female behavior being viewed as deviant or defective. This assumption makes it considerably more difficult for men to question the masculine mystique than for women to question the feminine mystique.

The second chapter deals with the view that giving up traditional standards of masculinity is both foolhardy and utopian, since it would leave us weak and "emasculated" as a nation, vulnerable to attack and takeover by foreign powers. I argue that it is in fact the adherence to the masculine mystique by men in power that contributes to the serious endangerment of our national security.

The third chapter deals with the idea that "boys will be boys" regardless of how we raise or socialize them, for they are naturally aggressive and violent. An overview and evaluation of sociobiological, hormonal, psychoanalytic, and social learning theory research on male violence are presented. The prevalence among males of problems (most often genetically based) that have a high correlation with violent and criminal behavior is discussed. About 40 percent of prison inmates suffer from learning disabilities and close to 30 percent are mildly retarded.

While there is some overlap between these two groups, these figures are still very high. The main thrust of this chapter is that while there appears to be some biological base to greater male violence, this potential can be reinforced or diminished depending on socialization. *An underlying thesis of the book is that it is precisely because many men have a strong potential for violence that we must do everything possible to discourage it and encourage the development of empathy and other qualities which are inversely related to violent behavior.* Violence can be very significantly reduced. It is never claimed that it can be completely abolished.

The second part of the book deals with the kinds of changes in child-rearing and socialization that represent first steps in the direction of raising significantly less violent male children. One of the main purposes of this book is to stimulate more research and discussion of these issues.

The first section addresses the question of what kinds of changes we must make in how we rear male children—from infancy—to discourage character traits and values conducive to belligerence and violence, and more generally to the acceptance of violence as a legitimate way of resolving international conflicts. This section draws heavily on research in psychology, sociology, and anthropology indicating that a father's nurturant involvement in rearing boys plays a major role in discouraging violence in them. Undoubtedly, many parents will be concerned that if they act in accordance with some of the recommendations made in this book, they will be increasing the likelihood of their sons becoming homosexual. I argue that in fact, the present narrow definition of masculinity and the ensuing socialization encourage homosexuality. The kinds of recommendations I make would, if anything, have the opposite effect.

The second section deals with changes that must be instituted in our schools. Existing classes in child-rearing and conflict resolution in public and private schools are described. I recommend that such classes be made mandatory in all schools. Innovative social studies curricula that emphasize critical thinking and self-examination with respect to racism, ethnocentricity, and xenophobia are described and discussed. I recommend that such classes become the norm.

The third section focuses on those activities that occupy a major part of most boys' free time—playing with toys, participating in sports, TV viewing, listening to music. The main thrust of this section is that instead of treating our children as our most precious national resource we have allowed them to be treated as a commercial market. A major part of their enculturation is now in the hands of people whose primary interest is in profit-making rather than in the well-being of children. I argue that this intolerable situation has much to do with our extraordinarily high rates of violence. Because of technological advances boys are being raised in a culture of violence of unprecedented magnitude, a culture which is qualitatively and quantitatively different from that in which their fathers and grandfathers were raised. This, in spite of the fact that on the basis of over two hundred research studies on TV and film violence there exists an overwhelming consensus among social scientists that the "catharsis" hypothesis has been disproven and that viewing violence encourages violent behavior!

We have a long tradition of laws for the protection of children. They must now be extended to encompass many areas of sports and entertainment. In the case of television, where regulation would interfere with the First Amendment rights of adults, I recommend that we create a Children's Public Broadcasting System dedicated to top-quality pro-social programming for children. Its creation would be accompanied by an educational campaign directed at parents and mandatory lock boxes enabling them to block out all other channels.

In researching the influence of the media, toys, and sports, I have repeatedly encountered an objection, from men, that in essence runs like this: "I used to play with war toys but now I work for the peace movement," or "I love boxing but I've never committed a violent act in my life."

One response is to point to the escalation of violence in toys and entertainment. But these men's argument gets to the heart of another very important issue which I shall address briefly here in order to make clear what is and what is not being said in this book.

It is not being said that any one of the factors described as reinforcing violent tendencies in boys will, by itself or in combination with any of the other factors, be either a necessary or a sufficient condition to lead a boy to commit an act of violence. For example, a boy may very well play with every conceivable war toy, be addicted to the most violent films imaginable, grow up in an extremely violent home, and still never commit an act of violence; while another boy who has been exposed to the most minimal violence may commit violent acts. This is analogous to a person smoking three packs a day, eating a cholesterol-ridden diet, and living to be eighty, while a nonsmoker on a low-cholesterol diet dies of either a heart attack or lung cancer at age forty.

In the social sciences, as in the medical sciences, the concern is with statistically significant trends. The boy who is addicted to violent films and toys and the person who smokes three packs a day and eats a high-cholesterol diet are at a significantly higher risk of acting violently or dying prematurely. No further claim is being made.

In the case of illness as in the case of violence, genetic factors and personality play a role in the effect that interaction with the environment has on a particular individual.

Part Three, the conclusion, outlines some of the basic premises upon which any serious long-range attempt to curtail violence must rest.

Notes

1. See p. 319 for violent crime statistics and sources.
2. Lee made this statement at a 1986 Freeze Voter meeting in New York City. Sagan's coments were made at the 1986 Shalom Center Annual Awards Dinner.

Introduction to the 2002 Edition

Back in the mid- to late 1990s, as I read about the schoolyard killers, wrote about them, and was invited to comment on them in the media, I found myself thinking frequently of Seth Maxell (fictitious name), who was the same age as several of the boys. Seth's story is the only case history that appears in *Boys Will Be Boys*. (The book's analyses and recommendations are based on a synthesis of research, not on anecdotal material.)

While the bulk of this 2002 introduction is focused on updating the material presented in the 1991 edition of *Boys Will Be Boys*, I begin with Seth's story because it captures so succinctly and vividly what the book is all about.

I met Seth Maxell, his parents, and his sister quite by chance in 1987, when he was five years old.

From the youngest age Seth exhibited a pronounced tendency toward violent behavior—kicking, biting, punching without provocation (see pp. 66–68). By the time he was three, his parents were deeply concerned and his mother took him to see a psychologist. The diagnosis was attention deficit disorder with hyperactivity—a condition that affects at least 3 percent of

American children and, according to recent studies, is five to eight times more frequent in boys than in girls. The condition is often a predisposing factor to serious teenage and adult violence. Given Seth's proclivity toward violence at such a young age, the psychologist warned Mrs. Maxell that unless something was done soon, Seth was at very high risk of developing into a violent man. By the time I met Mrs. Maxell, she estimated that with the help of the psychologist Seth's violent behavior had decreased by approximately 60 percent. "Behavior modification" in Seth's case focused on strict but non-violent methods of dealing with his violent behavior; intense, enthusiastic praise by his parents for any demonstration of kindness, generosity, empathy, and caring; and a ban on violent entertainment, which Mrs. Maxell, a former teacher, was able to enforce because she did not go back to teaching after Seth's birth.

In 1998, I rummaged through old date books, found the Maxells' phone number, and called his mother. "How has Seth been all these years? How is the violence problem going?" I asked. "There is no longer a violence problem," Mrs. Maxell responded. "Let me think when that came to an end." After a short silence, she said, "Nine—he hasn't committed any acts of violence since the age of nine. He's still thoroughly hyperactive but lets out the energy in sports." She then reeled off all the sports activities Seth was involved in—none of them combative, like football or boxing.

A few weeks ago, I checked in with Mrs. Maxell once again. Seth is now almost twenty years old and is a professional athlete. He is still hyperactive but completely non-violent. He is very kind and thoughtful, his mother told me, "a gentle soul."

The underlying argument of this book is that in this age of advanced technology that enables machine-gunning large numbers of people in seconds, hijacking planes and using them as lethal weapons, and annihilating all life on earth through nuclear weapons, we must move away from an obsolete concept of masculinity focused on toughness, dominance, emotional detachment, callousness toward women, and eagerness to fight. If Seth Maxell had been raised in accordance with these values, which I refer to as the "masculine mystique," there is little doubt that he would be a violent man today. Instead he is a poster child for how all boys should be raised in the twenty-first century.

Even though a majority of men never commit any significant acts of violence in the course of their lives, cross-culturally a vast majority of those who do commit violence, whether criminal or in warfare, are male. And a certain percentage of the male population, like Seth Maxell, is at particulary high risk for violence. But because the masculine mystique still dominates our culture, many boys with no particularly strong proclivity to violence find that part of themselves so strongly reinforced that they are led to acts of violence for which they and their victims often pay a high price.

Last year I received a letter from Paul, a Vietnam veteran, in which he described this process. It reads: "As a child, I trained as a warrior—it was a boy thing. We had little toy soldiers with guns and flame throwers, tanks, war ships, and fighter planes. This was normal and expected. Warrior play was reinforced by the movies I went to almost every Saturday afternoon. Messages and themes were about courage and winning. God was on our side and the cavalry always came in time. Two weeks after graduating from high school, I was in the Marine Corps. The four years I spent in the Marine Corps had a major influence on who I am. Since then I have gradually rebuilt my value system. . . . For a short time in the '60s and '70s there was a collective attempt to introduce new themes, but it seems like as a society we have already lost some of the lessons from the Vietnam war. This makes your work . . . even more critical. . . . My daughter and daughter-in-law are both having baby boys in May and I would like to give them a copy of *Boys Will Be Boys*."

Paul does not want his grandsons to be raised to be soldiers; he does not want them to wait until they are in their fifties and carry the heavy burden of having committed unnecessary acts of violence before they are able to fully experience empathy and caring and express it openly and without embarrassment.

Paul is a member of a Vietnam veterans group started by the Vietnamese Buddhist monk Thich Nhat Hanh. The group is very open and welcoming, and I—with my Holocaust survivor background and commitment to decreasing violence—have become part of it. Most of the men in the group are in their fifties and are still coping with the emotional fallout of their war experiences. Those who killed Vietnamese men, women, or children, or accidentally killed some of their comrades, tend to be in the greatest pain. In the group there is a lot of hugging, crying, caring—behaviors that would not have been acceptable when these men were eighteen years old, for they were reared on the masculine mystique.

Since the publication of *Boys Will Be Boys*, many men have accused me of being a "male basher." (I will get to this group shortly.) It has been heartening to have their anger and indignation more than balanced by the reaction of men like the ones in my vets group, who understand that male bashing means raising little boys to be soldiers and then sending them off to fight in unnecessary wars.

Judging by my mail and verbal accolades, men who have had firsthand experience with violence are the most likely to welcome me as an ally—like the Alameda county juvenile probation officer of close to thirty years who wrote to me, "I couldn't agree more with your book." He understands that male bashing consists of raising boys in an environment that encourages violence and then locking them up when they act criminally violent.

A high school teacher who had for many years served as football coach called to tell me how much he liked my sports chapter. He had stopped coaching, he explained, because he could no longer bear to see the damage that the boys were doing to their bodies. According to my dictionary, the literal definition of bashing is to "strike hard and violently." Large numbers of boys are bashed in high school sports, and many are left with permanent physical damage.

A young man from Arizona who had been a victim of male bashing wrote to tell me about how it had affected him: "I am seventeen years old, but I don't go to school. . . . When I was fifteen I quit high school because of the harassment from ultra-violent 'jocks.' " (As we shall see below, since the Columbine and other schoolyard killings, there is less acceptance of bullying as normal "boys will be boys" behavior.)

And then there are the many men who have escaped the narrow confines of the masculine mystique and just get it. One such man wrote to tell me, "I'm one of those atypical non-macho human males you wrote about. . . . I've been a single parent and raised a son mostly on my own. This is why I think the programs you outline that teach parenting skills to children of both genders are marvelous and ought to be encouraged. . . . The only way macho attitudes are ever going to change is through a conscious effort to change them in the child-rearing process."

A young man sent me a letter and a flyer that described him as "The Feminist Fullback," and told me about the "Real Men" group he had started in Boston with the goal of "working to end sexism and violence against women." His name is Jackson Katz, and his work in this field is now widely recognized.

A Wisconsin man wrote to thank me for writing the book, and then warned me that "unfortunately most men will not heed your warnings and observations, let alone pay attention to your suggestions for improving the quality of malehood. I fear this is the case because you are a woman making statements about men. And the kind of unhealthy man you write about will use this against you." He was right on target.

Even before the publication of the first edition, I had gotten a taste of the resistance to dealing with violence as a mostly male phenomenon. Some of this resistance is described and analyzed in the chapter entitled "When Male Behavior Is The Norm . . ." My first taste of the rage that was to follow completion came in the fall of 1990, when the manuscript of Boys Will Be Boys was copy edited and sent back to me. The job of copy editors is to correct grammar and punctuation, but I found margins sprinkled with angry, hateful comments about the book's content. My editor was stunned—in his many years in publishing he had never seen anything like it. It would delay publication by three weeks, but the text would have to be re-edited, he told me. This time he sent it to a female copy editor.

This introduction prepared me for the hostility I would encounter over the years, which included being dismissed as a "male basher" on national television and radio, and as a "well known man hating Lesbian Feminist who regularly rails against male children" on the Web. Some years ago, an acquaintance called to say that he had just heard Rush Limbaugh refer to me as a "feminazi."

On a more personal level, my experiences included a man at a small dinner party who became so enraged by my description of what Boys Will Be Boys was about that he left the table for twenty minutes to calm down. Nor was I the only one to experience such reactions. A Minnesota woman told me she had been reading *Boys Will Be Boys* on a plane when a man sitting across the aisle asked to see it. She gave it to him; he glanced through it and then handed it back to her, irate. "What are you reading this shit for?" he bellowed. His subsequent behavior was so frightening that when the plane landed she waited until well after he had left before she got up. A Rhode Island bookseller told me that a man who had done no more than glance at the title had become so enraged that he also had compared the book to fecal matter.

My pre-publication interview with author David Rothenberg (described on p. 11) prepared me for the reaction of some magazine editors. His comment that "The [*Village*] *Voice* had printed everything except my laundry list, but they rejected this piece [on masculinity and violence]" was to be reiterated almost verbatim by a writer I happened to have some personal contact with. His review of *Boys Will Be Boys* had been rejected by a leading left-wing intellectual magazine that he was on the editorial board of. The editor's comments about his review and his refusal to publish it "made no rational sense at all," he told me. "He's never rejected anything I've written; I think he just couldn't deal on an emotional level with your cultural critique of masculinity."

Fortunately, the mass media thrives on controversy and outrage, and so thanks to appearances on hundreds of TV and radio shows my recommendations reached a wide and diverse audience. And then there were the women and men who understood and helped me disseminate my recommendations through lectures, anthologies, articles, interviews, and Op-Eds.

That violence-prone men who fully adhere to the values of the masculine mystique would be enraged by even the title and subtitle of the book is not all that surprising, but that some progressive men strongly opposed to the unnecessary use of violence should be so deeply disturbed by it points to the depth of the resistance described in Chapter 1.

Again, I am not alone in experiencing these kinds of reactions. Colleagues whose work is also focused on traditional masculinity and violence have told me that because of the instant aversion on the part of so many progressive thinkers to any gender analysis of violence, they have decided to focus on the characteristics of violence-prone people without antagonizing their audiences by mentioning the gender of a vast majority of these people.

In the preface to his 2002 book, *War and Gender*, which focuses on the almost exclusively male nature of war and how it affects the construction of masculinity, International Relations professor Joshua Goldstein demonstrates his understanding of this aversion. He writes, "Recently, I discovered a list of unfinished research projects, which I had made fifteen years ago at the end of graduate school. The list included 'gender and war,' with the notation 'most interesting of all; will ruin career—wait until tenure.' "[1] Brian D'Agostino, whose Columbia University doctoral dissertation on gender and national security is discussed below, was not as cautious. He has been unable to obtain an academic position and teaches high school. In his recent book, *Misogyny*, anthropology professor David Gilmore describes and discusses the pervasiveness and intensity of misogyny in cultures around the world. In his preface he comments on "the utter lack of interest in this subject among my (all male) former anthropology professors. I brought up my observations with them time and again, only to be met with shrugs, smirks, and mumbled pronouncements about eternal verities and timeless commonplaces."[2] When issues of gender and violence are dealt with in academia it is mostly by women and relegated to Women's Studies.

The resistance to any gender analysis that reveals problematic male tendencies is a prime example of what the philosopher Jean-Paul Sartre described as "bad faith"—a form of knowing and not knowing something at the same time. It takes very strong blinders to dampen awareness of the obvious fact that violence is a predominantly male phenomenon. In recent years the increase in female violent crime has been used for that purpose. The fact is that the baseline for female violent crime was so low to begin with that even with the increases, in 2000, 89.4 percent of those arrested for homicide and 82.6 percent of those arrested for violent crimes were males.[3] So much for the myth that "women are catching up."

Another myth is that when it comes to domestic violence, women are the perpetrators as often as men. When sociology professor Michael Kimmel was invited by the Equality Committee of the Department of Education and Science to review the minority of studies that supported this view—a vast majority of studies indicate that the preponderance of domestic violence is perpetrated by males against females—he found serious flaws in them, including the fact that "these studies lump together violence, so that a single slap may be equaled with several intensive assaults." Kimmel points out that "women are six to seven times more likely to require medical care for their injuries than are men" and concludes that "the evidence is overwhelming that gender asymmetry in domestic violence remains in full effect."[4] When it comes to homicide, in 2000, 33 percent of female murder victims were killed by boyfriends or husbands, while 3.2 percent of male victims were killed by their girlfriends or wives.

While I welcome the recent focus on the cruel behavior that some girls exhibit toward other girls—when my older daughter transferred to a new school in fifth grade some of the girls were so nasty to her that I went secretly to see her teacher to ask for her help in stopping them—I also fear that it will be used to further facilitate denial and bad faith about male violence. The ongoing sloppy use of the term "aggression" (which is discussed on pp. 43–45) facilitates this. For example, in her recent book, *Woman's Inhumanity to Woman*, author Phyllis Chesler quotes a study of female aggression in 137 societies that "found that women engaged in physical, verbal, and indirect aggression 'around the world.' Women 'shriek, scream, scold, revile, and insult their (mainly) female opponents.' " The specific examples that follow include "kicking apart the clay cooking stoves of their rivals" and, at the extreme, "destroying her [rival's] house, uproot[ing] part of the garden, and wreck[ing] the fence." Or it is stated that "an Ute woman may kill her rival's horse."[5] To describe these acts as "physical aggression," when not one of them involves physically assaulting or killing a person, is misleading. I can already hear the voices of denial pointing to an anthropological study that shows that women worldwide engage in physical aggression just as men do.

I have dwelled at length on the denial and rage that a gender analysis of violence leads to in some men, because it serves to prevent or at least significantly delay change. Moving away from an obsolete concept of masculinity and the violence that it entails is at least as radical a change as the eighteenth-century movement away from absolute monarchy in favor of a concept of the rights of "man," the nineteenth-century abolition of slavery, or the twentieth-century granting of equal rights to women. In fact it is probably more radical. In order for significant steps to be taken in this new direction, strong support from a variety of quarters will be required. To have significant segments of the nation's thinkers be in a state of denial about the problem, to have an academic world in which, with the exception of women's studies, one is likely to be penalized for dealing with it, to have magazines, journals, and newspapers often averse to publishing articles about the problem, is an enormous handicap.

Along with men who "get it," women will have to play an important role in bringing about this change. While the denial of and discomfort with focusing on male violence is far more prevalent in men, it is not limited to them. In response to my focus, I have more than once heard women say, "but women can be so much more vicious than men," by which they are referring to malicious gossip, slandering, outcasting, and other forms of psychological cruelty. Surely these women do not really think that psychological cruelty is on a par with machine-gunning schoolmates; kidnapping, raping, and murdering little girls; or jealousy-driven killings of ex-wives or girlfriends. My hunch is that they are motivated by a fear—which may well be unconscious—of being dismissed as male bashers or man-hating bitches. Women will have to overcome these fears if we are to move forward toward a form of masculinity appropriate to the twenty-first century.

Interestingly enough, conservative thinkers often recognize what many liberals do not. This may be because they tend to accept a Hobbesian view of "man" as innately nasty and brutish. Males as a group, they believe, are hardwired for dominance and violence, and, while socialization plays a role, that role is quite limited. This can then be used as a justification for the status quo. For example, in an article entitled "Women and the Evolution of World Politics," political scientist Francis Fukuyama concludes that governments run by women would be less violent, but he warns that women would be unable to deal with ambitious, unconstrained men like Saddam Hussein. While he admits that "biology . . . is not destiny," he remains convinced that because dominance and violence are "bred in the bone" of men, men and "masculine" women like Margaret Thatcher will and must continue to control international politics. "Masculine policies will still be required."[6]

In the "Real Men, Wimps, and Our National Security" chapter, I address concerns about whether my recommendations for changing the socialization of boys would endanger our national security. I argue that, quite to the contrary, it is the masculine mystique and its "masculine policies" that lead to political decisions that endanger our national security and even help to create the likes of Saddam Hussein—more about this below.

WHAT'S CHANGED IN THE LAST DECADE?

VIOLENT CRIME

The good news is that in 2000 the murder rate was 43.7 percent lower than in 1991, with the number of victims down to 15,517. This is the lowest national murder rate since 1965, but it is still very high compared with other advanced industrialized countries. For example, in spite of its recent increases in violent crime, France's per capita murder rate is one-eighth of ours.[7] We Americans have become accustomed to extraordinarily high crime rates. While any decrease is to be applauded, surely 15,517 murder victims in a year is not something we can really rejoice about. Between 1991 and 2000 there was also a decrease in homicides and other violent crimes committed by boys under the age of eighteen. Here again, while this is good news, we must not forget that this decrease is from an all-time high—between 1967 and 1996, violent crime arrests for males under eighteen increased by 124 percent. The late 1990s brought us large numbers of schoolyard killings by young middle- and upper-middle-class white boys.

A variety of explanations have been given for the recent decreases in violent crime, including better policing, community policing, decreased unemployment, and long prison sentences (a large number of crimes are committed by recidivists). Another contributor to the decrease might be that so many inner-city boys grew up in the late 1980s and early '90s going to the funerals of their friends and siblings who were victims of violence. The role that school programs of the kind described in the "School Programs That Work" chapter might have played is largely ignored, even though there is good reason to believe that these have had positive effects in deterring violence. They could play a much larger role if funding were made available to expand them.

While it is too early to tell whether we are about to witness a new increase in violent crime, the FBI reports that the murder rate rose by 3.1 percent between 2000 and 2001—this figure excludes the victims of the September 11 terrorist attack. As long as no basic large-scale changes are made in the socialization of boys, violence rates will continue to fluctuate without any truly significant long-term reduction.

BOOKS ABOUT RAISING BOYS

When in the mid-1980s I began my research on how to change the socialization of boys to decrease violence, a feminist awareness had already led to critical writings (by both women and men) on men and patriarchy, and more generally on male values and attitudes. Without that awareness and these writings, my own work would not have been possible.

But, while quite a bit had been written on men, after an extensive search I was only able to find one book on raising boys—*The Little Boy Book*. It was a traditional child-rearing guide for parents of boys up to age eight. And so in the introduction to *Boys Will Be Boys*, I stated that "One of the main purposes of this book is to stimulate more research and discussion" on the topic of "raising significantly less violent male children."

Because no book is written in a vacuum, it is impossible to know how much of a role my own work might have played in stimulating the more than twenty books on raising boys and a few books on boys and violence that have appeared since the mid-1990s. Unlike *Boys Will Be Boys*, which deals extensively with political decision making, education, sports, and entertainment, and makes public policy recommendations, most of these books are written by mental health professionals and focus primarily on how parents or professionals need to change the way they raise or treat boys. Some, like William Pollack's 1998 *Real Boys*, present analyses that are very much in keeping with my own, and make recommendations that can only lead to decreases in violent behavior. The publication of these later books, most of them written by men, has helped to make the focus on gender and violence somewhat more acceptable than it was in 1991, when *Boys Will Be Boys* was published, but resistance still remains strong.

THE NATURE/NURTURE ISSUE

"Violence is best understood as developing out of an interaction between a biological potential and certain kinds of environment," I wrote in the conclusion to the "Boys Will Be Boys" chapter, which deals with the nature/nurture issue. I was well aware that for many feminists and others on the political left, any mention of biology playing a role in violent behavior would meet with total rejection and often intense hostility. Brown University professor Anne Fausto-Sterling, author of *Myths of Gender*, was among the experts I interviewed in researching this issue. She asserted that besides differences in sexual organs there are no biological differences between males and females, and rejected as futile research on this subject, stating that it will always be impossible to distinguish between biology and culture.

The intense reaction to any mention of biology grows out of a fear that biology might be used to justify reactionary, racist, and sexist social policies. Biology has indeed been used in just such ways. But denying the role that it plays in violence, not even allowing for discussion of the topic by experts, is no solution. (In 1992, a conference bringing together leading researchers on the subject was canceled because of protests; when it was held in 1995, it was disrupted.) It plays into the conservative assumption that any acceptance of the role of biology must be to the exclusion of, or the minimizing of, the role of environment. It is this misguided assumption that must be questioned. Francis Fukuyama is wrong: we live in an age of advanced technology, which, under "masculine" leadership, brought us over 170 million deaths from war and political violence in the twentieth century alone. If women as a group are less prone to turn toward violence to solve conflicts, this becomes a strong argument for their equal representation in government. If boys and men as a group are at higher risk of learning violent behavior, this lends a special urgency to doing everything possible to change their socialization—just as Seth Maxell's biologically based early violent behavior led his parents to do everything possible in raising him to discourage his tendency to violence. We need strong and numerous voices asserting the need for such change and working to bring it about. A denial that biology plays any role at all, which smacks more of a theological belief than a research-based one, does nothing to advance this cause. My own informal survey of parents indicates that a majority are convinced that biology does play a role in their sons' behavior. The focus on nurture to the complete exclusion of nature strikes them as naïve and pollyannaish. Unless people are educated to understand the interaction of nature and nurture, they will be more prone to accept uncritically the conservative "prisons not programs" view: that government should not waste money on preventive programs (of the kind described below) that cannot work because they defy "human nature."

The research I have examined since the publication of *Boys Will Be Boys* has further strengthened my conviction that the interaction of biology and environment best explains violent behavior. Now as then, it is the combination of cross-cultural studies, hormonal studies, brain research, and animal studies that leads me to this conclusion.

Cross-Cultural Studies

Studies continue to confirm that worldwide, from a young age, a larger percentage of boys than girls hit and insult each other. In play groups boys are more concerned with dominance and hierarchy. Several studies carried out in the 1990s also show that far more violent themes are present in stories made up by boys than by girls. Recent studies confirm that sex differences in aggression are relatively constant both historically and cross-culturally, and that recent changes in female gender roles have not led to significant changes in male/female levels of violence.[8]

Hormones

The relationship between testosterone and violent behavior is complex. Testosterone levels are affected by external circumstances—for example, rising when a man wins an important contest and falling when he loses it. Higher levels of testosterone may well be related to traits that increase the probability of violence, such as a tendency to be more easily frustrated, impatient, and irritable, rather than being directly linked to violent behavior. But continued evidence indicates that one way or another it plays a role. For example, in recent years, a number of researchers have studied testosterone levels of prison inmates, and most of them have found that men guilty of violent crimes had higher testosterone levels than those who had committed non-violent crimes.[9]

Brain Research

New technologies are facilitating brain research undreamt of in earlier times. While still in an early stage, this research suggests the existence of some differences between the male and female brain. For example, in a 1995 study, when glucose was injected into the brains of a group of men and women and a positron emission tomography (PET) scanner was used to see where it was absorbed most quickly, male and female brain images were alike except in the limbic system, where men's brains "glowed most brightly in a region linked to a quick physical response. Women's didn't; their limbic system was more active in a region linked to a quick verbal response."[10] This is suggestive of a physiological difference that would make men more likely to strike out physically and women to strike out verbally.

Our Close Cousins: Chimpanzees and Bonobos

Extrapolating from animal studies must be viewed with caution, but in light of our common origins—evolutionary biologists estimate that we parted ways about five million years ago—and the fact that we share more than 98 percent of our DNA with them, the behavior of chimpanzees and bonobos is particularly relevant to understanding human behavior. Bonobos were initially believed to be a variety of chimpanzee and were called pygmy chimps, but it is now clear that they are a different but closely related species. These two species are more closely genetically related to humans than to gorillas. According to Harvard professor of biological anthropology Richard Wrangham, out of four thousand mammals, only humans and chimpanzees live in patrilineal, male-bonded communities and indulge in "male-initiated territorial aggression, including lethal raiding into neighboring communities in search of vulnerable enemies to attack and kill."[11] Male bonobos act considerably less violently than male chimpanzees or male humans. Wrangham points out that this low level of male bonobo violence is due in large part to the fact that female bonobos form alliances, hold considerable power, and are able to influence the behavior of those male bonobos who exhibit violent tendencies—this should give us humans hope.

FATHERS' INVOLVEMENT IN CHILD-REARING

When I first began working on *Boys Will Be Boys*, I had no idea that the book would end up with three chapters on fathering. But the more I looked at research in psychology, sociology, and anthropology, the more convinced I became of the importance of an involved, caring, non-violent father (or father figure) in deterring violent behavior in boys. Recent developments in terms of father involvement are positive, but problems remain.

Joseph Pleck, at the University of Illinois, has compared the responses, over the course of sixteen years, of newly wed couples who were asked to rank the values they wanted to be part of their married life. The responses indicate that co-parenting has gone from being the eleventh priority out of fifteen in 1986 to being the second priority in 1997. In his book *Fatherneed*, psychiatrist Kyle Pruett informs us that "father care" has become as common as "all forms of day care combined," and that "acceptance of paternity by unmarried men is up threefold from 1995."[12] According to surveys conducted by The Families and Work Institute of New York, in 1977, working fathers spent 55 percent of the time that working mothers did providing child care during the week; by 1997, it had gone up to 77 percent. However, as the authors of the study point out, the results might be biased "by respondents' views of what is socially desirable."[13] Nevertheless, there can be no doubt that in a large percentage of dual-parent families, fathers are considerably more involved than they were in the past. This augurs well as long as fathers are modeling caring, non-violent behavior.

While the growing recognition of the important role fathers play in the development of their children is a major step forward, it can lead to abuses in child custody battles. Because the presumption is no longer that the child belongs with the mother, and because a higher percentage of men than women can afford expensive legal counsel, child advocate groups such as the National Coalition for Family Justice report that some men use custody battles as a means of decreasing their child support payments, and some obtain custody or visitation rights in spite of evidence of abuse on their part.

SCHOOL PROGRAMS THAT DISCOURAGE VIOLENCE

Parenting Education

In the chapter entitled "When Boys and Babies Meet," I describe school programs that teach child-rearing and recommend that such classes become mandatory in all our schools to encourage empathic, responsible, non-violent future fathering in boys (and mothering in girls). This chapter led directly to the creation of The Parenting Project, a non-profit organization dedicated to making child-rearing classes a standard part of school curriculum in the U.S. A lecture I gave in Toronto in 1995 led to the creation the following year of the Roots of Empathy school program. Currently in 191 classrooms in seven Canadian provinces, the program is in the midst of major expansion. While the Canadians chose in naming the program to emphasize the role that these classes play in encouraging empathy (which is inversely related to violence), their program is in fact very similar to the elementary and junior high school child-rearing program that I describe. When a group of Japanese psychologists and teachers came to Toronto in the late '90s and visited Roots of Empathy classes, they were enormously impressed. As a result, a one-year pilot program was completed in the spring of 2002 in Tokyo. In consultation with Roots of Empathy founder and president Mary Gordon, a full-scale plan of implementation is being worked on by Japanese educators and mental health professionals.

The Philadelphia-based Educating Children For Parenting program described in this chapter has by now reached more than 100,000 students throughout the U.S. By the 1999–2000 academic year, the program was in 294 classrooms in seven states, including Virginia, Louisiana, and New Hampshire. The Caring Project also originated in Philadelphia and was developed to encourage empathy and nurturance. It includes a "partnership" program in which older schoolchildren plan activities and help younger children with schoolwork. Family and Consumer Sciences classes (formerly known as Home Economics) have for a long time included a child-rearing component, but it is too often minimal since it is part of a broader life skills curriculum.

A variety of child-rearing programs have been developed since the early '90s, including the Houston-based Parents Under Construction and the Minneapolis-based Dads Make a Difference. More than a million teens have experienced the Baby Think It Over Program—a parenting education project that uses a computerized infant simulator in order to help teens improve their knowledge and attitudes about parenting, and serves as a teenage pregnancy deterrent. Most of these programs have had evaluations by teachers, or by tests such as the Adult-Adolescent Parenting Inventory (AAPI), which assesses child rearing attitudes particularly with respect to practices associated with abuse and neglect. The results have generally been very positive.

In 1999, New York became the first state to mandate child-rearing classes. By 2005, all students graduating from high school will have had some training in child-rearing. Unfortunately the mandate has not been accompanied by funding. The California state legislature has voted several times to make child-rearing classes mandatory in all California schools, but Governors Pete Wilson and Gray Davis have misguidedly vetoed the bill. Efforts are underway in Connecticut and several other states to pass such legislation.

Moving Away from Bigotry

In the chapter entitled "Taking the Glory Out of War and Unlearning Bigotry," I describe a Boston school program, Facing History and Ourselves. Its goal is to help students think critically, develop their capacity to empathize with people of a different ethnicity or race, and move away from the glorification of violence. The program has grown considerably, with regional offices in several U.S. cities, including Chicago, Cleveland, and New York, as well as program representatives in Europe. It now reaches an estimated one million students.

In 1996, Facing History was the recipient of a two-year grant from the Carnegie Corporation of New York. In the ensuing recently completed Carnegie study, the evaluation team concluded that as a result of the Facing History program, students showed increased maturity in relationships and less fighting behavior, racist attitudes, and insular ethnic identity relative to comparison students.

Resolving Conflicts Non-Violently

In the chapter entitled "Alternatives to Fistfights and Bullying," the Resolving Conflict Creatively Program (RCCP) is described. It is currently in ninety schools in New York City and has reached about 200,000 city children since its inception in 1985. New York City Educators for Social Responsibility, the group that developed it, has since introduced a series of other programs, including one for Pre-K children, that encourage pro-social behavior. Since the early '90s, Resolving Conflict Creatively has been extended to twelve school districts across the country, including New Orleans, Atlanta, and Anchorage.

Thanks to grants from the federal Centers for Disease Control and Prevention and private foundations, a rigorous evaluation of the program was carried out under the auspices of Columbia University's School of Public Health. The evaluation found that the program "had a significant impact when teachers taught a high number of lessons from the RCCP curriculum (on average twenty-five lessons over the school year)." The children who had gone through this training showed more positive social behaviors and emotional control and less aggressive behavior compared to children who had not gone through the curriculum or had had a low number of lessons.

While these and the other school programs described in *Boys Will Be Boys* can only serve to discourage bullying, that is not their primary focus. The introduction of anti-bullying programs into American schools is a recent development. "The schoolyard killings of the mid-1990s were a national wake-up call," Merle Froschl, the director of Educational Equity Concepts, which began to develop an anti-bullying program in 1995, told me. It soon became clear that most of the schoolyard killers had been victims of bullying and teasing, and schools around the country began introducing anti-bullying and anti-teasing programs. (Boys are both the victims and the perpetrators of most physical bullying; girls are both perpetrators and victims of most of the teasing.) Froschl's organization began by running a pilot site in a New York City elementary school that is racially, ethnically, and socio-economically diverse. After two years of intervention, bullying and teasing were reduced by 35 percent.

The positive evaluations of the Resolving Conflict Creatively and Facing History programs by rigorous independent researchers lend support to what common sense, anecdotal reports, and smaller studies and evaluations tell us—that quality school programs that encourage empathic, non-violent behavior can make a significant difference. Such programs cost a pittance compared to the cost of incarceration. (The RCCP program can be implemented for approximately $98 per child for the first year.)

SPORTS

When it comes to "Athletes as Role Models," one of the subheadings in the chapter on sports, there has not been much improvement. A small but significant minority of athletes continue to catch media attention for violent behavior. As I write, the sports pages are filled with stories about 76ers star player Allen Iverson's most recent run in with the law. In early July he allegedly barged into his cousin's West Philadelphia apartment yelling threats and equipped with a gun; he was looking for his wife, whom the police claim he had earlier thrown out of their home naked. He was charged with four felonies and ten misdemeanors. Like his earlier charges and those against so many other athletes, these charges have been reduced, and he will most likely face no more than probation. Iverson, who "moonlights" as a rapper, had an album in 2001 that was widely criticized for bashing women and gays.

In late July 2002, a bench-clearing brawl erupted during a Boston Red Sox–Baltimore Orioles game. It was triggered by a bean ball incident. In January 2000, NFL player Rae Darruth was arrested and charged with the drive-by shooting of his pregnant girlfriend. In 1997, Golden State Warrior Latrell Sprewell was suspended for one year after he attacked head coach P. J. Carlesimo. He lost both his $32 million Warrior contract and his contract with Converse sneakers. These were viewed as strong actions on the part of the NBA, the Warriors, and Converse, and as part of an effort to decrease the "quasi-criminal" violence on the court that was beginning to keep some families away. Nevertheless, there are serious limits to these efforts—Sprewell is now a star player for the New York Knicks! Along similar lines, while Indiana University basketball coach Bobby Knight finally got fired for his repeated violent and obnoxious behavior, he was soon hired by Texas Tech University in El Paso.

In the Sports chapter I wrote that "some preliminary studies indicate that athletes may well be overrepresented in college sexual assaults." In the mid-1990s, sports researchers Jeff Benedict and Todd Crosset published several articles based on their study of the prevalence of domestic abuse and sexual assault among athletes at NCAA schools that were again and again ranked in the top twenty in basketball and football. They were given access to these universities' records of internal judicial affairs, and found that between 1991 and 1993 male athletes were responsible for almost 20 percent of the sexual assaults, even though they represented only 3 percent of the student body.[14] In his 1996 book, *Public Heroes, Private Felons*, Benedict deplores the fact that while the NCAA and professional leagues have rules prohibiting and penalties for "drug use, gambling, and the use of performance-enhancing drugs," they have no rules or penalties governing off-the-field behavior with respect to "rape, assault, and other criminal violence."[15] In 1997, the NFL adopted an anti-violence policy that calls for a mandatory psychiatric evaluation and a fine or suspension for anyone convicted of or admitting to a violent crime. In a July 26, 2002 *New York Times* article entitled, "Fix Needed for Epidemic of Violence," sports writer Mike Freeman comments that "while [the NFL anti-violence policy] is a good start, it still carries the kick of skim milk."

In the area of youth sports, violence on the part of adults has continued to escalate. In 2002, in a highly publicized case, Massachusetts jurors found Thomas Junta guilty of involuntary manslaughter in the 2000 beating death of Michael Costin at a hockey practice attended by both men's sons. The men had gotten into two fights over rough play during the hockey drills. Stillman College Health and Physical Education professor Donald Staffo reports on a few other 2000 "incidents," which include a hockey dad in Hollywood, Florida beating another hockey dad to death, and a Pony League baseball coach in

Reading, Massachusetts breaking the jaw of an umpire whose calls he didn't like. He also relates that the National Association of Sports in Racine, Wisconsin "received about three calls a week from officials assaulted by parents or spectators."[16]

In the late 1980s, I reported that the emphasis on winning at any cost had gotten out of hand in youth and high school sports, with some high school boys playing with injuries that could permanently jeopardize their physical well-being. In a July 2002 interview with the author, Todd Crosset, now a professor of sports management at the University of Massachusetts, reported on a disturbing new trend. Many high school athletes are taking Creatin, a new muscle-enhancing drug, in addition to muscle-building hormones. (He also pointed out that this is not limited to athletes—some male students who are not athletes are also enhancing their muscles by these means simply to conform to an entertainment- and sports-driven, big-muscle, macho image of masculinity.) Crosset deplored the fact that budget cuts in education have led to even less money for certified trainers or persons with equivalent training at practices and games. As a result, even more boys are playing injured and risking permanent damage to their bodies than in the late 1980s.

On the positive side, by the year 2000, some steps were taken to move away from the "winning at any cost" mentality. The Positive Coaching Alliance (PCA) was formed at Stanford University. Its founder, Jim Thompson, wants to move youth sports away from its role as entertainment for adults. His goal is to create a grassroots campaign to refocus youth sports as a character-building activity. The PCA encourages and helps coaches to create a culture in which playing with sportsmanship rather than winning at any cost prevails. With that goal in mind, it holds workshops for coaches and sports organizations.[17]

The Mendelson Center for Sport, Character, and Culture was established by the University of Notre Dame with a similar goal. Professor Brenda Bredemeier (whose study of how college athletes think of morality on and off the playing field appears in the sports chapter) is the co-director of the Center. In a keynote address, she stated that the " 'win at all cost' mentality is a huge problem, even in youth sport. . . . Athletic trainers, sport psychologists and sports physicians are enticed, sometimes coerced, into enhancing athletes' performance at the expense of those athletes' health and well-being. Universities, even high schools, often find their educational mission compromised by sport programs that have bowed to commercial and entertainment 'requirements.' " The Mendelson Center's mission goals include generating "a grassroots movement for change in the culture of sport" and offering "professional training programs for those seeking to strengthen their moral education competencies in sport and physical education contexts."[18]

ENTERTAINMENT

By the late 1980s, over 235 studies had been carried out on the effects of TV violence. Several surveys of these studies, including one by the National Institute of Mental Health, concluded that a vast majority showed that viewing violence puts children at higher risk of committing acts of violence. In the 1990s, the American Psychological Association and the American Academy of Pediatrics, among others, arrived at the same conclusion. Most recently, a 2001 study by Stanford University researchers focused on elementary school children and a seventeen-year longitudinal study completed in 2002 by Columbia University and the New York State Psychiatric Institute further confirm that viewing violence puts children and teenagers at higher risk of violent behavior.

In spite of overwhelming evidence, much of the entertainment industry and many civil libertarians continue to claim that it is not so. Most often, they do this by erecting a straw man, claiming that the sole cause of violence is the media. They then dismiss this absurd claim and self-righteously point to the "real" causes of violence—guns, poverty, etc. This conveniently ignores that researchers do not claim that violent entertainment is the sole cause of violence, but only that it is one among several important contributing factors that interact to increase rates of violence.

The depth of the "deniers'" self-deception was brought home to me by none other than Arnold Schwarzenegger. In 1991, Schwartzenegger was visiting Vermont in his role as President George Bush's spokesperson for Physical Fitness and Sports at the same time that I was there on a lecture tour. I attended a press conference he gave at an elementary school and questioned his fitness as a spokesperson for this cause in light of the fact that many of his films encourage acts of violence that are highly detrimental to physical fitness. He was visibly irritated and refused to answer my question, but as several journalists continued to pursue the same issue, he became increasingly disturbed. In an attempt to demonstrate his responsible behavior he told us, "If you saw *Kindergarten Cop*, for instance; the original script . . . did not have any exercise program whatsoever. . . . And I insisted . . . that we put in around five to seven minutes of exercising as a means to get those kids in shape. I don't have to tell you what power for instance just a movie like *Saturday Night Fever* had. I mean, the whole world was disco dancing after that movie came out . . . " This comment was followed by stunned incredulity. How could he fail to draw the implications of what he had just said? The answer no doubt lies buried in the ten million dollars he was being paid at the time for his second *Terminator* film.

The gargantuan profits of the entertainment industry lead both to extreme denial and to enormous contributions to politicians that ensure that very little will be done to stop the continued treatment of our children as a commercial market to be exploited for profit rather than as a treasured national resource. Greed is draped in First Amendment hypocrisy. Even measures like placing warning labels on violent and pornographic CDs have been depicted as threats to the First Amendment.

Besides denial, the entertainment industry's major public response to the culture of violence it has created is that "it's up to the parents to monitor what their children play with or watch on the screen." Whenever I hear this response, I think of the parents who have told me over and over again, "We won't let our son watch violent movies or TV shows, or play with violent toys or video games, or buy CDs with rapist violent lyrics, but the boys at school and on the block won't play with him; they call him a geek and a nerd. He comes home so upset. We are in such a quandary. Should we go against all our beliefs and succumb, or do we let him continue to be ostracized by the other boys?" I will never forget the two professors I sat next to at a luncheon following a presentation at their university. They spent almost the entire time telling me about how exhausted they and their wives were from their efforts to protect their sons from the culture of violence. They were particularly concerned at that time about the video game *Doom*, one of the earliest "first person shooter" games, which permits boys to directly pull the trigger and kill rather than cause characters in the games to kill. (The game, which provides excellent training, rehearsal, and desensitization, was a favorite of the Columbine killers.) All the other boys had the game, and their sons had for months been on a campaign to get them to buy it. When we got up from the table, one of the professors sheepishly admitted to me that he and his wife had broken down only a few days earlier and gotten their son *Doom*.

In light of the fact that the industry promotes and thrives on this "pestering power" of young children, its self-righteous "it's up to the parents" borders on the sadistic.

Boys Will Be Boys' six chapters on entertainment and toys describe the culture of violence of the late '80s, but both the descriptions and the recommendations are as relevant today as they were then. (The last twelve years provide us with further evidence of the naïveté and futility of relying on the good will of the entertainment industry to reform itself.) While different TV programs, films, video games, etc. are popular now than in the late 1980s, very little has changed with respect to the level of violent content. For example, at a 1999 concert, rage rock band Limp Bizkit lyrics included " . . . I pack a chainsaw . . . I skin your ass raw / And if my day keeps going this way / I just might . . . break your fucking face tonight." (During the performance a woman was allegedly raped. By the end of the concert, gang rapes, looting, and fires were reported.) Compare these lyrics to some from the late '80s quoted in the "Music and Wrestling" chapter, like these from rapper Eazy-E: "I creeped on my bitch with my / Uzi machine / Went to the house and kicked / down the door / Unloaded like hell . . ." I also reported at the time that "at a concert in Los Angeles featuring the group X, a girl of seventeen was raped at knife point."

There is only one area in which radical change has taken place since the late 1980s. At that time the World Wide Web was in its inception; now, in 2002, it provides millions of young children and adolescents with access to material posted by hate groups that advocate violence and provide information on how to put together explosive devices, and by pornographers who provide graphic portrayals of violent sex. Chat rooms pose the danger of children and adolescents being lured into encounters with rapists and murderers.

The National Institutes of Health has commissioned a five-year project to examine the effect on children of viewing raw images of sexual violence on the Web. I see no reason to assume that its effects would be any different from those that have already been confirmed with respect to TV and film violence.

A July 23, 2002 *Wall Street Journal* article entitled "Porn-Blocking Software for Kids" evaluates various filters intended to protect children by blocking access to inappropriate sites. Two of them—including one that has "seven filtering categories (from 'hate speech' to 'weaponry')"—are judged highly effective. They provide parents with the possibility of protecting their young children from these materials. As demand grows, filters will undoubtedly become increasingly refined and accurate. Informal interviews with librarians lead me to believe that if the filters became more discriminating, most libraries would no longer object to them.

Television

When it comes to television, according to a 1999 Kaiser Family Foundation "Kids and Media" study, children spend an average of close to twenty hours a week watching TV, down somewhat from the twenty-four hours of TV watching in the late '80s. This decrease is no doubt due to the greater amount of time children now spend playing video games and on the Web. According to the American Psychological Association, the average child now watches eight thousand televised murders before finishing elementary school. That number more than doubles by the time he or she reaches age eighteen. These numbers are lower than the late '80s estimates of TV murders—this may be due in part to the fact that boys now spend less time watching murders and more time practicing them in the form of video games.

A recent drop in boys' interest in professional wrestling is good news but most likely temporary. The World Wrestling Federation has a long history of peaks and dips and is already working on coming up with some new themes and wrestling stars—having lost amongst others the popular Rock, who has moved into action films.

Since June 1997, all new televisions thirteen inches or larger must contain a V chip that permits parents to block programs rated V for violence by the networks. While 40 percent of parents now own a TV equipped with a V chip, more than half of them are unaware of it. Of those who are aware, about one in three has used it to block programs with sexual or violent content. These figures are not suprising, since no educational campaign accompanied the introduction of the V chip. The introduction of the ratings and the V chip has also been accompanied by an increase in material that is inappropriate for children. According to the conservative Parents Television Council, during prime time "in terms of sexual content, coarse language, and violent material combined, the per-hour figure almost tripled from 1989 to 1999."[19]

While the V chip is a small step in the right direction, it is not nearly enough. I stand by my recommendation that lock boxes that permit parents of young children to block all adult TV channels be mandatory in new TV sets, and that they be combined with the creation of a high quality Children's Public Broadcasting System (CPBS) and a major educational campaign aimed at parents. Ideally, parents of young children would be able to block all stations except CPBS. But even without CPBS, the lock box, combined with an educational campaign, would permit parents to block all channels except those more appropriate for children, such as Nickelodeon, Disney, and public television. This would represent a considerable improvement over the present situation.

Film

When it comes to films, gore-filled 1980s slasher series like *Nightmare on Elm Street* and *Friday the 13th* have been replaced with gore-filled 1990s series like *Scream*. *Halloween*, started in 1978, continues in 2002 with its eighth installment, featuring more dismemberments and piercings by Michael Myers, the series' psychotic killer. Arnold Schwartzenegger will be getting $30 million for his next film, *Terminator 3*. But he, Sylvester Stallone, and Steven Seagal are getting a bit old to go on playing violent adventure heroes, and so a crew of younger males are being brought in to star in these films. Newcomer Vin Diesel, with his action comics body, got $10 million to star in *XXX*, which opened in August 2002.

In the late 1980s, I reported on my own informal survey of movie theaters, which revealed that R ratings were rarely enforced. It was obvious to me that R-rated action adventure and horror/slasher films were in fact made for young male teenagers. In a report released in September 2000, the Federal Trade Commission (FTC) revealed that out of forty-four R-rated films the agency had examined, thirty-five were consciously aimed at and marketed to teenagers under the age of seventeen. Since the release of the FTC study, congressional critics have pressured filmmakers not to market R-rated films to young boys, and the National Association of Theater Owners has urged its members to keep young theatergoers from viewing very explicit or violent movies. Some members have complied with this request, and some filmmakers have produced a few somewhat less violent films, which—like XXX—are rated PG-13. But several gore- and violence-filled films are already scheduled for release in 2003, including Quentin Tarantino's Kill Bill. Young boys will undoubtedly flock to them. Will most theater owners keep them out? I doubt it. It is not surprising that even small improvements are not likely to be long-lasting, since, unlike film regulations in European countries, which are buttressed by law, the enforcement of the Motion Picture Association of America (MPAA) ratings is entirely voluntary.

In 1992, when I gave a lecture on the culture of violence to a group of Americans working and living in Europe, one of the women in the audience told the story of how her husband had snuck their nine-year-old son into a Brussels movie theater to see Batman, which was rated inappropriate for young children. The film was about to start when the lights went on and the manager came out. It had been brought to his attention, he said, that an underage child was present, and the film could not be shown until the child was removed. While the ACLU views such regulations as a major threat to the First Amendment, judging by the applause from my American audiences whenever I tell this story, regulations to protect children from violent entertainment would have considerable support in this country. In fact, these Americans in exile told me that they were making every effort to continue to live in Europe until their children were grown up in order to protect them from the American culture of violence. Unfortunately, Europe has in recent years been inundated by this culture, and many Europeans view this as a contributing factor to their violent crime rates, which, while still much lower than those of the U.S., have gone up considerably in the last few years.

I would not be surprised if the European countries, with their far greater commitment to the well-being of children, began in the not-too-distant future to extend their movie regulations to videos, video games, etc. The creation of a Children's Public Broadcasting System also seems more likely to happen in Europe than in the U.S. German television has already created exactly the kind of exciting, danger-filled adventure show for boys that I suggested could replace violent adventure films on CPBS. One of the most popular action shows on German television is a program called *Medicopter 117*. It is centered on helicopter rescue crews, which get people out of very dangerous situations— planes that have spun out of control, mountain climbers in life-threatening situations, people trapped in a depot for explosives, etc. The program has been running since 1998, and Peter Jännert, its editor-in-charge, explains "We predominantly get the younger audience, particularly little boys. They like the dangerous rescue missions, they like the helicopter and the technical feats involved. The presentation of positive heroes works."[20]

Toys

Since the late 1980s I have made repeated visits to Toys "R" Us. While many of the toys have changed over the years, the violence remains. In the late '80s, a few games offered historic military simulations. In 2002, military toys and games cover an entire large wall. The German WWII military is especially well represented—I counted a total of nine German soldiers on display, including a German Panzer Division Officer and a Luftwaffe General. Some German weaponry was also featured, including the Luftwaffe Stuka Dive Bomber. Swastikas were removed. (I am surely not alone in finding these offensive on a very personal level.)

In the late '80s, the very violent Transformers were extremely popular. In the '90s, the Mighty Morphin Power Ranger dolls (based on the very violent TV show) were at their peak, as were toys connected to professional wrestling. I did not see any Power Rangers, but wrestling dolls and Transformers were still around. "Spiderman Venom," which features a "Snap-on Battle Grip for Pummeling and Kicking Action," has taken center stage.

A major section of the boys' toys section is still devoted to killing, kicking, shooting, destroying, and blowing up. But in 2002, I found no outright sadistic toys, such as the "Dissect an Alien" and "Monster Lab" sets I describe in the toy store chapter. Sadism appears to be out—at least for the time being. Another positive development is the popularity of the Harry Potter toys. This points to the fact that boys do not have to kill and destroy in order to have fun. After the heroism that firefighters displayed on September 11, I was surprised not to find a single firefighter action hero.

Given the enormous financial power of the entertainment industry, it is unlikely that American children will receive any real protection in the near future. The industry's hiding behind the First Amendment continues to receive support from misguided civil libertarians. But the real threat to the First Amendment comes not from regulations to protect children but from the abandonment of antitrust laws, which has placed the media in the hands of a few large corporations free to manipulate political content.

Boycotts aimed at advertisers of undesirable TV shows may help for a while, until the heat is off and the industry feels free to relapse, but a CPBS and lock boxes are necessary to provide adequate long-term protection. For other forms of entertainment, only legislation to protect children will be truly effective. Undoubtedly, as children grow older, enforcement becomes more difficult. But even less-than-perfect enforcement would lead to a drop in the adolescent market for violence-filled films sufficient to decrease production.

Media education is the solution of choice of most of my colleagues. It can be helpful, but is not nearly enough. It is akin to accepting the absence of any enforced regulations to keep drinking water clear of pollutants, and recommending instead an educational school program aimed at teaching children about the harmful effects of their drinking water and what they can do to protect themselves.

WHAT ABOUT OUR NATIONAL SECURITY?

In the chapter entitled "Real Men, Wimps, and Our National Security," I argue that the men who run our country are often handicapped by their adherence to the values of the masculine mystique in making rational foreign policy decisions. The evidence presented in that chapter received further corroboration from the research done by Brian D'Agostino, who in 1990 conducted a survey on "self-perception and national security beliefs" as part of his Columbia University doctoral dissertation in political science. The survey indicated that male hawks apparently wanted to maintain high levels of military power in part in order to uphold an image of themselves as "not feminine." This appeared to be unconscious on their part. D'Agostino found that 44 percent of the variance of policy preferences with respect to militarism was explained by differences in self-perception. He points out that if political decision making were based on rational considerations, we would not expect a correlation between self-perceptions and hawkish beliefs, just as we would not expect to find a correlation among biochemists between their self-perception and their acceptance of competing biochemical theories.

Columnist Anthony Lewis captured this irrational motivation in a June 16, 2001 *New York Times* Op-Ed, when he wrote, "A single proposition . . . underlies President Bush's determination to destroy the ABM treaty. He does not believe in treaties limiting weapons of mass destruction, even though they have manifestly worked well, because they limit our freedom of action—as if somehow mutual security diminished American manhood."

In the first edition of *Boys Will Be Boys*, I wrote that the values of the masculine mystique and the equation of militarism with patriotism obscure the fact that many national defense decisions have more to do with the economic interests of the military-industrial complex than with defense needs. Nowhere is this more clear than in our government's failure, in spite of numerous terrorist attacks against Americans and repeated warnings by experts, to focus on the single most serious threat that has confronted us in recent years—terrorism. Already in the mid- to late 1990s, experts like Lawrence Korb, Assistant Secretary of Defense in the Reagan administration, now at the Council on Foreign Relations, and Vice Admiral John J. Shanahan, the former head of the Atlantic fleet, warned that much of the enormous Pentagon budget was being misdirected toward weapons systems and military forces that would have little value in protecting us from the real threat of terrorism.

In a recent speech, Shanahan stated, "Back then [in 1996], I said our greatest threat is from terrorists, and our massive military forces have little utility against such threats. We have to use diplomacy and economic power to eliminate the conditions that create terrorism. No one paid attention then. I was shunted aside by a bureaucracy unwilling to think outside the box. . . ."[21] In more recent years, a commission headed by former Senators Gary Hart (Democrat) and Warren Rudman (Republican) warned that terrorist attacks in the United States were the greatest danger confronting us. But instead of putting money into building the best possible intelligence capabilities, we continued to spend tens of billions every year on unnecessary nuclear warheads, a highly controversial missile defense system (many experts question its effectiveness), B2 bombers, and other weapons designed for Cold War missions.

It seems highly unlikely that terrorists could have scored their extraordinary September 11th level of destruction if our government had genuinely been addressing our national security needs. We are now tragically aware that the FBI and CIA have antiquated computers, that nothing was done to ensure indispensable communication between these two agencies and with the Immigration and Naturalization Services. Providing the FBI and CIA with the best up-to-date computers, and ensuring that agencies communicate properly and quickly, that counterintelligence aimed at terrorists is of the highest order, that large numbers of agents and future agents are learning Arabic and becoming expert at understanding the mindset of terrorists, and that airport security is significantly upgraded, does not win the support of the weapons manufacturers who donate millions every year to politicians. There is no moneyed lobby whose goal is to ensure the safety of Americans.

The tragic events of 9/11 have served as a further bonanza to the weapons industry. In a post 9/11 interview with the *Wall Street Journal*, Boeing vice chairman Harry Stonecipher stated, "The purse is now open; any members of Congress who oppose the new [weapons] spending frenzy by arguing that we don't have the resources to defend America . . . won't be there after

November."[22] In keeping with his analysis, the Senate and the House voted overwhelmingly on June 2002 to give the Pentagon another $40 billion, which brings the military budget up to close to $400 billion for next year. Representative Jerry Lewis, Republican of California and the chairman of the House Defense Appropriations Subcommittee, said it was the largest vote in support of a military spending bill in recent memory, and demonstrated that even lawmakers who in the past had argued that the military was getting too much of the federal budget were making defense a top priority after 9/11. "The vote today is a reflection of the public's strong support for the military," he asserted.[23] What the public is not told is that much of this money will go to projects that help to line the manufacturers' pockets, but do little if anything for our safety. Admiral Shanahan points out that the National Security Agency (NSA) and intelligence-gathering operations will only get about one-twelfth of the funds allocated to the Pentagon. He notes that "funding for the Immigration and Naturalization Service has also been cut!"[24]

Along similar lines, in discussing the June appropriation to the Pentagon, Colonel David Hackworth, best-selling author and our nation's most decorated living soldier, argues that we should not "allow the Pentagon to spend big on Cold War stuff —designed to take down the Soviet Union, which crashed a decade ago—like the half-billion-dollar heavy Crusader artillery system, the billion-dollar new reconnaissance helicopter, or the $5 billion budgeted to buy F-22 Stealth fighters . . ." He goes on to comment that "Most of the congressional porkers are afraid to stand tall and stop this the-enemy-is-at-the-gates spending spree. They don't want to come off as opposing a military buildup when their fickle constituency has war fever. And besides, there's the dough that'll be pumped into their states—

not to mention their re-election coffers—for all this so-called 'urgent anti-terrorist war gear.' We've got to start putting our money in the right places, not the right pockets. Like making our cities and our ports of entry—air, sea and ground—terrorist-proof instead of wasting another $60 billion on Star Wars II. Why shouldn't our ports be at least half as tight as the Super Bowl? And why aren't the Marines, Special Operations, Coast Guard, FBI and Border Patrol more sensible investments than most of those gold-plated toys at the top of the Pentagon's shopping list?"[25]

In keeping with the values of the masculine mystique, patriotism is equated primarily with weaponry, regardless of how unnecessary the weaponry might be to our national security. In the fall of 2001, Attorney General John Ashcroft placed the gun lobby above national security by refusing the FBI's request to use records of gun background checks to investigate suspected terrorists. It has been revealed recently that Ashcroft's claim at the time that it would be illegal to make these records available to the FBI was contrary to his legal staff's opinion.[26] Yet Ashcroft was not then, nor is he now, stigmatized as an unpatriotic wimp endangering our national security. But opposing weapons or wars, however unnecessary they may be to our national security, leads to just that kind of labeling.

Taking measures to prevent wars or terrorist acts is not viewed as patriotic, either. Jessica Stern teaches at Harvard's Kennedy School of Government and is the author of The Ultimate Terrorists. She points out that "effective counter-terrorism policy design requires an understanding of how terrorist leaders mobilize their constituency."[27] But understanding how the enemy thinks and wins adherents, so that we can better prevent future attacks, does not appear to be of more interest to our government now than it was in earlier times. Thinking ahead, except for spending on weapons, is just not part of the game.

Moorehead Kennedy, who served as a Foreign Service officer and the Acting Economic Counselor in Iran, was one of the hostages taken at the U.S. Embassy in Tehran and held from 1979 to 1981. When the hostages returned to the U.S., our government had a rare opportunity to consult with Americans who had been in daily contact with Islamic terrorists for over a year. But Kennedy tells us that "when we came back, the State Department didn't even want to debrief us. They didn't want to know the names of our captors."[28] The Reagan administration's lack of interest in understanding the terrorists' thinking and the conditions that bred them in order to better deter future attacks was matched by its lack of interest in thinking through the long-range effects of arming that sadistic, megalomaniac dictator, Saddam Hussein. Instead of using American influence to deter European countries that had already begun to arm Saddam, our government allowed the Hughes Aircraft Company to sell sixty of its helicopters to Hussein in 1982, and went on to allow U.S. firms to supply much of the technology for Iraq's weapons of mass destruction. Nor did Saddam's 1984 use of poison gas against his own people, the Kurds, serve as a deterrent. This policy continued during the next administration. According to author Alan Friedman, President Bush and Secretary of State Baker were convinced that it would be in the interest of American business to maintain a close relationship with Saddam Hussein, and so they secretly committed taxpayers' money to assist him and allowed U.S. companies to help him develop further his lethal weapons projects. Friedman comments that "More than anyone else, Bush and Baker must bear responsibility for paving the road to Operation Desert Storm, a war they justified as necessary in order to wipe out the very

nuclear weapons capacity the U.S. had helped foster in Iraq."[29]
Now, in 2002, George Bush II threatens to wage a preventive
war against Iraq in order to get rid of Saddam Hussein, who we
are told represents a major threat to our national security.

Volumes will undoubtedly be written in future years on how
our support of the Taliban and our failure to do anything about
the Saudi Arabian financing of Al Qaeda facilitated the events of
September 11, 2001. Already in a recently published book,
French intelligence consultant Jean-Charles Brisard reports that
in a July 2001 conversation at New York's Plaza hotel, John
O'Neill, the former head of the FBI's unit in charge of investigating Al Qaeda, told him that "all of the answers, all of the
clues allowing us to dismantle Osama bin Laden's organization,
can be found in Saudi Arabia."[30] O'Neill was so frustrated by the
State Department's lack of support—which he attributed to corporate oil interests—for his efforts to dismantle the Al-Quaeda
network that after twenty-five years with the Bureau he
resigned his post, and in August 2001 became the head of security at the World Trade Center. O'Neill died on 9/11 while trying to rescue others from the Twin Towers. When Francis
Fukuyama states that "masculine policies" are necessary in
order to deal with the likes of Saddam Hussein or Osama bin
Laden, he overlooks the fact that it is these short-sighted "masculine policies" that help to arm and support these kinds of
leaders in the first place—and, in the case of bin Laden, to tolerate him even after he instigated terrorist attacks against
American embassies and military personnel.

Our national security depends not on continuing "masculine
policies" that have proven to be disastrous in the past, but on
moving away from them. The simplistic reliance on military
buildup and military actions to defend our nation has been
equated with manhood (as defined by the masculine mystique)

and patriotism. But it only serves to hide the fact that our defense policy is often driven not by a careful thinking through of the long range consequences of our actions, but rather by a macho mentality combined with corporate interests.

IN RETROSPECT, WHAT WOULD I CHANGE?

ABOUT HOMOSEXUALITY

The etiology of homosexuality is in no way a central issue of *Boys Will Be Boys*. My decision to address it at all grew out of my realization that the single major barrier to changing the way boys are raised is parents' fears that these changes could lead their sons to become gay. Since I devoted only a few pages to this topic, I did not do the extensive interviews with experts and intensive survey of research that I did on other topics. My discussion of homosexuality is the only area in which I was presented with knowledgeable criticisms and concluded that some were well taken. Several mental health professionals wrote to me, and one psychologist even included a one-and-a-half-page bibliography. While they all expressed their otherwise very positive reaction to the book, their major objection was to my quoting Charles Socarides as an authority on the topic of homosexuality. Socarides, they informed me, had in 1972 led the opposition to the removal of homosexuality from the American Psychiatric Association's list of mental disorders, and fought throughout the 1980s to have it reclassified as such. His and psychologist Henry Biller's attribution of homosexuality to inadequate father/son relationships, they went on to point out, was not grounded in any solid research and had been rejected in recent years by, among others, the American Psychiatric Association and the American Psychological Association. They universally characterized Socarides as a homophobe. With the exception of John Stoltenberg, author of *Refusing to be a Man*, who wrote that he sees "almost all of men's sexuality and sexual behaviors as the product of social construction," my critics pointed to the increasing scientific research supporting the view that there is a strong biological component to homosexuality. What they failed to realize is that almost all of this research was published starting in 1991—after the publication of *Boys Will Be Boys*. For example, Simon Levay's article "A Difference in Hypothalamic Structure Between Heterosexual and Homosexual Men," which received considerable attention, appeared in the August 1991 issue of *Science* magazine. Michael Bailey and Richard Pillard's study of twins, which showed when one identical twin is gay there is a 52 percent chance that the second twin is gay, versus a 22 percent chance with fraternal twins, was also published in 1991.[31] In my discussion of homosexuality, I do present psychoanalyst Richard Isay's view that homosexuality is constitutional, that it is not fathers' rejection that causes sons to become gay, but rather that fathers sense that their sons are "different" and then reject them. But this view—based on his therapeutic treatment of over forty gay men—had not yet received support from scientific studies. Now, in 2002, I am inclined to believe that biology plays a significant role in the development of homosexuality.

While some felt that my wording was at times unfortunate, almost all the men who wrote understood why it was necessary for me to reassure parents that following my recommendations would not lead to their sons' becoming gay: "I understand your very legitimate concern that homophobia will be employed to attack your arguments in favor of curtailing the violence encouraged in boys and men by our culture and institutions," one of them wrote. John Stoltenberg went as far as to say, "The biggest value of your book, I feel, is that it deconstructs parental panic about not raising boys to be 'real boys.' " In 2002 as in 1990, there is no doubt in my mind that taking on homophobia as well as patriarchy would have been foolhardy and destructive. I have no regrets about this. The issue of parents' negative reaction to their sons' being gay is further complicated by the fact that for some this reaction is based at least in part on the fear of AIDS.

WOMEN'S ROLE IN SUPPORTING THE MASCULINE MYSTIQUE

"During the mid-1960s there was a bumper sticker that read, 'Girls Say Yes To Boys Who Say No.' It was speaking about the Vietnam War, but something of the same attitude needs to happen today. This is where the women must be educated. If we really want what you term the "masculine mystique" to wither away, then it has to not be successful. Men will have limited motivation to change so long as the macho guys and the rich guys still get the girls *and they do*." A male reader made this comment in a letter he sent me soon after the publication of *Boys Will Be Boys*. Around the same time another man wrote, "I can tell you from many years of experience in law enforcement (and other fields) that violent sexist men inevitably have numerous women attracted to them."

I addressed this issue very briefly in the conclusion to the book, stating that the traditional definition of masculinity leads many women "to admire and reinforce just those traits that are conducive to rape, wife abuse, child abuse, and murder." It deserved more attention.

With the advent of the second women's movement of the late 1960s and '70s, the patriarchal social structure was challenged, and enormous changes were made, but cultural attitudes that have been held over millennia do not change easily, especially when they receive support from entertainment and sports industries that glamorize tough, violent men. There is no doubt in my mind that much progress has been made in women's attitudes in the last thirty years, but women still have a distance to go, and they must learn to distinguish between positive traditional male traits, such as courage, strength, and sense of adventure, and destructive traits, such as emotional callousness and the desire to dominate. Women must learn to value caring and empathy more than muscles, wealth, and social standing.

CHILD NEGLECT

In the conclusion to *Boys Will Be Boys*, I wrote "Most working mothers must conform to a marketplace designed for men with homemaker wives. This leaves millions of children unattended and emotionally deprived—a good breeding ground for anger and violence. Inadequate day care compounds the situation." There has not been much change since then. Compared to other advanced industrialized countries, the United States continues to have the least family-friendly parental leave policies and the most mediocre day care. Far too many of our children continue to receive inadequate care at home and in day care. This problem also deserved more attention.

THE MASCULINE MYSTIQUE AND MERGER MANIA

I deeply regret that due to an error on the part of my publisher, the hardcover 1991 edition of *Boys Will Be Boys*, with its thirty-two pages of endnotes and bibliography, was published without an index, rendering it far less likely to be used for research purposes. As I see it, I was an early victim of the mergers and acquisitions movement. Doubleday was bought by the German company Bertelsmann, and the firing spree began—that inevitable attempt, regardless of consequences, at cutting costs after paying billions for the acquisition of a company. As my book was going into production my editor was "retrenched" and replaced with an employee who had seniority. I have it from a reliable source that a lack of communication between the two editors on the topic of the index led to it not being ordered.

The compulsion to acquire more and more corporations—often in the form of hostile takeovers—strikes me as a non-violent manifestation of the desire to dominate. My publisher's reaction when I requested that the flawed printed copies be destroyed and a new round printed with an index also seemed connected to the theme of the book. The company could not afford the $40,000 that this would cost, I was told; Doubleday had just signed a $5 million contract with General Norman Schwarzkopf for his Gulf War memoirs. I eventually paid to have indexes sent to a thousand libraries around the country, with the hope that at least some of them would take the trouble to rebind the book and insert the index.

CONCLUSION

While I am convinced that we can create a society in which violence, both criminal and in warfare, would be enormously diminished, I do not believe that we will ever achieve a completely violence-free society, just as we have not achieved a perfect democracy, or a society in which all citizens are truly equal. Nevertheless, enormous progress has been made since the days of absolute monarchy, slavery, and the subjection of women. This progress would not have been possible were it not for the extreme adaptability of human beings. How many Southerners in the year 2002 think that black people should be enslaved; how many men think that women should not be allowed to vote or serve on a jury? One hundred and fifty years ago, a majority would have held these views. Along similar lines, imagine a baby boy born and raised in Saudi Arabia—he will very likely think it normal for women to be covered from head to toe and not be allowed to leave the house or travel without their father's or husband's permission. Take the same boy and raise him in the U.S., and he will have an entirely different set of values and outlook—he may still have a desire to be in control and dominate women, but it it will take a greatly mitigated form. It is this adaptability that makes it possible to create a far less violent world than the one we know.

I began by pointing to Seth Maxell as a poster child for how to raise less violent boys. But Seth is blessed with concerned, educated, affluent parents who have done everything possible to help him grow up to be a non-violent man, and such circumstances are rare. If we are serious about moving boys away from violence, we need societal changes. We must introduce the kinds of school programs described in this book—child-rearing classes that will decrease the early abuse and neglect that put boys at higher risk of violence, and conflict-resolution, anti-bigotry, and anti-bullying classes that will move boys away from a concept of masculinity focused on dominance and violence and provide them with non-violent ways of resolving conflicts. A common objection to these kinds of programs is that they are "frills," and that schools need to focus on the three R's. This overlooks the fact that so many children's failure in school is due to parental neglect, abuse, or just plain ignorance about early childhood development; and that classes in social skills lead to decreases in anti-social classroom behaviors that hamper learning.

We need regulations to protect children from entertainment that encourages violence—parents need to be helped, not hindered, in raising their children. We need family-friendly policies in the workplace that ensure extended leaves after childbirth, and quality, affordable day care of the kind that exists in France and other European countries, where day-care professionals undergo years of training in child development and health, and are paid on the same scale as schoolteachers. How can we possibly afford all this? We squander tens of billions every year on unnecessary weapons systems, and tolerate a level of Pentagon unaccountability that would be inconceivable in any other government agency—a 1999 audit by the Department of Defense revealed that $2.3 trillion in Pentagon spending could not be accounted for. The answer lies in moving beyond the values of the masculine mystique that dominate our government policies and spending priorities.

Notes

1. Goldstein, *War and Gender*. Cambridge: Cambridge University Press, p. xiii

2. Gilmore, *Misogyny*. Philadelphia: University of Pennsylvania Press, p. xii

3. Violent crime statistics quoted here and below are taken from the annual FBI Uniform Crime reports.

4. Kimmel, "Violence and Gender," in *Brother*, Spring 2002

5. Chesler, Woman's Inhumanity to Woman. Thunder's Mouth Press/Nation Books, pp. 38–39

6. Fukuyama, in *Foreign Affairs*, September/October 1998, pp. 39, 28, 37

7. "Not Only in America: Gun Killings Shake the Europeans," *The New York Times*, May 11, 2002

8. See Eleanor Maccoby, *The Two Sexes*. Cambridge, Massachusetts: Harvard University Press, 1998, pp. 40–41, 56; and Alfons Crijnen, et al., "Comparisons of Problems Reported by Parents of Children in

12 Cultures" in Journal of the American Academy of Child and Adolescent Psychiatry, 36:9, September 1997. See Richard Lippa, Gender, Nature, and Nurture. New Jersey: Lawrence Erlbaum Publishers, 2002, pp. 117, 118

9. See James McBride Dabbs. Heroes Rogues and Lovers: Testosterone and Behavior, McGraw Hill, New York, 2000, p. 78. See also Lippa pp. 108–112, and Deborah Blum, Sex on the Brain: The Biological Differences Between Men and Women, New York: Penguin Books, 1997, pp. 174–176

10. See Blum, pp. 60–62

11. Richard Wrangham and Dale Peterson. Demonic Males: Apes and the Origins of Human Violence. Boston: Houghton Mifflin, 1996, p. 24

12. Fatherneed. New York: The Free Press, 2000, p. 1. Pleck's findings are also reported in Pruett, p.1.

13. The 1997 National Study of the Changing Workforce, pp. 38–41

14. These articles include: Jeff Benedict, Todd Crosset, Alan Klein, "Male Student-Athletes Reported for Sexual Assault: A Survey of Campus Police Departments and Judicial Affairs Offices," Journal of Sport and Social Issues 19:2, May 1995

15. Benedict, p. 222

16. Staffo, The Tuscaloosa News, July 21, 2000

17. AP Sports, Breaking News, March 9, 2000

18. Bredemeier's speech and the mission goals are from the Mendelson Center website.

19. V chip information is from "Parents and the V-Chip 2001," a July 2001 Kaiser Family Foundation Survey. Information about content is from "What a Difference a Decade Makes," a Parent Television Council 2000 special report comparing prime time language, sex, and violence in 1989 and 1999.

20. I am indebted to Hannfried Von Hindenburg, who at my request interviewed Peter Jännert in April 2002 and transmitted this information and quotes from Jännert by e-mail, and to Jännert for agree-

ing to the interview.

21. "Admiral Questions Bush Defense Spending," *The Baltimore Chronicle*, June 2002

22. See William Hartung, "Pentagon Spending Spree," *Multinational Monitor Magazine*, November 2001

23. "Budget Increases For Pentagon Pass Easily," *The New York Times*, June 28, 2002

24. *The Baltimore Chronicle*, June 2002

25. From David Hackworth's Web site

26. "Ashcroft's Words Clash With Staff on Checks," *The New York Times*, July 24, 2002

27. From KSG Media Experts, December 7, 2000 (online interview)

28. Comments made at a John F. Kennedy Library and Foundation Forum on "The Roots of Terrorism," November 5, 2001

29. *Spider's Web: The Secret History of How the White House Illegally Armed Iraq*. New York: Bantam Books, 1993, p. xviii

30. Jean-Charles Brisard and Guillaume Dasquie, *Forbidden Truth: U.S.-Taliban Secret Oil Diplomacy and the Failed Hunt for Bin Laden*, New York: Thunder's Mouth Press/Nation Books, 2002

31. "A genetic study of male sexual orientation," *Archives of General Psychiatry*, 48, 1089–1096

The Problem:
The Acceptance
of Violence
as a Way of Life

1
When Male Behavior Is the Norm...

It is a universal fact of human existence that what we know best, that which forms part of our everyday mental landscape, is also that which we most take for granted, and question the least. And so some of the strongest jolts to our awareness, the deepest reorientations in our thought, often come from being confronted with the obvious.

Any child that ever shot a marble, any adult that ever played billiards, already knew the gist of Newton's first law of motion—that in the absence of an externally applied force a body continues in motion in a straight line. But it wasn't until seventeenth-century thinkers such as Galileo, Descartes, and Newton focused on the study of objects in motion that a real awareness and understanding of this obvious fact developed. Its detailed characteristics, its consequences and implications, its connections with other natural phenomena, were studied; and a revolution in our thinking about nature was started.

In the late 1950s and early 1960s, when Martin Luther King and other civil rights activists demanded equal rights for African-Americans, the facts of racial segregation were well known and, with few exceptions, taken for granted by conservatives and liberals alike—they were part of the sociocultural landscape in which people grew up. Before the civil rights movement there was no major outcry, no loud moral outrage about the fact that in the South, and very often in the North, African-Americans were not allowed into the same restaurants, apartment buildings, or universities as whites. Few Americans were disturbed that African-American soldiers served in segregated units and African-American actors and actresses could aspire to little more than playing Step'n Fetchits or fat mammies.

Just as early scientists focused attention on the motion of objects, civil rights leaders focused attention on the plight of African-Americans. In both cases these facts were then no longer taken for granted; they were critically examined. In one case they were studied and laws of nature were discovered; in the other case they were examined and found to be contrary to our legal codes and moral convictions.

The development of the women's movement is another example of a mental landscape that was jolted by an examination of what had been taken for granted. When Betty Friedan published *The Feminine Mystique,* people already knew that millions of talented, creative women—many of them graduates of the best universities in the country—were spending their lives shining floors and wiping noses. As a result of her pointing out and questioning the obvious, the self-images and lives of millions of women were radically altered.

When the exploring of the obvious impinges on our sociocultural institutions and traditions—as in the case of the civil rights and the women's rights movements—it often meets with deep resistance. The questioning of assumptions, values, and patterns of behavior that have been taken for granted for so long can be threatening to people's sense of identity and self-worth; it can create feelings of guilt.

Today we all know that most acts of violence are committed by men. This knowledge is so much part of our mental landscape that we take it for granted. But the time has come to focus our attention on it so that we can begin to explore ways of significantly reducing the incidence of violence.

The resistance to this focus is enormous. I became aware of its depth soon after I started working on the topic of male violence. "What are you writing about?" a male acquaintance inquired. I had barely started to explain when he informed me that he felt personally offended by my topic. *He* had never committed any acts of violence. He responded this way in spite of my having made it clear that I was in no way suggesting that all men are violent or have a propensity to violence. *To say that men as a group are more violent than women is by no means to assert that all men are violent, violence-prone, or accepting of violence as a way of resolving conflicts and attaining power. It means only that a significantly higher percentage of men than women exhibit these tendencies.* This in no way denies that a large percentage of men are not violent at all, that a certain percentage of women are violent, or that some women are more violent than some men.

Shortly after this exchange, I was asked the same question by a male colleague. When I answered him, he expressed surprise that I had chosen this topic since women were also very violent. When I pointed out that approximately 89 percent of violent crimes are committed by males, that approximately 1.8 million women a year are physically assaulted by their husbands or boyfriends, and that wars have always been, and continue to be, initiated and fought almost exclusively by men,[1] he changed the subject. Changing the subject turned out to be a frequent reaction when the subject of my book came up.

While more women reacted to the topic with enthusiasm, I was surprised at how many were put off. "Isn't it divisive to harp on the fact that men commit most acts of violence?" was one reaction. But it is an elementary rule of research in the physical and social sciences that to deal effectively with a problem one must first identify the population that is afflicted with it. It would greatly hamper their work if medical researchers and practitioners didn't "harp on" the fact that in the United States, AIDS afflicts primarily gay people and intravenous drug users, or if psychologists didn't take cognizance of the fact that females are more frequently victims of depression than are males. If we are to understand the causes of violence and work on finding a cure, we must identify the high-risk population.

Another typical response was "But women can be just as violent as men if they are given a chance." Or more emphatically: "But women can be even more vicious than men when they are given a chance." In fact, as we shall see in Chapter 3, there is some reason to believe that *as a group* men have a greater biologically based potential for violence than women. This is not to deny that women are capable of violence. The number of women arrested for violent crimes went up by 41 percent between 1986 and 1990. But the baseline for female violence was so low to begin with that 88.7 percent of persons arrested for violent crimes in 1990 were nevertheless male. My hunch is that if we continue to allow our children to be raised in a culture of violence, female violence, while remaining small by comparison to male violence, will continue to increase.

But whatever the future might reveal with respect to the female potential for violence, at present it is overwhelmingly male violence that leads many men and women in our country to live in fear of murder, rape, and assault, which has led to the death of millions in war, which threatens us with nuclear annihilation. In light of this, it seems to make no sense that the immediate reaction of many women is that if given a chance, women would be just as violent. It is as if I told people I was writing a book on the problem of malnutrition among impoverished Americans, and they instantly protested, "But wealthy Americans would be just as malnourished if they grew up in similar conditions."

These reactions are so intense because we live in a society in which men have not traditionally been subject to generic criticism. In recent years there has been a growth of literature dealing critically with such issues as patriarchy or the traditional definition of masculinity, but these works have yet to become part of mainstream thinking. Books about men who suffer from the "Peter Pan syndrome" or have difficulty expressing emotions have been popular. But they are usually written from a very personal and practical female perspective (how to deal with or avoid such men), and do not represent a systematic critical analysis of masculinity.

And so with few exceptions, men have never been subject to the kind of scathing generic criticism to which women have been subjected throughout history. In literature and opera; in religious, philosophical, and psychological texts, women have been depicted as deceitful, fickle, childish, irrational, untrustworthy, morally inferior. Female inferiority has been certified by some of the greatest thinkers in our cultural tradition.* "The male is by nature superior, and the female inferior," wrote Aristotle.[2] One of the major female defects, according to the early Greek philosophers, was a lower level of rationality than the male.

In Western history, females have been viewed as emotional and passive, and have been identified with nature and the body. Males have been viewed as active and rational, not allowing emotions to interfere with their thinking or decision making.

It should come as no surprise that St. Thomas Aquinas, the brilliant thirteenth-century synthesizer of Aristotelian and Christian thought, categorizes women together with children and insane persons with respect to their inability to give reliable evidence because of their "lack of understanding."[3] While echoing the Aristotelian tradition, Aquinas was also influenced by the biblical view of woman. In Genesis, God creates Eve to provide Adam with "a helper fit for him." Eve's moral weakness is such that shortly after her creation she succumbs to the temptation of eating the forbidden fruit. She is responsible for the expulsion of Adam and all humankind from the Garden of Eden.

This mind-set continues to influence our thinking. Freud believed that women "show less sense of justice than men . . . they are less ready to submit to the great exigencies of life . . . they are more often influenced in their judgments by feelings of affection or hostility."[4] This moral weakness, so reminiscent of Eve's, is no longer taken for granted solely on the basis of

* It is true that many of the virtues which our society ostensibly prizes—sacrifice, service, charity, self-abnegation—are "feminine" virtues and women have at times been considered the morally superior sex. But, as philosopher-theologian Mary Daly has pointed out, while lip-service is given to sacrifice and charity, ambition, power, and ruthlessness are the true values of those in socially dominant roles. The self-sacrificing virtues of mothers and wives are recognized and encouraged, while at the same time women are viewed as morally, and in every other way, inferior (reflecting their true position in society).

religious myths or traditional views. Now it is buttressed by psychoanalytic theory. As Harvard psychology professor Carol Gilligan points out, Freud and other prominent psychologists, such as Jean Piaget and Lawrence Kohlberg, base their theories of moral development exclusively on the study of boys. When it is discovered that girls do not conform to the boys' model, they are declared defective.

So it is easy to see why many men and women feel uncomfortable focusing on violence as a male problem. Men's behavior is assumed to be paradigmatic and so men are not accustomed to questioning it. Women, who are accustomed to being viewed as defective, have no difficulty with self-criticism, but are not used to criticizing men. To criticize men, the way so many men have criticized women, is consciously or unconsciously perceived as aggressive, emasculating behavior. So while we all know and take for granted that most acts of violence are committed by men, many of us refuse to allow ourselves to focus on it. To do so would imply criticism of an aspect of male behavior which is at the core of some our most serious domestic and international problems.

This lack of focus on violence as a male problem can be seen clearly in well-known works on aggression and violence. Ethologist Konrad Lorenz devotes two chapters at the end of his book *On Aggression* to the problem of aggression in modern society, but never focuses on the fact that *male* aggression is the core of the problem. Lorenz writes about his hope "of improving the chances of permanent peace by arousing, in young *people*, militant enthusiasm for the ideals of art, science, medicine and the like"[5] (my emphasis). But it is clear from all of human history, and from his book, that it is not young people, but some young men, who threaten peace.

It is easy for Lorenz to ignore this because he is part of a cultural tradition in which women—their behavior, feelings, life situations, values—are seldom, if at all, included, in books about "mankind." When women appear in books or research, it is almost invariably in relation to men, either to be declared defective by comparison—as in Aristotle, Freud, or Kohlberg—or as men's helpers, lovers, wives, mothers. But most of the time, as in Lorenz's work, women are invisible, forgotten. Human behavior is equated with male behavior and it never occurs to the author or the readers that the book or study that is supposed to be about "mankind" or "human beings" or "people" is really only about men. Since women are not part of the author's consciousness, he or she has nothing to contrast men's behavior with, and so that behavior is taken for granted, perceived as normal "human" behavior.

Psychiatrist Anthony Storr, in *Human Aggression,* argues that women are naturally passive. To understand the significance of this title one must reverse the situation. Is it imaginable that a book primarily about female passivity and very secondarily about male aggression would bear the title *Human Passivity?*

The unconscious omission of women is further facilitated and obscured by the use of "man" and "men" to refer to males exclusively as well as to both males and females. When I recently reread a large number of books *(On Aggression* and *Human Aggression* among them), it became clear to me that they were about men only. Yet this had never occurred to me previously, although I had used some of these books in classes I had taught, and had read them with utmost care. Like everyone else, I was so accustomed to the omission of women that I had remained completely unaware of it.

In her essay entitled *On Violence,* Hannah Arendt points out, "In the last edition of the Encyclopedia of the Social Sciences 'violence' does not even rate an entry." She goes on: "this shows to what an extent violence and its arbitrariness were taken for granted and therefore neglected; no one questions or examines what is obvious to all."[6] But while Arendt herself no longer takes violence for granted and focuses her essay on it, she never shows the slightest awareness of the equally obvious fact that it is almost exclusively male violence that she is writing about.

In his essay *The Moral Equivalent of War,* William James argues for universal conscription—in what we today would call a Peace Corps—as a way of chaneling those aggressive tendencies that throughout history have gone into war making. He writes of the "conscription of the *whole* youthful population" (my emphasis), but there is no question that he is thinking of the male youthful population only: a few paragraphs later he points out that as a result of "their" conscription to public service "the women would value them more highly, they would be better fathers and teachers of the next generation."[7] As usual, women make their

pearance in the text as an afterthought, in relation to men
nly.

In a 1989 article, physicians Perri Klass and Lila Wallis point
out that "in medical school the paradigm patient is known as
the 70 kilogram man.' "[8] He is "all man"—never suffers from
endometriosis or other female problems. Studies of diseases
that afflict both men and women "have typically used male subjects exclusively, with the results generalized—as if males were
the generic humans . . . No one does a study on a group of
women and then assumes the results apply to men, but the
reverse happens again and again." The authors conclude that
"in medicine, women have been a variant, a deviation from the
concept of the human norm." Their view is supported by a 1985
Public Health Service study which states that lack of data on
women has led to a limited understanding of women's health
care needs. By 1989, three members of Congress were calling
for an investigation of whether federally funded medical research excludes women from clinical tests.

The development of in-depth awareness that male is the norm
leads to permanently altered perceptions. With respect to violence we are now at a stage analogous to the pre-Newtonian
billiard player who knows that a moving object continues in a
straight line unless deflected. It is obvious that acts of violence
are committed largely by men, but since we continue to take for
granted that male is the norm, we remain unaware of it: we pay
very little attention to this fact in our attempts to understand
and deal with crime, war, or the threat of nuclear annihilation.

To recognize violence as a primarily male problem we would
have to focus equal attention and place equal value on the behavior of women. This would change our entire perspective. It
would make it as impossible to write a book about male aggression entitled *Human Aggression* as it is to write a book about
"female passivity" entitled *Human Passivity*. The resistance to
doing so is enormous. The reactions to my book topic are a
testimony to this resistance, as are the reactions encountered by
David Rothenberg when he wrote an article on essentially the
same topic.

Rothenberg is the founder and former director of the Fortune
Society, a highly successful and respected nonprofit organization for ex-convicts. Over a period of fifteen years he talked with

thousands of adult and teenage male criminal offenders, and found "an amazing similarity" in their explanations of what led them to commit crimes: "I wanted them to know that I was no sissy" and "I had to prove that I was a man"[9] were among the most frequent explanations given. (Rothenberg's experience is with lower-class, mostly ghetto men. In a February 17, 1986, *New York Times* article that reports on high rates of gang rape on college campuses, an administrator at the University of Florida explains this behavior in the following way: "The men almost cannot say no, because if they do their masculinity will be in question.")

Wanting to share his experience and insights, Rothenberg wrote an article in which he pointed out, "Child abuse, racism, drugs and alcohol habits, and poverty are at the top of lists in any study about anti-sociability. Yet daughters grow up in the same homes as sons. But the young girls rob, steal, and kill with one-tenth the frequency as their male counterparts."[10]

Rothenberg sent the article to *The Village Voice,* a publication for which he had been writing for years. "The *Voice* had printed everything except my laundry list," he told me, "but they rejected this piece." After collecting a few more rejections he published the article in his own Fortune Society newspaper.

Rothenberg was equally unsuccessful in getting experts concerned with crime control to focus on why half the population is so much less violence-prone than the other half. It is because male behavior is tacitly accepted as the norm and is not subject to generic criticism that Rothenberg encountered so much resistance to dealing with and learning from this discrepancy in male and female behavior.*

Imagine the reaction if close to 90 percent of all violent crimes were committed by women! If tabloid headlines carried stories,

---

* This is not to deny that sex differences in criminal behavior have at times been acknowledged by criminologists. Cesare Lombroso, one of the founders of the field, attributed women's lower crime rates to their passivity, lack of male vigor, and lower position on the evolutionary ladder which led to their being less differentiated biologically and therefore less vulnerable to the "atavism" which he thought made some men natural criminals. This theory testifies to the depth of commitment to women's defectiveness. It is no small feat to turn a lower level of criminality into a symptom of evolutionary inferiority! More recently James Q. Wilson and Richard J. Herrnstein devoted a chapter in their book *Crime and Human Nature* to gender differences, but they focused on biological differences without examining the role that socialization plays.

with some regularity, of man-hating women leaving behind them cross-country trails of murdered men's bodies; of ex-wives, driven by fits of jealousy, killing their former husbands and their children; of groups of women killing each other in rival gang fights. Imagine the scorn that would be heaped on women for killing *each other* off at such high rates! How quickly such behavior would be perceived as an aberration, a deviation from the norm of male behavior, a "women's problem" to be dealt with urgently! Think of the fuss made about menstrual emotional stress and menopausal hot flashes as reasons for keeping women out of top political decision-making situations—this in a century which has given us Hitler and Stalin and more recently Khomeini, Idi Amin, and Saddam Hussein.

But when so many men commit violent crimes, or when nations led by men engage endlessly in armed conflict, there is no awareness that we are faced with a "men's problem."

What could be more immoral than the taking of innocent human lives? Yet we find a dearth of theologians, philosophers, or psychologists deploring this behavior. There is no Aristotle or Aquinas telling us that in light of men's historical record of bloodshed, we are compelled to view man as "an imperfect woman afflicted with natural defectiveness."

The power of deep-set cultural assumptions is so overriding, the glorification of war so all-pervasive, that in spite of the fact that many more men than women commit acts of violence, thinkers such as Freud, Piaget, and Kohlberg can comfortably adhere to the view that it is women who are morally deficient. The reverse is unthinkable, for as long as male behavior is taken to be the norm, there can be no serious questioning of male traits and behavior. A norm is by definition a standard for judging; it is not itself subject to judgment. So while individual men can be found defective in light of a paradigm of manhood, they cannot be found defective by comparison with women, who stand outside the paradigm and are seen as secondary and defective to begin with.

Since male behavior is the norm, warfare and violence are not only accepted as central, normal parts of human experience but they are transformed into heroic, exciting events.

When my older daughter was in fifth grade and studying Latin American history, she came home from school one day and asked: "Mommy, why did Pizarro want to go to South America and kill people? Why did he want to conquer Incas? Why didn't he stay in Spain with his family and get a job? If he wanted to travel he could have, without killing all those people."

Had she been studying European or ancient history she probably would have asked the same type of questions about Alexander the Great or Napoleon. Or she might have wondered why the French and English couldn't resolve their differences peacefully rather than kill each other in the endless battles of the Hundred Years War. Closer to home, she might have been perplexed as to why Alan Seeger and so many other young American males were eager to die in World War I, a war for which historians are still trying to figure out a rationale. Seeger was the young Harvard graduate who wrote the well-known poem beginning with the lines:

> I have a rendezvous with Death
> At some disputed barricade,
> When Spring comes back with rustling shade
> And apple-blossoms fill the air—

When World War I started, Seeger and two hundred other young Americans living in Paris marched to the Hôtel des Invalides and joined the Foreign Legion. Flowers were thrown and handkerchiefs fluttered as the intrepid young American heroes signed up for the Great War. Less than thirty of them survived. Seeger met his "rendezvous" in 1916 in the July offensive along the Somme. Casualties at the battle of the Somme alone have been estimated at roughly 650,000 Germans, 420,000 British, 195,000 French. The total casualties of the war came to approximately 37.5 million.

All of this would no doubt have been as incomprehensible to my daughter as Pizarro embarking for South America to kill and conquer Incas.

What struck me about her questions was that I had never heard them raised in any elementary, high school, or college history class I had attended. In the context of hundreds of pages describing endless rivalries, struggles for power, and then the inevitable wars, there might be a passing remark on the terrible waste of lives in a particular war or at a certain battle, but the very idea of conquest as an acceptable goal and war as an acceptable way of settling conflict or enhancing power was taken for granted in books and lectures. Just as it was, and still is, taken for granted that Alan Seeger and his comrades were heroes rather than deeply misguided young men who excitedly went off to kill total strangers. These young men should be viewed as tragic victims of a very primitive value system, one that elevates to a virtue the mutual killing of people of different nationalities and/or conflicting views and interests.

The linking of manhood with toughness and destructive aggression goes far beyond the real need for strength and courage in standing up to a genuinely life-threatening attack, or the survival value of being prepared to cope with possible threats. This linking transcends nationalities. A maxim from Ireland tells us: "Bloodshed is a cleansing and sanctifying rite and the nation which regards it as a final horror has lost its manhood." A Spanish saying goes: "When a nation shows a civilized horror of war it receives directly the punishment for its mistakes. God changes its sex, despoils it of its common mark of virility, changes it into a feminine nation, and sends conquerors to ravage it of its honor."[11] Such maxims and attitudes are geared to encouraging young men to sacrifice their lives in *unnecessary* wars.

There have been through the centuries men and women who have experienced and conveyed the absurdity of the ceaseless violence that has characterized human history—the insanity of bearing sons, caring for them, loving them, only to see them go off when they reach manhood to risk death over issues which a few years later are hardly remembered, over issues which could have been resolved through negotiation and compromise. Aristophanes saw it in the fifth century B.C. In his play *Lysistrata,* the women of Athens and Sparta withhold sexual favors from their husbands until they stop their endless and senseless fighting. When the horny men, pointing erections rather than swords at each other, finally agree to stop fighting, Lysistrata serves as mediator and in a few minutes resolves the disputes which have caused endless deaths for years.

Jonathan Swift described the absurdity of war in *Gulliver's Travels.* In it the empires of Lilliput and Blefuscu are engaged in a long and bloody war caused by a disagreement over which end of an egg should be cracked when opening it.

Director Philippe de Broca captured it in his film *King of Hearts*. Set during World War I, the film portrays the relative sanity of the inmates of an insane asylum compared to the insanity of the soldiers slaughtering each other in the outside world.

But as long as male behavior is seen as the norm and the waging of war as the ultimate manifestation of masculinity, war will continue to be a normal part of human existence and people will remain blinded to its absurdity.

Since women have throughout history been predominantly nonviolent, it makes sense to look to them both to play a larger role in the political arena and to provide men with a different kind of role model.*

One would expect women, and feminist women in particular, to be most intensely aware of the need to imbue society with female values and to play a major role in bringing about this social transformation. But this has not always been the case.

No contemporary movement has done more to question traditional male-female roles and relations than feminism. Yet paradoxically, because the assumption that male is the norm was so deeply embedded in our culture, many women assumed that to be liberated meant to be like men.

A distinction needs to be made here. Insofar as women felt free to adopt positive male traits such as initiative, action, independence, and commitment to work, and tempered them with positive female traits, this was a major step forward. But especially in the early days of the movement, some feminists accepted and sought to emulate the caricatures of these positive male traits.

Their tacit assumption that male was the norm, prevented them from seeing that the male excesses of emotional detachment, toughness, and extreme competitiveness could be just as detrimental to the individual as the female excesses of self-sacrifice and dependency.

Had it not been for this assumption, feminists would not have felt so threatened by the possibility of biologically based psycho-

---

* Female political leaders such as Margaret Thatcher or Indira Gandhi have not provided a different role model. Gro Brundtland, the prime minister of Norway, has. As long as male behavior is the norm, those women who share male values and behavior are most likely to attain the highest political positions.

logical differences between the sexes. They would have realized that in a nuclear age, if differences were discovered, women's biological makeup might very well turn out to be more viable than men's.

Feminists have increasingly become aware and critical of the assumption that male is the norm. Psychiatrist Jean Baker Miller, novelist and social critic Marilyn French, and psychology professor Carol Gilligan are among those who have argued for recognition and appreciation of the differing values, attitudes, and behavior of women. At the 1984 National Women's Conference to Prevent Nuclear War, speaker after speaker echoed actress Joanne Woodward's opening remarks that "women are much more inclined than men to put a priority on peace and social stability."

In 1964 Betty Friedan wrote in *The Feminine Mystique* that "the feminine mystique has succeeded in burying millions of American women alive."[12] Friedan was speaking figuratively about the psychological thwarting of women. *By the 1990s, an increasing number of us had come to realize that the masculine mystique, if it remains unchecked, may eventually succeed in burying all of humanity not figuratively but literally.* We are becoming aware that what has until now been taken as normal male behavior and therefore as normal human behavior is the result of an historically outmoded and destructive masculine mystique, just as the normal 1964 female behavior described by Friedan was the result of a historically outmoded and destructive feminine mystique.

In each case the mostly positive traits that have traditionally been associated more with one sex than the other have been caricatured into thwarting images of what men and women should be like.

Nurturing, caring, sensitivity, spontaneity, a sense of connectedness with others, a concern with one's physical environment, were turned into childlike, empty-headed dependency, passivity, baby-producing, and homemaking, all geared toward consumerism.

Initiative, action, independence, curiosity, courage, competitiveness, abstract thinking, were molded into toughness, insensitivity, eagerness to fight and to seek out danger, callous attitudes toward sex, thinking detached from goal or purpose, all of it geared toward an egocentric and often obsessive need to be dominant and to win—whether it be wars, women, or higher ranks in the social pecking order.

The qualities that make up the masculine mystique have varied somewhat in both form and emphasis in different historical periods and social classes. The extreme competitiveness which is an important component of today's masculinity would have been highly repugnant to early nineteenth-century gentlemen who inherited the land and wealth that assured them a dominant position in society. But despite these differences there has been an ongoing thread of continuity in the paradigms of masculinity which have been taken for granted and have constituted the norm of human behavior for millennia. To achieve widespread questioning of some of the core characteristics of that paradigm, such as the need for dominance, toughness, and eagerness to fight, will not be an easy task. But it is perhaps one of the most important to confront us.

2
"Real Men," "Wimps," and Our National Security

The original intent of this chapter was to answer the objection that raising "wimps" would endanger our national security.

I could hear the sober warnings of the "realists": These ideas sound good in theory, but they won't work in the real world. If we stop imbuing our boys with the values of the masculine mystique, we'll end up raising nice, decent, sensitive men who'll do just about anything to avoid war and violence. But what about the Hitlers, the Khomeinis, the Husseins, and all the rest of the belligerent unliberated world? They'll go on raising strong, tough men ready to fight at the slightest provocation—or without any provocation at all. Our nice "wimpy" leaders will be sitting ducks as far as the international political scene goes. We can't afford this kind of experimentation, the "realists" will say; our national security is at stake.

I wanted to put this type of objection to rest. But the present focus of the chapter is quite different from its original intent. For the more research I did, the more experts I interviewed, the more I reflected on my findings, the clearer it became that our national security was already endangered. The "real men" who run our country are handicapped by the values of the masculine mystique in their ability to make rational foreign policy decisions.

These values also serve as a facile cover for self-serving economic interests. They help mask the fact that many national defense decisions have more to do with the economic interests of the military-industrial complex (which President Eisenhower warned of in his Farewell Address) than with defense needs. This further endangers our national security.

The chapter now focuses on the ways in which the masculine mystique hampers the "real men" in our government in their ability to deal rationally with national security issues. This is followed by a discussion of how it influences many citizens to support wars *unquestioningly,* and encourages young boys to sacrifice their lives in them, often unnecessarily.

PATRIOTISM, MANHOOD, AND WAR

Through much of our history, the failure to place "pragmatic" over moral concerns, the failure of a person in government to fully embrace a policy of unquestioning belligerence and/or full-scale war toward whoever "the enemy" might be at any particular historical time, has led to that person—or the governmental branch voicing opposition—being called pusillanimous, soft, weak, unmanly, unpatriotic, an abettor of the enemy, and most recently wimpish.

In 1848, then Congressman Abraham Lincoln was vilified in the Illinois press for his stance against the Mexican-American War, a war waged by the United States in order to take from Mexico some of its provinces. *The Register,* a newspaper in the district Lincoln represented, deplored "the foul disgrace" that "moral traitors" like Lincoln had brought on the nation's name and honor.[1]

In 1987, when I interviewed *New York Times* columnist Tom Wicker, he recollected that during the Vietnam War he was regarded by many as being unpatriotic because he opposed the war, but columnist Joseph Alsop, who supported the war, was not considered unpatriotic. Wicker explains: "You can't be considered unpatriotic if you're for a war . . . General LeMay said that the thing to do was to bomb them [the Vietnamese] back to the Stone Age . . . He was a national hero almost for that . . . whereas someone who demonstrated for peace at that time was regarded as sort of a wimp . . ."

To be deeply committed to negotiations, to be opposed to a particular war or military action, is not only considered unpatriotic, it also casts serious doubt on one's manhood.

Paul Warnke, chief American negotiator of the 1979 Salt II Arms Control Treaty between the United States and the Soviet Union, remembers being called a "weak wimp" by the Committee on the Present Danger, which succeeded in preventing the ratification of the treaty by the Senate.[2]

In the Contragate secret jargon, the name for the State Department was "Wimp." This was due to then Secretary of State Shultz's disapproval of the sale of weapons to Iran and diversion of profits to the Contras.

When Woodrow Wilson showed reluctance to enter World War I, Theodore Roosevelt charged that Wilson has "done more to emasculate American manhood and weaken its fiber than anyone else I can think of."[3]

In such a context, men in power are often eager to prove their manhood and patriotism through a willingness to send young men to war.

In his book *The Best and the Brightest,* which profiles the men who ran the Vietnam War, David Halberstam informs us that "the thing [Lyndon] Johnson feared most was . . . that his manhood might be inadequate."[4] In an interview with author Mark Gerzon, Halberstam confirmed that President Johnson wanted more than anything "to be seen as a man . . . he wanted the respect of men who were tough, real men . . ." When Johnson was told that a member of his administration was "going soft" on the war, he dismissed him with the comment

"Hell, he has to squat to piss." According to Halberstam, Johnson was by no means alone in these concerns. "Manhood was very much in the minds of the architects of [the Vietnam War]. They wanted to show who had bigger balls."[5]

In June 1985 when TV interviewer Larry King asked Speaker of the House Tip O'Neill (who was a personal friend as well as a political opponent of President Reagan) why the President wanted to intervene in Nicaragua, O'Neill responded, "It's his being a man." He went on to explain: "[The President believes] America has to show a firmness of manhood." "Do you think it's macho?" King then asked. "Yes," O'Neill responded.

After the 1989 United States military intervention in Panama, the *New York Times* ran a front-page story entitled, "War: Bush's Presidential Rite of Passage." The article pointed out that "for better or for worse, most American leaders since World War II have felt a need to demonstrate their willingness to shed blood to protect or advance what they construe as the national interest . . . All of them acted in the belief that the American political culture required them to show the world promptly that they carried big sticks."[6]

A year later, the press was discussing President Bush's need to prove his manhood as a motivating factor in his threats to go to war with Iraq. For example, in the January 7, 1991 issue of *Newsweek*, Washington correspondent Evan Thomas commented on Bush's tough talk about Saddam Hussein getting "his ass kicked," and reported that "some pundits have wondered if the President is still fighting the wimp factor."

These concerns are confirmed by former Defense Department consultant Richard Barnet's descriptions of the inner sanctums of power: "One of the first lessons a national security manager learns after a day in the bureaucratic climate of the Pentagon, State Department, White House, or CIA is that toughness is the most highly prized virtue . . . The man who is ready to recommend using violence against foreigners, even where he is overruled, does not damage his reputation for prudence, soundness, or imagination . . ."[7] As an example, Barnet points out that during the Vietnam War those generals who urged the destruction of numerous Chinese targets or the mining of Haiphong Harbor, including any Soviet ships that might have been there, were neither reprimanded nor did they lose their jobs when their advice was rejected by President Johnson.

On the other hand, "the man who recommends putting an issue to the U.N., seeking negotiations, or, horror of horrors, 'doing nothing' quickly becomes known as 'soft.' To be 'soft'— i.e., unbelligerent, compassionate, willing to settle for less—or simply to be repelled by mass homicide, is to be 'irresponsible.' It means walking out of the club."[8]

Barnet points out that since the onset of the Cold War "the outstanding bureaucratic casualties . . . have all been men who took modest risks to promote conciliation rather than confrontation."[9]

Among them are President Truman's Secretary of State, James Byrnes, who was accused of being an "appeaser" because he favored exploring the exchange of scientific information with the Russians at a Moscow conference in 1945.

In the 1950s George Kennan, former ambassador to the Soviet Union and father of our Soviet "containment" policy, lost political influence when he expressed the view that the Soviets did not represent a serious military threat in Europe and that negotiations with them were preferable to continued confrontation.

In 1962 Chester Bowles developed a reputation for "woolliness" because of a plan he proposed for the neutralization of Southeast Asia. For this and other suggestions intended to downgrade the use of force in the pursuit of the national interest (he was also opposed to the disastrous Bay of Pigs invasion of Cuba) Bowles soon lost his position as Undersecretary of State. Barnet points out that "ten years later [Bowles's plan] would look like a blueprint for a U.S. victory."[10]

It is not lost on career bureaucrats that "wimpish" advice is likely to lead to dismissal while "tough" advice is not. "That reality sustains a bureaucratic atmosphere that supports permanent military involvement," Barnet tells us.[11]

It is difficult to think clearly and rationally, to entertain all the possibilities objectively, when taking a "wimpish" position endangers one's high position in government and one's livelihood, and puts one at risk of being considered unpatriotic. Only men of exceptional courage will do so.

As long as those who favor negotiations and are reluctant to enter armed conflicts are put on the defensive, are considered "wimps," it will be exceedingly difficult to pull away the cloak of patriotism in which our military-industrial-congressional-academic complex is wrapped, and clearly analyze our military needs for the future.

In the early 1980s, conservative Republican Senator Charles Grassley of Iowa looked into Pentagon spending, and concluded that a sixty-to-eighty-billion-dollar *cut* from the military budget would enhance our national security. For only if the Pentagon stopped being a military welfare state would our weapons systems grow out of defense needs rather than the economic needs of manufacturers and "revolving door" officers.

Pentagon waste and unnecessary spending as well as the extraordinarily shoddy quality of many of the weapons that are manufactured under this system have been documented extensively.[12]

In summary, the equating of militarism with patriotism, the need to prove manhood through support of war, the fear of losing one's job if one is opposed to military intervention, the existence of powerful economic interests in keeping the military budget high, all serve to prevent a rational analysis of whether a particular war, military intervention, or weapons system is really necessary to our national defense.

THE DANGERS OF A ONE-DIMENSIONAL PERSPECTIVE

Richard Barnet is convinced that our national security managers suffer from a severe handicap in conducting foreign relations because they have no "training or incentive to develop understanding, compassion, or empathy for people in different circumstances from their own."[13] They are so removed emotionally from the desperate conditions that afflict billions of human beings that they cannot understand why people engage in any revolutionary activities. "Revolutionaries must be agents, dupes, or romantics."[14]

An important part of what enabled Chester Bowles and other "wimps" like him to foresee that getting involved in a war in Vietnam would be a calamitous mistake was their ability to empathize with the Vietnamese people, to see things from their perspective. They understood that Ho Chi Minh (the man who led the Vietnamese revolution against the French colonialists) was a national hero for the Vietnamese, and that the Viet Cong, which was the offshoot of the revolutionary army, had the enthusiastic support of the Vietnamese people. Because they understood this, they realized that it would be close to impossible for the United States to win in Vietnam.

To the architects of the Vietnam War, empathy was a "soft," "irrational," "effeminate" quality antithetical to their "rational," "hard-nosed" thinking. And so they were unable to develop a realistic understanding of the situation in Vietnam.

Robert McNamara's judgment was severely impaired by these values when he served as Secretary of Defense and played a major role in escalating the war. He was renowned for being a cool, cerebral administrator who never let emotions interfere with his thinking. McNamara seems to have learned from experience. He now speaks of "the necessity of looking at your actions through the eyes of your opponent—that is absolutely fundamental and we don't do that." McNamara made this point in a 1987 interview with the author in the course of explaining that instead of automatically looking at every Soviet move as a hostile and threatening act we must not forget how our acts influence them. One then becomes aware that a lot of what they are doing is reactive and defensive rather than aggressive. He is now convinced, he told me, that "much of what the Soviets have done [in the nuclear arms race] is reaction to what we've done."

Roger Fisher is a Harvard Law School professor and the director of the Harvard Negotiation Project, a research project devoted to the development and dissemination of improved methods of mediation and negotiation. William Ury is its associate director. In their bestselling book, *Getting to Yes*, Fisher and Ury argue that in conflicts between individuals or nations "the ability to see the situation as the other side sees it, as difficult as it may be, is one of the most important skills a negotiator can possess." They point out that in negotiations, especially when there is considerable bitterness, "feelings may be more important than talk." It follows that "failing to deal with others sensitively as human beings prone to human reactions can be disastrous for a negotiation."[15]

One of the methods of negotiation described by Fisher and

Urey is the "one-text procedure," in which mediators consult with the negotiating parties and develop a list of interests and needs, with options for dealing with them. Negotiations are then based on this "one-text procedure," instead of on conflicting proposals. This method was successfully used by American mediators to help Egyptians and Israelis arrive at the Camp David agreements.

They emphasize that being strong, not allowing others to take advantage of you, and not trusting anyone unless you have good reason to are essential ingredients of successful negotiation. But strength and realism, according to them, are very different from the concern with dominance and ego that characterizes the masculine mystique and leads to a greater commitment to scoring points and posturing than arriving at a truly advantageous agreement. These concerns, combined with a lack of empathic understanding of how the other side feels and thinks, are typical of "positional bargaining," which they reject as both irrational and ineffective.

The authors also reject "soft positional bargaining" in which the tendency is to put too much trust in the other side and make concessions too readily. (Perhaps the best-known example of "soft" positional bargaining was the Munich Pact in which Chamberlain made disastrous concessions to Hitler.)

In "principled bargaining," which Fisher and Ury advocate, the focus is on interests, not on positions, so that the participants do not lock themselves into stances with which their egos are identified. Participants are viewed as problem solvers and the goal is to arrive at a fair agreement that will be acceptable to all sides. The emphasis is on long-range effects. An unbalanced outcome is bad for *both* sides. An example of this is the Versailles Treaty, in which the victors of World War I imposed hard positional bargaining on the Germans, which led to economic disaster and intense humiliation for Germany. These factors then played a major role in Hitler's coming to power. Approximately twenty years after the treaty was signed, Germany attacked those very countries that had forced it on them. Fifty-five million lives might well have been saved and the endless destruction and suffering of World War II avoided had the Versailles treaty been more equitable.

When one side is committed to using force in order to get

exactly what it wants, negotiations will not work. This was the case in the tragic uprising of Chinese students and workers in 1989. But this does not detract from the fact that in a large percentage of situations where there is at least some desire to avoid violence, using principled empathic negotiation can lead to an equitable solution, whereas positional negotiation leads to stalemate or war.

During much of our history, the tendency has been to identify political rationality with hard positional bargaining and the willingness to go to war when such bargaining fails. Being weak, irrational, and "wimpish" has been identified with soft positional bargaining and a disinclination toward war.

But if we look carefully at the distinction between weak positional bargaining and principled bargaining, we realize that many of the men maligned as being "wimps" have in fact been much closer to the latter in their way of thinking about foreign policy than to the former. They have often shared with the Harvard Negotiation Project a concern with long-range effects, with arriving at a fair solution based on objective and ethical criteria in conflict situations. They have been aware of the need to understand and empathize with the other side in order to arrive at a realistic long-range solution. They have tended to shun the kind of macho posturing and concern with ego and dominance that characterize hard positional bargaining.

For example, there is far more reason to believe that Chester Bowles's plan for the neutralization of Southeast Asia grew out of these qualities as well as the "skill at inventing options," which Fisher and Ury consider to be "one of the most useful assets a negotiator can have,"[16] than from any weakness of character or tendency to cave in and make unnecessary concessions.

WHEN THERE IS NO EMPATHY FOR THE VICTIMS OF WAR

Ron Kovic is the Vietnam War veteran whose autobiography, *Born on the Fourth of July*, was made into a film with the same title. Kovic returned from the war a paraplegic, and became increasingly enraged as he realized that his sacrifice had been unnecessary. In the book he writes:

He had never been anything but a thing to them, a thing to put a uniform on and train to kill . . . They were smooth talkers, men who wore suits and smiled and were polite, men who wore watches and sat behind big desks sticking pins in maps . . . They had never seen blood and guts and heads and arms. They had never picked up the shattered legs of children and watched the blood drip into the sand below their feet.[17]

Toward the end of his service as Secretary of Defense Robert McNamara would sometimes weep in public ceremonies honoring Vietnam war heroes. Yet in engineering our Vietnam policy McNamara was the epitome of emotional detachment, never allowing emotions to influence his thinking. Richard Barnet explains that "he could function as the famous McNamara machine only after the object of his attention, notably the two to three million victims created in Vietnam during his Pentagon service, were quantified and dehumanized."[18]

If McNamara had allowed himself, *from the beginning,* to feel empathic toward the young Americans who would lose their lives there or return maimed and crippled, or if President Johnson and the men around him had been more concerned with saving lives than showing who had "bigger balls," Ron Kovic might not be spending his life in a wheelchair.

But, as we have seen, saving lives is not a top priority in the halls of power. Being compassionate and concerned about human life can cause a man to lose his job. It can cause a woman not to get the job to begin with. Women's reputed empathy and compassion are viewed by many as rendering them unqualified for high offices that involve "tough" international decision-making. (The German Nazi party was strongly committed to this point of view. Author Mark Gerzon tells us that at its first meeting in 1921 a resolution was passed that a woman could never be accepted into the leadership of the party and the governing committee. Only men possessed the required "strength of hardness.")

David Evans, a former Marine lieutenant colonel who is now the military correspondent for the Chicago *Tribune,* vigorously rejects this callous, unempathic attitude. He is convinced that it leads to a thoroughly unrealistic foreign policy based on fantasy and denial.

Evans describes the postcombat "hamburger"—the pieces of

legs, arms, and guts strewn around the battlefield—in terms almost identical to Kovic's. After his combat experience in Vietnam, he came away feeling that the widely accepted concept of war as an extension of politics—put forth by the German military theorist Clausewitz—was "complete rubbish." He is now deeply convinced that "there is no difficulty on this planet that could not be worked out at some lower level of confrontation . . . It is absurdly out of proportion to the issues for men to do this [go to war]."[19]

He is convinced that direct involvement in combat leads most men away from a macho, belligerent response to political conflict. War becomes a nightmarish reality, not a patriotic, flag-waving, exciting demonstration of manhood. A relatively small percentage (Oliver North comes to mind) are excited by battle and cannot get enough of it.

Evans is fond of pointing out that many of the men in our government who take the toughest, most macho positions on foreign policy and nuclear strategy have never seen any form of combat. McGeorge Bundy, Robert McNamara, and Walt Rostow served in World War II, but their service was limited to planning and analysis. They all supported the Bay of Pigs invasion of Cuba and the Vietnam War.

In the Reagan administration, Pat Buchanan, Elliott Abrams, and Richard Perle favored support for the Contras and more American involvement in Nicaragua. They took "tough" positions on the nuclear arms race. None of them has been in the service.

The social conditioning that romanticizes war and teaches young boys to repress empathy, to be tough, to be fearless, not to cry, to value winning more than anything, leads to the development of "mental machismo" among politicians who make decisions unencumbered by emotional or moral scruples. Their machismo requires the "courage" to make decisions without concern for the human suffering they will bring to others. This "detached" decision-making, which is in fact deeply attached to the values of the masculine mystique, is then viewed as the epitome of male "rationality."

After having spent three years at the Pentagon, David Evans is convinced that our most dangerous failure to deal with reality is in the area of nuclear policy. He describes the men who develop our nuclear strategy and our defense policy as suffering from severe "denial psychosis." The fact that most of them have never experienced any war at first hand makes it easier for them to shield themselves from any concrete sense of what fifty million casualties or the destruction of ten of our major cities might really mean.

Their tendency to look at war "as a huge football game" further facilitates avoidance: Evans describes an ad by the manufacturer of the F-15 fighter that compares its uses to football plays, stating that "we've gone to a long deep pass from a nuclear line of scrimmage." Star Wars is perceived as "blocking the kick."

We have all heard of the briefcase that contains the secret codes needed to authorize the launching of our nuclear weapons. It follows the President everywhere, day and night, enabling him to react immediately in case of nuclear attack. But how many of us are aware that this all-important briefcase, whose contents hold the key to destroying all life on earth, is called the *"football"*?

The use of sports, especially football language, among men in power when dealing with international politics is both striking and frightening in terms of the mind-set it reveals. In the Vietnam War, the May to October 1972 bombing of North Vietnam was named "Linebacker I"; the December bombing was "Linebacker II."

In describing the White House reaction to Mikhail Gorbachev's July 1985 announcement of a unilateral nuclear test ban, then National Security Advisor Robert McFarlane stated that it led to "a sense that they were more agile now, so we had to become more agile ourselves. It's like being a member of the Notre Dame football team and you're used to playing Davidson. And all of a sudden Davidson recruits some players from the New York Giants. You have to adapt and move quicker yourself."[20]

In the chapter on sports we shall see how the obsession with winning, and the notion that you can never go wrong being too tough, owe much to the training in extremely competitive sports that so many American boys receive from the youngest age, both as participants and as spectators.

The obsession with winning is so strong that when Steven

Kull, a psychologist attached to the Center for International Security and Arms Control at Stanford, interviewed seventy-seven people in the field of national defense (including Pentagon and Defense Department officials, members of the National Security Council, senators, and nuclear theorists), he found that while most of them recognized that it didn't matter in a military sense whether we or the Soviets had more nuclear weapons, they still were committed to our having more.*

Kull quotes a Rand corporation analyst who, after acknowledging that all his security-related rationales for nuclear parity did not work, answered the question, "So why do you feel a need to maintain equality with the Soviet Union?" by saying: "I don't know. I just *feel* better that way . . . I just do [my emphasis]." Kull comments: "It seems that he was genuinely reporting the emotional gratification derived from maintaining American status relative to the Soviet Union independent of its security relevance."[21]

Many of the men Kull interviewed volunteered almost identical statements. To them, on a very personal emotional level, the strategic balance was a symbol of America's stature as a superpower and *maintaining this stature was seen as intrinsically worthwhile regardless of our national defense needs.*

In sports there is no further goal, no purpose, beyond winning. *It seems that for many men in government the goal of "winning," of having more than "they" do, becomes a substitute for a carefully considered foreign policy based on an analysis of the effects that various policy decisions are likely to have on human beings.*

Carol Cohn is a research fellow at the Center for Psychological Studies in the Nuclear Age, an affiliate of the Harvard Medical School. She recently spent a year at the MIT Center on Defense Technology and Arms Control, a nuclear think tank.

* Almost every expert agrees that when the average nuclear bomb has a destructive power thirty times that of the Hiroshima bomb, roughly two hundred to four hundred impregnable (submarine-based) nuclear devices are enough to deter any conceivable enemy attack. Everyone I interviewed, including former Secretary of Defense Robert McNamara, former CIA Director William Colby, and former Assistant Secretary of Defense for International Security Affairs and Salt II negotiator Paul Warnke, was in basic agreement with this view. Steven Kull's book *Minds at War,* and his article "Nuclear Nonsense" shed light on why we have approximately fifteen thousand more nuclear devices than we need.

Like Evans and Kull, Cohn is convinced that the thinking of nuclear theorists is based on the avoidance of nuclear reality. In an article based on her experiences at MIT, she explains how both the limited subject matter they deal with—in their "war games," nuclear strategists are concerned primarily with the survival of weaponry, not human beings—and the "techno-strategic" language they have created make it possible for these normal, decent men to talk about and plan nuclear holocaust as though it were just another job. The use of "abstraction and euphemism" allows them to talk about nuclear holocaust without having to deal with the reality behind their words. In their language the incinerating of cities is referred to as "countervalue attacks." "Collateral damage" is the term most often used to refer to human deaths. A "surgically clean strike" refers to "attacks that can purportedly 'take out'—i.e., accurately destroy—an opponent's weapons or command centers, without causing significant injury to anything else."[22]

The MX missile, which carries ten warheads, each with the explosive power of 300 to 475 kilotons of TNT—*one missile is the bearer of roughly 250 to 400 Hiroshimas*—is referred to as a "damage limitation weapon."

The nuclear strategists are detached from reality in yet another way. Their theorizing is about weapons, not about people.

If asked about human survival, they will explain that they don't deal with those issues. They consider the separation of technical knowledge and theorizing from social, psychological, or moral issues to be legitimate and necessary. This separation enables them to talk about weapons that are supposed to protect people "without actually asking if they *can* do it, or if they are the best *way* to do it, or whether they may even damage the entities you are supposedly protecting."[23] While they will admit that these are valid questions, they see them as separate, outside their realm of concern or expertise. To get involved in these broader questions would allow emotions to interfere with their thinking.

The false equation of rationality with absence of emotion or concern with moral issues or questions about goals leads to their dealing with the nuclear issue as a calculus of weaponry. It requires that they not allow themselves to imagine what nuclear destruction would be like, what it would mean concretely to have some of our major cities wiped out or, very possibly, all life on earth destroyed.

Many of the men Cohn worked with occupied high advisory positions in the government. One was a science advisor to the President, another was the head of the Arms Control and Disarmament Agency, another had been writing the Secretary of Defense's Report to Congress for the last twenty years.

The thinking of our defense intellectuals—which is the foundation of our nation's nuclear policy—lives up to the highest standards of the masculine mystique. It is tough-minded, "sober," "rational," untouched by any feelings of empathy or moral concerns. It is also based on the most extreme psychological avoidance, which is justified by the erroneous idea that rationality requires absence of emotion and moral concerns.

The masculine mystique teaches men to be tough, to repress empathy, and not to let moral concerns weigh too heavily when the goal is winning. These qualities have become identified with rational, realistic political thinking, or "political realism."*

But what is rational or realistic about not allowing the human cost of war to be a major factor in political decision-making? Why is *not* weighing the suffering of the Ron Kovics who fight wars or of the civilians who are innocent victims, a condition of rationality? Why does political realism require a lack of concern with moral issues?

Could it be that if politicians allowed themselves to feel empathic they would feel so sorry for the soldiers who might be maimed or killed in war that they would be paralyzed, unable to do what they rationally understand to be necessary to defend our nation against dangerous enemies? Would empathy and moral concerns about killing civilians lead them down an irrational road to appeasement and enslavement? Is this how emo-

---

* The basic ideas of "political realism" can be traced to interpretations of the writings of Thomas Hobbes and Niccolo Machiavelli. Hobbes's basic premise is that "man's" natural state is to live in a world entirely dominated by fear, force, and manipulative calculations. Machiavelli believed that human beings are naturally inconstant, untrustworthy, and power-hungry, and so only a naive, idealistic politician would be influenced by moral concerns. Political realism serves as a self-fulfilling prophecy. It reinforces the human potential for selfish behavior and discourages altruistic behavior. The fact that the female half of the human race spends much of its time in life-promoting, caring activities is ignored.

tion would interfere with rationality? Is this why they must repress empathy and moral concerns?

The answer is quite clearly no, for the tendency to defend oneself against attack is so strong, both in terms of individuals and groups, that it is almost unthinkable that leaders imbued with empathy and moral concern would allow our nation to be attacked and not respond. The bloody history of our species suggests that much greater effort is required to restrain violent response than to encourage it.

The main function of repressing empathy and moral concerns is that it permits men in power to pursue goals that are in the national interest—as *they* define it—*regardless of the human or moral cost.*

The claim that theirs is an "instrumental" rationality that does not get involved in questions of values and goals detracts from the fact that their goals and values are almost entirely limited to what they take to be national power, prestige, and economic interests. (As we have seen, their definition of our national interest often grows out of their own ego needs, their needs to prove manhood, or the desire to secure their position of power.) The claim to "instrumental" rationality permits them to avoid fundamental questions. For example, if our national interest is related to the safety and welfare of our citizens (isn't that what the Constitution tells us?) then what could be more contrary to it than a callous and cavalier disregard for the lives of young Americans who are sent off to fight in wars whose need has never been rationally assessed?

THE JOHN WAYNE SYNDROME, OR RAISING BOYS TO BE SOLDIERS

The belligerent policies of the "real men" in power are made possible through public support given by citizens raised to believe that being patriotic means supporting their nation's wars and military actions without questioning. The values of the masculine mystique prepare boys, from the youngest age, to someday willingly risk their lives in battle. Boys find out at a very early age that war is respectable. There are endless role models of great conquerors, heroic warriors, and brave soldiers.

It would be unthinkable for a respected children's publishing house to publish a book for children entitled *Famous Public Hangings,* or *Famous Witch Burnings,* "excitingly illustrated in full color." Western society has rejected public hangings and witch burnings together with slavery and gladiatorial fights, and sees itself as having progressed toward a more civilized set of values and attitudes. But a book entitled *Famous Battles of World History,* "excitingly illustrated in full color," is perfectly acceptable. (I found a copy in the waiting room of my daughter's pediatrician.)

It is not only patriotism that leads so many parents to acquiesce in the sacrifice of their sons in unnecessary wars, but also pride in their sons' manhood. (Many young women raised with the image of men as tough and dominant find men in uniform sexy, thus further reinforcing the values of the masculine mystique.)

In a letter published in the *Ladies Home Journal* during World War I, a father writes to his son: "Don't forget that the biggest thing that a war can do is to bring out that man [in you]. That's really what you and the other chaps have gone over for: *To demonstrate the right kind of manhood.*"[24]

The opportunities for exercising heroism and demonstrating manhood in a major war are greatly diminished in a nuclear age, but excitement over violent conflict continues. In 1984, when my younger daughter's sixth-grade class voted on a nuclear freeze (after having studied the issue), out of twelve girls, eleven supported a nuclear freeze, one was undecided. Out of seventeen boys, six were pro-freeze, three were undecided, and eight opposed a freeze. "Nukes all the way!!!!!" one boy wrote. "I say yes to total Global Thermonuclear Missiles build up (in other words NUKES)," wrote another. Some of these very bright twelve-year-old boys brought to the development of nuclear missiles the same enthusiasm which Alan Seeger and his comrades brought to fighting the battles of the Great War.

Ron Kovic's book *Born on the Fourth of July,* and the film based on it, depict this atmosphere and the values that led Kovic to enlist when he was seventeen to fight in a war he knew very little about. One scene in the film captures it perfectly. When Kovic visits the family of one of the men in his battalion who died in Vietnam, the soldier's father confesses that he doesn't understand what his son gave his life for; he doesn't grasp the purpose of the Vietnam War. But he does not question any further. He proudly tells Kovic that his own father fought in the First World War and that he fought in the Second. On screen we see his young grandson, who will never know his father, practicing with his toy rifle for his turn to prove patriotism and manhood.

Like this young boy—like most young boys—Kovic started his practice for war at a very young age. The film opens with him and his friends playing war in the woods with their toy machine guns, helmets, grenades. Later we see Kovic's high school physical education teacher calling the boys "ladies" and screaming at them to sacrifice their bodies. (In the book it is the drill sergeant in boot camp who constantly threatens the young marines' manhood by calling them "ladies.") We also see a young Kovic despondent when he loses a wrestling match and jubilant when he plays an important role in winning a baseball game. This constant competition prepares boys to think in us/them and win/lose terms. They become so imbued with the glory of winning that it hardly matters to them, later, what military contests are about. They are mainly a chance to fight and win.

The romanticization of war through war toys, in books, in films, on TV, and the extreme emphasis on competitiveness, winning, and sacrifice in sports, all prepare young men to sacrifice their bodies and often their lives years later in warfare.

Once Kovic understood this he felt duped and enraged that he had been sold a fantasy of war and patriotism, that he had been treated as "a thing to put in uniform," that he had lost his body for nothing.

For Kovic, one of the major symbols of war as romanticized fantasy and hollow patriotism is John Wayne.

As part of the research for his book *A Choice of Heroes,* a work dedicated to questioning obsolete paradigms of masculinity, Mark Gerzon interviewed a large number of Vietnam War veterans. He found that living out a John Wayne fantasy was foremost in the minds of many of those who had embraced the war. Typical was author Phil Caputo, who enlisted because he had wanted "the chance to live heroically . . . I saw myself charging up some distant beachhead, like John Wayne in *Sands of Iwo Jima,* and then coming home a suntanned warrior with medals on my chest."[25]

Gerzon tells us that "the John Wayne syndrome is an explicit, if unwritten, code of conduct, a set of masculine traits we have been taught to revere since childhood." These traits include being "hard, tough, unemotional, ruthless, and competitive."

In a New York *Times Magazine* article, author William Manchester, who fought in Asia in World War II, tells us that when his rifle company was polled on why they had joined the Marines, a majority cited a war fantasy with John Wayne called *To The Shores of Tripoli.*

Manchester recalls, "after my evacuation from Okinawa, I had the enormous pleasure of seeing Wayne humiliated in person at Aiea Heights Naval Hospital in Hawaii . . . Each evening, Navy corpsmen would carry litters down to the hospital theater so the men could watch a movie. One night they had a surprise for us. Before the film the curtains parted and out stepped John Wayne, wearing a cowboy outfit—10-gallon hat, bandanna, checkered shirt, two pistols, chaps, boots and spurs. He grinned his aw-shucks grin, passed a hand over his face and said, 'Hi ya, guys!' He was greeted by a stony silence. Then somebody booed. Suddenly everyone was booing."

"This man was a symbol of the fake machismo we had come to hate, and we weren't going to listen to him. He tried and tried to make himself heard, but we drowned him out, and eventually he quit and left."[26]

In the second part of this book, we will see how we can change the socialization of boys so that war is no longer seen as a romanticized fantasy but rather as a grim reality.

WHO ARE THE *REAL* WIMPS?

Throughout this chapter the terms "wimps" and "real men" have been surrounded by quotation marks to indicate their usage in accordance with how they or their equivalents—"pusillanimous," "weak," "effeminate," "emasculated," "soft," etc. —have been used through much of our history, with respect to men in government.

If we look at Webster's dictionary for definitions of the terms "manly" (the closest one can get to "real man") and "wimp" we find that "manly" is defined as "Not effeminate or timorous: bold, resolute, and open in conduct or bearing; of undaunted courage." "Wimp" is defined as "a weak, ineffectual, or insipid person."

It should be clear by now that many of the "real men" who often act out of extreme competitiveness and concern with ego, or out of fear of losing their positions of power, and who deal with the horror of war through avoidance are in fact far more weak than are the "wimps" who often courageously take unpopular positions they believe are for the good of our nation, at the risk of losing their prestigious positions.

It is the "real men" who are not "open in conduct or bearing" when they make amoral decisions based on supposed political realism while at the same time justifying their policies to the public in the loftiest moral and patriotic language.

The "real men" seem unable to distinguish between (on the one hand) determination, resoluteness, and boldness in the ability to make decisions that are difficult precisely *because of human and moral concerns,* and (on the other) making decisions without regard for moral concerns, without empathy for those who will suffer the consequences. They have mistakenly confused the latter with manliness. By their definition, Mafia members who are without moral scruples, but are tough and determined in their pursuit of money, are prime examples of "real men." (There is a certain irony in the fact that men who in the political arena dismiss concern with human life or morality as "soft" are outraged, or at least claim to be outraged, by crime, rape, and domestic violence, for it is the same values and attitudes that guide them that also lead to male brutality in the home and crime on the street.)

It seems that if we are to respect the dictionary meanings of the terms "manly" and "wimp" we must reverse their use. It is the supposed "real men" who most often act as immoral wimps. It is the supposed "wimps" who most often act in a moral, manly fashion.

If the so-called "wimps" are often ineffectual in terms of changing our foreign policy, it is not for lack of determination, but because they are struggling against the values of the masculine mystique which are deeply embedded in our political establishment. These values have, however mistakenly, become almost synonymous with patriotism and masculinity.

We have come full circle. If the major objection, from a national security perspective, to our moving away from the masculine mystique and rearing sons who will not place intrinsic value on toughness, dominance, emotional detachment, fierce competition, is that such men will not be able to function well and defend our nation in the real world, then our response is that the thinking and actions of the men who determine our national security policy now are based on the confused thinking, dangerous unreality, and self-deception that grow out of their attachment to the values and attitudes of the masculine mystique.

Just like a John Wayne war movie, it's all fake machismo. Real strength, real courage, are based on dealing with reality, not denying it. The thinking of the "real men" who are supposed to be defending our national security is based on avoidance and remains attached to atavistic, non-functional values. All their talk about "toughness," about "surgical strikes" and "collateral damage," is a form of verbal swaggering as unconnected to reality as John Wayne's physical swaggering on the screen.

3
"Boys Will Be Boys"

The goal of this chapter is to answer the common objection that nothing much can be done to diminish male violence because it grows out of an inexorable aggressive instinct.

The research and writings of sociobiologists are often used to buttress the view that the male of the species has, through natural selection, developed highly aggressive and territorial drives that are unalterable and have led to conflict and violence throughout human history. Hormonal studies are marshaled to support this "killer instinct" view of male aggression. Here the culprit is the male hormone testosterone. Some turn to

Sigmund Freud's hypothesis of an aggressive instinct to support the thesis that violence and war are inevitable.

It is a far cry from the simplifications of some of the popularized versions of these theories to what the most respected researchers in the field are saying. With the exception of a minority of psychoanalysts, there is a broad consensus that while violent behavior is based in human biology, it can in no way be considered an inexorable instinct or drive.

That males *from a very young age* act more aggressively than females is not the issue in any of this; for here agreement is almost universal. In 1973, psychologists Eleanor Maccoby and Carol Jacklin published *The Psychology of Sex Differences.* After analyzing thousands of research studies they concluded that there were only a few areas in which the evidence warranted the conclusion that male-female differences did exist. Aggression was one of them.

While studies of American children represent the bulk of their data, Maccoby and Jacklin also reviewed cross-cultural data, animal studies, and hormonal research. They found that both in the United States and in other cultures, boys from a very young age hit and insult each other more frequently, respond faster and more strongly when they are insulted or hit, and engage in more rough-and-tumble play. Studies of monkeys and rodents show that injections of testosterone increase aggressive behavior.

Maccoby and Jacklin emphasize that this male-female difference is not a dichotomy; it is a difference in tendencies. This conclusion follows quite clearly from an analysis of the ninety-four studies on aggression in children which they reviewed. While a majority (fifty-two) of these studies showed that boys are more aggressive, a substantial number (thirty-seven) showed no difference. Only five studies showed girls to be more aggressive. Males as a group are more aggressive, but many males are no more aggressive than most females.

Although aspects of *The Psychology of Sex Differences* have been subjected to considerable criticism, it is still considered the "definitive" study to date on male-female differences.

The issue, then, is *why* are men more violent than women? Is there an *inevitability* to high levels of male violence?

In this chapter I review some of the best available answers to these questions, beginning with hormonal, sociobiological, and psychoanalytic theory. After it is made clear that these theories do not buttress the view that it is hopeless to attempt to significantly diminish violence, I focus on what we can learn from psychoanalytic theory and social learning theory (the dominant school of psychology in American universities) about the causes of violent behavior. Finally, I examine some of the literature on physical disabilities that affect boys primarily and put them at higher than average risk of violent behavior.

Since the literature and research on violence is vast, I limit myself to the work of a few of the most highly respected thinkers in each field whose work is particularly relevant to the issues that concern us. *This is not to say that their positions are to be regarded as definitive.* When we are physically ill, we consult physicians even though we know that there is disagreement among them both on diagnosis and on treatment. We also know that fifty years from now medical knowledge will be considerably changed. In the same way we must look to the best available present-day knowledge, with all its limitations and tentativeness, to help us begin to grapple with the social disease of violence.

The synthesis of this research will serve as the basis for many of the proposals for diminishing violence presented in later chapters. But before embarking on this project, some semantic clarifications are necessary.

I have very consciously chosen to use the term "violence" rather than "aggression" throughout this book to refer to the use, or the threat, of physical force to hurt or gain power over another person, or to obtain another person's property.*

My decision to use the term "violence" grows out of the ambiguity of the term "aggression." This ambiguity tends to make acts of violence more acceptable when they are called "aggressive" rather than "violent." The reason for this is that the term "aggression" can be used in several highly divergent senses, some of which have a very positive connotation.

President Franklin D. Roosevelt acted aggressively—he

---

* I am aware that some thinkers refer to the infliction of emotional pain as violent. Others focus on the importance of what they call "structural violence" growing out of inequality in the distribution of power. While these topics are beyond the scope of this book, it should be clear that the kinds of recommendations made in later chapters can only have very positive results with respect to both.

started federal work programs, introduced Social Security, etc. —to meet the problems of the Great Depression. At the turn of the century Julius Rosenwald's aggressive and innovative marketing techniques led to the success of Sears, Roebuck & Company. I recently found myself telling a friend that she needed to be much more aggressive in her efforts to find a job. These are just a few of many examples of useful, constructive aggression. Constructive aggression has much to do with assertiveness, determination, personal strength. It has nothing to do with violence unless a person, an organization or group, or a government decides to use violent means to achieve the goals it is aggressively pursuing. But there is no necessary connection between the two. Apple and IBM are often extremely competitive and aggressive in their efforts to corner a larger part of the computer market, but they do not use violent means in their efforts to do so.

Even when the desire for power is a major motivation, it is still possible to refrain from violence in order to achieve one's goal. This point can be illustrated by contrasting our own electoral history with that of countries in which men regularly use force to overthrow those who hold power. Surely the desire for power, prestige, and dominance has been a major motivation for many of the men who have sought the presidency of the United States. But as long as our nation has existed no man has staged a coup or assassinated the man in power in order to take power. In our political tradition, there is a clear separation between the desire for political power and using violent means to obtain it.

It is a major human tragedy that no such tradition exists in international politics. Instead, it is traditional that nations use violence as a method of satisfying their desires for power and prestige, economic benefits, or religious dominance.

When boys are encouraged to be not just assertive and determined, but almost obsessionally competitive and concerned with dominance, it becomes more likely that they will eventually use violent or other antisocial means to achieve dominance. (They are also likely to be abusive verbally and intimidating in their "body language.") Nevertheless, violence and the desire for power are not inextricably linked. Most human beings are capable of extraordinary self-control with respect to acts that are considered deeply shameful and humiliating. We are able to control our body functions, however pressing they may be, because we would be mortified if we didn't. *If human beings are to survive in a nuclear age, committing acts of violence may eventually have to become as embarrassing as urinating or defecating in public are today.*

For our purposes, it is sufficient to distinguish three different senses of the term "aggression": constructive aggression, as in assertiveness and determination; antisocial aggression, as in extreme competitiveness and concern with dominance; and destructive aggression, which is synonymous with violence.

When people talk or write about aggression, it is often not clear whether they have constructive, antisocial, or destructive aggression in mind. They are often not clear about it themselves. This lack of clarity allows for the use of the term "aggression" with all its positive connotations instead of the much more negative term "violence" when one is in fact describing violence. For example, to say that football is a very aggressive game sounds much better than to say that it is a very violent game. If basketball and baseball were commonly described as aggressive and football as aggressive and violent, more parents might be inclined to encourage their sons to play basketball or baseball instead of football. For while many parents want their sons to play team sports so that they will learn to be assertive and determined, teaching them to be violent is not usually one of their goals.

Since the principal researchers and theorists whose work I discuss mostly use the word "aggression," I frequently use the term in this chapter in order to do justice to their work. The use of "aggression" to cover both aggression and violence facilitates the misinterpretation and misuse of their theories by the general public.

Within the category of destructive aggression, or violence, a further distinction needs to be made between defensive and offensive violence. When a person or a nation is attacked and mounts a defense against the aggressor, we look upon this as justified defensive behavior. For example, we might say of a boy who was involved in a fight, "He isn't really violent, he was just defending himself against the school bullies." My concern in this book is exclusively with offensive violence.

IS TESTOSTERONE THE CULPRIT?

In their book *Man and Woman, Boy and Girl*, a study of the influence of hormones on male and female behavior, John Money and Anke Ehrhardt are so intent on emphasizing the role of the environment in human development that they devote an entire chapter to this topic. They present both case studies and anthropological data showing the enormous culture-dependent human variability with respect to gender behavior. In several recent articles, Ehrhardt argues that behavior and environment can have a strong and direct influence on hormone levels, and suggests that testosterone levels may well be affected by environmental factors.[1]

What then is the contribution of hormones to aggressive behavior, according to Money and Ehrhardt?

Before addressing this question, a few basic definitions and facts of endocrinology have to be set forth.

The male hormone testosterone leads to the formation *in utero* of the male's sexual anatomy. If for some reason testosterone is not released, the embryo develops into a female even if it is genetically a male. This is the case with genetic males suffering from androgen insensitivity.

In order to determine the role of prenatal hormones in influencing male and female behavior, Money and Ehrhardt studied these genetic males who received no testosterone *in utero* and therefore looked like girls at birth and were raised as girls.*

Almost all of them scored very high in terms of "feminine" traits. They were less tomboyish than controls, and conformed to a high degree to the feminine stereotype in American culture at the time they were growing up. It seems that the complete absence of testosterone *in utero* leaves a child with dispositions that can easily be molded by society into "feminine" traits.

---

* It is not clear at this point precisely how higher levels of testosterone *in utero* affect behavior. Research suggests that it may be that the release of the male hormone during the critical period of fetal brain development "masculinizes" the brain, influencing the nervous system permanently. Sex hormones produced in adulthood appear to play a role in activating behavior that was preorganized at an earlier developmental phase. In normal boys, testosterone levels increase sharply at puberty. Adult males have about ten times as much testosterone as women.

When Money and Ehrhardt studied a group of girls who received high levels of testosterone *in utero* (as a result of either an enzyme defect or their mothers' taking progestin), they found that the genetic males who had not been androgenized *in utero* were more "feminine" than the genetic females who had been androgenized.

Money and Ehrhardt's studies indicate that these androgenized girls who are born with ambiguous genitalia (usually a grossly enlarged clitoris; in rare cases a penis and empty scrotum which are surgically corrected shortly after birth) tend to exhibit more "tomboyish behavior" than control groups. This behavior includes more rough-and-tumble play, more interest in outdoor physical activities, and more self-assertiveness in competition for dominance.

From our perspective, one of the most interesting facts about the androgenized girls studied by Money and Ehrhardt is that while they engaged in significantly higher levels of tomboyish activities than did control groups, their behavior was not any more violent than the control groups in terms of their picking fights. This suggests that for many little boys, in order for their predisposition to rough-and-tumble play and their concerns with competition and dominance to become translated into violent behavior, some form of social condoning and probably encouragement is required. While it is acceptable for girls to be tomboys, it is not acceptable for them to fight.

When I interviewed Ehrhardt in 1986, she suggested that the biologically based difference between males and females may amount to no more than a general tendency to more rough-and-tumble, physical activity, and self-assertiveness on the part of boys.

The possibility that testosterone may be linked to characteristics that tend to be *precursors* to violent behavior rather than to violence itself is also entertained by Norwegian psychologist Dan Olweus. In discussing a study he and colleagues carried out to see what effects differences in testosterone levels had on a group of adolescent boys in terms of antisocial and violent behavior, he comments that the boys with higher levels of testosterone tended to be more easily frustrated, more impatient, and more irritable than the boys with lower levels. These traits increase the probability of these boys engaging in antisocial or violent behavior.[2]

This theorizing based on hormonal studies receives confirmation from behavioral studies. Eleanor Maccoby points to increasing evidence that males as a group, from a very young age, are more easily frustrated, and act more impulsively, than females.[3]

It may turn out that an important part of the biological base of male violence boils down to a lower threshold for frustration, greater irritability and impulsiveness, and a tendency to rough-and-tumble. While rough-and-tumble is usually not violent—boys often roughhouse as a way of establishing friendly contact—it would tend to encourage the expression of anger or frustration through physical activity rather than verbal reaction.

It is also probable that these dispositions are often magnified by the way boys are reared. Studies indicate that from birth boys and girls are treated differently. In a 1989 interview with the author, New York University professor emeritus of clinical psychology Robert R. Holt pointed out that boys are often overstimulated from a young age. Parents, especially fathers, toss them about more and act loud and tough rather than soft and gentle as they do with girls. Such treatment may very well decrease a sense of calm and patience, and increase irritability.

A LEGACY FROM OUR HUNTING-GATHERING DAYS?

Sociobiology is an application of the theory of evolution to human behavior. Sociobiologists ask the same kinds of questions about social behavior that Darwin asked about physical characteristics. Why do some species exhibit highly aggressive behavior while others are very unaggressive? How did humans develop feelings of love, hate, envy? How did altruistic or aggressive behavior patterns come to be? As with anatomical traits, behavioral traits are explained largely in terms of natural selection. Individuals possessing advantageous traits have a better chance of surviving and passing them on to their offspring.

Aggression, sociobiologists argue, was advantageous for humans. As early hunting and gathering societies competed for limited resources, the more aggressive groups with better warriors tended to survive. These warriors were male—for males did the hunting and fighting while the females, frequently pregnant, stayed back tending to food-gathering and children. This, they believe, explains why males as a group are more aggressive than females.

Harvard professor Edward O. Wilson is the author of *Sociobiology: The New Synthesis,* perhaps the major work in the field, and *On Human Nature,* which won the Pulitzer Prize. Wilson stresses again and again that while human behavior is based on biology, and its origins can be traced through evolutionary theory of adaptation, it can only be fully understood through the interaction of biology and culture, and the weight of culture is enormous.

Wilson distinguishes between different categories of aggression, comprising both violent and nonviolent behavior. In the discussion below, the term "aggression" always includes violent behavior.

Wilson makes it clear that violent aggression does not grow out of an instinct or drive. He does describe aggression as being innate, but he defines innateness as referring to "the measurable probability that a trait will develop in a specified set of environments, not to the certainty that the trait will develop in all environments."[4] For example, bands of hunter-gatherers in all parts of the world act aggressively in their defense of land that contains a reliable source of food. Males fight over females when they are scarce in numbers.

Wilson distinguishes his own understanding of violent aggression from those who believe, like Freud or Konrad Lorenz, in the "drive-discharge" model. They see it as an active drive or instinct that constantly seeks release. Wilson, by contrast, tells us that we must not picture aggression as a fluid constantly applying pressure against the walls of its containers (the Freud-Lorenz model), but rather as a preexisting mix of chemicals that can be transformed by specific catalysts if they are added at some later time. This is the "culture-pattern" model, which is based on the interaction of genetic potential and learning:

> . . . aggressive behavior, especially in its more dangerous forms of military action and criminal assault, is learned. But the learning is prepared . . . we are strongly predisposed to slide into deep, irrational hostility under certain definable conditions. With dangerous

ease, hostility feeds on itself and ignites runaway reactions that can swiftly progress to alienation and violence.[5]

The ethnocentrism and xenophobia that develops among rival bands and tribes is another widespread cause of warlike policies. In general, primitive people divide the world into their own villages, composed of friends and kin, and foreign villages, composed of enemies who are reduced to frightful and often subhuman status, which makes it easier to kill them. For Wilson the fact that the belligerent behavior and motivations of "civilized" societies so closely resemble those of "primitive" societies lends weight to the argument for a biological underpinning to aggressive behavior.

Sociobiologists often support their generalizations about humans by pointing to similar behavior in other species. Wilson points out that more than anything the sight of a stranger, especially a territorial intruder, elicits aggression in animals. This has been documented in almost all animals exhibiting higher forms of social organization.

In animals, as in humans, a major cause of aggression among members of the same species is competition for vital resources. But aggression is only one competitive technique among many, and some animals don't exhibit it at all. Its existence in those species closest to humans adds weight to the argument that males have an underlying predisposition to act aggressively under certain conditions.

Wilson is fond of pointing out that radical changes in human aggressiveness have taken place within specific groups, going from nonaggressive to aggressive and vice versa. The Semai of Malaya seemed not even to have a concept of violent aggression. Murder was unknown in their society and there was no explicit word for killing. But the British colonial government recruited Semai men to fight Communist guerrillas in the early 1950s. After some of their kinsmen had been killed by Communist terrorists, the previously completely peaceful Semai men became extremely bloodthirsty and violent.

A change in the opposite direction occurred among the Maori of New Zealand, who in pre-European times were among the most violent people on earth. The introduction of European firearms in such a belligerent group was catastrophic. During the approximately twenty years of the resultant musket war, one quarter of their population died from causes related to the conflict. By 1830 the use of fighting for revenge was beginning to be questioned. Eventually the old values crumbled, and by the late 1830s and early 1840s warfare between the tribes had stopped entirely.

It is clear that in looking for the causes of war one must look not only to the combination of a genetic disposition to learn violent behavior and conditions of scarcity leading to violent competition for resources, but also to previous history and cultural conditions that can predispose a group to seek violent solutions to conflict. The Maori had a tradition of violence; the Semai had a tradition of nonviolence. Yet under changed social conditions, each group underwent radical changes in its behavior.

Wilson is telling us that sociocultural conditions conducive to violence can and must be transcended. We must consciously undertake to master and reduce "the profound human tendency to learn violence."

He quotes the Yanomamo (a particularly violent South American tribe) as saying: "We don't want to kill anymore. But the others are treacherous and cannot be trusted." He sees this as one example of a universal tendency to xenophobia, and advocates that studies in anthropology and social psychology be used to help us overcome it. Political and cultural ties "that create a confusion of cross-binding loyalties"[6] must be promoted.

In his book *The Biology of Peace and War* German sociobiologist Iraneus Eibl-Eibesfeldt deals at length with the kinds of social and economic changes that need to be made if we are to eliminate war. Like Edward Wilson, he believes that we must begin by recognizing those underlying biological dispositions—xenophobia and territoriality—that lead to aggression and war, so that we can deal with them better. He argues that we must take concrete measures to help fulfill the basic economic needs of all people, so that nations will no longer resort to war in order to obtain the territories and raw materials they need for survival. We must combat xenophobia and learn to appreciate our own culture without automatically disparaging other cultures and systems of values and creating enemy stereotypes. We need education that socializes aggression so that it is not used destructively.

As Eibl-Eibesfeldt sees it, aggression is initially neutral and can through socialization be linked with territoriality and xenophobia, and turn into violence, or it can be put to work in positive ways to tackle human problems.

Many sociobiologists, including Edward Wilson, have been the target of scathing attacks, some of them personal as well as intellectual. The more virulent attacks grow out of the critics' fears that any attempt at grounding human emotions and behaviors in evolutionary theory will be used to justify reactionary, racist, and sexist social policies.* It is true that simplistic genetic and evolutionary theories have at times been used as the basis of discriminatory policies.

Since the goal of this chapter is limited to showing that according to the best contemporary research and thinking in relevant fields, male violence is not inexorable and unchangeable, there is no need to embroil ourselves in this controversy. For while Wilson and Eibl-Eibesfeldt do believe that "genes hold culture on a leash," they also believe, in Wilson's words, that "the leash is very long."[7] It is long enough to have made it possible for the Maori, with their history of extreme violence, to give up warfare altogether within a relatively short period of time. As far as Eibl-Eibesfeldt is concerned, the leash is long enough to enable all human beings to abolish war. For our purposes that is more than sufficient, for the claim made in this book is that it is possible to diminish male violence significantly, not to abolish it.

IS THE "DEATH INSTINCT" A DEAD END IDEA?

Many if not most schools of psychoanalysis reject the hypothesis of an aggressive drive altogether. Most Freudians accept it. I

---

* In light of the rejection of sociobiological theory as reactionary, it is worth noting that sociobiologists' emphasis on scarcity of economic resources as the moving force behind human evolution, and Eibl-Eibesfeldt's emphasis on economic factors as the underlying cause of wars, are not so far removed from Marxist theory. The sociobiologist sees human biology as having been determined by the same economic struggle for survival that Marxists see as *the* determining force in human social and political organization.

have chosen to focus primarily on Freudian theory because among the general public it is the most influential and best known of the psychoanalytic theories.

Freud does not distinguish between males and females as to aggression. As usual the model of "man" is male, but this is not recognized. What is important for our purposes is that this theory is used to justify the view that there isn't much we can do about violence, and leads to mistaken beliefs about catharsis.

Freud's "death instinct" and the "aggressive drive" postulated by some of his disciples have been subjected to such scorching criticism from within and without the Freudian movement that it is difficult to argue that they represent anything more than the very tenuous views of some Freudians. Further, an analysis of these concepts reveals that they are so broad that much of the time they have little if anything to do with violence.

The death instinct, according to Freud, is fueled by an internal energy that exists spontaneously, and is originally aimed at the self. He argues that all living matter carries within itself the desire to self-destruct. When we direct our death instinct toward the outside world rather than toward ourselves, it becomes an aggressive instinct. "The living creature preserves its own life, so to say, by destroying an extraneous one."[8]

Most contemporary Freudian psychoanalysts no longer accept Freud's concept of an inwardly directed death instinct, but many continue to adhere to the notion of an aggressive instinct directed against others, although, to distinguish human behavior from animal behavior they describe it as a drive rather than an instinct. They recognize that whereas animal instincts lead to predetermined behavioral responses, drives interact with experience and reflection in determining behavior. Nevertheless, they remain committed to the view that aggressive behavior grows out of an internal aggressive drive that creates excitation or tension in the individual and must then be released.[9]

In *Civilization and Its Discontents,* Freud admits that the assumption of a destructive instinct "is not entirely proof against theoretical objections." He goes on to say that "this is how things appear to us now in the present state of our knowledge; future research and reflection will undoubtedly bring further light which will decide the question."[10]

"Future research and reflection" have revealed that the psychoanalytic theory of a death instinct or aggressive drive fueled by psychic energy does not satisfy any of the conditions that normally corroborate theories in the social or physical sciences. It has neither predictive nor explanatory value nor is it supported by clinical or other data.

The Absence of Supporting Data

Robert R. Holt, who has written extensively on Freud, zoologist Patrick Bateson, and Edward Wilson are among those who are convinced that the underlying and mistaken model for Freudian instinct and drive theory is the hydraulic image of, as Wilson puts it, "a fluid that continuously builds pressure against the walls of its containers."[11] Holt and Bateson are even more explicit. Bateson tells us that if an aggressive drive exists "it is emphatically not like urine which builds up and has to be discharged from time to time."[12] Holt rejects the "model of urination" and points out that there is no evidence that "a psychic energy or anything else . . . accumulates when a person is peaceable and gets discharged via aggressive behavior."[13]

One obvious distinction between urination and aggression is that urination is a universal human function. Aggression is not. Nor does aggression have remotely the same level of universality as sex or hunger, to which it is often compared. Apart from those suffering from anorexia nervosa, or starvation, all human beings eat and drink regularly, and almost all engage in sexual activities for significant portions of their lives. But a large percentage of people, including males, go through life without spontaneously committing any significant acts of violence.

One reason that violent behavior seems universal is that nonviolence is rarely reported. No one puts a man who never batters his wife and children, and never gets into fights or kills anyone on the evening news. Peaceful countries like Switzerland or Norway rarely make the front page of the *New York Times.*

Besides this, people who are willing to use violence often wield an inordinate amount of power and so they are much more visible than those who don't. I would venture to guess that very large numbers of Lebanese want nothing more than a cessation of the violence that has devastated Lebanon, but they are unable to influence the course of events.

Yet in spite of the lack of evidence that aggressive behavior is in any way as universal as sexual behavior, eating, drinking, or the evacuative functions, Freud argues that it grows out of a universal instinct, the repression of which leads to unhappiness. In *Civilization and Its Discontents,* he states that the repression of sexuality *and aggression* required by civilization makes it "so hard for men to feel happy in it."[14]

Why the Aggressive Drive Explains Nothing

Besides a lack of behavioral data to support it, the Freudian theory of aggression also does a poor job of explaining violent behavior when it does occur.[15] It is based on the mistaken assumption that there must be an inner entity that corresponds to the concept "aggression." But in fact there is no one entity that the term "aggression" refers to. To think that there is provides us with the illusion that we are explaining the causes of violence, as if we could explain why one man is more violent than another by saying that he has a higher quantum of aggressive drive energy.

Since it is widely thought that Freud introduced the aggressive instinct in part to explain the death and destruction of World War I, I shall illustrate this point with the following analysis of that war.

Certainly men's willingness to start wars, and to fight in them, needs explanation. For while the willingness to fight can sometimes be explained in terms of genuine defense—they and their loved ones' lives would be endangered if they were conquered by invaders—it is safe to venture that this is very often not the case, as in World War I.

If we cease to deal in generalities, and get down to the specifics of what led some men to start that war and others to participate in it we find that the concept of an aggressive instinct or drive explains little. There is no reason to believe that most men volunteered for the war because they had an internally driven urge to kill and maim other human beings.

In her autobiography *Testament of Youth,* British writer Vera Brittain describes her brother and her fiancé, both of whom volunteered to fight in World War I (and lost their lives in it). There is no evidence at all that these sensitive, decent young men were driven by anything other than fantasies of glory, heroism, and excitement, as well as peer pressure and patriotism. Once these fantasies were replaced by the grim reality of war, doubts set in. Brittain writes of her fiancé, after he was sent to the front: "He certainly had no wish to die, and now that he had got what he wanted, a dust-and-ashes feeling had come. He neither hated the Germans nor loved the Belgians; the only possible motive for going was 'heroism in the abstract,' and that didn't seem a very logical reason for risking one's life."[16]

In a letter from the front he writes: "I used to talk of the Beauty of War; but it is only War in the abstract that is beautiful."[17]

Brittain's book corroborates the evidence presented in earlier chapters. Whether it be young American men like Ron Kovic going off to fight in Vietnam spurred by images of John Wayne in *Sands of Iwo Jima*, or young Englishmen going to fight on the continent spurred, no doubt, by poems and epic stories of heroic wars, the prevailing feeling is that going to war is exciting, patriotic, and proof of courage and manhood.

Boys are raised to be soldiers. They are prepared from the youngest age to view war as a thrilling adventure. Their play with war toys is great fun without pain. The books they read (and today the TV shows and films they see) focus on exciting violence. In schools all over the world, little boys learn that their country is the greatest in the world, and the highest honor that could befall them would be to defend it heroically someday. The fact that empathy has traditionally been conditioned out of boys facilitates their obedience to leaders who order them to kill strangers.

J. Glenn Gray is a college professor who served in Europe and North Africa in World War II and later wrote a book about his own and his comrades' experiences. As Gray sees it, the intense feelings of power and excitement, the delight in destruction that many men experience in war, are often reactions to the boredom, the emptiness, the lack of meaningful goals that characterize so many men's daily lives. The sense of camaraderie is another major attraction.

Little boys are taught to be strong and brave and not to cry. The ensuing tendency to deny fear and vulnerability, as well as greater male impulsiveness, tend to make the excitement and ego rewards predominate in men's minds over the fear of death.

We must not forget that many, if not most, of the men who fight in wars are drafted. Their choice is between the most intense social disapproval and rejection, questioning of their manhood, prison or death; and fighting. But many who are drafted no doubt never question their orders because of their obedience to their leaders. If, instead of declaring war, Kaiser Wilhelm had announced in 1914 that England and Germany had become close friends and allies and that large numbers of young Germans would be conscripted and sent to England to help the English build urgently needed hospitals and schools, in all likelihood most men would have gone and built hospitals and schools.

Sociologist Stanley Milgram's well-known experiment on obedience to authority is more helpful in attempting to understand what makes men go to war than the concept of an aggressive drive. When a psychologist asked subjects to give ever more intense electric shocks to a person as part of a study on learning, a majority of the men kept obeying orders even though the victims were screaming in pain and *even though many subjects expressed emotional and moral concern about what they were doing.* When the victim was in the same room, considerably fewer gave the shocks. (The electric shocks and the pain were of course simulated.)

When men first go to war, the enemy is abstract and distant; so are death and suffering. As the enemy and their own pain become more real, many change their attitudes. It is a well-documented fact that in World War I, once they were in the trenches, many of these men supposedly driven by a death instinct in fact established a truce with enemy soldiers. It was only after their superior officers got wind of what was happening and intervened that these truces were ended.

None of this is to deny that for some men war is an opportunity to express their anger, rage, and hostility, and to give legitimate vent to their desire to do physical harm to others.

Some may be venting chronic rage at parents who battered, neglected, abandoned, or humiliated them. Others may suffer from one of the genetic disabilities described below that can play a role in predisposing boys to violence. These men may make up the bulk of those who truly enjoy death and destruction. It also seems likely that their behavior encourages and sanctions such behavior in other men who on their own may not be so violently inclined. Their daring, recklessness, and violence make them role models of manhood.

What about the leaders who started World War I? Does it help us understand their motivations to say that they were led by an aggressive drive? There have been some leaders, Stalin and Hitler among them, who seem to have suffered from extreme psychopathology and enjoyed seeing others suffer. But there is no reason to believe that any of the leaders involved in World War I—Kaiser Wilhelm, Raymond Poincaré, David Lloyd George, Woodrow Wilson—fit this bill. Their motivations probably had much more to do with maintaining prestige and power, and saving face, than an urge to kill and maim.

In a world dominated by the values of the masculine mystique this meant exhibiting toughness and a willingness to use force. Underlying it all is a lack of empathy for the victims of war.

To argue that postulating an aggressive instinct or drive does not explain World War I, as Freud apparently thought it did, is not to deny that human beings, especially men, have a strong innate biological *potential* for violence.

For example, a very young boy may spontaneously respond to frustration by hitting the cause of his frustration, whether it be mother or father refusing a cookie or another child grabbing a toy away. But there is no necessity to this response. It is one of several possible responses to frustration. For temperamental reasons some boys will probably have more of a tendency than others to express anger, and react to frustration, irritation, or attack by hitting, kicking, or biting. But regardless of a boy's natural inclinations, how these inclinations are responded to by his caretaker, the basic quality of the boy's relationship with the caretaker, the values and attitudes of peers, and society's attitudes toward the use of violence will be major determinants of whether the boy continues to react with violence or finds other ways of dealing with difficulties whenever possible.

To say that violence has innate roots in biology, can be provoked by certain types of situations, but is subject to enormous variations based on environmental conditions, is very different from saying that it emanates from an instinct or drive made up of aggressive energy that creates internal tension and demands release regardless of external conditions.

False Predictions

We have seen so far that the aggressive drive theory is not based on data and lacks explanatory value. What about its ability to predict?

If the aggressive drive theory were correct, we would feel relief of tension after releasing aggressive energy and would not have to engage in violent behavior for a while. And indeed Freudian psychoanalysts have maintained that the catharsis of aggression either through direct acts of violence or through substitute activities such as participating in or viewing very aggressive sports, or viewing violent films, will diminish violent behavior. But this view has been proven incorrect through empirical research: these substitute activities in fact increase violence, as we shall see in Chapters 11 and 12.

Based on the hypothesis of the aggressive instinct or drive, one would also predict a decrease in violence in nations that have just been at war, since the war will have furnished either a direct or vicarious outlet for aggressive energy.

Social psychologist Dane Archer tested this hypothesis by comparing prewar and postwar homicide rates. Both in a study of the two World Wars and in a study of twelve other wars, he found that nations that had just been at war had increased homicide rates when compared with control nations. This was so even though the combatant nations had lost large numbers of young men, who are the group most likely to commit homicide.

Archer concluded that the catharsis hypothesis was refuted by the results of his study. Authorized wartime killing in fact legitimizes and encourages violence in peacetime.

In summary, the instinct or drive theory of aggression cannot be derived from data on human violence. It is lacking in explanatory value. Its predictions are disconfirmed by data on sports, entertainment, and postwar violence.

The Many Meanings of "Aggression"

Besides the problems outlined above, much of what has been written on aggression by Freudians is simply irrelevant to the problem of violence, since both Freud and his successors adhere to a definition of aggression that encompasses far more than violence. Freud writes that the death instinct can also be called "the destructive instinct, the instinct for mastery, or the will to power."[18]

In keeping with this broad definition of aggression, Freudians describe the aggressive drive as the psychic source of the infant's and child's individuation, of its sense of self. For instance, psychoanalysts Gertrude Blanck and Rubin Blanck, in writing about children, state that "aggression severs connections for the purpose of propelling growth."[19]

When Freudian psychoanalysts write about the aggressive drives and their emotional and behavioral consequences, they sometimes have a "violence drive" in mind—violence is clearly Freud's major concern both in his letter to Albert Einstein on the causes of war and in *Civilization and Its Discontents*—but much of the time they do not. Their writings are the epitome of the kind of ill-defined, all-encompassing and therefore potentially misleading use of the term "aggression" that was pointed out earlier.

THE ROLE OF EARLY CHILDHOOD DEPRIVATION

If there is any one kernel of agreement among various schools of psychoanalysis on the issue of violence, it may well lie in the idea, supported by considerable clinical and observational data, that a child who suffers emotional neglect, humiliation, or physical abuse in the early years of life is more likely to act violently in later life than a person whose childhood has been benign or relatively benign. This greater tendency toward violence can also express itself in support of violent leaders and governments.

A very brief survey of three psychoanalysts—Erich Fromm, Heinz Kohut, and Alice Miller—who hold such a view follows.

• • • •

In *The Anatomy of Human Destructiveness,* which is probably the most systematic attempt to deal with the problem of aggression from a psychoanalytic perspective, Erich Fromm analyzes the sadistic personality. Stalin and Nazi henchman Himmler are two examples of such personalities.

Fromm asserts that the sadistic personality gets pleasure from having total life-and-death control over others in order to compensate for an extreme sense of powerlessness experienced as a child. The sadist has often been sadistically beaten as a child, and has grown up in a situation of psychic scarcity: ". . . there is an atmosphere of dullness and joylessness, the child freezes up; there is nothing upon which he can make a dent, nobody who responds or even listens, the child is left with a sense of powerlessness and impotence."[20]

Fromm is quick to qualify this statement by saying that extreme powerlessness in childhood does not necessarily result in a person's developing a sadistic character. Whether or not this happens depends on many other factors. But it is one of the main sources contributing to the development of sadism.

Heinz Kohut also believes that when a child's caretakers do not listen or respond to the child, when they neglect essential emotional needs, or show no admiration for achievements, the chances of violent behavior in later life are greatly increased. The very deep need that every child has for recognition, love, and admiration is referred to as a narcissistic need by Kohut. When such needs are not satisfied in childhood, people carry narcissistic injuries with them through their entire lives, and "narcissistic rage" often occurs in adulthood.

Kohut tells us that while narcissistic rages can take many different forms, they all share certain characteristics: "The need for revenge, for righting a wrong, for undoing a hurt by whatever means, and a deeply anchored, unrelenting compulsion in the pursuit of all these aims . . ."[21]

Kohut begins to sketch out some suggestions as to how narcissistic injury and rage may affect group psychology. He suggests, for example, that Germany's "thirst for revenge after the defeat of 1918 came close to destroying all of Western civilization."[22] In Adolf Hitler the German people found an idealized, omnipotent leader with whom they could identify and so assuage their own feelings of narcissistic injury.

Swiss psychoanalyst Alice Miller is also convinced that the neglect of young children's emotional needs is connected with violent behavior in later life. In her book *For Your Own Good,* she attempts to trace Nazism and the enthusiasm with which it was embraced by so many Germans to the "poisonous pedagogy" by which many Germans had raised their children since the eighteenth century. She quotes extensively from respected German authorities on child-rearing. For them, the breaking of the child's will at a very early age was a major goal. This was achieved through physical punishment, extreme repression of spontaneity and life-affirming feelings, and by teaching unquestioning obedience to authority. It was believed that expressions of love or admiration would spoil the child and create an excessive degree of self-esteem, which was considered harmful.

Children raised in this way often grow up to be emotionally detached and incapable of empathy, as well as filled with unexpressed rage at the pain and humiliation they suffered as children. This rage, turned inward, can lead to self-denigration, masochism, and even suicide, or it can be turned outward.

As she sees it, the Nazis furnished many Germans with a "legitimate," patriotic outlet for their rage. Feelings could be displaced from unconsciously hated parents to Jews, Gypsies, homosexuals, and other alien enemies. People who as children had been deprived of any sense of worthiness or self-esteem could now bask in the glory of membership in a triumphant master race. Millions of German women raised on "poisonous pedagogy" welcomed Hitler and Nazism with enthusiasm.

Throughout history, many women have supported wars and proudly sent off their husbands and sons to fight in them. But traditionally women have not served in the military or at least not in active combat, and so they have not participated directly in government-sanctioned violence. Even more significantly, their participation in criminal violence has been minimal compared to men's. (A survey of male and female arrest records for all crimes in twenty-five countries reveals that men are five to fifty times as likely to be arrested as women. The gender gap is even greater for serious crimes.[23]) Since girls suffer from emotional neglect, humiliation, and physical and sexual abuse at least as much, and probably more, than boys do, one would expect psychoanalysts to deal with the discrepancy in male and female levels of violence. In fact it has received very little attention. In recent years, several psychoanalytically oriented social scientists, among them Dorothy Dinnerstein, have begun to address it.

Dinnerstein argues that traditional child rearing, in which male children are raised from birth by females, results in a lower level of male sensitivity and caring, and a higher level of male aggression.[24] I examine her work in detail in the following chapter.

FOCUSING ON THE SOCIAL ENVIRONMENT

Social Learning Theory explains human behavior by focusing on the role that familial, communal, social, and cultural aspects of the environment play in influencing individual behavior.

One of its leading figures is Albert Bandura, professor emeritus of psychology at Stanford University, who has been researching and writing about aggression for the last thirty years. Bandura's basic definition of aggression is a broad one, but in the following discussion his primary concern is with violence.

While he believes that biological factors set the parameters of aggressive responses, and individual genetic endowment influences the propensity to learn aggressive behavior, Bandura's focus is on what he takes to be the three main sources of aggression in the social environment: the modeling and reinforcement provided by family, the subculture in which a boy grows up, and the mass media, TV in particular. (Since Bandura's conclusions on the influence of TV and film violence are similar to those of the researchers whose work is summarized in Chapter 12, I will discuss only the first two sources of aggression here.)

Modeling oneself on parents is an important source of aggressive behavior. Studies indicate that boys whose fathers are criminals are more likely to become criminals, especially if the father is cruel and neglectful. A much higher percentage of delinquent boys have had aggressive fathers as models than nondelinquent.

Abused children have a high rate of abusing their own children. But most aggressive boys do not have criminally or severely violent parents. What causes them to act violently?

Bandura and Richard Walters did a study in which the families of adolescent boys who repeatedly displayed antisocial aggressive behavior were compared with the families of boys who were neither particularly aggressive nor particularly passive.

It was found that parents of nonaggressive boys encouraged their sons to be strong in defending themselves, but they did not accept physical aggression as a method of settling quarrels. In family interaction these parents behaved considerately and relied heavily on reasoning in dealing with social problems. On the other hand, while parents of the aggressive boys did not display much antisocial aggression, they did repeatedly exhibit and reinforce combative attitudes and behavior. They did not tolerate aggression toward themselves, but almost invariably they encouraged their sons to be aggressive toward peers, teachers, and other adults.

Bandura's findings that physical abuse, parental modeling of aggression and permissiveness toward aggressive behavior encourage aggression in boys are supported by numerous studies by other researchers.[25]

Modeling and reinforcement by the family play an important role in causing aggression, but research indicates that the highest rates of aggressive behavior are found in surroundings where aggressive models are numerous and where aggression is highly valued. Growing up in a neighborhood where gangs dominate and where status is based mainly on fighting skills puts a boy at very high risk for violent behavior.

Bandura's emphasis on the importance of subcultures is shared by many of his colleagues. For example, in a 1987 interview, Eleanor Maccoby expressed her conviction that male peer groups are a more important influence on boys' behavior than their families. Recent research, she pointed out, shows that there is a great emphasis on dominance, hierarchy, and prestige in boys' play groups, much more so than in girls' play groups. Compared to the behavior of boys alone, there appears to be a qualitative leap in the level of aggressive behavior of boys in groups.

While Maccoby agrees with Bandura that many boys who are not particularly aggressive are highly influenced by male subcultures, she believes that family pathology will predispose a boy to greater aggression. Those boys who carry with them a heavy dosage of hostility will be the quickest to be aroused and to fight. They are the more likely candidates for gangs or other groups that further reinforce aggressive behavior.

Bandura points out that the role of the environment goes far beyond providing immediate role models and reinforcement for aggression. From an early age, young children internalize the social pressures and role models they are presented with and develop a concept of the kind of behavior that is expected of them. A pattern of behavior can be stored cognitively and only acted on at a much later date when external conditions are conducive. Behavior learned in the family, from peers, or from the media may not manifest itself until years later.

PHYSICAL CONDITIONS THAT PUT BOYS AT RISK

The emphasis on numbers and statistics in this section is not accidental. It is often argued that the influence of mass media violence on boys is negligible because only a small group of disturbed boys already disposed toward violence will be affected. But, as we shall see, statistics indicate that millions of boys and men in the United States are at risk for violent behavior. The list of conditions described below is intended to give the reader an idea of the magnitude of the problem. It is not exhaustive. There are other conditions, for example, severe head injuries or psychomotor epilepsy, that also seem to put boys at greater risk for violent behavior.[26]

To say that they are at risk is in no way to suggest that all of them or even close to a majority of them are, or ever will be, violent. Most of the boys and men who suffer from these conditions lead and have led useful, productive, nonviolent lives. (Among them are Albert Einstein and Nelson Rockefeller.) Nevertheless *as a group* they are significantly more vulnerable to violent behavior than other boys and men.

Attention Deficit Disorder With Hyperactivity

Seth Maxell [fictitious name] was a difficult child from birth. By the time he was six months old he invariably woke up from naps crying and kicking. His response to cuddling was a stiffening of the body or more kicking. "It could easily take an hour to calm him down," his mother remembers.[27]

As he grew older, Seth would often lash out without warning. He might throw his toys or his spoon at people, punch his mother, or kick a door. Seth's attention span was very short and his tolerance for frustration very low. His physical energy level seemed unbounded. By the age of three Seth was having at least three major hysterical temper tantrums a day.

Mrs. Maxell emphasizes that Seth is not devoid of positive traits. He is often very generous and affectionate, but nevertheless she confesses that by the time he was three, she often would wake up in the morning "angry and not wanting to be Seth's mom."

Seth's parents are college-educated professionals. Mrs. Maxell, a former teacher, now devotes herself full-time to Seth and his sister. She is a sensitive, intelligent, high-energy person.

Seth was three years old when his mother took him to see a psychologist. I would guess that the diagnosis of attention deficit disorder with hyperactivity (ADDH a.k.a. ADHD) was not a difficult one to make, for Seth had many of the characteristic traits of this disorder, which affects at least 3 percent of American children: hyperactivity, impulsiveness, short attention span, temper outbursts, engaging in dangerous activities, low frustration tolerance.

The psychologist told Mrs. Maxell that unless something was done about it soon, Seth was very likely to develop into a violent man.

While violent behavior at a young age is not typical of all boys suffering from ADDH, the disorder is often a "predisposing factor" in the development of aggressive conduct disorder, which usually occurs around puberty and is characterized by acts of physical violence such as vandalism, rape, arson, mugging, assault.

In adolescence and adulthood, ADDH is a predisposing factor

for antisocial personality disorder (sometimes referred to as sociopathic or psychopathic personality), whose distinguishing characteristics include delinquency, theft, vandalism, repeated physical fights or assaults, and repeated drunkenness or substance abuse. Approximately 9 percent of American boys under the age of eighteen suffer from aggressive conduct disorder and about 3 percent of men suffer from antisocial personality disorder. Both are far more common among males than females.

According to current research, ADDH (which until recently was referred to as "minimal brain dysfunction" or "minimal brain damage"), appears to be approximately six to nine times as prevalent among boys as among girls. Based on this, my estimate is that well over one million American boys may be afflicted. (Throughout this section estimates are intended to give the reader some sense of the magnitude of the problems described. No claim to exactitude is made.)[28]

By the time I met the Maxells, Seth was five years old. One year of work with the psychologist, which consisted mainly of receiving very concrete advice on how to handle Seth, had led to significant improvements. His mother estimated that between the ages of three and five, his violent behavior had decreased by approximately 60 percent.

As I write, Seth is starting second grade. His mother tells me that in first grade he hung out with rough boys and got into quite a few school yard brawls. However, he would come home and tell his parents that he didn't really like getting into these fights. "He didn't know how to get out of it," Mrs. Maxell comments. "He says that this year he really wants to try and do well. He wants to stay away from 'the boys that are bad' as he puts it . . . He wants to do well in school. He wants the praise from the teachers; he wants the praise from me, to be told that he's good."

In spite of his school yard brawls and the fact that he still at times flies into a rage when he is frustrated (it's worse if he's hungry and tired), Mrs. Maxell estimates that Seth's violence level is about the same as when he was five—about 60 percent below what it had been when he was three or four. He now has enough self-control to be able to behave well when he is at a friend's house. He knows that if he doesn't he won't be invited back. Besides his school yard fights, it is mostly at home that he still hits, punches, and kicks.

Mrs. Maxell carefully monitors Seth's TV and film watching. She explains that "if he watches a violent show on TV he goes crazy, directly imitating whatever he sees." The most violent film he has ever seen is *Jaws*.

Even for the Maxells, who are able to afford whatever help they need, are informed on how best to deal with Seth, and have only one other child (who is good-natured and easy to raise), having a son who suffers from ADDH is extraordinarily trying. Mrs. Maxell admits that "every once in a while Seth gets a good whack," even though she and her husband are troubled about using violence to control his behavior.

Children with ADDH are prime candidates for child battering. If they can drive concerned, educated, patient, loving parents crazy, it is frightening to think what effect they would be likely to have on a poor teenage mother with no husband, no professional help, and no understanding of why her son behaves the way he does.

While genetic factors play an underlying role in the etiology of ADDH, it seems that other biological factors such as injury to the brain at time of birth, and maternal alcoholism, play a role as well in some cases. Parents' negative reaction to these difficult children can in turn worsen their condition.[29]

Seth Maxell provides us with an example of how a boy's symptoms, even when they are severe, can be alleviated by parents who have the emotional and financial ability to deal optimally with the situation.

Besides being fortunate in terms of his parents, Seth is also lucky in that he is very intelligent and does not suffer from any learning disabilities. "He comes home with either A+'s or F's depending on his concentration level," his mother comments.

While estimates vary considerably, there is a significant overlap of ADDH and learning disability, as well as ADDH and mental retardation. Each one of these conditions significantly increases the chances of violent behavior.

Learning Disability

It is estimated that approximately 32 percent of delinquent boys and 40 percent of the jail population in the United States suffer from learning disability (LD).[30]

Learning disability seems to afflict roughly 5 to 10 percent of the population. While boys are at least twice as likely to be identified by teachers as suffering from learning disability, recent research reveals that dyslexia (the most common of the learning disabilities) is in fact as prevalent in girls as in boys.* Assuming, conservatively, that boys make up no more than half of those suffering from *all* learning disabilities, I estimate that as many as six to twelve million American males may be afflicted.

According to the National Joint Committee for Learning Disabilities, learning disability refers to "a heterogeneous group of disorders manifested by significant difficulties in the acquisition and use of listening, speaking, reading, writing, reasoning, or mathematical abilities. These disorders are intrinsic to the individual and presumed to be due to central nervous dysfunction."[31]

A child can have a very specific learning disability, such as reversing letters when reading or severe difficulty with spelling, and yet be perfectly normal or even above average in every other way. In fact, the range of individuals suffering from learning disabilities goes from genius to retarded.

While many middle-class and upper-middle-class boys are afflicted, learning disability is considerably more common in lower socioeconomic classes. This may be due in part to complications at birth, which are more common among the disadvantaged.†

* We saw earlier in this chapter that boys are apparently more easily frustrated, act more impulsively, and are more interested in rough-and-tumble and outdoor physical activities than girls. These traits would make it more difficult for boys than for girls to deal with a learning disability. Boys would tend to concentrate less, make less effort, and act out more. Teachers are then more likely to identify them as suffering from a learning disability. An unobtrusive girl, working to the maximum of her capacity, may just be viewed as slow.

† According to Danish and Swedish studies, crime rates among adopted boys are more closely related to their biological parents' crime rates than to those of their adopted parents. (see S. A. Mednick et al., M. Rohman et al., and S. Sigvardsson et al.). These findings are corroborated by an American study (see R. R. Crowe). The fact that adopted

Mental Retardation

The incidence of mental retardation is much higher among prison inmates than among the general population. In fact, some experts have estimated that up to 30 percent of criminal offenders are mentally retarded.[32]

Approximately 3 percent of the American population suffer from mental retardation, which is nearly two times as prevalent among males as among females. Irritability, aggressiveness, and temper tantrums are often behavioral concomitants of mental retardation.

Since most extremely retarded people are either institutionalized or highly supervised if they live at home, it is safe to assume that criminal offenders come from the category of mildly retarded individuals, those with IQs of 50 to 70. About 80 percent of retarded people fall into this category. This means that as many as four million males may fall into the category of mildly retarded and be at high risk for violent behavior.

Mildly retarded children are born almost exclusively into economically disadvantaged families. The cause appears to be one or more of these factors: genetics, maternal alcohol or drug addiction during pregnancy, environmental factors such as malnutrition, and early child-rearing experiences.

Mentally retarded children are three to four times as likely to suffer from ADDH as the general population.

XYY Boys and Asperger's Syndrome

Several less common disabilities that affect only boys, or affect boys more often than girls, seem to have some link to violent behavior.

Research indicates that about 0.1 percent of males suffer from a genetic abnormality that consists of their having two Y chromosomes instead of one. This means that there are over 100,000 XYY men in the United States.

Young XYY boys are prone to severe temper tantrums and

---

children, who tend to come from deprived backgrounds, are four times as likely to suffer from learning disability than nonadopted children, may help to explain these findings.

behavior problems. Their IQ is lower than average, and approximately half of them have problems with speech and reading at school.

While early reports that large numbers of male prison inmates were XYY were vastly exaggerated, studies do indicate that there are far more XYY men among inmates than would be expected by chance.[33]

Asperger's syndrome, according to most experts, is a mild form of autism in high-functioning individuals. Autism is characterized by a lack of interest in other human beings and a lack of empathy for them. Several specialists have suggested that the link between Asperger's syndrome and violent behavior needs to be explored.

One study describes a young man named John who, according to his father, even as an infant "did not seek affection," and "always lacked an ability to know what other people are feeling."[34] As a young man John tried to strangle his brother. Over a period of four years he battered his girlfriend sometimes two or three times a day.

It would not be surprising to find a significant correlation between Asperger's syndrome or mild autism and violent behavior, since studies show that empathy and aggression are inversely related. In *The Anatomy of Human Destructiveness,* psychoanalyst Erich Fromm devotes a chapter to Adolf Hitler. He speculates that Hitler might have had a "semi-autistic streak."

Approximately two to four people out of ten thousand suffer from infantile autism, which is three times more common in boys than in girls. Approximately 30 percent of autistic individuals have IQs over 70. Many of these relatively high functioning, mildly autistic people (somewhere between 11,000 and 22,500 of them are male) are part of mainstream society.

Special Services or Incitement to Violence?

Millions of American boys and men suffer from conditions that put them at risk for violent behavior. Whether or not they engage in such behavior is to a significant degree a function of the familial, social, and cultural environment in which they are raised. Unfortunately, our society blindly encourages their worst tendencies.

Violent television programs and films, war toys, and even some sports provide boys and men with detailed role models of violence, and help desensitize them to the suffering of others.

According to at least one study, children who are mentally retarded, learning-disabled, or emotionally disturbed watch even more TV in general, and more violent programs in particular, than nonhandicapped children.[35] The values of the masculine mystique encourage violence in all men. Promoting these values among boys and men who suffer from physical conditions that put them at increased risk for violent behavior is a bit like throwing lit matches into a tank of gas.

The masculine mystique's emphasis on extreme competition and dominance can only serve to exacerbate this group's frustrations and increase their humiliation and anger in the face of their difficulties in school.

The mystique's glorification of danger and physical conflict provides highly impulsive and easily frustrated boys, many of whom are already predisposed to violence, with a legitimate arena in which they can prove their superiority. In fact, they may well become role models for some of their peers. If they can't do well in class, they can certainly assert their dominance in school yard brawls. As they get older, depending on their socioeconomic background, they find opportunities to affirm their masculinity by joining gangs, committing violent crimes, going on joy rides, engaging in group rape. All of this is facilitated by the masculine mystique's ban on crying and "soft feelings," which discourages feelings of empathy for their victims.

It may well be that a significant number of these men find a natural home in groups or organizations in which risk-taking and violent behavior are particularly valued. Teacher and Vietnam veteran Chris Wilkens writes that "During a brutal war, civilized customs are left behind. Violent, restless men—psychopaths—find themselves in a world suited to their character. Their actions are often admired and they become leaders."[36] As we saw earlier, ADDH is often a precursor to "psychopathic personality."

Is it possible that groups like the Nazi brownshirts, the Haitian Tonton Macoute death squads, and the Ku Klux Klan tend to attract inordinate numbers of men who suffer from one or the other, or a combination of several, of the conditions described above? Is it possible that these men are especially likely to rise to leadership positions in such groups and that they are perceived as paragons of courage and manhood by those who serve under them and seek to emulate them? These questions are worth exploring if we are serious about decreasing violence.

Our national lack of interest in and lack of respect for child-rearing, our abysmal neglect of medical and social services for poor pregnant women and young mothers, and our failure to curtail teenage pregnancies can only serve to increase the numbers of boys suffering from these conditions and ensure that many of them will indeed become violent. Child-battering, emotional cruelty, and neglect increase the odds that any boy will grow up to be violent. Many of these boys are particularly prone to being battered—they can drive even the best, most patient, parent crazy.

The situation is now aggravated by the fact that more and more drug-addicted women are giving birth. Recent studies indicate that children born to mothers who are cocaine or crack addicts "show symptoms similar to those in children with mild autism or those with personality disorders . . ."[37] They are described as withdrawn, lacking in emotion, not interacting with other children. Their ability to concentrate is very low. In addition many addicted mothers subject their children to extreme emotional and physical neglect, or abandon them. Very few of these children have ever had any fathering.

Because of his parents' sensitivity, caring, and ability to get good psychological counseling, it is unlikely that Seth Maxell will be a violent adult. He is already considerably less violent than he was a few years ago. He himself has expressed negative feelings about his violent behavior at school. His mother is very careful to reinforce his generosity and kindness and to encourage empathy. When he has been particularly rude, difficult, or violent she sends him to his room and tells him to think about what he has done. Later he will often make comments like: "I don't like it when I have to think about what I did . . . It makes me feel sad that I've hurt you or that I wasn't nice." Seth Maxell is highly motivated to please his parents, whom he loves, and so there is a part of him that very much wants to control his violent behavior.

But imagine Seth Maxell born to a fifteen-year-old single mother in an urban ghetto. Can you imagine his *not* becoming a violent adult?

If enacted, the recommendations made in the second part of this book would play an important role in discouraging violent behavior in all boys. However, special services for children with these conditions and their parents are necessary. I would venture to guess that the cost of such services would add up to a fraction of what we pay to process large numbers of these boys through the judiciary system and incarcerate them, not to mention victim-related costs and suffering.

NATURE OR NURTURE?: A FALSE DICHOTOMY

Eleanor Maccoby and Carol Jacklin's work confirms what most of us already suspected. Boys, from a very young age, act more aggressively than girls. But the belief that "boys will be boys" and so the fighting and killing will go on regardless of what we do has no foundation in the best available knowledge. It is based on the erroneous belief that violent behavior grows out of a drive or instinct akin to hunger or sex.

But to say that violence is not an instinct or drive is not to deny that it has a biological basis. We are physical beings and so all of our behavior is grounded in biology. If we had not been biologically programmed with the ability to learn to be violent, then violent behavior could never have developed. Much as some of us may want to fly like birds, we shall never do so, because our biology forbids it. Intensive efforts have been made in recent years to teach language to chimps. The efforts failed. Chimps are not biologically wired to learn more than a few concrete terms; concepts and abstractions are beyond their potential. But we can learn concepts and abstractions. We can also learn violence.

We must begin to move beyond a simplistic view of violence in which one side contends that it is biological and therefore nothing can be done about it, while the other side asserts that human beings are naturally good and violence is caused by socialization alone.

Violence is best understood as developing out of an interaction between a biological potential and certain kinds of environments. In comparing males and females, the different treatment of boys and girls from birth makes it difficult to assess what is due to biology and what is due to socialization. It is the *combination* of evidence from such diverse and independent sources—studies in the United States, cross-cultural studies, hormonal and animal studies—which leads me to conclude that the potential for violence appears to be greater in males.*

Higher levels of testosterone seem to be a factor in greater male violence, but it may be that these are not so much linked directly to offensive violent behavior as to a lower threshold for frustration, more irritability and impatience, greater impulsiveness, a tendency to rough and tumble, and perhaps a greater concern with dominance, all of which can easily be precursors of violence. These tendencies can only be reinforced by the rougher treatment that boys receive from an early age. Hormone levels appear to be affected by the environment. A boy's involvement in a dominance- and violence-oriented group may cause increases in his testosterone levels.

The violence gap between boys and girls is enlarged by the fact that boys, more frequently than girls, suffer from physical disabilities which put them at greater risk for behaving violently. Nevertheless, when we speak of male-female differences with respect to violence we must remember that we are referring to tendencies which are more pronounced in one group than the other, not to separate, nonoverlapping groups. The fact that a majority of men lead essentially nonviolent lives, in spite of living in a society that applauds the values of the masculine mystique, testifies to the lack of any intense inclination towards violent behavior on their part.

Early childhood experiences are important. Boys who are

* Many parents of boys have shared their experiences and views on the nature/nurture issue with me. A majority are convinced that nature plays an important role in their sons' high level of interest in rough play, war toys, and violent entertainment. On the other hand a significant minority—perhaps as high as 40 percent—have told me that their sons have no or very little interest in these areas. A few have told me that their sons are far more gentle than their daughters. I have been struck by the similarity between these very informal findings and the data collected by Maccoby and Jacklin. While a majority of the ninety-four studies they examined showed boys to be more aggressive, a large number showed no difference and a few studies showed girls to be more aggressive.

emotionally neglected, humiliated, or battered, boys whose parents encourage combative attitudes and behaviors, are more likely to be violent.

Peer pressure is important. Concerns with dominance and proving manhood through fighting can lead boys in groups to commit acts of violence that they would not commit on their own.

Human beings easily learn xenophobia and territoriality. Governments often encourage and exploit these tendencies for their own purposes, including the waging of wars. Research indicates that wars serve to legitimize and encourage other forms of violence.

The enormous influence that government, society, and family have in terms of encouraging or discouraging the potential for violence is clear both from changes which take place within the same culture and differences in levels of violence between different societies.

Anthropologist Peggy Sanday's cross-cultural study of ninety-five societies revealed that 47 percent of them were free of rape. Robert R. Holt reports that there are at least thirty-three societies in which war as well as interpersonal violence are extremely rare.[38]

People who live in violent societies tend to assume that high levels of violence are inevitable. Now that we have, hopefully, been cured of this mistaken belief, we shall focus our attention on what can be done to make our society less violent.

Toward a Solution: Raising Sons for the Twenty-first Century

I
Bringing Up Baby When It's a Boy

4
Where Have All the Fathers Gone?

Pop psychology, as embodied in Alfred Hitchcock's film *Psycho,* tends to reinforce the image of the violent male as having had an overbearing, domineering, hypercritical mother. Father isn't mentioned.

Inadequate mothering is undoubtedly a significant factor in the etiology of male violence. As we have seen, a boy whose mother is cold and indifferent, or subjects him to humiliation and irrational criticism, or batters him, is more likely to become violent than a boy who has a loving, sensitive, respectful mother.

However, the best available data also suggest that high levels of violent behavior are frequently linked to a boy's having had inadequate fathering.

Sociological studies of juvenile delinquent boys indicate that a high percentage of them come from families in which either there is no father in the household or the father is on hand but abusive or violent. Cross-cultural anthropological studies suggest that violent behavior is often characteristic of male adolescents and adults whose fathers were absent or played a small role in their sons' early rearing.

Psychological studies of families in which child-rearing is shared by the parents or in which the father is the primary caretaker reveal that the sons in these families are more empathic than boys raised in the traditional way. In a twenty-six-year longitudinal study of empathy, researchers found that the single factor most highly linked to empathic concern was the level of paternal involvement in child care.[1]

Dorothy Dinnerstein, professor of psychology at Rutgers University, has developed a theory (summarized below) that links greater male violence and lack of empathic, nurturing qualities with the fact that boys are reared almost exclusively by women. However speculative her theory may be, it receives considerable corroboration from diverse and independent findings in the social sciences.

This chapter explores how the very secondary role of fathers in child-rearing and in many cases the absence of any involvement, are linked to male violence. It examines how fathers' and mothers' adherence to the values of the masculine mystique encourages violence in their sons.

In addition to its direct effect on boys, a lack of fathering can also have a profound impact on the quality of mothering a boy receives. A woman who is able to share the emotional and financial burdens of child-rearing with a supportive husband is more likely to be a loving, affirming mother than the woman who is on her own and often resentful and angry at the boy's father. *It may well be that in order to improve the quality of mothering one of the most important things we can do is encourage boys and men to be good fathers.*

Some of the recent literature concerning the effects on boys of having father as the primary or coequal caretaker is examined. I argue that raising boys to become nurturing fathers would help to decrease violence among all men.

Chapter 5 is devoted to answering some of the common objections to the idea of greater male participation in child-rearing.

The conclusion of this section is clear: *major nurturant paternal involvement in child-rearing would play an important role in reducing male violence.* It would signal the end of adherence to the masculine mystique and would lead to significant improvements in mothers' behavior toward their sons.

SWITCHING IDENTIFICATIONS, OR WHY IT'S DIFFICULT TO BECOME A MAN WHEN YOU ARE RAISED BY A WOMAN

In the traditional family, girls are raised by a woman, a person with whom they can remain identified for the rest of their lives. Boys are not.

Dorothy Dinnerstein points out that while both male and female babies identify with their mother, internalizing her basic qualities, by the time the little boy is approximately eighteen months old he has already developed some sense that he is male and different from his mother. As he gets older he realizes increasingly that unlike his mother he will not be wearing dresses when he grows up, nor will he develop breasts or give birth to babies. He will not become the nurturant primary caretaker of children, the person who feeds them, changes their diapers, toilet trains them, empathizes with them when they get hurt. This feminine world is the only one that he is intimately familiar with; it is the center of his universe, but in order to become a man he must distance himself from it.

He learns from his father, if he is around, and from the outside world—media, peer group, school, books—that being a man means working outside the home, being strong and tough, not crying, and being willing to fight or go to war. He also learns that men are more important and dominant in the adult world—they run it. A vast majority of political, professional, and religious leaders are male. Men's jobs are more prestigious and pay more than women's jobs. In their relations with women, men are dominant. They initiate relationships; they "take women out" and pay for them. Married women take on their husbands' names, and in spite of the fact that women do all or most of the child-rearing, their children go through life bearing their fathers' surnames.* Without anything ever having to be said, the little boy quickly realizes that in the adult world, the power structure is the reverse of that in the nursery.

It becomes imperative that he separate himself from the less powerful, less prestigious world of women and find his place in the world of men. In order to become a man he works hard at not crying or showing fear, at being tough and strong. This means repressing early feelings of attachment, dependency, vulnerability, intense love and hate. It means repressing his desire for the warmer, softer, more empathic world of women he has grown up in. These qualities are dismissed as feminine and unfit for a "real man."

The reward he will receive for denying his deepest emotions and needs is a higher position in society, simply by virtue of being a man. Even if he spends his entire life at the bottom of the social ladder, he still will have someone to feel superior to. (Nineteenth-century British philosopher John Stuart Mill was ahead of his times in recognizing the significance of this reward. He wrote: "Think what it is to a boy, to grow up to manhood in the belief that without any merit or any exertion of his own, though he may be the most frivolous and empty or the most ignorant and stolid of mankind, by the mere fact of being born a male he is by right the superior of all and every one of an entire half of the human race . . ."[2] Mill was convinced that the discrepancy in male and female power served as *the* basic model for inequality.)

Raphaela Best is an educator who studied and worked with children in a suburban elementary school from 1973 to 1977. In her book *We've All Got Scars,* which is based on that experience, she tells us that by the second grade, in order to be accepted by his peers, "a boy had to overcome and root out anything in his own actions, feelings, and preferences that could be viewed as

---

* Some changes have taken place since the advent of the women's movement. There are more female professionals, more women running for political office. Some women do not take on their husbands' names at marriage. More men are involved in child-rearing and household chores. But these changes are not significant or widespread enough to change the basic picture for most boys.

remotely female." Displays of affection, playing with girls, help-ing to clean up the classroom were no longer acceptable: "What-ever females did, that was what the boys must not do."[3]

What did the boys do to prove their manhood? "First, of course, to be a man you had to be willing to fight, whatever the odds. If a boy did not like to fight, it was important to act as though he did . . ."[4] Besides fighting, the boys' major concern in terms of proving their manhood was being first in everything from physical strength to sports, from schoolwork to being the class line leader. Best's observations on the role of dominance in boys' play groups corroborate the research discussed in Chap-ter 3.

Many parents actively reinforce these values. Research reveals that fathers, especially, tend to become deeply disturbed by any behavior in their sons that is not typically "masculine."[5] This kind of father provides a role model that fits the masculine mystique even though he may not be violent, at least not uncon-trollably violent—he may use physical punishment to discipline his son. He does not express much emotion. He doesn't cry. He is very concerned with dominance, power, being tough. His taste in movies runs to John Wayne and Sylvester Stallone. On TV he watches violent shows like "Miami Vice" and "Hawaii Five-O." Whatever his actual behavior may be, he is likely to indulge in callous sexual talk about women. He may feel that a high level of involvement in child care is unmanly. As a result, his son is likely to be less empathic. This kind of father is proba-bly typical of a large number of basically decent American men who reinforce in their sons just those qualities that serve to desensitize them and make them more prone to commit violent acts or condone them.

As mentioned earlier, parents, especially fathers, who want to make sure that their sons grow up to be strong and tough often overstimulate them from an early age. They toss them about more, act loud and tough rather than soft and gentle as they do with girls. Robert R. Holt points out that there is evidence from animal and human studies that in order to be able to take this kind of treatment, the organism becomes less sensitive. He em-phasizes that "part of callousness, part of toughness is not being sensitive, not having as much pain sensitivity and not having as much general awareness of feelings."[6]

Holt also points out that in their efforts to encourage the values of the masculine mystique many parents in fact encourage violent behavior in their sons by not setting distinct limits, by not making it clear that violence will not be tolerated. It is the often basically decent sons of such parents who can succumb to peer pressure and engage in gang rape; or "join the boys" in beating up a member of a disliked minority group; or, if they are in positions of power, make decisions that unnecessarily endanger the lives of people.

By contrast, even within the traditional family, a loving, supportive father who is not afraid to show tenderness, empathy, and tears, who, together with his wife, does not condone violence and does not try to mold his son into the traits of the masculine mystique, is most likely to have a son who will not use unnecessary violence. For such a boy, the separation from the "feminine" emotions is less sharp, for he can identify with his father and still retain some empathic, loving qualities.

Such a boy will in all likelihood experience sharp contradictions between the way his father behaves and the way many of his peers behave. His willingness to fight will grow mainly out of self-defense: if he does not *appear tough,* he will become easy prey for bullies. As an adult he will not be prone to violent behavior.

There are no such contradictions for the boy whose father is emotionally or physically abusive. He may well model himself on his father and become unacceptably abusive to his peers—he may become the class bully.

For boys without fathers, the mass media and their own peer group tend to be the main sources of their concept of what it is to be a man.

Les Willis runs a program for teenage fathers at a hospital in Philadelphia. The population he works with is 98 percent low-income and African-American. Most of the boys have no experience of a nurturant father. One of the major hurdles Willis must overcome in order to get the boys involved in fathering is "the stigma of being a nurturer." They fear being perceived as effeminate by their peers if they push a baby carriage or hold their baby close. Once the counseling and peer support groups at the hospital help them get over this fear, many of these young men will say: "I've always wanted to do this but I was afraid of being called gay."[7]

Willis's program is highly successful both in terms of getting the boys to accept their paternal responsibilities—82 percent of them see their child regularly, with 76 percent of them paying some child support—and in terms of helping them get and keep jobs—79 percent of the young men are employed. It is also successful with respect to turning these "high-risk" young men away from lives of violence. Their involvement decreases the chance that their sons will be violent. Studies of delinquent boys have convinced many sociologists that boys raised by mothers alone are particularly prone to violence because of their susceptibility to "hypermasculinity."

Sociologist Walter B. Miller tells us that the extreme concern with toughness in lower-class culture probably originates in the fact that for a significant percentage of these boys there is no consistently present male figure whom they can identify with and model themselves on. Because of this, they develop an "almost obsessive . . . concern with 'masculinity'."[8] A preoccupation with homosexuality is also very prevalent. It manifests itself in the common practice of baiting and often physically attacking gay men.

In *The Myth of Masculinity*, sociologist Joseph Pleck takes a critical look at hypermasculinity theories. One of his major criticisms is focused on the assumption in these theories that the traditional dichotomy between male and female roles is valid, and the problem with delinquent boys is that they don't have a traditional father in the home.

As Pleck sees it, the problem lies not in the absence of the father but in the imposition of rigid sex roles: if our ideas of what constitutes acceptable male and female behavior were more fluid, boys raised by mothers would not have to act "hypermasculine" in order to prove that they are real men, for it would be acceptable for "real men" to be empathic, caring, emotionally connected.

The difficulty with Pleck's position is that the findings in anthropology, sociology, and psychology described in this chapter suggest that the lack of paternal involvement plays an important part in the development of rigid, dichotomous, and hierarchical sex roles, with the male role including a considerable degree of violence. As we shall see, it may be that male involvement in nurturant fathering is *a condition* of more fluid sex roles and decreased violence.

Anthropologist Beatrice Whiting carried out a study of six cultures, focusing on the relation of child-training practices to personality. One of her findings was that in the two cultures that were the most violent, the fathers were most loosely connected with the family and had least to do with rearing of children. The husband and wife seldom slept or ate together, and seldom worked or played together. Her findings are corroborated by other cross-cultural research.[9]

As Whiting sees it, "It would seem as if there were a never-ending circle. The separation of the sexes leads to a conflict of identity in the boy children, to unconscious fear of being feminine, which leads to 'protest masculinity,' exaggeration of the difference between men and women, antagonism against and fear of women, male solidarity, and hence to isolation of women and very young children."[10]

The view that the more exclusively a boy is reared by his mother without the presence of a male figure, the more he will need later on to deny his identification with her and her feminine qualities to prove his masculinity through "hypermasculinity," is further corroborated by anthropological research on initiation ceremonies into manhood.

Anthropologists Roger V. Burton and John W. M. Whiting tell us that societies that combine almost exclusively female child-rearing with strong male/female role differentiation and higher male social status create a strong conflict in boys. The conflict is resolved in favor of manhood by often excruciatingly painful initiation rites: "The initiation rites serve psychologically to brainwash the primary feminine identity and to establish firmly the secondary male identity."[11] The tests of manhood often include painful genital operations, sleep deprivation, and hazing. To give an idea of how traumatic these rites can be, one ethnographer reported that "boys returning home after initiation did not know their village or recognize their parents."[12]

In most societies with elaborate initiation rites there is one term that refers both to women and uninitiated boys and another term for initiated males. In these societies it is believed that a male is born twice: "once into the woman-child status, and then at puberty he symbolically dies and is reborn into the status of manhood."[13]

In some societies the boy acquires his "second identity" not through initiation ceremonies but by an abrupt change from maternal to paternal residence, or from maternal to paternal supervision and education.

Indian psychoanalyst Sudhir Kakar tells us that in traditional Hindu India, at around the age of five, boys are abruptly separated from their mothers. Until this age the boy is enveloped in his mother's protective and nurturing love. Now the men in the family take responsibility for his care and instruction: "Without any preparation for the transition, the boy is literally banished from the gently teasing, admiring society of women into a relatively stern and unfeeling male world . . ."[14]

For the American boy, manhood is not usually achieved through abrupt switching from maternal to paternal supervision or formal initiation rites. Perhaps the closest we come to initiation rites is a deer hunting ritual that is common in Mississippi and some other parts of the South. David Blankenhorn, the director of the Institute for American Values, grew up in Mississippi. In a 1989 interview with the author he explained that when a boy is somewhere between eight and twelve years old, his father will take him out hunting: "Your first deer is a big deal. It signifies you have done something significant approaching manhood." Blood from the deer is smeared all over the boy's face and photographs are taken and often displayed on family mantelpieces. Blankenhorn, who went through the experience himself, does not hesitate to characterize it as an initiation rite. He estimates that perhaps as many as 60 or 70 percent of boys in Mississippi undergo it.

But for most American boys, manhood is achieved through a series of informal tests. By not crying or associating with girls, by being strong, tough, good at sports, and willing to fight, boys prove to their peers—and often to their parents, especially fathers—that they are real men.

Raphaela Best tells us that as early as the first grade, the boys she observed held girls and girlish activities in such low esteem that they made it known that "they would never cook or sew or do any other housekeeping chore under any circumstances, *even if they starved to death or had to throw away their torn clothing or go without clothes* [my emphasis]."[15]

According to Diane Ehrensaft, a psychologist and author of *Parenting Together,* a study of families in which father and mother have shared child care, preliminary evidence suggests that boys raised by mother *and father* do not share this negative attitude. She describes an elementary school class with an emphasis on nonsexist education in which boys were asked to complete the phrase "If I were a girl . . ." and the girls "If I were a boy . . ." Those boys who had been raised in a traditional family came up with varying degrees of misogyny, the extreme being "If I was a girl I would hate it." There were no parallel responses of boy-hating from girls. On the other hand, the boys from shared-parenting families (of whom there were quite a few) did not show any such negativity. One of these boys wrote, "If I was a girl I would like to put on lipstick." Another wrote "If I was a girl I would have long hair and I would work at a traveling agency."[16]

When a boy is able from the earliest age to identify with his father, and when that identification includes loving, nurturing, and feeling connected with others, then his developing a masculine identity does not depend on his repressing his identification with his mother and her feminine qualities. He does not need to be contemptuous of women in order to solidify his identity as a man. Having had a nurturant father, he is more likely to be empathic toward others, including girls.

The lack of male involvement in child-rearing leads to decreased sensitivity and empathy, and greater violence, in another closely related way: young boys are not rewarded for those qualities that someday will make them nurturant fathers.

From the earliest age, girls are perceived as future mothers. They are taught to be nurturant, helpful, sensitive to the feelings of others. They rehearse their future role by playing with dolls, by playing house.

In the traditional family being a good father means primarily being a good provider. For a little boy, to rehearse for fatherhood is to rehearse for future work and financial success. Fathers are also expected to discipline their sons, imbue them with ideals of competitiveness and hard work, and play ball with them.

The boy who learns to be competitive, hard-working, and involved in sports is on his way to becoming a "good" father.

Since traditional fathers are not expected to nurture their children in the sense of directly caring for their physical and emotional needs, there is no need to develop the same degree of empathy, sensitivity, and caring in little boys as in little girls. Quite to the contrary, some parents, especially fathers, may become concerned if their sons exhibit these traits to any significant degree—the empathic, caring boy who lets himself cry is often seen as being too soft, too gentle. Parents are often uncomfortable if a boy rehearses the nurturing role by playing with dolls. As they get older, boys become increasingly aware that playing with dolls, being interested in babies, or exhibiting nurturant behavior is inappropriate for them, and they act accordingly. But several recent studies suggest that until the age of about five or six there is no difference in boys' and girls' interest in babies.[17]

The role that parents play, often unwittingly, in influencing their children's attitudes toward nurturance is revealed in a study done by psychologist Phyllis Berman.[18] Berman videotaped forty-eight boys and girls, two to three years old, as they played with dolls in the presence of their parents. She found that most of the mothers and fathers made comments encouraging the girls to think of themselves as the doll's mother taking good care of her baby. "You're such a good mommy" was typical. But only one or two of the boys' parents made analogous comments about the boys' being the doll's father. *The parents, a sophisticated group of professionals, were unaware that they were encouraging their daughters, but not their sons, to think of themselves as future nurturant parents.*

When Carol Ember, anthropology professor at Hunter College, studied the Luo community in Kenya, she noticed that mothers who did not have enough daughters or other female family members to help them with their feminine chores would assign their sons to help them. Ember compared the behavior of the boys who helped in child-rearing and other feminine tasks to those who did not and found that boys who helped their mothers inside the home were less aggressive and more pro-social than those who didn't. The difference was greatest among those boys who had assisted their mothers in child-rearing.

. . . .

Taking care of young children requires patience, self-sacrifice, empathy. Studies by psychologists indicate that when empathy increases, violence decreases.[19]

Martin Hoffman, professor of psychology at New York University, specializes in the study of empathy, altruism, and the development of moral principles. According to him, in recent decades psychologists with very different theoretical perspectives have all come to consider empathy as perhaps "the most significant factor in altruistic behavior."[20]

From an early age, girls act more empathically and altruistically than do boys. Hoffman explains that girls may possibly have a slightly stronger disposition toward empathy than boys, but the evidence is far from conclusive. Even if there proves to be some biological difference in the predisposition to empathy, it is significantly magnified by later socialization. Not only is empathy much more highly valued in girls than in boys, but also it is easier to be empathic with someone when one has experienced similar emotions. But boys are conditioned to repress feelings of weakness, fear, vulnerability. As a consequence, their emotional repertoire is much more limited than that of girls, and so is their ability to empathize.

Modeling themselves on their mothers, girls are quick to help other children who are in danger, or to warn them of dangers. Raphaela Best tells us that among the children she observed, the girls "offered emotional as well as practical support to those who needed it," including boys.[21] If a boy ever broke down and cried, or if he got very upset about something, it was almost invariably a girl who would comfort him: "the clear assignment of the nurturant role left the boys free to be receivers, not givers of emotional support."[22]

The boys, on the other hand, prodded each other on toward greater and greater risk-taking. The greater the risk the greater the proof of manhood. "We've all got scars," one boy proudly told Raphaela Best as he rolled up his sleeves to show off his symbols of manhood.[23] (Best observes that things haven't changed much since the days when young Prussian officers proved their manhood by acquiring facial scars from fencing.)

This behavior was baffling to the girls: "The girls could not understand what drove the boys to bruise their bodies on the playground so that they could acquire scars to prove their manhood." "What's so great about getting hurt if you don't have to?" one girl wondered.[24]

FATHERS WHO SHARE;
FATHERS WHO ARE PRIMARY CARETAKERS

While their numbers are still very small, there has been an increase in the last fifteen years in the number of men who either are primary caretakers of their children or share equally.

In *Parenting Together,* psychologist Diane Ehrensaft describes Adam, a four-year-old boy who, when asked what he wanted to be when he grew up answered, "Maybe just a daddy," and then added, "or maybe I'll be a ranger." For boys like Adam who are raised or partially raised by their fathers, nurturing—being a daddy in the fullest sense—is a natural part of being a man.

Both Ehrensaft and Kyle Pruett, a Yale psychiatrist who did a study of children raised in families in which the father was the primary caretaker, tell us that the children they studied seemed to have no difficulty in terms of viewing roles that traditionally are associated with one sex as perfectly normal for the other.

Typical was Henry, the "baby-doll-toting, Big Wheel stunt driver." His father's comment about Henry's "androgynous" behavior was: "Any kid who bombs around the neighborhood in his Big Wheel with his baby doll tucked into the jump seat is probably going to make out just fine."[25]

These boys' broader notions of appropriate or inappropriate male and female behavior in no way affected their sense of sexual identity—there wasn't the slightest doubt in Henry's mind that he was a boy. He and the other children raised by fathers or by both parents simply had a more fluid idea of what constitutes appropriate gender roles. As far as they were concerned boys play with trucks, helicopters, and dolls, just as men —like their daddies—take care of children, work, repair cars, and play baseball.

For the sons of nurturant fathers, achieving a masculine identity is easier, not harder. From the earliest age these boys experience a deep level of emotional closeness with someone of their own sex. As they get older, to achieve male identity they do not have to cut themselves off emotionally from their nurturer in order to identify with a far more remote figure. They can continue to remain emotionally connected to their fathers *and* identify with them. Boys raised by their fathers or by both parents have a *primary* masculine identification. For boys raised by their mothers, the masculine identification must always remain *secondary*.

Popular mythology tends to see the man who is heavily involved in child care as a weak and unassertive type, but this is not the picture that emerges from Pruett's and Ehrensaft's books or from other studies on the subject. In fact, Norma Radin of the University of Michigan reports that in one study when fifty-nine fathers who were primary caregivers were given the BEM Sex Role Inventory no significant differences emerged between them and the husbands of primary caregiving wives.

The BEM test is intended to determine how "masculine," "feminine," or "androgynous" a subject is. A characteristic is considered "masculine" if it is perceived in American society as more desirable for a man than for a woman, and "feminine" if it is considered more desirable for a woman than for a man. "Athletic," "analytical," and "self-reliant" are a few of the traits classified as "masculine." "Affectionate," "compassionate," and "gentle" are a few of the traits classified as "feminine."

It is possible that in our society those men who feel very secure in their traditional masculine traits are more able and willing to confront the enormous social pressure against men's becoming primary caregivers.

This is not to say that nurturing their children has no psychological effect on fathers. "In the past five years I've become a different person," one coparenting father asserts. "I am more accepting, have gained a great deal more patience, and am a lot more easygoing than before our daughter was born." Nurturing fathers learn to be "more patient, more tuned in, more sensitive to other people's needs," Ehrensaft comments.[26]

Pruett tells us that "primary caretaking fathers feel and express sex discrimination less acutely than do traditional fathers."[27] Since they themselves have moved away from traditional sex roles, it makes sense that they are less concerned with their sons' and daughters' conforming to rigid sex roles.

Both Ehrensaft and Pruett are convinced that tending babies puts men in touch, at the deepest level, with feelings of vulnerability, dependency, love, and forgiveness, feelings they learned to repress at an early age. Ehrensaft describes nurturant father-ing as a "corrective emotional experience." It permits men to make contact with the repressed child in themselves. *They no longer have to pretend.* They can be full human beings.

Kyle Pruett's book is not particularly concerned with violence, yet he concludes it in the following way:

> Since children both male and female are born with a vigorous predisposition to procreate and nurture, how wise and far-reaching it would be to encourage not just half but the whole human popula-tion to embrace this precious endowment . . .
>
> Imagine what such a man could do for his society, his family, his son, his daughter. He would be loving and nurturing without em-barrassment or fear, open and vulnerable without being a victim. He could foster in his children the freedom to be strongly feminine or tenderly masculine but, above all, abidingly human.
>
> *In so doing, he will help bring forth increasingly humane familial and social environments bent more on nurturing and the fulfillment of meaningful rela-tionships than on the obscene violent posturings of power, envy, and domina-tion* [my emphasis].[28]

MAKING MEN PART OF LIFE-GIVING RATHER THAN LIFE-TAKING

Since women carry the fetus *in utero,* give birth, and take care of their young, children perceive the realm of child-bearing and child-rearing as feminine. Since the ability to give life is viewed as awesome by young children, many young boys feel excluded from the greatest power of all. Psychoanalyst Karen Horney coined the expression "womb envy" to capture their feelings.

As boys begin to reject identification with their mothers, these feelings are repressed together with so many unacceptable early feelings, but on an unconscious level they continue to influence men's behavior. For some men the power to destroy life be-comes the equivalent to the female power to create life. Vietnam War veteran and author William Broyles, Jr., states it clearly: "[War] is, for men, at some terrible level the closest thing to what childbirth is for women: the initiation into the power of life and death."[29]

Carol Cohn tells us that the history of the atomic bomb proj-ect is permeated with imagery which equates creation with destruction and suggests men's desire to appropriate women's life-giving power. At Los Alamos, the atom bomb was referred to as "Oppenheimer's baby." When Henry Stimson, Secretary of War during World War II, received a telegram informing him of a successful atomic bomb detonation, it read, after decoding: "Doctor has just returned most enthusiastic and confident that the little boy is as husky as his big brother. The light in his eyes discernible from here to Highhold and I could have heard his screams from here to my farm." Edward Teller's telegram to Los Alamos announcing the successful test of the hydrogen bomb (named "Mike") read, "It's a boy."[30]

But while some men derive a sense of power from having the ability to destroy life, war gives many men a sense that they are preserving and improving life for their families, friends, and country. Irrespective of the facts, wars are commonly portrayed as defensive, or essential to a nation's well-being, by those in power. Women may have a monopoly on giving life, but men have a monopoly on defending it against the enemy.

That willingness to defend one's country, to risk one's life in battle, to ensure the safety and freedom of others, then takes on a higher value than the life-giving and life-nurturing activities of women. Monuments, churches, parades, history books, are all a testimony to the all-important activity of defending one's nation against the enemy. There are few if any monuments testifying to the life-giving activities of women.

Pruett tells us that a major difference between traditionally raised boys and boys raised by their fathers is that the latter show more curiosity and interest in father as procreator. For the boys he studied, "father is seen as a *maker* of human beings along with mother, who makes *and* births them."[31]

In a traditional family or in a single-mother family, the fact that the mother cannot have a baby without the father's sperm is easily forgotten, for it has an abstract, distant quality. There is no tangible reality that corresponds to it. When the father is as much a nurturer as the mother, having a baby is experienced as a *joint* enterprise with father giving mother the seed that enables her to carry the baby. Father's importance in the process is experienced directly.

It seems likely that boys reared or coreared by fathers would experience men in general and themselves in particular as givers of life in a very profound way. *The essential role of the male of the species in creating life would be fully recognized and experienced.* *

Experiencing the power to give life may well come to replace the need to experience the power of taking life. Killing in war may seem less exciting to men who are excited by and feel intimately connected to giving life.

As we saw in Chapter 3, according to J. Glenn Gray the intense feelings of power, excitement, delight in destruction, and camaraderie that many men experience in war are reactions to the boredom and lack of meaningful goals in their daily lives. What could replace war for men, Gray asks? An important part of the answer lies in "the growth of that preservative love and care which is in strongest opposition to destructive lusts . . ."[32]

Gray was writing in the early 1950s, when it was almost unthinkable that one of the deepest forms that love and care could take for a man would be a profound and ongoing involvement in the rearing of his children.

Men who are guided by the values of the masculine mystique find it difficult to develop deep emotional bonds not only with their wives and children, but also with other men. The hollow quality of their lives is then alleviated by the excitement and camaraderie of war.

Men who are deeply emotionally connected to their children —as well as their wives and friends—will be more reluctant to send their sons and their friends' sons off to war, or to go to war themselves.

Kyle Pruett tells us about a Mr. Blue (not his real name), who after the birth of his son decided to give up one of his favorite activities, motorcycle riding. He told his wife: "It's just too crazy to go out there now that I have a kid. It feels nuts to be bombing around the streets just asking people to bump you off like that."[33]

Mr. Blue's reaction will be familiar to many women who after

---

* Another likely benefit would be a closer connection in men's minds between the sexual act, procreation, and nurturant fathering. For many men, sex has much more to do with power and aggression than with love and procreation. The use of the word "fuck" as an insult, or as a synonym for being abused, attests to this, as do statistics on rape. For some boys—especially in our ghettos—impregnating girls is a sign of sexual prowess and manhood. The interest in their offspring stops at that.

becoming mothers and experiencing how utterly dependent their children are on them become far more concerned with their own safety.

It seems likely that fully nurturant fatherhood would imbue many men with a newfound sense of responsibility that would be passed on to their sons. (An increase in responsibility and concern with future generations would also, in all likelihood, make men less prone to engage in the destruction of the environment.)

WOMEN AS GODDESSES AND WITCHES

Men kill each other in staggering numbers in wars, in gang warfare, in random criminal acts, but there is also a form of male violence that is directed specifically at women.

In 1990 30 percent of all female murder victims were slain by husbands or boyfriends; there were 102,555 *reported* rapes. About 1.8 million women are assaulted by their husbands every year.

Women are frequently the victims of what would appear to be the most painful types of abandonment. Young women are often left by husbands or boyfriends who refuse to take any economic or other responsibility for their young children. Older women are often cast aside when their husbands become interested in younger women. Yet as newspaper headlines and statistics attest, *it is jilted men who cannot deal with abandonment.* It is they who with regularity kill their ex-spouses or girlfriends. Jean Harris, who was convicted of killing her lover, Dr. Herman Tarnower, is one of the few exceptions. For every Jean Harris there are hundreds of male murderers. Within a recent period of one week, three Long Island women were murdered by their ex-husbands.

Why is there such an extraordinary discrepancy between males and females in crimes of passion? Why do so many men batter their wives and girlfriends? Why do so many men experience such intense rage *at women?*

One factor is the adherence to traditional views on male and female sex roles. A man who believes that males are naturally dominant and females submissive will not only feel deeply hurt if his wife or girlfriend leaves him or if she does not submit to his wishes, but he will also experience her behavior as a humiliating insult to his manhood.

Another part of the answer lies in the fact that women take care of children from birth. At the deepest psychic level, the completely helpless, dependent baby experiences the person who fulfills its needs as all-powerful. Since even the most caring mother is unable to fulfill all of her baby's needs, the mother is experienced alternately as Goddess and Witch.* *It follows that as long as solely women fulfill the needs of young children, men's emotional reactions to women will be overdetermined.* If Freud's observation that repressed emotions influence behavior on an unconscious level and often in an intensified and diffuse way is correct, then it would follow that the boy who has repressed very strong feelings of early rage against his mother will as an adult be influenced by these feelings in his relations with women.

If the little boy is reared by both parents, he does not have to switch identifications in order to become a man, and so there is less need for him to repress his emotions. He carries fewer undealt-with early feelings of anger, love, and dependency. The object of such feelings as remain is no longer the mother alone. He is also likely to be more empathic, which decreases the probability of his being violent.

At the deepest psychic level, men would no longer experience women as the *sole* omnipotent life-giving figures of their infancy and early childhood. Each child's psyche would contain Goddesses and Gods, Witches and Satans. But with less early repression, these feelings would be less intense in the adult male personality. Fathers' involvement in nurturance would lead to less anger and violence on the part of the son in yet another way. A boy whose mother is unloving and neglectful of his needs is much more likely to develop strong feelings of rage against her than is a boy whose mother is loving and caring. Given how extraordinarily demanding child-rearing is, it is the exceptional woman who as sole caregiver will be able to fulfill her child's emotional and physical needs satisfactorily. Nurturant male participation in child-rearing would tend to decrease unconscious rage against women by making it easier for women to satisfy their children's needs.

A woman who is completely without emotional or financial

* Psychoanalyst Melanie Klein was the first to focus attention on the baby's experience of its caretaker as all-powerful and the ensuing split in the child's psyche between the good and the bad mother.

support from her child's father has the hardest task and runs the greatest risk of incurring her son's rage.

In his research on hyperaggressive children, psychologist Brent Willock has found that often the emotional and physical abuse that these children have experienced results from having mothers "who became overwhelmed and depressed by stressful life circumstances combined with a lack of emotional support (poor marital relationship or none at all, lack of extended family etc.)"[34]

Some mothers seem to be displacing onto a son the rage they feel against the boy's father, and against their own abusive non-nurturing fathers.

When I visited a Parenting Class for teenage mothers at Manhattan's West Side High School, Marie Bronshvag, who teaches the class, told me beforehand that single teenage mothers abandoned by their boyfriends "often take it out on their sons; the sons then take it out on their girlfriends."

The girls' anger at their boyfriends, at their fathers, and at men in general was highly visible in the class I observed. One student started making fun of a girl she knew who "brags on a nigguh all the time—'he's my man; he loves me.'" The girls all laughed at this girl's naïveté and stupidity. "Some girls are so dumb," a few of them chanted. They nodded their heads as someone commented, "They have to learn on their own."

After listening to some of their stories, I began to understand the depth of their negative feelings. In one case the girl's boyfriend started going out with a friend of hers when she was seven months pregnant. She told the class that her subsequent boyfriend in a fit of irrational jealousy "kicked my door in—after that I left him." Another girl described how her boyfriend punched her out of jealousy. "Some men is crazy," she concluded. The girls all seemed to agree that irrational jealousy was a major problem in their men. One girl was so angry at her child's father that she said, "If he comes near [my baby] I kill him —it's too late." Another girl's father "beat the shit out of my mother for drugs; he was gonna sell me when I was three months old." She announced, "I hate mens; I'm plannin' to be a butch."

Another common tale was that of the boyfriend who encouraged the girl not to use contraceptives or not to have an abortion because he wanted a child. He promised that he would stay around and help, but once the baby was born and his manhood proven, he disappeared.

When I asked the girls if they thought these experiences and angry feelings had any influence on how they felt about their sons, one girl said, "Some people do treat them mean 'cause they come out lookin' like their father." Some of the other girls nodded their heads in agreement.

After speaking to Les Willis about his program for teenage fathers I thought of how different these young women might feel, and how different their childrens' lives might be, if *their* boyfriends had been contacted shortly after impregnating them, and had been recruited to join a fathers' group in which they were encouraged to give emotional and physical support to their pregnant girlfriends, and to be present at their children's birth. What if their boyfriends had been persuaded that nurturing one's child is not effeminate, and had been helped to get jobs and to support their children?

DECREASING VIOLENCE BY INCREASING NURTURANCE

If we want to effect *a fundamental and long-lasting change* with respect to violence, if we want it to become an occasional aberration instead of part of our everyday lives, then coparenting must be fully accepted and encouraged.

This is not to say that in every family mother and father must share child-rearing equally. As coparenting increasingly becomes the norm, the norm for male behavior will change. Empathy, emotional connectedness, concern for others, will come to be accepted as masculine qualities. This will lead to a significant decrease in men battering their wives and children. Fathers will no longer feel compelled to treat their sons roughly in order to make sure they become "real men," nor will they tolerate violent behavior in them. *These changes would have a profound influence on the behavior of all men, including those who do not fully share parenting and those who never become fathers.*

While the number of young fathers who play an important nurturant role in raising their children has increased in recent years, there has, unfortunately, also been a trend in the opposite direction. In the last forty years there has been an enormous increase in the percentage of unmarried women giving birth. Among white women it is now over 16 percent; among African-American women, over 62 percent. While some unmarried fathers are involved in raising their children, these statistics nevertheless indicate a significant decrease in paternal involvement. Divorce rates remain high, and for many fathers divorce leads to very little or no contact with their sons.

If we adopt the kinds of recommendations made in the following chapters with respect to teaching child-rearing and conflict resolution in our schools, and presenting boys with pro-social, nurturant male role models in the media and in their toys, we would begin to reverse these trends.

5
"You Can't Trust Men with Kids" and Other Objections Answered

"Thank God men aren't more involved in child-rearing! Child-molesting and battering rates are bad enough already. Imagine what it would be like if they spent as much time with kids as women do!" This comment was made by a woman after a talk I gave on men and child-rearing.

The age-old assumption is that men, lacking some biologically based nurturing instinct, are incapable of connecting emotionally with infants and children the way women do. The care they would give their children would be at best inferior to that given by mothers, and at worst it would include child-battering or child-molesting. Statistics seem to lend weight to the idea that men are not suited to child-rearing. Men are responsible for almost all child sexual abuse. It is estimated that one million American women over the age of eighteen have been involved in incestuous relationships with their fathers. Approximately sixteen thousand new cases occur each year. It is likely that many cases go unreported.

Men and women are about equally responsible for child-battering. But since men spend a much smaller portion of their time with their children, one must conclude that they are considerably more given to battering them.[1]

It is not surprising that when psychiatrist Kyle Pruett began his study of children raised by their fathers, he was somewhat skeptical as to whether these children would do as well on the Yale Developmental Schedule as those from traditional families. (The schedule enables researchers to record progress in a young child's motor functions, language and social skills, and ability to solve problems.) He was shocked to find these children doing *better* in all areas. While he speculates as to a number of reasons why they did so well, he concludes that the most likely reason is that these children had *two* highly involved parents. The mothers were fully committed to their children's well-being and growth, even though they had full-time jobs outside the home. In the traditional family the father is not usually as intensely involved with his children.

One might think that these children did so well because only a man highly dedicated to children, and nurturant to begin with, would become primary caretaker, whereas for mothers there is no such selection process. But one third of the men in Pruett's group became primary nurturers not out of any desire to do so but for purely practical reasons, and often as an interim measure —until a wife who was ill came out of the hospital, or until they could get a job. They then continued far longer than anticipated. This makes Pruett's book of particular interest.

Typical of a number of the men in the group is Mr. Blue, who says: "I love looking after my son. But I would never have guessed it. In fact, if my high school jock buddies ever knew I was doing it, they'd fall over dead from laughing."[2]

These men's children did just as well as the children of men who had a prior commitment to child-rearing. Pruett tells us that the "clearest change over time had occurred in those fathers who'd been economically forced into the primary parent role, and who were often initially quite anxious, if not unhappy, with their lot. They thawed most slowly to their task, but . . . their children were indistinguishable from the 'early choosers' by age two. Of the seven fathers still at it after four years three were from this group of 'last choosers.' "*[3]

Pruett explains this in terms of the father's "engrossment" with his child. *The father who connects with his child at a very early age, who participates in the nurturing of the child, forms a deep emotional bond which seems to elude most traditional fathers.*

A study done by Hilda and Seymour Parker of the University of Utah lends support to Pruett's views on engrossment and its consequences for the quality of the father's child-rearing. The Parkers did a comparative study of fifty-six men who were known to have sexually abused their minor daughters and fifty-four men with no known child sexual abuse in their backgrounds. They found a very significant correlation between lack of involvement in child care and nurturance, and child abuse.[4] While the study corroborated previous findings that stepfathers have a considerably higher rate of child abuse than natural fathers, it also revealed that there was no significant difference in sexual abuse between those stepfathers who had been present and involved in nurturing their stepdaughters during the first three years of life and natural fathers who were involved in nurturing their daughters. The higher rate of stepfathers' sexual abuse seems to be related to their higher rate of absence and lack of opportunity for nurturance during the early years. The authors conclude that it is quite possible that "if primary child care were shared more equally by men and women, one basis for . . . the sexual exploitation of females might be eliminated."[5]

But, the skeptic may ask, isn't there still an element of self-selection in all this? Aren't there some fathers who, unlike the men studied by Pruett, would *never*—under any conditions— agree to play a major role in nurturing their children?

It may well be that some men are thoroughly unsuited to child-rearing. In some cases they may refuse the responsibility because they fear they may physically or sexually abuse their

---

* A total of sixteen families participated in the study. As for the other fathers, after four years, three were sharing child care with their wives. In six of the families the mother had become the primary caretaker.

child. (Some of these men may end up abusing their children anyway.)

In today's society when the masculine mystique reinforces in boys those qualities that work against being a good father, many more men than women are unsuited to being good nurturers. This disparity is certain to decrease once men are reared and socialized to become fathers. However, since there appears to be some biological basis to greater male violence, stemming at least in part from some boys' and men's lower tolerance for frustration, and greater impulsivity and irritability, then it may well be that the percentage of men unsuited to be fathers will always be somewhat higher than the percentage of women unsuited to be mothers. Since men suffering from the disabilities described in Chapter 3 are particularly susceptible to these dispositions, it is probable that a higher percentage of them would not be well suited to fathering.

It is important for the well-being of our children that both now and in the future men not be pressured into caring for children if they are deeply reluctant to doing so. It is also important that women not be made to feel that motherhood is the only means to feminine fulfillment, for this entices ill-suited or ill-prepared women to become mothers.

WOMEN'S REACTIONS: DON'T ENCROACH ON OUR TERRITORY

Pruett reports that women's reactions to his findings were mixed, to say the least. Some women feared that if men got involved in child-rearing they would take over and proclaim their superiority at it. Others questioned the validity of the study. Some feared that further male encroachments in child-rearing would permit men to use custody battles as a means to gain concessions from their wives in divorce and child custody proceedings. It makes sense that many women would fear and resent men's entering the world of child-rearing. After all, this is one of the very few areas of life in which female superiority has been proclaimed. The concern about battles over custody is particularly warranted. Some men who have shown no great interest in their children during the marriage use custody battles as a means of getting financial concessions from wives who, above all, want their children.

Deep cultural and socioeconomic changes are always difficult for those who are caught in the transition, and there are frequently severe problems and abuses. Many, if not most, judges are traditional men and their decisions are sometimes outrageous. But the solution is not turning back but rather changing attitudes, and laws, and choosing more enlightened judges.

But, in the long run, women have much more to gain than to lose from male involvement in child-rearing. What woman would not welcome a significant decrease in male violence? Women and children are the victims of rapists, of child molesters, of battering husbands, of jealous and often murderous ex-husbands and lovers, and of serial murderers, not to mention gender-blind muggers, burglars, and murderers. Women are especially concerned about war and the threat of nuclear annihilation.

Another benefit—for women and children—of major male involvement would be that child-rearing as an occupation would gain prestige and attention. In our society any kind of work undertaken solely or mainly by women tends to be low in prestige and low in pay. (We are by no means unique in this: for example, in the Soviet Union, where a vast majority of medical doctors are women, and almost all bus drivers are men, bus drivers earn two to three times as much as physicians.) Not surprisingly, "homemaker" was rated at the lowest possible level—together with poultry-offal shoveler, rest-room attendant, and parking-lot attendant—in the United States Department of Labor's 1965 Dictionary of Occupational Titles, which ranks twenty-two thousand occupations according to the complexity of skills involved.

If a majority of men became deeply involved in child-rearing, there would be far greater recognition of the skills, sensitivity, emotional control, patience, and scrupulous attention that the job requires. Its importance in transmitting moral and social values and determining the quality of life for each generation as it ages would be genuinely appreciated instead of receiving lip service. Raising children would become as respected an occupation as being a stockbroker or a corporate chief executive is today. It might even outrank trading pork belly futures on the job prestige ladder.

With men involved in child-rearing, social policies would begin to reflect its vital social importance. It would become unthinkable for parents to raise their children without any training in child-rearing, without ongoing medical, psychological, and child care support systems. It would be unthinkable to pay day care center staff an average salary of twelve thousand dollars per year.

Once a large number of men experienced fully how demanding and important child-rearing is, parents of newborn babies would routinely be given maternity and paternity leaves and shorter workdays later on. These changes would lead to decreases in violent behavior. Latchkey children, children who are lonely, emotionally undernourished, and lacking in loving adult supervision and discipline, are likely candidates for rage and violence.

If being a father in the fullest sense were seen as a major part of a man's life, if boys were reared at home, educated in school, and encouraged by media images to be nurturing, responsible fathers, we could expect a significant decline in the feminization of poverty (which is due in large part to men not taking responsibility for their children). While fathers would be required, by law, to assume financial responsibility for their children and would have part of their salaries withheld if they failed to do so, such extreme measures would in all likelihood not be frequently necessary. Fathers who are genuinely bonded to their children do not usually abandon them emotionally or financially after divorce.

If all of this seems ridiculously implausible, one has only to think of the changes in child-rearing that have taken place in the last two centuries.

In eighteenth-century colonial America, children whose parents could afford it were often sent away from home during infancy to be cared for by wet nurses; after weaning they were sent to schools, often far from home. In nineteenth-century America, lower-class children could be found working in factories at the age of six.

In this era of mass media, social change takes place at a much faster rate. One can imagine the scorn and derision that a person would have met with if he or she had predicted in the late 1950s that in twenty years or so most American universities would have coed dorms and chartered gay student organizations, and that a large percentage of women with young children would be working full-time.

WHAT ABOUT MASCULINITY, HOMOSEXUALITY, AND ROLE CONFUSION?

Our notions of masculine and feminine behavior or attire are culturally determined and highly subject to change. In eighteenth-century France, noblemen wore fancy hats, frilly lace, and high heels. In Scotland soldiers wear skirts. In nineteenth-century America all the professions except teaching and nursing were considered to be for men only. Even secretaries were male.

This is not to deny that in times of cultural change, behavior that is not in keeping with traditional expectations can cause confusion and discomfort. While the connections between the roles we play and our sexual identity—our sense of being male or female—are arbitrary, we are conditioned to believe that these connections are inextricably linked. When we step beyond the bounds of the acceptable, we meet with disapproval.

Many of the nontraditional couples studied by Ehrensaft and Pruett and other researchers suffered from criticism and sometimes rejection by family members and friends. How could this not, at the very least, cause discomfort? In school, children raised by their fathers but aware of the social norm would sometimes write stories in which Mother stayed home and Father went to work.

There has never been a significant historical change without pain. It is not difficult to imagine the external rejection and moments of inner confusion and doubt that must have beset the first women who chose to attend universities and enter professions in the nineteenth century. Then, there were experts warning that women who attended universities would suffer from sex-identity confusion. Now there are experts warning that men who are primary caretakers or who share child-rearing with their wives will experience sex-identity confusion, and so will their children. Underlying this fear is often a deeper anxiety that raising boys as future nurturing fathers unafraid to show emotion and tenderness will increase homosexuality.* "If I encourage boys to play in the dollhouse, the community will run me out," a school principal told educator and researcher Raphaela Best.[6] The parents had no analogous qualms about girls playing ball with the boys or playing with construction material.

A sophisticated young mother of four told me that while she and her friends didn't like their sons to play with guns, they still worried that if the boys didn't, if they preferred arts and crafts and dolls, perhaps they were developing homosexual tendencies.

There is an irony in these fears in that there is reason to believe that encouraging nurturance and empathy in boys and discouraging aggression would diminish, not increase, homosexuality. While there is much disagreement about causes, and there is no reason to believe that there is a single etiology of male homosexuality, an examination of the literature does reveal one recurrent theme—*most homosexuals have rejecting or emotionally unavailable fathers.*

Charles W. Socarides is a psychoanalyst who specializes in the study of homosexuality. He tells us that "for almost all prehomosexual children the father is unavailable as a love object for the child."[7]

Psychiatrist Richard Green, author of *The Sissy Boy Syndrome,* tells us that "male-affect starvation" operates as a continuing force from early childhood in men who had poor relationships with their fathers and with male peers: "This hunger may motivate the later search for love and affection from males. It may be fed in a homosexual liaison."[8]

In the last twenty years, psychoanalyst Richard A. Isay has seen over forty gay men in therapy or analysis. He relates that "the majority of gay men, unlike heterosexual men who come for treatment, report that their fathers were distant during their childhood and that they lacked any attachment to them."[9] Isay is convinced that homosexuality is constitutional and believes that the fathers reject their sons because they sense that they are "different."

---

* The following pages do not imply any value judgment of homosexuality. They are meant to address what may be one of the deepest psychological barriers to the acceptance of major male involvement in child-rearing.

In reviewing the literature on the subject, psychologist Henry Biller concludes that "an inadequate father-child relationship often appears to be a major factor in the development of homosexuality among males."[10]

This is not to say that the connection between a poor father-son relationship and homosexuality is universal. There are no universal connections in psychology. Human beings bring their unique temperaments and dispositions to any situation, so that given the same environment the outcome will be different for each person. One can only speak of tendencies. Many men have poor relationships with their fathers and do not become homosexual. Some men have good relationships with their fathers and become homosexual.

While few experts would agree with Isay that homosexuality is entirely biologically based, it seems that for some boys there may well be a biological predisposition. Many of the boys followed by Richard Green in a longitudinal study seem to fall into this category. From the youngest age they showed an *extreme* and constant interest in wearing their mother's clothes, playing with girls and playing only girls' games; so much so that Green points out that girls who behaved similarly would be considered extremely feminine. Three quarters of these boys became homosexual. *Green is very clear in distinguishing these boys from the numerous boys who occasionally like to put on Mother's clothes, sometimes play girls' games, and don't like to play baseball or football.*

Studies indicate that traditional fathers are much more concerned with their sons' masculinity than are mothers. Ironically, this attitude often has an effect which is diametrically opposed to the father's wishes. The father's disappointment with and rejection of a son who prefers reading to playing baseball, or who would rather paint than work on the car, discourages the boy from identifying with his father. He will identify more with his mother, thus increasing the chances of his becoming homosexual.[11] The boy is also getting the message that he is not a "real man"—he behaves like a girl. This can become a self-fulfilling prophecy.

A mother describes the rift between her husband and one of their sons who did not want to play football or go deer hunting: "I don't think his father could accept the fact that he had a son that wasn't masculine as he would have preferred . . . When those guys were young, it was black and white. You had to be a jock to be a male; it was a hard thing for his father to accept. I could see the gap widening . . ."[12]

Unfortunately, not much has changed since her husband was young. While more people today would agree with her when she comments, "It takes much more of a man to shed a tear than it does to shoot a deer," many people still see masculinity and femininity in old-fashioned, rigid "black and white" categories.

These rigid, stereotyped categorizations lead not only to boys being rejected by their fathers, but to rejection by their peer group as well. Macho male images in the media confirm what father and peers are saying. The boy who does not like football, or baseball, or hunting, or fighting finds out from all sides that he is not a real man. If he is not a real man, then he must be homosexual.

Over fifty years ago, in *Sex and Temperament,* Margaret Mead argued that societies that set up rigid categorizations of male and female behavior thereby encourage homosexuality. She pointed out that there was no homosexuality among either the Arapesh or the Mundugumor, two of the societies that she studied and described in the book, and attributed this to the fact that these societies had very fluid definitions of male or female behavior. She contrasted this with European and American society, where "masculine" and "feminine" temperamental traits, interests, and behaviors are sharply distinguished. As a result a man whose interests and traits tend toward the "feminine" side is made to feel that he is not really a man, and identifies with women.

There is no intrinsic connection between sex roles and sexual orientation. Heterosexual poets and gay football players attest to that. Dave Meggyesy, director of the West Coast Office of the National Football League Players Association, estimates that the percentage of gay football players is about the same as the percentage of gay men in the population at large.[13] We have created a situation that pressures boys whose inclinations do not fit into our narrow definition of male roles into becoming homosexual.

CHANGING PARADIGMS OF FEMININITY
AND MASCULINITY

In the nineteenth century it was commonly believed that due to their smaller head size women were not cut out for intellectual activity. Besides their natural inferiority in this area, it was feared that if women were allowed to be educated as men were, they might die from mental overexertion. Those who survived would be "masculinized" and unable ever to attract marriageable suitors. Today, when more women than men attend college, and maintain higher grade point averages, these beliefs seem ludicrous. It may well be that by the middle of the next century the view that child-rearing is a female task that males can't handle will seem just as ludicrous.

If we put ourselves in the position of people in the early nineteenth century, we see that their concerns about women's intellectual abilities grew out of circumstances very similar to those surrounding our concerns about men's nurturing abilities. While upper-class women were taught to read and write, most of their education focused on becoming good wives, mothers, and homemakers. Boys studied mathematics, history, philosophy, law, medicine. Girls learned needlepoint and piano. As they grew up they were discouraged from engaging in intellectual or political discussions. One would expect that when a woman with this kind of background occasionally attempted to participate in such a discussion, her contributions would tend to be less well informed than those of men; and one would expect women's intellectual, scientific, literary, and artistic achievements to be far less than men's.

But instead of realizing that the discrepancy in male and female performance was related to social conditioning that squelched girls' and women's potential, people attributed the discrepancy to women's smaller heads. George Eliot, Berthe Morisot, Marie Curie, and others were seen as extraordinary exceptions rather than as indications of vast unfulfilled female potential.

Today we encourage in little girls from the earliest age those traits that make for good mothering. We do nothing of the sort for boys. We encourage in them traits that will make them good breadwinners and brave soldiers. Then when men show little interest or ability in fathering, we say they lack nurturing instinct. When a man is very deeply involved in caring for his children, we see him as exceptional.

Just as men and women in the nineteenth century feared that educated women would be masculinized and unattractive to men, today it is feared that nurturant men will become too feminine and will be unattractive to women.*

In the nineteenth century the paradigm of femininity was a delicate, weak, dependent, obedient, sexually pure creature whose interests focused on home, husband, and child. Today's woman who takes her work seriously, goes on unchaperoned vacations, and wears pants much of the time would have seemed highly unfeminine in 1837.

In the twentieth century the paradigm of masculinity is a strong, dominant, tough man who asserts his power through prowess at fighting or talent in making lots of money. Perhaps by the middle of the twenty-first century, being in touch with one's feelings, being empathic, caring, and nurturing of one's children, will be seen as an acceptable part of being a normal male. Perhaps by then a concept of masculinity associated with John Wayne and Sylvester Stallone will seem as outdated as a concept of femininity that involves fainting spells, smelling salts, and an inability to handle anything outside the home seems today.

---

* While we do not know what men would be like if fully freed of the masculine mystique, there is no reason to assume that they would be identical to women, except for the obvious anatomical differences. It may be that under any circumstances, more boys than girls will want to play with helicopters, planes, and cars. Perhaps more women will always be interested in reading novels and more men inclined toward sports. Perhaps not.

II
School Programs
That Work

Most students at the Germantown Friends Lower School in Philadelphia take child-rearing classes starting in kindergarten. By sixth grade each child is assigned to the school's day care center to take care of a toddler for several hours a week.

In seven New York City school districts, elementary school students take classes in conflict resolution. After two years the children choose several classmates who go through mediation training and then help schoolmates resolve conflicts nonviolently.

At Roxbury High School in Succasunna, New Jersey, some seniors are taking a course called "The Vietnam Generation." It stresses critical thinking, empathy, and the deglorification of war; and deals head-on with difficult, controversial issues of the kind that many social studies textbooks shy away from.

Programs and classes like these exist here and there around the country. If we are serious about reducing violence, they must become the norm rather than the exception.

The first three chapters in this section describe existing programs, including the ones mentioned above. I discuss the important role they can play in curbing violence. The last chapter answers objections to some of these programs.

6
When Boys and Babies Meet

It was clear to me from the research discussed in the last chapter that teaching child-rearing would have to be part of any major effort to decrease male violence. It would reinforce empathy and caring, legitimize young boys' interest in babies, and encourage them to think of themselves as future nurturant fathers. It would give them some understanding of child development and heighten their awareness of the importance and responsibilities of fatherhood, thereby decreasing the likelihood of their becoming teenage fathers. If and when they did become fathers, their sharing in the demanding task of nurturing children would make it considerably easier for their wives or girlfriends to be good mothers. The quality of mothering would also be vastly improved if girls took child-rearing classes.

The affirmation of boys' empathic, caring feelings of connectedness with others, and their intimate connection with life-giving, would tend to decrease the need for the excitement, power, and camaradrie found in youth gang fights and warfare.

At the same time my research made me intensely aware of the fact that by the age of four or five most boys have found out that an interest in babies is "girl's stuff." In order to prove that they are "real boys" they must repress it. I expected to find considerable resistance to child-rearing classes on the part of boys. I was stunned by the level of enthusiasm I found. The very fact that their school offers classes in child-rearing and encourages boys to take them helps boys overcome the intense pressure to repress their interest in the subject. This holds especially true when the classes are required.

In the following pages I focus on two programs in child-rearing.

EDUCATION FOR PARENTING: STARTING AS EARLY AS KINDERGARTEN

Education for Parenting was started in 1979 at the initiative of Sally Scattergood, who was, at the time, a teacher at the Germantown Friends school in Philadelphia. In an interview Scattergood explained that she was disturbed by the fact that child-rearing, which is probably the most important task that most human beings will ever undertake and one of vital importance for society, is ignored in our school curriculum. Her goal was to develop a curriculum that would teach children what it means to be a responsible, caring parent.

There exists a mistaken and highly dangerous assumption that good child-rearing is instinctive: mothers just naturally know what to do and what is best for their children. The increasing research on the history of childhood is enough to cure anyone of such fantasies.

From Roman times until the late Middle Ages European children were abandoned in great numbers by parents of all social classes—because of poverty or illegitimacy, or because they were female, or simply unwanted.

As we saw earlier, as late as the eighteenth and nineteenth centuries, upper-class infants were frequently sent away from home to be cared for by wet nurses. The physical abuse of children by mothers and fathers has been and continues to be widespread. Mental abuse is perhaps even more common.

Most parents have the capacity to love and nurture their children, but that capacity must itself be reinforced and nurtured by the environment. The wealth of information that psychologists and psychoanalysts have gathered on the needs of young children must be conveyed to future parents.

Influenced by the writings of psychiatrist Henri Parens, who was convinced that very young children could be taught a lot about child-rearing, Sally Scattergood was inclined to start conveying that information in the early grades. It was decided after meetings with educators, psychotherapists, and social workers that child-rearing classes would start in late kindergarten and go through sixth grade.

The underlying pedagogical premise of the program is psychologist Jerome Bruner's concept of a spiral curriculum in which the same concepts are reintroduced year after year, and become more and more enriched as the child grows older.

The program at the Germantown Friends school basically follows this recommendation. At the nine Philadelphia public schools—all in poor ghetto areas—that have adopted the program, its structure varies depending on the wishes of each principal. One principal may require all fifth- and sixth-grade teachers to teach parenting; another will leave it up to individual teachers. One school, now in its fourth year of parenting classes, has the program running from kindergarten through eighth grade.

The academic goals of the program are to teach the children that babies go through a developmental process based on a combination of biological readiness and interaction with parents and the environment. Students come away with a deep sense of the vital role that parents play in all aspects of the child's development—emotional, physical, verbal, intellectual, etc.—and how parents can either promote or hinder that development. They are made aware of temperamental variations between babies and between parents, and how these variations affect parent-child relationships.

The students also develop emotional and practical skills that are required in child care. They do this through the central component of the program: the baby visits. At the Germantown Friends school, starting in late kindergarten, a parent brings his or her baby or toddler to class once a month. Often the visits start when the mother is pregnant.

Students are instructed to observe what parents bring with them to class: bottles, diapers, toys, favorite blanket or stuffed animal. This gives them a sense of the kind of careful thinking ahead and planning that is required of parents. They also learn by asking questions: "What do you have to take along when you go away for a weekend?" or "Can you ever leave the baby to play alone in her room?"

Before the baby and its parent come to class, the children plan for its visit. They must ensure that the classroom will be safe. If they cannot "childproof" the room, or they decide not to, then they must be on the alert to prevent the toddler from hurting him or herself. The planning is always based on their predictions of what the little visitor will or will not be able to do. If an infant is not yet able to crawl, there is no need to childproof. They often learn a lot from erroneous predictions.

To facilitate these predictions and to provide an overview of what a child's development looks like, a chart is kept. It is divided into six areas of development: physical, object, social, intellectual, emotional, and language. In each area there is a subdivision where the role that the parents play in the child's development is recorded. The chart is based on careful observations. The children are made aware of the difference between observing and interpreting. One set of exercises in their workbook helps them distinguish between observations, such as "He cried at naptime and didn't sleep," and interpretations, such as "He clung to me because he loves me." The goal of these particular exercises is to help children to listen and observe more carefully, and to be more aware of the difficulties involved in interpreting a child's behavior.

The children's workbooks, called guided journals, encourage close observation, psychological insight, and sensitivity. Other typical exercises include: "Describe a situation that occurred during infant's visit," and then "Tell how you think the baby may have been feeling. Give two ways, if you can." Or "List three ways you would try to make friends with a twelve-month-old" and "How would you expect the twelve-month-old to show s/he was learning to trust? How would you expect a twelve-month-old to show mistrust?"

In fourth and fifth grade the students at the Germantown Friends school spend about half an hour a week observing babies and parents who come to a parent-infant support group held at the school. The group is led by a psychologist. Each child is assigned a baby to observe and reports his or her observations on a worksheet that includes questions like "What does the mood of your child appear to be? List evidence." Or "Think about the child you observed last time. How is this week's child like last week's, or unlike last week's?"

From time to time the students must shift their attention away from the babies, for the worksheet also tells them, "Listen to the conversation between the various parents. What is the focus? What does this tell you about the interests and concerns of the parents?"

When I was visiting, the mothers talked about how hard it was to find any time for themselves. "The only time I have to reflect on anything is when I'm washing dishes," one woman commented. After a while the discussion turned to sibling rivalry problems. From listening to such conversations, children get a sense of the reality of parenting, of the sacrifices and demands as well as the joys. They get a sense of how deeply a child affects every aspect of the parents' lives.

I observed two parent-infant groups, once with a fourth-grade class and once with a fifth-grade class, and in each case went back to class with the children to observe a follow-up discussion of about twenty minutes. In the first class the discussion starts off with observations of changes in babies' behavior. "Ana was sitting in her mother's lap last time and this time she was walking around, exploring more," a girl remarks. "She can talk better," a boy adds. The teacher tells the children that Ana was a premature baby and so has been somewhat delayed in doing things, but she is now catching up. She explains that if a child is born at six months or seven months or earlier it is premature and will tend to have slower development and sometimes more serious problems.

After a while the discussion shifts from the babies to the

mothers. One boy comments on how much less time you have for yourself when you have a child. Another boy comments on how hard it is to be a mother—you have to learn how to put on diapers and so many other things. The teacher then chimes in to say that when she had her baby she had no idea how to change a diaper. She was afraid to give her a bath, and didn't know how to get her to stop scratching herself. "When you become a parent, trivial things are important and things that seem unbelievably boring become so interesting." One of the girls nods in agreement and describes how excited she was the first time her baby brother smiled.

In the second class discussion I attend, the children focus on a baby named James. Several comment on how much more active he was this time: "really awake," "full of pep," "moving and jumping around." Several of the boys agree. One of the boys starts mimicking the faces that James and some of the other babies make. He gets a lot of laughs. Another boy comments on how Ana cried because her diaper was wet. "Some diapers don't absorb as well as others," one boy observes. The teacher agrees with him, but points out that there are temperamental differences between babies. What is very disturbing to some is only mildly so to others. The discussion moves on to developmental differences. The teacher explains that older babies tend to get quite upset when they are left with new people; very young babies usually don't mind.

By the time they are in sixth grade, most of the students at the Germantown Friends school have had close to six years of observing, studying, and interacting with babies. They are now ready for caretaker responsibilities. Once a week, for a period of about twelve weeks, each child takes care of a toddler that he or she is paired with in the day care center that the school runs for its employees.

Before they start their caretaking assignment, students call parents and get information about the child's likes and dislikes, interests, favorite toys and games. They are expected to do some research on child development and relate their findings to their child. They also have class discussions on how to handle young children—how to get acquainted, how not to scare the toddler. They learn about not stepping in too fast to do things for the toddler even if he or she is very slow. The little ones need to do things on their own. Each sixth grader makes a toy for his or her child. "They have come up with some pretty creative ideas for toys," Sandra Meyer, the program coordinator, tells me. At the end of their twelve weeks they write a report about their child and give it to the child's parents. They then receive a child-care certificate.

I spend some time at the day care center watching sixth graders with "their kids." When I comment to one of the liaison teachers on how well one of the boys is getting along with his child, she tells me he is a troublesome boy with considerable academic and behavioral difficulties. Often children who have problems in other areas are able to relate very well to little children, she explains. The experience enhances their self-confidence, especially when the little ones become very attached to them and look forward to their coming.

I ask her if she has observed any differences in level of involvement and interest between boys and girls. She thinks for a moment and then says "No, the differences are more in individual children; some older children might just not relate that well to little children." She also points out that "some little kids aren't that friendly." She gives me the example of one little girl who remained aloof in spite of her caretaker's efforts to befriend her. "I don't think she likes me," the boy in charge of her finally concluded sadly.

I cannot help thinking how valuable such experiences can be for children when their meaning is fruitfully explored with the help of a teacher. Not all babies are friendly, not all babies are easy. How helpful to know this by the age of twelve! How helpful to have had six years of experiences both positive and negative with young children! With most work choices we make we at least have an inkling of how we may like an occupation from our school experience. The child who hates math is not too likely to want to become an accountant. The child who loves writing may someday consider looking for a job in journalism. But when it comes to raising children, most of us are devoid of the experience and knowledge that would help us make an informed decision about bringing a new life into existence and caring for it.

Everything I have described so far is mandatory at the Friends school. But there is one optional program: partnering. In partnering an older child is paired with a younger child.

Sandra Meyer tells me that her daughter, who has just completed first grade at the school, is paired with a sixth grader. Besides going to Quaker meetings together, they plan parties for holidays and play together for a half hour during recess on Friday afternoon. Her daughter loves it. The partner is her "special person." Sally Scattergood tells me that when she asked her five-year-old grandson what his favorite activity was at school, he answered "partnering."

Some of the partnering is more focused and extends to the upper school. Young children whose parents are getting divorced may be partnered with an older child who has gone through the same experience; some older children tutor younger children who need help in a particular subject.

"Very impressive," the reader might think, "but isn't this a select group? Since most Quakers are pacifists they are not too likely to inculcate the values of the masculine mystique in their sons. Wouldn't these boys naturally be less resistant to becoming interested in and caring for babies and younger children?"

I had these doubts myself after my first visit to the Germantown Friends school. Even when I was assured that most of the children at the school were not Quakers, I remained somewhat skeptical. They were, after all, learning Quaker values at the school. But as I visited diverse schools and spoke to a variety of people involved in parenting programs, I became convinced that this unabashed, just-below-the-surface interest in babies was not limited to any special group.

The metamorphosis that I witnessed in one particular special education class at a Philadelphia public school has come to symbolize for me the enormous potential interest of boys—of all socioeconomic, religious, and ethnic backgrounds—in young children and in child-rearing. Here was a group of African-American males of twelve and thirteen, most of whom came from low-income families without a father, and yet they came alive when a twenty-month-old toddler came into their classroom.

The class has seven boys and two girls. Many sit slouched over their desks. Some look as if they might doze off at any moment;

others seem to be dozing already. "Kids in this class seem depressed, most listless class I've been to," my initial notes say.

"How is she ever going to get these kids interested in anything?" I wonder as Mary Jane Miller, the liaison teacher from Education for Parenting, starts pointing to twenty-month-old Jayjay's developmental chart on the board. Once a month since the beginning of the semester, Mrs. Glover has been bringing her toddler Jayjay to the class for a visit of approximately half an hour. Jayjay and his mom are expected shortly.

It is now time to go over last month's chart notations and make predictions about what Jayjay will be able to do this visit. Earlier that day I have observed a public-school kindergarten class in parenting where the children are enthusiastic and prolific in their predictions, but here only a few seem to wake up enough to respond to Ms. Miller's and Ms. Calvin's (the regular class teacher) quest for ideas. Nevertheless, by the time Mrs. Glover and Jayjay arrive, Ms. Miller has managed to elicit a respectable list of predictions.

Jayjay, clad in bright red pants with a blue and green shirt, struts in. He is full of energy, curiosity, affection. The contrast with the children in the class is striking.

Mrs. Glover sits down in front of the class and places a variety of toys on the floor. At first the children remain largely oblivious to Jayjay. When he picks up an eraser and starts erasing the board there is a mild show of interest. His mother hands him a toy and explains to the children that distracting him with a toy doesn't always work, but it is the first thing she tries when he does something he is not supposed to do. Sometimes she just has to remove him from the situation.

When Jayjay, who is eager to get the children's attention, grabs one of them in a leg grip, one of the boys volunteers that this looks like a wrestling grip. "He likes to watch wrestling on TV with his dad," Mrs. Glover explains, and he imitates what he sees. She goes on to tell them how much his behavior is imitative: "If I put lotion on him, then he takes lotion and puts it on his E.T. doll."

A few of the kids are sitting up straight now. They are beginning to respond to the discussion and to Jayjay's efforts to engage them in some sort of interaction—throwing his ball to them is one way. Pretty soon one of the boys who only a few minutes earlier was slouched over his desk is picking Jayjay up and hugging him. Some of the kids are smiling at them. They smile too when Jayjay keeps running over to the liaison teacher and hugging her.

Within ten minutes of Jayjay's arrival the class has come alive, with one exception. One boy continues to stare into space, apparently unmoved and uninterested. The other children are laughing, smiling, playing ball with Jayjay. They listen with interest when the teachers and Jayjay's mother discuss his behavior. They ask questions: "If we hit him with no reason, does he hit back?" "He will hit you if you hit him," Mrs. Glover responds. "What feelings are created when you hit him?" Ms. Calvin asks. The kids agree that he is likely to feel angry, and that he may hit back either because he is angry or because he imitates the behavior of others. Ms. Calvin recommends that when the children are at home they think of what emotions their behavior creates in their younger siblings.

Pretty soon it is time for Jayjay to leave. The disappointment on the children's faces is expressed by the boy who has been picking Jayjay up and hugging him. "I thought he was staying until two forty-five," he says, and then tries again: "Aren't we going to measure him?"

Whether it be a required child-rearing class in a ghetto school, a six-year program at a Quaker school, or an elective baby-care course offered at New York City's highly prestigious and traditional all-boys Collegiate Prep School—where fifth- and sixth-grade boys enthusiastically learn how to diaper, feed, and play with babies—boys when they are given permission can become enthusiastic and tender in relating to babies and younger children.

While Sally Scattergood's original goal in starting the Parenting Center was to teach children what it means to be a responsible, caring parent, and in so doing to make them more caring in their relations with their peers and others, she is now convinced that the program also prevents early pregnancy.

Her conviction is corroborated by informal data collected from the nine public schools in poor minority neighborhoods in which the Parenting Center runs classes. For example, Elaine Francis, a teacher at the George Washington School, writes: "I developed a need for the Parenting Program because of my concern about the many pregnancies that were showing up among our seventh and eighth graders . . . This year, with only a few teachers using some of the activities brought back from the [parenting] sessions, we have not had one pregnancy yet. It is not uncommon to hear one student tell another, 'No baby for me yet, it's too much responsibility. I need more education for a decent job.' These statements are coming from male and female students. *The male students understand that they also have a responsibility to a child they sire* [my emphasis]."

Les Willis, whose work with teenage fathers was discussed in Chapter 4, is convinced that the Parenting Center's program prevents pregnancies. Once young people are made aware of the responsibilities of parenting, once it becomes a reality to them, they will think twice before rushing into it. He gives me the example of his own program. In the five years since he started it, the recidivism rate for the teenage fathers in his group has been six percent. The national recidivism rate for teenage births ranges from twelve to twenty-two percent depending on geographical location.

TEACHING TEENAGERS ALL ABOUT KIDS

"This is a great class, Mr. Howort. I'm glad I took this class. I can't tell you how much it means to me. Sometime I leave this class and start to cry. For only one reason: happiness from taking this class." "It is essential to have a class like this taught, even mandatory." "This course is one of the most important courses I have took this year." "I think this class is one of the best course in 'the Humanities.' This class help me to understand and raise my sister Julie."

These are the kinds of student evaluations that teachers' dreams are made of.

When Lou Howort, who teaches a class in Child Development and Parenting to eleventh and twelfth graders at the High School for the Humanities in New York City, opened his filing cabinet and pulled out a set of evaluations from one of the previous year's classes, I found that with one exception they ranged from positive to ebullient. The exception was a student who "thought that it [the class] was boring . . . I didn't get any value except that I learned you shouldn't hit your kids." *

My guess is that Lou Howort is not dissatisfied with that negative evaluation, for if there is one thing he wants his students to learn, it is not to hit their kids.

He tells me that the main goal of his class is "to cut down on physical and mental abuse [of children] and to prevent teenage pregnancy." Like Scattergood and Willis, he is convinced that there is nothing like giving kids a sense of the importance, the demands, and the responsibilities of parenting to dissuade them from becoming parents too early.

Howort first became aware of the need for such a class when he was teaching health to boys in their junior year at a vocational and technical high school in Brooklyn.

In the course of explaining how the nervous system is slow in developing in children and how they are often clumsy as a result, he used the example of a five- or six-year-old who might reach over for a napkin on the dining room table and knock over a glass of milk accidentally. "What would you do if that happened?" he asked. "I'd beat the shit out of the kid" was the most common response. "Why?" he asked. "How else are you going to teach them?" was the boys' answer.

Howort was shocked by this response. He realized that "these were perfectly decent kids—I liked them a lot—and they were going to go ahead and abuse their own kids someday and think they were doing the right thing," simply because they had no knowledge of child development or of children's needs. "That's what really got me started thinking about a parenting class. I knew I had to expand what I did in health to include child development."

A few years later, Howort heard Dr. Margaret Kind, a psychiatrist who had done work in this area, give a talk on the subject. The two of them got together and developed a curriculum in parenting.

In the fall of 1985, Howort, who was by then teaching at the High School of the Humanities in Manhattan, taught his first Parenting and Child Development Class. In 1990, the New York

* Student evaluations of the class are done at the end of the semester and are supposed to be anonymous, but some students sign their names anyway. Several highly enthusiastic comments were signed by boys.

City Board of Education published the course curriculum. It is now being used in thirty-three high schools. The class is an elective taught every semester with an enrollment of about twenty-five to thirty students in each section. Initially Howort taught one section, but enrollment was so high that a second section was opened in the fall of 1987. It is a sequential course in child development that starts with prenatal care and includes topics like "Infancy: Emotional-Social Development, Including Attachment, Separation-Individuation, Separation Anxiety, Stranger Anxiety" and "The Toddler (Age 1 to 3 Yrs.): Intellectual and Language Development, the Need for Parental Stimulation; Parent Development: The Authority Stage."

As in the elementary school classes I visited, the boys here seem as interested and involved as the girls. However, there are sixteen girls and ten boys in class when I visit. Howort tells me that this is quite typical—the enrollment is about two-thirds female and one-third male. The female-to-male ratio at the school is roughly 55:45. Given our society's values and attitudes it is inevitable that as long as parenting classes are not mandatory more girls than boys will enroll in them.

The High School of the Humanities is highly integrated racially and socially: approximately 44 percent white, 20 percent African-American, and 36 percent Hispanic and Asian. Some of the students come from expensive private schools and include the children of celebrities; others come from impoverished ghettos. Many of the students have grown up being routinely spanked or hit for any undesirable behavior.

Dr. Kind comes in a few times a year to teach the class. I sit in on her class on battering, in which she draws heavily on her experience as staff psychiatrist at Metropolitan Hospital. When she talks about some of the mothers at the hospital who hit their babies when they drop their bottles, it is clear that many of the students know from firsthand experience what she is talking about. One of the major challenges of the class is to break this cycle of physical punishment, to make the students aware that there are other ways of disciplining children besides hitting them.

In both the classes I observed the students were constantly tying the material to their own experience and seemed to feel free to argue and challenge their teacher with tough cases: How do you deal with "my cousin who keeps pulling the cat's tail? My cat hides, now she's a nervous wreck." Or "My little brother likes to drop eggs." Or "How can you not be negative if a kid keeps knocking a cage with a bird in it?"

Howort and Kind are opposed to physical punishment under any condition, but they make it clear that some child-rearing experts think it is acceptable in some limited and extreme situations. Judging by class discussion, evaluations, and what Howort tells me, most of the students conclude that physical punishment should not be used at all. The minority view is that it's okay to use it as a last resort and in moderation.

When I sit in on one of Mr. Howort's classes, the primary focus is on the toddler's needs for self-respect and self-esteem. "Toddlers need praise and admiration," he tells the students. "If they don't get it, if they are ignored, if they don't feel any love, if they are physically abused, they may have narcissistic rage for the rest of their lives." "But how do you praise a toddler?" a student asks. "You can admire their scribblings," someone suggests. "You can say, 'Gee, you ate a lot' admiringly" is another suggestion.

Howort engages the students in a lively discussion of how such narcissistic rage manifests itself in adults. "Like someone who argues with you about everything," one student offers.

In a class evaluation, one of the students writes: "What I like most about this course was the discussion on emotional damages and a child's self-esteem. Now as I said before I know why I act furiously towards people sometime without me knowing why. And the reason I sometimes wake up in the night crying and hurting emotionally." The same student writes that one of the most important class topics was "Children's self-esteem—how to be careful so that you do not destroy your child's self-esteem. So that in the future your child can have security within him or herself."

I ask Howort if the class, which for some students seems to bring up a lot of painful early feelings, creates problems between some of the students and their parents. "Do you get any irate phone calls from parents?" I inquire.

Howort assures me that he has never gotten such a call. Quite to the contrary, on parents' conference day, the basic response is "I really wanted to meet you; my kid's learned so much in your class; we talk about it all the time at home." This corroborates what the students tell him—that their relationship with their parents is better because they discuss a lot of issues openly: "Kids tell me they go home and ask their parents questions like 'how did you treat me around toilet training?'" As they study various developmental milestones they are instructed to ask their parents when they reached that milestone. Their relationship with their parents tends to improve as a result of the course. As they become aware of how difficult and demanding child-rearing is, they appreciate what their parents have gone through.

They understand that their parents had not benefited from a course like this when they raised them. Their parents were never assigned articles discussing "Problems of Parental Narcissism" or "An Infant's Feelings," nor were they required to read a textbook on child development (Draper's *See How They Grow*), or to write papers based on careful observations of children. In most cases their parents meant well. They thought that hitting was the right way to discipline a child, just as most of the students assumed until they took this class.

In studying about the two-year-old's conflicting needs for autonomy and dependency, and the parents' difficulty in supporting the child's autonomy, many of the students become aware of the similarity to what they are going through now. "What about parents who won't let go later when you're a teenager?" a young woman asks. "These issues come up again and again as a teenager demands more independence," Mr. Howort responds, and a discussion ensues on the conflict they experience between their desire for autonomy and their dependence on their parents. They talk about how their parents must feel about this. It's not easy for them either.

After several visits and talks with Howort and Kind, it becomes clear to me that besides directly increasing the likelihood that these students will be better parents someday by imparting essential knowledge about children, this course benefits them in several other ways. It seems to help them open up emotionally, putting them in touch with their own childhood pain. This is particularly valuable for the boys who have been taught not to cry, and to repress feelings of vulnerability, fear, and weakness, in order to become "real men."

When confronted with serious emotional problems, these young people will be more likely to seek professional help rather than act out and make others pay the cost. This will help them be more sensitive parents and less likely to repeat deleterious patterns.

Besides improving their relationship with their parents, the class also improves their relationship with their siblings. They become more interested, sympathetic, and understanding, and many of them share their newfound knowledge with their parents. "I have a 20 month baby sister. My mother and I really never knew what was going on with the baby but we have reduced many things that her grandmother did with her," one student writes. "I have two little brothers ages 2 and 5 and I learned a lot about what they do and how to deal with it . . . I understand the stages my brothers go through and I try to help them through it," another student says.

Some write about the improved quality of their baby-sitting. "I never found baby-sitting exciting until I came into this course," one student writes, and goes on to talk about finding "new ways to communicate to children."

Sally Scattergood points out that one of the main benefits of teaching parenting is that "teaching it will make it important." This shows clearly in the comments made by many of Howort's students. Some of the recurrent comments in their class evaluations are "This course has been the most valuable course I've taken this semester"; "My life has been changed by it"; "This course should be expanded to all schools in the country"; and "It is essential to have a class like this taught, even mandatory." *Regardless of how much detail these boys and girls remember by the time they become parents, the class has made them aware of the enormous importance that early childhood development has* both in terms of the quality of the child's life when he or she becomes an adult and in terms of social consequences. Taking the course has imbued them with a deep sense of the importance of parenting.

7

Alternatives
to Fistfights
and Bullying

In Aristophanes' satirical play *Lysistrata,* the leading lady, serving as mediator, resolves in a few minutes the disputes that have brought years of bloodshed to Athens and Sparta. Of course, we know that in real life it takes more than a few minutes to resolve a long-standing conflict. In New York City, since 1985, approximately four hundred elementary school teachers, at fifty New York City public schools, have spent about forty hours each learning that skill so that they can teach it to their students.

The teaching guide they use suggests that they explain to students that "handling conflict well is a skill like riding a bike or using a computer." Such an explanation is necessary, because the ability to resolve conflicts in a mutually satisfactory and nonviolent way has never been thought of as something one learns in school. Until recently it was not thought of as something one learns at all.

The field of conflict resolution originated in the business world about seventy years ago with the goal of helping business managers handle interpersonal conflicts in the workplace. Starting in the 1960s, people in other fields began to develop an interest in it. Lawyers and community activists started to set up community mediation programs dealing with everything from landlord-tenant disputes to environmental issues.

The Resolving Conflict Creatively Program (RCCP), which is described in the following pages, is a joint venture of the New York City Board of Education, Educators for Social Responsibility,[1] and the seven school districts that have adopted the program. The RCCP draws heavily on Fisher and Ury's *Getting to Yes,* discussed in Chapter 2. It was introduced in 1985 in three Brooklyn schools. In the spring of 1987 a ten-session course for training student mediators was added to the curriculum. Twelve fifth graders were chosen by their peers to become mediators and help settle disputes between fellow students. By the spring of 1989 the program had expanded to over forty elementary schools and six junior high schools in Brooklyn, Manhattan, Queens, and the Bronx. In New York City, where crime rates in some schools are so high that the Board of Education has installed metal detectors to help keep guns and knives out, the RCCP's main problem is keeping up with the demand for its program.

In 1988, at the request of Community School District 15, an evaluation of the RCCP was done by an independent evaluation consulting firm. Its findings can only serve to increase that demand. It concluded that "even in this early stage of implementation, there was an observable and quantifiable positive impact on students, participating staff, and classroom and school climate."[2]

The RCCP's teaching guide warns teachers that "children tend to have vivid concepts of war and violence, fed by images from television. By contrast, they often see peace as the absence of excitement rather than the presence of anything interesting. They see peace as okay but boring; or worse, something for 'sissies.' " Transcending this negative concept of peace is one of the goals of the program.

When I visit a second grade RCCP class at P.S. 261 in the Cobble Hill area of Brooklyn, a predominantly low-income, ethnically diverse neighborhood, the day's agenda on the blackboard includes: "What is a peacemaker? What can you do to make peace? What is a pledge?" and "What is a peace pledge?" The children's definitions reflect their lives. One little girl explains that there is "a lot of shooting where I live because people take drugs. Those who don't are peacemakers." The students' suggestions for peacemaking include "helping people to stop taking drugs," "help mother if she gets burnt," "help someone with their homework," "help people be more friendly if they have an argument; help them say they're sorry and shake hands again," "stop people from littering the water."

When it comes to the peace pledge, the teacher explains that it involves making a very specific and realistic commitment to doing one thing that will help create peace. The children are given peace pledge forms on which they fill out their names and addresses and then make a peace pledge and draw a picture illustrating it. The teaching guide gives samples: Jonathan pledges that he "will stop fighting with my sister," and Samantha that she will "bring peace in the world by not fighting with my friends . . ." In the discussion of their peace pledges some of the children in this second-grade class express goals like: "If someone's taking drugs, I'd help him to stop taking drugs," and "I would put cops in every corner to prevent crime." By the time they fill out their peace pledges the teacher will no doubt have persuaded them to set more realistic goals.

A lot of the RCCP's program centers on taking activities that tend to be ignored or perceived as passive and hence not worthy of any special attention and showing students how doing them well involves activity and skill, and leads to decreases in conflicts, and better ways of resolving them when they do occur.

When I visit a sixth-grade class in the same school, the lesson is focused on good and poor listening. The teacher, Mr. Brooks, starts out by asking the children if they've seen any movies they've liked lately. The response is enthusiastic, and he chooses a girl named Maria to come to the front of the class.

They sit down facing each other and she starts telling him with enthusiasm about Eddie Murphy's latest movie. Mr. Brooks plays with his pen as she talks, his gaze wanders around the room; he stares vacantly at the ceiling, smiles at the students in the class. As she is in the middle of a sentence, he starts telling her about another Eddie Murphy film he saw. When Maria starts again, he interrupts her to ask her if a pen on his desk is hers. She is looking more and more exasperated. When they are done he turns to the class and asks: "Was I a good listener?" The answer is a loud "No!" All the children are waving their hands in response to the next question: "What made me a poor listener?" "You kept interrupting." "You avoided looking at the speaker," and so on.

Mr. Brooks then asks Maria how she felt. She does not mince words in explaining how upset and angry she was " 'cause you weren't listening; then you interrupted me."

The second exchange involves a student describing *Robocop*. This time Mr. Brooks is listening carefully. When he is done he asks the class: "What was I doing? What are good listening skills?" Again a flurry of hands: "You were concentrating"; "No interruptions"; "You looked her straight in the eye"; "You summarized what she said"; "You nodded—communicating understanding."

When Mr. Brooks asks the students how many of them have had the experience at home of having their parents pretend to listen, almost all raise their hands and tell anecdotes about their parents not listening to them. When he asks, "What about teachers?" he is met with another flurry of anecdotes about teachers —including himself—not listening.

When the RCCP coordinator asks the children what they have learned from this lesson, a discussion of what constitutes good, active listening ensues. She goes on to explain that if people don't really listen to each other, conflicts often result. *Learning how to listen well is a means of avoiding some conflicts and a building block for resolving those conflicts that do occur.*

"Improving Communication Skills" is the second unit in the program's teaching guide.

Besides the teaching of active listening the section includes a variety of very specific communication-related skills that tend to decrease conflict. There is a section on manners: "if your class doesn't regularly say 'please,' 'thank you,' and 'excuse me,' discuss their use and importance." There is a section that distinguishes between "I-messages" and "You-messages." An example of an "I-message" is "I'm angry that you borrowed my bat and lost it because it was my favorite." The "You-message" way of stating this is: "I can't believe you lost my favorite bat. You're such a stupid jerk. I should never have lent it to you."

Besides increasing the children's sensitivity to how our remarks and our way of delivering them make others feel, the communications program seeks to heighten children's awareness of how different people perceive things differently, and to increase their ability to understand other people's point of view, particularly in conflict situations. At the same time, the authors of the teaching guide make it clear that while "it's important to understand both sides of a conflict ('to walk a mile in the other person's moccasins') before deciding who's right and who's wrong," this does not mean "that everything is relative, that good cannot be distinguished from evil, or that destructive actions should be excused because they grow out of a certain point of view."

There is a section on put-downs. Teachers are instructed to "have the class brainstorm all of the mean, nasty words or phrases they've ever heard or said," and then discuss how these words make people feel, why we say them, and "what would be the effect on the class if everyone always put everyone else down." The authors conclude that "to counter such behavior in our students, we have to model the opposite by taking every opportunity to 'put students up.' "

The importance of affirming people in terms of a conflict resolution program is that people who have a sense of self-worth find it easier to see the good in others, even if they are in a conflict with them. They are also less likely to get into conflicts to begin with. "Put-ups" in early childhood are part of the groundwork of a person's psychological well-being. (The reader may recall the students in Lou Howort's class discussing how to praise a toddler.) Children who do not get the affirmation and love they need are likely to experience narcissistic rage, which can express itself in a tendency to seek out conflict.

· · · ·

At the same time that I am visiting conflict resolution classes in public schools, I also sit in on several classes in conflict resolution taught by Linda Lantieri in the Graduate School of Education at Hunter College.

Lantieri works for the Board of Education in the Division of Curriculum and Instruction. She was instrumental in launching the RCCP and continues to work for the program. Her students at Hunter are all teachers, mostly in public schools.

I am struck by how receptive these adults, ranging in age from their twenties to their sixties, are to the same concepts that the elementary school children are learning. They seem to be trying to make up for lost time: these are the first students I have known to ask for extended class hours in order to cover more material.

In the first class I attend we all partake in a two-minute active listening exercise analogous to the one I observed in the sixth-grade class at P.S. 261. Each person takes a turn telling the person next to him or her a story. The listener then has to summarize the story and the person who told it appraises both the accuracy of the summary and the listener's demeanor.

Afterward the class discusses what they have learned from this experience. Gregory Whyte, a physical education teacher at Evander Childs High School in the Bronx, is particularly articulate and expressive in stating his reaction. He shakes his head in dismay as he tells his classmates that this exercise has made him intensely aware of what a poor listener he is. He's got to do something about it, he asserts with conviction. Many of the other students have similar reactions.

This class is very much a consciousness-raising experience for these students, many of whom have been teaching for years. In a paper one student writes: "My consciousness was raised to the fact that I often 'put down' my students without even realizing it. This is another area that I've been working on in the classroom. I'd really be interested in finding out whether any activities ["put-up" exercises] exist that could be utilized on the high school level."

They become aware of how they have misinterpreted students' behavior or remarks: "There have been times when a student said something that I reacted very strongly to only to find out that her remark was made in an innocent manner. It is therefore necessary to 'put yourself in their shoes' and try to understand their feelings before jumping to a hasty conclusion,'' another student writes.

If these teachers spend a lot of time becoming aware of their shortcomings, they spend even more time acquiring new skills—skills that those children fortunate enough to be in the RCCP program are learning in elementary school. They learn to become good listeners; they learn to "put people up" instead of putting them down; they learn to use "I" statements instead of "you" statements. They learn to deal with difficult, sometimes infuriating students without overreacting, but not ignoring their unacceptable behavior either.

Lantieri tells them a story about her early teaching days when she had a disturbed, violent boy in one of her classes. She didn't know how to handle him and so she ignored him, letting him get away with poking and bothering other students. One day he picked up a microscope and threw it.

She realizes now, she explains, that her "If I ignore it, it might go away" style of dealing with conflict had led to this incident. His violence needed to be dealt with from the beginning.

At P.S. 261, when I visit a sixth-grade special education class, the children are learning the kinds of skills that would have made life a lot easier for Linda Lantieri—and I suspect for millions of other teachers—had she learned them in elementary school.

The children are learning about different ways people react when they are angry. One way is to ignore the other person. The teacher explains that she sometimes does this when her husband comes home from work in a bad mood. "I ignore him until he gets better." Sometimes, as in this case, ignoring helps, but a lot of the time it doesn't. The teacher and the liaison teacher now act out a skit in which one teacher comes over and pushes the other. The "assaulted" teacher meekly walks away. The "assaulting" teacher yells at her, "You're chicken," and "No guts." The consensus after discussion is that in this situation ignoring is not the best reaction. The "assaulter" continues her verbal abuse and may attack again.

Another common expression of anger is acting mean, the teacher explains. Before the teachers even have a chance to act this one out, a boy raises his hand with a very personal example: "My sister punched me on the chest when I woke her up at six this morning like my mother told me."

The teachers now dramatize acting mean when provoked. The "assaulted" teacher calls the "assaulter" names, and pretends to attack her physically. The consensus is that this kind of reaction can easily lead to more violence and someone's getting hurt.

A third way of dealing with one's anger is saying clearly what your feelings are in a strong but not mean way. The teachers act this out: "I don't like it when you push me," the "assaulted" teacher says in a loud, strong voice. "I feel like it," the "assaulter" says. "You're in a rotten mood but don't push me. I don't like it" is the response.

The kids ask about situations where none of this works. Several of them describe a boy named Jerry who rides the school bus with them and likes to grab kids' necks in a headlock. The teacher says this is a situation where you need help. Get a teacher involved in stopping Jerry, she suggests.

When I discuss these kinds of "bully problems" with Tom Roderick, the Executive President of Educators for Social Responsibility, who is one of the founders and administrators of the RCCP, he tells me that there are some situations where conflict resolution doesn't work and one has to resort to power —as in the case of a child seeking a teacher's help—or to physical force. *The point is to exhaust all other means first.* *

The conflict resolution program opens new possibilities for boys. Normally boys are expected to fight back both verbally and physically if attacked. If they don't, they're not "real men." Boys who have gone through the program have experienced a devaluation of violence as a way to solve conflicts, and have been presented with alternatives. For many of them, fighting becomes a last resort.

Shomen is a sixth grader at P.S. 230, also in Brooklyn, who went through the RCCP in fifth grade and then became a school mediator. This is how he explains the difference the program has made for him: "I've become less violent and I used to have a

---

* In Norway a nationwide intervention program designed specifically to combat bully-ism was introduced in the schools in 1983. According to University of Bergen psychology professor Dan Olweus, who conducted studies of the campaign, the frequency of bully-victim problems decreased by 50 percent within two years.

lot of fights and arguments. Now instead of fighting I talk things over. But if you have to fight you have to. This kid was picking on me, pushing me, doing everything. First I got angry, then I thought 'I'm a mediator' so I tried to talk things over, but he wouldn't listen to me and kept going so I had to fight."

Gregory Whyte had to wait until he was in his thirties to develop the awareness and skills that Shomen learned in fifth grade. Lantieri's class "gave me an awareness that there are other ways [besides fighting] of doing things," Whyte tells me. At Shomen's age he had been a very rough kid. "If [someone] hit me, my object became revenge. I never thought of finding out why he did it; [there was] no room for understanding, no room for compromise . . . You fight fire with fire—like in the Western movies." As he sees it now, movies and TV represent "a form of indoctrination that affects most kids [in a way] opposite of this class . . . In my own experience, because of movies I believed that only the strong survive. Someone does something to you, your only purpose becomes revenge." When he was a boy, Whyte's favorite kinds of movies were "John Wayne, Green Berets, and kung fu."

Whenever possible, Whyte tries to apply his newfound skills to helping students at Evander Childs resolve their conflicts nonviolently. He explains that when teachers see students arguing or fighting, they usually grab them and try to separate them. That's all he ever did before taking Lantieri's class. Then the students just went outside and continued the fight.

As Whyte tells me this my mind flashes to the fifth-grade class I observed at P.S. 230, in which future student mediators were acting out practice mediation skits in front of their classmates. The mediators were criticized by several students when they agreed that two students who had been fighting in the hallway should simply stay away from each other. "Just staying away isn't enough of a solution—sooner or later they'll bump into each other," a boy commented. "If they just stay away from each other, there's no opportunity to change and get to like the other person," a girl offered. These kids seemed to think that more attention had to be paid to the underlying problem if the conflict was to be resolved successfully.

Whyte has come away from his conflict resolution training with the same conclusion. Instead of just separating fighting students, Whyte now tries to talk to them, to determine what happened, and to help them arrive at a nonviolent resolution of their conflict. He tells me that "on two specific occasions it worked." Since he has only been in Lantieri's class for a few months, this is not a bad record. In one case "two guys were in a basketball game and got into a big argument. They started pushing each other. I took them back into the gym, determined that one guy did something he wasn't supposed to do, but he wasn't aware that what he did was wrong." Thanks to Whyte's mediation, the two students shook hands and went back to their basketball game. This anecdote illustrates one of the RCCP's basic tenets, that conflicts often grow out of poor communication, not hearing, not listening.

As we have seen, eradicating the passive, sissy image of nonviolence is one of the goals of the conflict resolution program. One way in which this is done is to counter the exciting images of John Wayne, Sylvester Stallone, Chuck Norris, and the like with information about real people who have practiced nonviolence in order to bring about social change. From this the children get a sense of the kind of courage, initiative, and determination that is involved.

The teaching guide suggests class discussion of a number of peacemakers. One of them is Rosa Parks, the Montgomery, Alabama, black woman who in 1955 refused to give up her seat in a bus to a white man. When she was booked and eventually found guilty of violating the city's segregation law, black leaders in Montgomery decided to appeal her case to the Supreme Court if necessary and to boycott the city's buses. It was through his leadership of this successful campaign that Martin Luther King, Jr., achieved national prominence. King is another representative of courageous, active, nonviolent behavior.

The teaching guide suggests a class play about Rosa Parks and the Montgomery bus boycott as an appropriate way to bring the story and the peacemakers in it alive. Such a play also serves the function of sensitizing the children to the suffering caused by racial or religious prejudice. Developing understanding and empathy for people who are different from us is one of the goals of the program.

By the time the children are done learning about Rosa Parks,

Martin Luther King, Gandhi, and others, it becomes much more difficult for them to think of nonviolent conflict resolution and peacemaking as passive activities for sissies. I suspect that for many of them—especially the boys—a reversal takes place. They start to see fighting as an immature way of resolving conflict and nonviolence as mature and courageous.

Besides learning about peacemakers and making peace pledges, the program's teaching guide recommends that teachers get their classes involved in a class project of a socially useful nature: "Begin with a brainstorming discussion in which children are invited to think of areas for improvement in the world and possible ways to address the problems . . . have the children talk with friends and family about their choice of a 'making a difference' project." Eventually the children settle on a class project. It could be visiting a nursing home, helping to clean up or repair a local playground, raising money for UNICEF, or almost any other socially useful program.

Just as King, Parks, and Gandhi serve as antidotes to Wayne, Stallone, and Norris, these projects serve as an antidote to the values of unabated competitiveness and self-centeredness that so many children seem to learn from the media, their family, and their peer group. Another antidote to these values is the fostering of cooperative activity in the classroom. The unit in the teaching guide devoted to this topic starts with an anecdote by a staff developer who went into a kindergarten class in order to work with the children on "Cooperative Monster Making," a project in which the class was divided into several groups, each of which created a group monster. The author writes that she had barely finished explaining the project when several children expressed negative reactions to it: " 'I want to make *my own* monster!' said one, expressing the feelings of many. The idea of working with a group of other people to create one product seemed to be a new idea for them."

The teacher explained that this time they had to work on the monsters cooperatively. They did, and had a lot of fun. They produced some very original monsters, and each group took pride in its accomplishments.

The author concludes, "The anecdote illustrates the fact that in our competitive society, children rarely have the opportunity to experience successful cooperative activities. Yet when given the opportunity, they enjoy being part of a team that has produced something larger than any one of its members could have produced individually."

Some Americans may question the value of teaching cooperation to children. "How will these children be able to compete in the marketplace?" they may wonder. Isn't it the American emphasis on individualism and competition that turned us into one of the world's most enterprising, innovative, and wealthy countries? Even Communist countries such as China and the USSR are now seeking to integrate these qualities into their failing economies.

These concerns can be answered by distinguishing between a healthy level of competition tempered by a sense of social responsibility and fair play, and an extreme or even obsessive concern with winning. For the last twenty years unabated competition and "looking out for Number One" have become a common ethos in this country. During the same period of time, we have been plagued by Watergate, numerous indictments of Reagan-era government officials on corruption and bribery charges, Wall Street insider trading scandals, and endless "corporate raiding" which harms rather than helps our nation's economic well-being.

Studies of the relationship between competition and achievement indicate that success is closely related to the individual's involvement in and commitment to his or her work, and love of challenging tasks. Extreme competitiveness is often associated with poorer performance. It can lead to short-sightedness, cheating and lying, inability to work well with others, and a very high level of anxiety, all of which detract from real achievement.[3]

It is essential for the well-being of our nation that we learn to temper our obsession with winning and competitiveness, and teach our children the value of cooperation and social responsibility.

8
Taking the Glory Out of War and Unlearning Bigotry

In January 1988, eight veterans who had suffered severe emotional trauma related to the Vietnam War returned to Vietnam with two therapists. The hope was that going back might help them face and deal better with their painful wartime experiences.* On March 15, 1989, several of those vets appeared on Ted Koppel's "Nightline." They talked about their guilt, depression, recurrent nightmares.

---

* While severe traumatic reaction to warfare seems to be particularly frequent among Vietnam vets, it is in no way unique to them. After the World Wars I and II many men suffered from what was called respectively "shell shock" and "combat fatigue." It is now called post-traumatic stress disorder.

Jake Lafave saw six Americans die hideous deaths in a mortar attack. He still suffers from a recurrent guilt-ridden nightmare in which his faceless dead comrades sit around a campfire and refuse to let him enter their circle. Ed Marcin talked about dreaming "of the enemy that I buried . . . and I see their faces, and I see their clothes, and I see their bodies. And I can still feel them . . . they've never gone away." Bill Koutrouba, a combat medic who was decorated for heroism and nominated for the Medal of Honor, felt enormous guilt over both the Americans he lost and the Vietcong soldier he killed. He described how members of his unit once fired into a village, for fun, to celebrate New Year's Eve. The next morning they saw the villagers bring out "seven small packages wrapped in plastic that were seven small children they had killed." "When I get depressed," he said, "I start taking a .44 magnum pistol and put it in my mouth, and I play Russian roulette with it, hoping that I'll die."

At the end of the show, the men pleaded with today's young men not to repeat their mistakes. "I understand that bravado and glory and wondrous things are a part of youth," said Ed Marcin, "[but] there's no glory in war. All there is, is dead. And there's no glory in being dead. If . . . you have to search for glory, please don't look at war for glory. Look somewhere else. There are many more wonderful and glorious things you can do with your life except go to war. And if you've got to go to war, at least know why you're going." The men all expressed their love of country while at the same time hoping that young men in the future would exercise more caution before enthusiastically going off to wars they know nothing about.

Koutrouba emphasized: "It's never the movies . . . it just isn't make-believe. It's very final," and added, "[when it] comes time to go to wars, maybe people need to take a hard look and understand, learn how to spell the name of the place we're going to fight, and understand what it is that we're paying a price for." Dave Roberts suggested that "one of the keys to future situations is education."

Roberts is joined in this view by numerous educators across the country who have committed themselves to creating realistic, honest social studies curricula in which difficult, controversial issues are not avoided. Like the Vietnam vets on Koppel's show, these educators believe that if young Americans might be asked to sacrifice their lives for their country at some point, then they should at least have had the opportunity to gain the knowledge, understanding, and ability to think critically. They must not be sacrificial lambs on the altar of adolescent war fantasies. They must not be allowed to kill first and then realize—and suffer endless guilt over the fact—that their victims are real people, not subhuman "gooks" or abstract "enemies."

They must be educated so that they can vote intelligently, so that their vote will be based on knowledge and understanding rather than a knee-jerk reaction of approval for whichever candidate sounds the most like John Wayne.

These educators are fighting a long tradition of avoiding controversial, difficult issues in textbooks and in social studies classes. This tradition is built on a deeply misguided and dangerous concept of patriotism.

In *America Revised,* a study of United States history textbooks, Frances Fitzgerald points out that the standard elementary and secondary school history textbooks "are essentially nationalistic histories."[1] She argues that an important part of the anger of college students in the 1960s grew out of their awareness that not only government officials but also teachers and textbooks had hidden the truth about United States history and policies from them.

Vietnam vets who are still suffering the aftereffects of their involvement in what now seems like a senseless bloodbath that cost over a million lives, and the families of soldiers who died in Vietnam, have even more reason to be furious.

This is how Fitzgerald describes the textbooks on which these men were raised:

> According to these books, the United States had been a kind of Salvation Army to the rest of the world: throughout history, it had done little but dispense benefits to poor, ignorant, and diseased countries. In the nineteenth century and the beginning of the twentieth, it had opened doors for the Chinese, saved Cuba from the Spanish, protected Puerto Rico, separated Panama from Colombia in order to wipe out yellow fever, and taken on the Philippines in order to "educate" and "civilize" the Filipinos—just as President William McKinley said. American motives were always altruistic

. . . In the twentieth century, the United States had spent most of its time—apart from a short period of isolation—saving Europe and Asia from militarism, Fascism, and Communism.[2]

With such a view of America's role in the world combined with John Wayne as hero and role model, it is easy to see how men like Koutrouba, Marcin, Roberts, and Lafave enthusiastically went off to Vietnam seeking glory and then, after encountering real-life war and understanding our misguided involvement, returned feeling deeply depressed and guilty.

While some textbooks of the 1980s have tempered their "nationalistic histories" with a higher dose of reality, many have not. This became clear to me as I spent an afternoon at the New York City Board of Education's Social Studies Library perusing textbooks approved for use in the city's public schools.

One book analyzed the Mexican-American War as resulting from "the restlessness" of the American people. The text explains that this "restlessness," which also manifests itself in Americans' moving frequently, "gave the country most of its present land before the middle of the nineteenth century."[3]

Another textbook concludes a section on our relations with Latin America between 1898 and 1918 by pointing out that

> The Americans brought important benefits to the countries they protected. They took care of the sick and hungry, restored law and order, and established honest government. They built roads, schools, hospitals, water supply and sewage systems. They stamped out tropical diseases and developed natural resources.
>
> Yet the people of Latin America disliked America's stepping into their affairs. They seemed to prefer their own governments, corrupt and weak though they might be, to honest and efficient administrations run by "norteamericanos."[4]

The same textbook has the following laconic comment on one of the most momentous events in human history:

> In August, 1945, American planes dropped two A-bombs and destroyed two Japanese cities. Japan surrendered and the Second World War finally came to an end.[5]

Nothing more is said about events that have been the subject of endless moral debate and marked the beginning of the nuclear era and the arms race.

These quotes and Fitzgerald's analysis reveal a concept of patriotism as the uncritical, unquestioning acceptance of United States policy, particularly military action, as being invariably right both politically and morally.

The absurdity and danger of such a concept can be illustrated by the following analogy: if one accepts this definition of patriotism, then a present-day Soviet citizen or Soviet textbook critical of the Stalin era with its brutal purges of millions of peasants and generalized terror would have to be considered highly unpatriotic. Germans who criticize Hitler and the Nazi era would be equally unpatriotic.

It is natural to identify strongly with and care about the community one grows up in and lives in. Since the inception of unified political states this identification has expanded to one's nation. But this deep emotional tie is very different from blind acceptance of everything that is done by government in the name of one's country.

The best and most useful kind of patriotism is one that holds one's country up to high moral and social standards and imbues citizens with a sense of responsibility for maintaining these standards. Such patriotism leads to active involvement in trying to improve one's community and country.

The mistaken identification of patriotism with blind obedience to the state, and unquestioning support for all military endeavors, probably grows out of the fear on the part of statesmen that without it men would be far less willing to fight in wars, and women would not so readily accept the sacrifice of their sons and husbands.

They are partially right. For without such blind patriotism it would be much more difficult to sacrifice the lives of our young men (and increasingly young women) in wars which are not really necessary for our national security. In light of the human propensity to self-defense and identification with one's community, there is no reason, however, to believe that they would be unwilling to fight when our nation is genuinely threatened.

In fact, the fear that teaching young people to think critically about our foreign policy and military actions would lead them to an unwillingness to support and fight in wars directly contradicts another tenet often held by the same people: that military conflict and war grow out of "human" nature and so there isn't very much that can be done about them. If "human" nature is so naturally violent that war is inevitable, then why fear that teaching young men to think critically about our foreign policy would decrease their "natural" enthusiasm for strife and violence to the point that they wouldn't even be willing to defend their country against real aggression?

LEARNING ABOUT VIETNAM: A CURE FOR RAMBOISM

Chris Wilkens is a Vietnam veteran with a deep commitment to relaying to young men the sober realism expressed by the vets on Koppel's "Nightline." He also has a special opportunity to do so, for he is a social studies teacher at Roxbury High School in Succasunna, New Jersey.

Like that of the men on "Nightline," Wilkens's desire to teach young men to think differently grows out of painful personal experience. Wilkins served three years in Vietnam. He was involved in the Tet offensive, in which half the men in his attack unit lost their lives. He tells me that for two or three years he suffered intense survivor's guilt: "I had a lot of difficult nights. It's still there but I'm able to deal with it now; before it was debilitating at times."

In the fall of 1988, Wilkens started to teach a course entitled "The Vietnam Generation."

The course is an elective for seniors, and the first class I sit in on consists of boys only. The second class has eight boys and three girls. Wilkens explains that the boys sign up because of the "macho-image attraction"—"they come in thinking they're going to get Rambo." They are in for disappointment. The course is intended as a cure for Ramboism.

During my visit the lesson focuses on Vietnamese culture. Wilkens informs the students that 85 percent of the people are farmers. Family, land, and traditions, including reverence for the old, are central to their way of life. He frequently draws analogies to American society and also points out differences. Until 1905 we also were primarily an agricultural society. People came to the United States to get land. Like the Vietnamese, we used to care for our elderly at home.

Slides, which accompany his lecture, give a vivid sense of

everyday life in Vietnam. The students see farmers planting rice in the Mekong Delta. Vietnamese fishermen at work, traditional Vietnamese women's clothes. These stand in sharp contrast to slides of young men and women in Western clothes on their scooters and mopeds in Saigon.

Slides of Buddhist temples and Buddhist monks begging are accompanied by a brief history of the development of Buddhism and its introduction to Vietnam. Some of the basic tenets and practices of Buddhism are contrasted with Christian beliefs.

After listening to Wilkens's lecture and seeing the slides, one has a sense of the Vietnamese as real people. His intent is clearly to cure students of the kind of attitude expressed by General Westmoreland, the Commander in Chief of United States Forces in Vietnam. In a documentary film entitled *Hearts and Minds,* Westmoreland states, "The Oriental doesn't put the same high price on life as the Westerner. Life is plentiful; life is cheap in the Orient."

In an interview, Wilkens tells me that one of his favorite educational tools is a picture of two dead soldiers, an American and a Vietnamese. Lying next to the Vietnamese soldier's body is a picture of his girlfriend.

"How many of you have pictures of your beaus or your girlfriends in your pockets right now?" he asks the class. Invariably hands are raised. Wilkens points out that what they see in the picture is not any different from them: "A young man who fought in battle, died, and he had a girlfriend at home. If you died someone would find [your picture]. What we want out of life is no different from what they want. We're at a different level of technology; our toys are different, but we basically all want the same thing."

For Wilkens the analysis of this picture serves as a springboard for one of the basic themes of his class: there is no glory in war; it is not a Ramboesque adventure. It involves killing real people like you and me, people you have nothing against, and risking your own life.

The conclusion Wilkens draws from all this is not pacifism. He describes himself as very conservative on foreign policy. "I would probably make Ronald Reagan look like a liberal." There is no doubt in Wilkens's mind that sometimes war must be fought. He has no problems with our maintaining a strong military. He considers the United States Marines to be "the finest."

Wilkens's goal is to take the glory out of war and provide his students with the proper tools for assessing whether or not they think a particular war is necessary. He deplores the fact that "we don't condition our kids to think; we kill their creativity." One way in which he gets his kids to think is to make them imagine the consequences of their spontaneous reactions to foreign policy issues. They are not allowed to get away with just suggesting that we should have bombed Hanoi. They must think through what would have been some of the possible consequences of our bombing Hanoi. Chinese or Russian intervention? Loss of the few allies we had? Negative world opinion? What might the effects of each of these consequences be?

Wilkens points out that after Ayatollah Khomeini's death sentence against novelist Salman Rushdie, some of his students came into class asserting that the best solution was to assassinate Khomeini. Wilkens made them go through a step-by-step analysis of the likely consequences of that action, including loss of oil for ourselves and our allies, with resulting economic shocks.

Wilkens also deplores the fact that besides being unable to think critically, students are frightfully uninformed about the world beyond our borders.

Until 1988, apart from one seventh-grade world geography and history class in which each teacher could choose which area to cover—many of them would choose ancient history—New Jersey students had no required world history classes whatsoever. A student there could graduate from high school with absolutely no knowledge of any contemporary foreign nation except for its involvement in American history. And yet, Wilkens and several other teachers at the school assure me that New Jersey is one of the better states educationally.

There has been some improvement recently. New Jersey now requires a world culture class in the ninth grade. New York State has instituted a global history requirement. A growing number of states are recognizing the need to give American students some sense of the fact that there are other nations out there with cultures and values different from our own. In 1987 the National Governors' Association formally endorsed global education.

New Jersey's world culture class is a highly interdisciplinary year-long survey course that includes the socioeconomic and cultural study of the Middle East, Africa, Asia, and South America. The nearby Morris County Museum makes available to world culture teachers in the area "artifacts boxes" that contain replicas of statues, paintings, ceramics, and so on from different parts of the world. These serve as a springboard for discussing the values, art, and cultures of various societies.

When I visit Robert Magnuson's world culture class at Roxbury High School, he is doing the unit on the Middle East and is covering the three major religions. Judaism was discussed the day before and this class begins with slides of Jewish religious practices—the blowing of the shofar, the laying of tefillin, and so on.

Chris Wilkens is delighted that New Jersey has finally made some teaching of foreign history and culture mandatory. But learning bare facts is not enough. There must be a willingness on the part of schools and teachers to deal with controversial issues that are often glossed over. As examples, Wilkens points out that in discussing World War II most teachers avoid raising questions about why the Allies didn't bomb the railroads leading to concentration camps—which they knew about from 1942 on. They discuss the Nuremberg war trials but avoid raising questions about our bombings of Dresden, Hamburg, Hiroshima, and Nagasaki. The question whether some of our leaders were also guilty of war crimes is too controversial for most schools and teachers. Wilkens wishes there were more critical examination along these lines.

He does not see raising such questions as either unpatriotic or endangering our national security. He is simply encouraging young people to think for themselves. The next time our nation sends soldiers to war, he would like our young men—and women—to be able to think through whether it is a worthwhile endeavor, indispensable to our nation's well-being.

Half the men in Vietnam had no idea where they were or why they were there, Wilkens tells me. For too many of them the desire to go to Vietnam grew out of watching John Wayne heroically walking off into the sunset after a glorious battle.

Wilkens is confident that if young people were informed and able to think critically, we would have no shortage of men willing to fight and die in a genuinely necessary war. There would be an "understanding that it had to be done." He contrasts soldiers' reactions in World War II and in Vietnam. In the one case there was a general conviction that the war had to be fought and won. Men like his father risked their lives again and again. They had confidence in the cause and in their orders. But in Vietnam, after a certain point, there was a growing sense that the war was a mistake. Soldiers were far more likely to question orders. In some cases soldiers refused to comply with officers' orders to head down trails where they knew there would be booby traps. Wilkens sees this as beneficial: "Often officers realized . . . that they had to think through more carefully what they were ordering."

For Wilkens, one of the problems with blind obedience to superiors grows out of the fact that in war "civilized customs" tend to be forgotten and "violent, restless, men—psychopaths" are often admired and become leaders. This warning is from a unit on My Lai which Wilkens contributed to "The Lessons of the Vietnam War," curriculum—the text which forms the basis of his class.

The Vietnam War curriculum is the brainchild of Jerry Starr, professor of sociology at the University of West Virginia. Starr was dismayed at how so many textbooks neglected the war, or gave only a very limited and superficial account of it. By the late 1980s more textbooks were covering the war, but the treatments still tended to be superficial and did not deal with difficult issues such as My Lai or the use of chemical warfare.[6]

The Lessons of the Vietnam War Curriculum does not avoid difficult issues. Besides My Lai, its twelve units include one dealing with the question of the legality of the war. A section entitled "Who Fought for Us in Vietnam" analyzes the socioeconomic makeup of the military. Another unit discusses in some detail the effects on the Vietnamese and on Americans of Agent Orange.

Each unit of the curriculum is written by a different contributor. Wilkens explains that Starr wanted a politically balanced curriculum and sought him out because of his conservative views on foreign policy.

An important concern of many educators who develop alternate social studies curricula is achieving a political balance, exposing young people to a variety of political and social points of view. They do this both because they see it as being the most effective way to get students to think critically—one of their primary goals—and because they are intensely aware of critics who see almost any departure from nationalistic histories as being unobjective, biased, and unpatriotic.

Besides balancing contributors politically, Starr further assured a diversity of views by encouraging writers to include personal statements by a variety of participants—not just academic and political leaders but also American GIs, Vietnamese soldiers and peasants, and American civilians. Poetry, letters to the editor, and court testimony are included.

Starr uses the curriculum in a class he teaches at the University of West Virginia. Like several of the educators I spoke to, he believes simulations are an excellent way of getting students to think through complex social, political, and military problems. When he teaches the Gulf of Tonkin resolution, his classroom becomes the floor of the Senate with some "senators" arguing for the resolution and some against. The debates are lively and informative. The students develop an understanding of the kinds of pressures that senators experience when it is claimed that an attack on American vessels was carried out—whether on the *Maddox* in 1964 or the *Maine* in 1898.

TEACHING ABOUT PAST GENOCIDES TO COMBAT TODAY'S BIGOTRY

In 1976 two Brookline, Massachusetts, junior high school teachers, Margot Stern Strom and William S. Parsons, set out to do something about the fact that American social studies textbooks ignored the Holocaust and the early twentieth-century Armenian genocide. With the help of funding from the U.S. Department of Education, they developed a program that was eventually adopted by other Brookline schools. By the 1980s the project had evolved into the Brookline-based national nonprofit organization, the Facing History and Ourselves National Foundation. Its Resource Center provides educators in more than fifteen hundred schools and communities, including Canada, Portugal, Germany, and England with services and resources for teaching a course entitled: "Facing History and Ourselves, Holocaust and Human Behavior."

Like the Lessons of the Vietnam War curriculum, the Facing History program has educational goals that go far beyond teaching children about specific historical events. They both are concerned with deglorifying violence and with developing the ability to think critically, to empathize, to put oneself in another's shoes.

Facing History explores the question of why people embrace racism and its often violent consequences. It also focuses on the individual's responsibility for social action or inaction when confronted with injustice.

While the course is being taught at highly diverse schools and communities, it is frequently introduced in schools where there is a history of racial conflict, such as South Boston High School, which was the scene of enormous strife and violence during the integration of Boston schools in the mid-1970s. Students who are unwilling to confront directly the racial problems that affect them begin to deal with them by learning about racism at another time, another place.

South Boston High, says teacher Virginia Ordway, is not an easy school to teach at. "I think this is as tough as it gets in terms of maintaining control in a classroom. These are not kids who come to school ready to learn with notebook and pen." The school is highly integrated, and a majority of the children—African-American, white and Hispanic—are from families on welfare. The course's goals of getting kids to think critically and to develop empathy present enormous challenges. "My students for the most part don't want to think," Ordway tells me, but then adds that of all the classes she has taught in eleven years "the Facing History class is the most effective at making kids think critically."

As for empathy, "they have had such tragic, traumatic lives and they're so wounded that their empathy for anyone else is limited." At the end of the semester she invites a Holocaust survivor to come to class. "With the kids I teach, if I brought the person in at the beginning they would be rude; they wouldn't care to listen to what she has to say; they wouldn't care if the woman was bleeding up there." But something changes and by the end of the semester the students are interested in her, listen to her, and empathize with her.

One change is that at the beginning of the semester roughly 30 percent of the boys of all races "identify with the Nazis totally. They think Hitler is just the swellest guy. He didn't win but people loved him." They admire "anybody that can mobilize people the way he did regardless of the result." Ordway attributes this admiration to the fact that most of her students consider themselves victims and "they certainly don't want to identify with the victim." However, while the girls are as much victimized as the boys, they do not identify with Hitler.

Ordway assures me that by the end of the course all these would-be Nazis have "mellowed out." They have developed enough empathy for the victims so that Hitler and the Nazis are no longer attractive figures.

One factor that leads to their change of heart and mind is a partially autobiographical book they read, entitled *Friedrich,* by Hans Peter Richter. The book is about two little boys, one Jewish and one Gentile, growing up in Nazi Germany. Through the events in these boys' lives the students experience a personal reflection of what is happening politically in Germany: "The kids really identify with these characters; it becomes like somebody they know that this is happening to . . . They begin to see the consequences of the actions."*

Before Ordway even begins to teach the course she has her students read a novel called *Friends* by Rosa Guy about two little African-American girls in New York City. The novel serves as a springboard for discussing, in a context that is close to home, most of the basic issues relevant to the Holocaust—racism, scapegoating, how people act differently as individuals and as part of a group, people's reactions to violence, the social responsibility of the individual.

One of the unique features of the Facing History and Ourselves program is its emphasis on understanding the processes

---

* A paper by an eighth-grade student captures beautifully the change that many of the children experience as a result of being confronted with the real-life consequences of violence. He writes: "A long time ago, I sat in a 7th grade class. I was dumb then, or at least that's what I feel now. Oh, I couldn't wait to see all those movies with these armies blowing up cities and shooting at each other . . . I didn't mind watching all those innocent people die in battle. I couldn't wait to see pictures, and learn about different planes, tanks, and battleships. Yup, that's what I thought I was going to learn during 8th grade social studies . . . what I did learn will probably change the way I think, and look out on life for the rest of my life."

by which a group of "normal" people—and in the case of the Germans, exceptionally well-educated people—is able to acquiesce in the persecution and eventual genocide of millions of people.

The program begins with an examination of questions that are at the heart of racism and genocide. This is done in part through self-examination—the students are required to keep journals—and in part through readings, which include primary sources, materials from victims, victimizers, and bystanders, films, and class visitors. Students examine issues such as how individuals attain a sense of identity through family, religion, political groups, and so on. The roles of propaganda and blind obedience to authority are analyzed, along with the roles of nature and nurture in violent behavior.

Toward the end of the semester many of the teachers show a film about the Ku Klux Klan Youth Corps and discuss what leads the young people in the film to join the Klan.

I observed a videotaped discussion of the film in a class taught by Linda Nathan in the Fenway Program at Boston English High School. Part of the discussion centered on the issue of whether one of the young men in the film whose father was a Klan member had a real choice about joining.

"His kid would be forced to join," one boy points out. "Yeah, 'cause the father was like that so the son has to be like that. He wouldn't have no choice."

"Are you just like your father?" Nathan asks.

When one of the boys responds, "If your father tells you since you're a boy to hate blacks, you're gonna hate blacks," a girl counters with "My mother tells me to go to church but I don't go." She argues that "they all had a choice not to go."

Ordway tells me that after she has shown and discussed the film, she has the students make up a list of ten reasons why someone their age would join an organization like the Ku Klux Klan. A composite list is then put on the blackboard. The last time they did this only one out of thirteen reasons listed was racism. Others included peer acceptance, family values and tradition, and the need for group identity.

From such discussions, from their previous study of how important group approval is for people's sense of identity, and from studying how decent Germans who were not especially anti-Semitic acted against Jews (or did nothing) out of fear, peer pressure, or wanting to feel part of the crowd, the students develop a sense of how the same thing could happen anywhere.

By analyzing the psychological, historical, and philosophical bases of prejudice and group action, and by increasing self-awareness, the course decreases the chances of the students' getting involved in such behavior themselves. "We don't produce Mother Teresas, but they [the students] become a bit more tolerant of one another and their cultural differences by the end of the course," says Ordway.

She emphasizes that she does not let students get away with believing that Germans are bad and Americans good. The book of readings used in the course encourages dealing with the uncomfortable questions that most history textbooks and teachers avoid: Why didn't we or the Allies bomb the railways to the concentration camps? Why, even after the 1938 Evian conference on how to aid refugees from Axis countries, did the United States and most other Western nations refuse to change their immigration policies and admit Jewish refugees? Why, in 1939, did the United States Congress vote down a bill to admit twenty thousand German Jewish children to the United States on a special quota?

Students are stimulated to think about the role that the Allies' inaction played in encouraging the Nazis. After the Evian conference a Nazi newspaper commented on the fact that no state was prepared to accept "a few thousand Jews" and concluded, "thus the Conference serves to justify Germany's policy against Jewry."[7] On several occasions Hitler cynically offered to send the Jews to any nation that would accept them, knowing that the offer would not be taken up.

The implications of ignoring the genocides of the past are brought out in Hitler's speech to his troops before the invasion of Poland in 1939: "I have sent to the East only my 'Death Head Units,' with the order to kill without mercy all men, women, and children of Polish race or language. Only in such a way will we win the vital space we need. *Who still talks nowadays of the extermination of the Armenians?* [emphasis added]"[8]

By the time they are done with the program many of the students have developed more of a sense of social responsibility. They have begun to understand that for nations as well as for individuals, not doing anything when others are being persecuted, when others are in need, is a form of action that has its consequences just as much as doing something has consequences.

None of this is rendered in a simplistic way. The readings include excerpts from a German who in 1935, after some agonizing, signed an oath affirming his loyalty to Hitler. The oath was a requisite for keeping his job. Part of his reasoning was that by doing so he would be better able to help Jewish friends and others in need. He did in fact later on save many lives by hiding people in his apartment. But in retrospect he felt that he had made a terrible moral mistake, for it was the decision by decent people like him to sign the oath, to go along, that made it possible for Hitler to attain the power he did. Had they all said no right from the beginning, not a few thousand but millions of lives would have been saved.

While the students discuss this moral dilemma, what is not at issue is the notion that doing something to help others when they are in need is the morally correct thing to do.

One year some students who had taken Linda Nathan's class decided to do a big fund-raiser for a local food bank and for Oxfam, a nonprofit organization dedicated to helping poor and often starving people around the world. Their persistent efforts led to their raising three thousand dollars. When some of the students were interviewed by a local university radio station and were asked what had prompted them to do this, one girl explained that studying the Holocaust made her realize that you couldn't be a bystander, that you had to do something.

A CORNUCOPIA OF INNOVATIVE PROGRAMS

While they reach only a small segment of our total student population, more innovative social studies programs have been created in recent years than could possibly be described in these pages. What follows are the outlines of a few sample curricula which, like the two described in some detail above, do not avoid difficult, unpleasant issues. They are geared to increase critical thinking, empathy, and the ability to see things from the other side's perspective. By combating prejudice and xenophobia, by taking the glory out of war and violence, by offering alternatives, they help young men sever their destructive attachment to the values of the masculine mystique and the cinematic fantasies that portray them. These are the kind of educational experiences that, I suspect, men like LaFave, Koutrouba, Roberts, and Marcin wish they had had.[9]

Moorehead Kennedy is the former Acting Economic Counselor at the American Embassy in Tehran and was one of the hostages taken by the Iranians in 1978.

The 444 days he spent as a hostage left him with a deepened sense of the importance for American foreign policy of being able to understand how the world looks from the perspective of other countries and cultures. The inability on the part of many Americans, including politicians and diplomats, to do this, combined with our national obsession with winning, leads to misinterpretations, failures to seize opportunities, and a tendency to see foreign policy issues in simplistic, immature terms: we are right, they are wrong; we are good, they are bad. These tendencies make it very difficult to negotiate nonviolent solutions to international conflicts. Kennedy is quick to point out that not all situations can be resolved nonviolently. Sometimes the use of force cannot be avoided.

Under the auspices of the Myrin Institute and the American Forum, Kennedy and educator Martha Keys have developed a series of simulation curricula that have been used in a variety of educational settings, from ninth grade through college.

Drawing on Kennedy's personal experience, he and Keys started out by developing a hostage crisis simulation. After reading a book on terrorism, the students play the roles of terrorists, hostages, government officials, and so on. They begin to understand what it is that drives some young Middle Easterners to become terrorists. To understand is not to condone. Understanding helps one deal better with the other side in attempts to work out a settlement and to formulate a future foreign policy that may prevent hostage-taking.

Colman McCarthy, a Catholic pacifist and columnist for the *Washington Post,* has developed and teaches courses called "The Politics of Nonviolence" and "Peace and World Order" in several high schools and universities in Washington D.C., and the surrounding area. McCarthy has taken on the task of introducing students to the thinking of proponents of nonviolence such as Dorothy Day, Tolstoy, Gandhi, King. He is appalled that in a century in which seventy-eight million human beings have lost their lives in wars, students continue to learn about "war heroes" like Napoleon, Custer, and Patton, but remain ignorant of "peace heroes." He is trying to bring a small measure of balance to what he sees as a very lopsided curriculum.

In New York City, at the Brooklyn Friends School, Lawrence Gibson teaches the history component and Don Knies the literature component of an elective called "Faces of War." With about 80 percent of the students taking it, the course is the most popular elective at the school. Besides reading historical texts, students gain a realistic view of what war is like from reading poems by German and American World War I soldiers, and novels like Ron Kovic's *Born on the Fourth of July.* A woman's perspective on war is presented in Vera Brittain's *Testament of Youth.* Students also read Phillip Knightley's *The First Casualty,* an analysis of how the needs of national security affect censorship and the press during war.

On the Pacific Coast, at South Eugene High School in Eugene, Oregon, social studies teacher Bob Veeck teaches a course on Soviet-American relations. He begins with the study of American foreign policy and interests since World War II, and threats to these interests. He then teaches exactly the same topics from the Soviet point of view. Once the class clearly sees issues from both perspectives, he introduces a unit on nuclear weapons. Veeck also teaches a semester-long elective on the arms race.

In 1984 the National PTA at its annual convention voted in favor of preparing curricular materials examining issues relating to the nuclear age. In a world that holds close to sixty thousand nuclear warheads and in which some students think they may not live to become adults because of the threat of nuclear war, an increasing number of parents and teachers feel that our young people must be educated to understand nuclear issues. According to Phyllis La Farge, author of *The Strangelove Legacy: Children, Parents and Teachers in the Nuclear Age,* as many as twelve to fifteen percent of elementary schools and high schools have a formal curriculum on nuclear education. La Farge points out that nuclear-age education at its best emphasizes process at least as much as content. It teaches children to ask fundamental questions about assumptions, biases, and evidence underlying positions on an issue. The ability to ask such questions will enable them someday to make sound evaluations of complex problems such as the nuclear issue.[10]

Alan Shapiro, retired from teaching at New York's New Rochelle High School, spends much of his time working on a United States–Soviet Education Collaboration Project, a joint venture of Educators for Social Responsibility (ESR) and the Soviet Academy of Pedagogical Sciences, and the Soviet group Educators for Peace and Understanding. Since 1988, these groups have met annually, and have produced classroom material for use by Soviet and American teachers. One of their major goals is to diminish mutually held stereotypes.

Shapiro and other Americans involved in similar cooperative ventures are convinced that in addition to the direct contributions they are making to improving the social studies curriculum in both countries, they are also playing an important role in helping Soviet educators reform their system of education in light of *perestroika*.

9
Changing
the Male Mind-set

In each of the three areas of education discussed in this section the primary focus has been on a different part of life. The child-rearing section is centered on the family; the conflict resolution section on peer relationships, and the social studies section on international relations. A closer examination reveals that the kinds of programs advocated would in fact influence young boys' thinking and behavior in all three areas.

Boys who have studied conflict resolution have learned to be good listeners, to "put up" rather than put down, to cooperate, to see things from the other side's perspective. They are more likely to become patient, empathic, nonviolent fathers.

As we have seen, reinforcing boys' empathic, caring feelings toward children, and encouraging them to feel the intimate connection with life-giving that grows out of being a nurturing father, would tend to decrease the need for the excitement, power, and camaraderie found in youth gangs and war.

Nationalistic history courses legitimize such role models as John Wayne and Rambo, who teach boys that being tough, dominant, and ready to fight at the drop of a hat is what manhood is all about. Men who perceive masculinity as consisting of these qualities are more likely to commit acts of violence at home and on the streets. Social studies programs that reinforce critical thinking, deglorify war, and decrease xenophobia remove the legitimization of violence that is provided by the acceptance of warfare as a normal, even glorious, way of resolving international conflict. It is not lost on young boys that nations routinely go to war in order to achieve their economic and political goals. If so, then why is it not acceptable for schoolboys to resolve their disputes in school yard fights, or for rival gangs to resolve their difficulties and achieve their goals through warfare?

Boys who have studied conflict resolution will be less inclined to look to the willingness to fight as a proof of manhood. They will be less likely to assume that the only proper patriotic response to international conflict is belligerence.

But there are those who have no fondness for these programs and are disturbed, not heartened, by their compounded effects. The conflict resolution and innovative social studies programs have drawn the sharpest criticism. Opponents argue that these kinds of programs are politically biased; that the critical thinking they teach can lead to moral and political relativism; and that the emphasis on empathy, cooperation, and putting oneself in the other side's shoes can weaken us as a nation and represents an unacceptable form of "psychologizing."

At any particular time in history, attempts at questioning traditional ways of doing and thinking will be met with animosity. One can easily imagine what the reaction would have been in 1840, in the South, to a social studies curriculum questioning the morality of slavery, or encouraging students to think critically about women's suffrage.

To those who accept the status quo, nationalistic histories

seem "objective." Any in-depth questioning of the way things are and have been will seem politically biased.

The Facing History program described above has been attacked on just these grounds. While the program received a top rating from the U.S. Department of Education in 1987, Shirley Curry, then head of the Department's Recognition Division, refused to fund it. A Special Program Significance panel appointed by Curry, a former political associate of anti-feminist and conservative activist Phyllis Schlafly, found among other problems that "the program gives no evidence of balance or objectivity. The Nazi point of view, however unpopular, is still a point of view and is not presented, nor is that of the Ku Klux Klan."

Apparently, opponents of the program also had "discomfort with its psychologizing" and thought it was "antiwar, anti-hunting" (the sourcebook uses a story about a little boy whose father takes him hunting, against his mother's and his wishes, to start a discussion of how children develop values and behavioral patterns) and likely to "induce a guilt trip."[1]

The concern with giving equal time to the Nazi and Ku Klux Klan positions is particularly perplexing in light of the fact that one of the objections to innovative programs raised by critics like Curry is that getting young people to think critically can lead to moral and political relativism.

Yet what could be more relativistic than to give equal time to antidemocratic movements dedicated to racism and genocide? One wonders if these critics of the Facing History program also favor the inclusion of the study of Satanism in religion courses at government-funded universities in order to give a "balanced," "objective" view of world religions.

Our nation is built on the values of life, liberty, pursuit of happiness, equality, the general welfare. Our two-hundred-year history represents a slow progress toward their greater fulfillment. The Facing History program is not neutral about these values, nor are the other curricula described. They teach children to think critically about the means by which they can best be achieved. They help them think through why these values are so important. The conflict resolution programs help children develop the kinds of attitudes—tolerance, aversion to gratuitous

violence, respect for others, ability to listen to the other side—
that are the foundation of a viable democratic society.

The Facing History program's "psychologizing" helps children understand the kinds of psychological needs that make
people like themselves, like all of us, susceptible to racist, murderous demagogues. By doing so and by encouraging empathy
and identification with the victims it decreases the likelihood
that these children will fall prey to such values and such leaders.

We live at a time when the possibility of nuclear escalation
renders any armed conflict particularly dangerous. We live in a
century in which wars have taken the lives of close to eighty
million people and wounded millions more. We live in a country
in which approximately twenty thousand people are murdered
each year and over nine hundred thousand are assaulted. In
such a context it would seem that giving students the intellectual
and emotional tools to think through life-and-death issues that
affect them directly, and enhancing their ability to cooperate
with each other and to resolve conflicts nonviolently, would be a
moral necessity. What greater evil is there than the unnecessary
taking of human lives?

But critics fear that encouraging critical thinking, cooperation, and empathy, helping students understand racism and xenophobia, and letting them experience the real effects of war
and violence, will undermine our ability to effectively deal with
and defend ourselves against enemies. These same critics often
believe that political reality consists of a Hobbesian "dog eat
dog" world.

The contradiction in their thinking was pointed out earlier: If
people are by nature mean, selfish, belligerent, and untrustworthy, then trying to mitigate these qualities with a bit of sensitivity
to the other side can hardly lead to our becoming a nation of
Pollyannas naively trusting all others—unless we are the only
nation on earth exempt from the Hobbesian portrait of human
nature which these critics adhere to.

In fact, human beings are extraordinarily malleable and demonstrate a potential for empathy as well as violence from the
earliest age.

Isn't it time to help boys who are attracted to the power and
dominance of demagogic figures such as Hitler to think through

and *experience* what the concrete consequences of such leaders' actions are?

Violence and insensitivity have been reinforced throughout most of human history, especially in men. Isn't it time that we began to counteract cruelty, xenophobia, war, and genocide with lessons in empathy and critical thinking?

Do we really need to worry that teaching conflict resolution will, as some critics contend, give children the mistaken idea that conflicts between countries are just like conflicts in the school yard? While such an analogy could be used simplistically, the kinds of analogies that many men in power use today are far more simplistic and dangerous. As we saw in Chapter 2, sports' values and attitudes, especially football, often provide the underlying mind-set that men bring to foreign policy issues. As we shall see in the following chapters, from the youngest age, boys learn from violent cartoons and TV shows, from films and war toys, that conflicts get resolved through fighting and wars.

III
Our Children: Commercial Market or Precious National Resource?

10
The Culture
of Violence

Anyone who has ever taken a cultural anthropology course is aware that different societies weave different patterns of culture, and that the different threads—religion, music, sports, children's games, drama, work, relations between the sexes, communal values, and so on—that make up the cultural web of a society are usually intricately related.

If a tribe's songs and dramas are centered on violence and warfare, if its young boys play war games and violently competitive sports from the earliest age, if its paintings, sculptures, and potteries depict fights and scenes of battle, it is a pretty sure bet that this is not a peaceful, gentle tribe.

Every child in the world is born into a particular culture and "from the moment of his birth the customs into which he is born shape his experience and behaviour," we are told by anthropologist Ruth Benedict.[1] Throughout history people have known this intuitively and so they have been careful to acculturate their children from the youngest age into a pattern of behavior that is acceptable to the group. We have in our own society some very clear and simple examples: Christian groups like the Hutterites and the Amish, or Jewish groups like the Hasidim want their children to grow up to be devoted primarily to religious rather than material values, to be sexually modest and completely chaste before marriage. They share a strong sense of community and commitment to taking responsibility for the well-being of all their members. Among the Hutterites and Amish there is a strong emphasis on nonviolence. None of these groups allows their children to participate in the mainstream culture.

Sometimes societies develop customs that become highly detrimental to their members. A cultural trait that may be of considerable value in a limited form or that was of value at an earlier point of history is elaborated and continued in a form that is socially deleterious. Ruth Benedict refers to this as the "asocial elaboration of a cultural trait."

A prime example is the incest taboos and marital customs of the Kurnai tribe of Australia. Many a student of anthropology has laughed or at least chuckled at Benedict's descriptions. Benedict explains that all human societies have incest taboos, "but the relatives to whom the prohibition refers differ utterly among different peoples."[2] The Kurnai, like many other tribes, do not differentiate "lineal from collateral kin." Fathers and uncles, brothers and cousins, are not distinguished, so that "all relatives of one's own generation are one's brothers and sisters."[3]

The Kurnai also have an extreme horror of "brother-sister" marriage. Add to this their strict rules with respect to locality in the choice of a mate and the right of old men to marry the attractive young girls, and a situation is created in which there are almost no mates for young people, especially young men. This does not lead the Kurnai to change their incest taboos or rules of marriage. Quite to the contrary, "they insist upon them with every show of violence."[4]

As a result, the usual way for tribe members to marry is to

elope. As soon as the villagers get wind of this crime, they set out in pursuit of the newlyweds with the intent to kill them if they catch them. That probably all the pursuers were married in the same way does not bother anyone. Moral indignation runs high. However, if the couple can reach an island traditionally recognized as a safe haven, the tribe may eventually accept them as husband and wife.

Cultural webs and irrationalities are simpler and easier to see in small, isolated tribes or small communities than in large industrial societies, but they exist in both.

Industrialized societies are made up of different socioeconomic classes, and often different ethnic groups. In a large country like ours, differences in geography and climate affect people. Nevertheless, there are certain aspects of our culture, besides a common language, that are widely shared. Children and adolescents from coast to coast play with the same toys, see many of the same films and TV shows, listen to the same rock music, play many of the same sports.

I suspect that if the Kurnai were to send a few anthropologists over to study contemporary American society, they would be as amused by our irrationalities as we are by theirs.

On the one hand, they would find in our Declaration of Independence a deep commitment to life, liberty, and the pursuit of happiness. An examination of the Constitution would reveal that the goals of our government include "justice," "domestic tranquility," and "the general welfare." An examination of contemporary society would reveal that we deplore murder, assault, wife- and child-battering, sexual abuse of children, and rape.

On the other hand, our newspaper headlines, our TV news with its daily roundups of murders and rapes, our crime statistics, and the fact that over six hundred thousand of our citizens —mostly male—are in prison would inform them just how deeply these problems afflict us. Having established this strong contradiction between our professed goals and beliefs, and our reality, our Kurnai anthropologists would begin to wonder what we teach our boys that makes them become such violent men. They would ask, "Who are your young boys' heroes, who are their role models?"

Rambo, Chuck Norris, Arnold Schwarzenegger, would be high on the list.

"Do your boys watch only violent adventure films?"

No. They like comedies too, but when they reach adolescence many of them become particularly fond of "slasher" films in which they can watch people being skinned, decapitated, cut up into chunks. Wanting to experience all aspects of our culture, the Kurnai anthropologists would undoubtedly watch a few slasher films. They would find out that the perpetrators are practically all male, and the films frequently center on the victimization of females.

"What about the rest of their leisure time, what do your boys do with it?"

Our young boys spend about twenty-eight hours a week watching TV. By the time they are eighteen, they have seen an average of twenty-six thousand TV murders, a vast majority of them committed by men.

"Do they listen to much music?"

They certainly do. They spend billions of dollars a year on records and tapes, not to mention radio and MTV. The Kurnai anthropologists might be advised to turn on MTV to see what the young boys like. They would find that the programming often consists of very angry-looking young men singing lyrics that are hard to make out, but the music sounds as angry as the men look. Women on the shows are often scantily clad, and sometimes it looks as if they are about to be raped.

"Can we see the texts of some of these lyrics?"

Samples of popular hits might include an album by Poison that reached number three on the Billboard pop charts and has sold over two million copies. Its lyrics include, "I want action tonight . . . I need a hot and I need it fast / *If I can't have her, I'll take her and make her* [my emphasis]."

Switching channels from MTV, the Kurnai would find that a considerable amount of American television is devoted to sports. Brawls and fistfights are common at these events, particularly in hockey but also in baseball and basketball. The main tactics in football, tackling and blocking, look exactly like bodily assault.

The anthropologists would find out that our high rates of violent crime have been exacerbated by an ever-growing drug problem. In light of this they would note that drug and alcohol abuse are common among athletes and the heavy metal musicians that many young people admire and emulate.

"What about your sons' toys?" the Kurnai might ask next.

A trip to the playground or a look under Christmas trees—religious symbols used to commemorate the birth of the deified founder of the nation's leading religion who preached a gospel of love and nonviolence—would reveal that while little girls get dolls and carriages and dollhouses; little boys get guns, "action figures" like GI Joe, and violent space-age toys and games.

By now the Kurnai would no doubt have discovered that rates of violence in our society are highest among boys and men raised by single mothers. Being anthropologists they would not be surprised since they would be aware of cross-cultural data indicating that the presence of a caring, involved father decreases the chances of a son being violent.

Delving deeper, they would find out that many boys who start out with fathers lose them along the way through divorce. They would hear divorced women, social workers, psychiatrists, and other professionals complain bitterly that a large percentage of divorced fathers never or rarely see their children, nor do they make child support payments.

Increasingly stunned by the irrationalities of our society, they might inquire of these professionals: In light of the lack of interest of so many of your men in nurturing and taking responsibility for their children, and the subsequent increases in rates of violence and other social problems, why don't you encourage your little boys to become good fathers by buying them dolls and baby carriages and dollhouses? Why don't you encourage them to play house instead of training them to become warriors?

"Parents would never stand for that," professionals and parents would explain. "They are much too afraid that their sons might grow up to be gay if they played with 'wimpy' girls' toys."

At this point the visiting anthropologist might emit a cry of disbelief. Is it not obvious to these strange people who deplore violence, yet do everything possible to encourage it in their sons, that gay men do not have children? They don't push baby carriages, change diapers, or give bottles to their babies. Only heterosexual men become fathers and do these things. What could be more absurd than to think that little boys will become gay by rehearsing the quintessentially heterosexual role of being a father?[5]

Having established the deep contradictions and absurdities of our customs, the Kurnai would look for their origins. They would find that like many warrior societies, we have a long tradition of raising our boys to be tough, emotionally detached, deeply competitive, and concerned with dominance.

These traits, they would note, have gotten out of hand. The enormous escalation of violence that Americans are experiencing seems to coincide with the development of a vast system of communications technology that has led to the creation of a culture of violence of unprecedented dimensions, much of it directed toward or available to children. Instead of treasuring their children as a precious national resource to be handled with the utmost care, Americans have allowed them to be exploited as a commercial market.

How could they let this happen? the Kurnai would wonder. Surely they must understand that one of society's most important tasks, the socialization of the next generation, should not be left in the hands of people whose main concern is financial gain, people who will not hesitate to exploit the basest human tendencies for profit?

In their efforts to understand this puzzle they would be helped by their understanding of their own culture. The Kurnai would see that our "laissez-faire" attitude toward our children can be traced to the asocial elaboration of some of our most beneficial and admirable values, just as their absurd marital rules can be traced to originally useful taboos.

A system of largely unfettered free enterprise led to the extraordinary economic development of the nation. The subsequent commitment to free enterprise is so deep that the economic exploitation of children is taken for granted. Companies manufacture toys for six-year-olds that encourage reckless violence, sadism, and torture, and few people question their right to do so.

The Kurnai would turn next to the First Amendment, the embodiment of the national commitment to free speech.

It would not escape their attention that with respect to pornographic and "indecent" material, it has long been acknowledged that the First Amendment cannot apply equally to children and adults. Long-standing laws protect children from such material. That is why there are no Saturday morning pornographic TV programs.

For some strange reason, the Kurnai would conclude, these people have blinded themselves to the fact that what makes sense with respect to sex makes at least as much sense with respect to violence. And so they have allowed their children to be raised on tens of thousands of TV murders, detailed depictions of sadistic mutilations on the screen, and song lyrics that advocate rape.

What a perfect example of an asocial elaboration, they might exclaim! Everything is justified in terms of free enterprise and free speech, but this freedom as interpreted in present-day society contributes to the nation's enslavement!

Don't these Americans see that boys raised in a culture of violence are not free? Their basest, most destructive tendencies are reinforced from the youngest age to the detriment of their altruistic, pro-social tendencies. Then when they commit serious acts of violence they are sent to prison.

Don't they see that millions of Americans, especially women and elderly people, live in great fear of being mugged, raped, or murdered? Many are afraid to leave their homes after dark.

A survey of national crime statistics published by U.S. government agencies would inform the Kurnai that about twenty thousand Americans a year suffer the greatest loss of freedom. They are deprived of their lives through violent deaths. Their families and friends are permanently deprived of someone they love.

How long will it take these people, the exasperated anthropologists might wonder, until they realize that an interpretation of freedom that allows for no restraints with respect to the commercial exploitation of children is self-destructive?

The Kurnai would note that in other areas Americans acknowledge there is no such thing as absolute freedom. Ordinances prohibit people from playing loud music in the middle of the night if in doing so they deprive others of sleep. Laws restrict the freedom of chemical companies to dump pollutants into streams and rivers. But when it comes to producing a culture of violence that pollutes the minds of their young and encourages violence, these strange people act as if freedom were an absolute!

. . . .

In Section III, I argue that if we want to stop our national bloodbath, we cannot continue to leave the enculturation of our children, without regulation, in the hands of people whose major concern is financial profit.

11
Sports:
When Winning
Is the Only Thing,
Can Violence
Be Far Away?

Boys are influenced by sports as participants and spectators.

Outstanding athletes like Rickey Henderson, Joe Montana, Wayne Gretzky, and Magic Johnson serve as role models for millions of boys. But the influence of athletes is by no means limited to a few exceptional players. Starting in high school, boys who are good enough to make varsity teams, especially the football team, tend to be highly admired. For many of their peers, male and female, they represent the essence of masculinity. The same is true in college.

When it comes to music or film stars, there is often a generation gap in the taste of adolescents and their parents. But athletes get parents', especially fathers', stamp of approval. In fact, for many American fathers having a son who is neither interested in sports nor athletically inclined is little short of a tragedy.

Athletes also have society's approval and admiration. Many major sports events begin with the playing of our national anthem. The President, or a member of his family, opens the baseball season, and it has become a tradition for him to invite college and professional athletic champions to the White House.

By the time children are three or four years old, they watch about twenty-eight hours of TV a week. Most little boys watch sports on TV, and many are taken to games long before they participate in them. Their earliest image of what sports is all about comes from being spectators rather than participants.

The first part of this chapter focuses primarily on the influence of spectator sports on young boys. Spectator violence is also discussed. The second part focuses on youth sports and high school sports. It is followed by a section on football and foreign policy. The chapter ends with recommendations for changes to reduce sports violence and encourage pro-social behavior.

I limit myself to the most popular sports viewed by the largest audiences and played by large number of boys across the country: football, baseball, basketball, ice hockey, boxing. The major emphasis is on football because of its enormous popularity and high level of violence.

In his book *Violence and Sport,* Professor Michael D. Smith of Toronto's York University divides sports violence into four types:

Brutal Body Contact: This comprises acts of assault performed in accordance with the official rules of a sport: "Tackles, blocks, body checks, collisions, legal blows of all kinds"[1] are included. This kind of violence is inherent in sports such as football, boxing, ice hockey, and lacrosse; and to a lesser degree in games like basketball, soccer, and water polo. The game as officially defined cannot be played without it. Knocking your opponent unconscious is the goal of boxing. Tackling or blocking the members of the other team, which in ordinary English means knocking them down to the ground, is at the core of football.

Borderline Violence: This comprises assaults that are prohibited by the formal rules of a sport, but occur routinely. They are more or less accepted by officials, players, and fans. They include the hockey fistfight, late hitting in football, high tackling in soccer, the baseball brushback pitch, and basketball "body language." Referees and umpires sometimes penalize this kind of violence, but the penalties are not usually severe enough to deter. In theory, criminal statutes also apply; in practice, athletes are not prosecuted. So the violence often escalates.

Quasi-Criminal Violence: This frequently leads to serious injury and is usually brought to the attention of top officials. Penalties can range from suspensions to lifetime bans. Civil and criminal suits are becoming more common, but convictions are infrequent. One well-known case was that of Houston Rockets basketball player Rudy Tomjanovich, who was given a severe punch in the head by Kermit Washington of the Los Angeles Lakers during a 1977 game. Tomjanovich suffered a broken jaw and a fractured skull. He sued the Lakers, won, and eventually settled out of court.

Criminal Violence: This takes place before or after a game among fans. An example is the June 16, 1990, killing of eight people as part of the "celebration" in Detroit after the Pistons won the National Basketball Association Championship. One hundred and twenty-four people were treated at a hospital.

From the perspective of influencing young boys, brutal body contact and borderline violence are probably much more important than quasi-criminal and criminal violence. For while the latter are relatively rare and usually evoke outrage and punishment, body contact is intrinsic to the game and borderline violence is widely accepted as unavoidable.

The acceptance of body contact and borderline violence seems to be based on the idea that sports is an area of life in which it is permissible to suspend usual moral standards.

In a study of how college athletes think about morality and how their thinking relates to their moral judgments and behavior, Professor Brenda Jo Bredemeier of the University of California at Berkeley found that athletes commonly distinguish between game morality and the morality of everyday life. A male college basketball player says, "In sports you can do what you want. In life it's more restricted . . ."² A football player says, "The football field is the wrong place to think about ethics."³

Bredemeier expresses concern about the social implications of this lower moral standard in such an important and influential area. She points out that sports gives us a wealth of metaphors in other activities: the language of sports is often used in discussions of business, politics, and war.

Bredemeier voices concern over the influence of an ethical double standard on adult men, but the influence begins at a much earlier age.

ATHLETES AS ROLE MODELS

We know from research in psychology that young children tend to model their behavior and attitudes on those of adults, particularly adults they admire. Some professional athletes have described the role that their fathers' admiration of athletes played in developing their own interest in sports and their desire to become athletes. Michael Oriard, former Notre Dame and Kansas City Chiefs football player, now a professor of English literature, tells us that "from watching those Sunday football games with my father I learned . . . to associate football with masculinity. Those football players on the TV screen were ideal men, and my father who watched and enjoyed them was doing what a man did. Though my father was a nonathlete himself, the role model he projected included the importance of football."⁴ For boys who have little or no contact with their fathers, athletes may well seem like the most widely accepted and applauded male role models. Even Presidents admire them.

Imagine a young boy watching an ice hockey game. In addition to the pushing and shoving which are part of the game, it has become standard for hockey players to regularly hit each other with hockey sticks and get into fistfights.

"I went to a fight and a hockey game broke out" has become a stale joke. But how many boys, or adults, are aware that a majority of hockey players want to abolish this violence?

To spectators, hockey violence is presented as the kind of brawl that men naturally get into when they are in high-intensity competition. But Richard Lapchick, the director of Northeastern University's Center for the Study of Sport in Society, informs us that in recent years, at annual meetings of the National Hockey Players Association, a major issue has been violence, with players asking owners to impose much stiffer penalties (including expulsion) on those players who persist in violent behavior. Lapchick explains that there are a small number of hockey players who are genuinely violent—"There are eight or ten players in the league who are in fights every night. The Players Association wants those guys out of the League permanently."

But club owners refuse to discourage the violence, because it attracts spectators who come to see "red ice." Players who don't participate in the violence endanger their jobs. For example, when former Los Angeles Kings hockey player Paul Mulvey refused to participate in a fight between his team and the Vancouver Canucks, he was ordered off the team and immediately shipped to the minor leagues.[5]

Imagine a young boy watching football. Normally, running into someone with all your weight and force and knocking that person down with a good chance of injuring him is viewed as bodily assault and could subject a person to arrest. But in football this behavior is called tackling or blocking and is widely admired and respected. If a player can get away with late hitting or spearing—both of which are illegal—he will be considered particularly clever and adept. (Late hitting refers to a blow dealt after the referee's whistle has declared that a play is over. Spearing is when a player uses his head as a primary instrument to spear another player who is already on the ground. In an interview, former Patriots football player Keith Lee told me that he had seen "flagrant spearing" go unpunished on the football field: "Nothing's illegal unless you get caught. That's the rule.")

Dave Meggyesy played football for Syracuse University and the St. Louis Cardinals. He is now director of the West Coast Office of the National Football League Players Association. When I asked him how unnecessary football violence might be curtailed, he pointed to greater control of the game by players. "Most players . . . don't want to see a game where their lives are in jeopardy or they have to put other people's careers in jeopardy," he explained. That pressure ultimately comes from owners "who are into making profits."[6]

Why should football players increase the danger to their bodies? The game is intrinsically dangerous enough. Under present-day conditions three hundred thousand football-related injuries per year are treated nationwide in hospital emergency rooms. In the National Football League, an average of sixteen hundred players miss at least two games a year because of serious injuries.[7] A recent survey reveals that 78 percent of retired professional players suffer physical disabilities. The average life expectancy of a former professional football player is about fifty-six years.[8]

Injuries that to most of us would seem quite serious are routine. In his autobiography, *Out of Their League,* Dave Meggyesy points out that "one of the justifications for college football is that it is not only a character-builder, but a body-builder as well." As he sees it, "this is nonsense . . . Young men are having their bodies destroyed, not developed. As a matter of fact, few players can escape from college football without some form of permanent disability. During my four years I accumulated a broken wrist, separations of both shoulders, an ankle that was torn up so badly it broke the arch of my foot, three major brain concussions, and an arm that almost had to be amputated because of improper treatment. And I was one of the lucky ones."[9]

When Jim Otto, a former center for the Oakland Raiders, appeared on a January 29, 1988, "20/20" program dealing with football injuries, viewers were informed that he "had one knee replaced three times and is about to get an artificial knee for his other leg as well. He's also broken his nose more than twenty-five times." Lynn Sherr then asked Otto, "In all, what was broken?" Otto: "Well, my nose, my jaw. I had both elbows operated on because I tore up the bursas in both elbows, knee surgeries, broken ribs, naturally, I've had back surgery . . . I think I've had sixteen, sixteen surgeries."

In football as in hockey there are some brutally violent men. Too often other players are pressured to emulate their behavior. If a football player refuses to "take players out" (i.e., to injure an opponent so badly that he cannot finish the game), or to play while injured, there are plenty of others who won't refuse and are waiting to take his job. And so a game that is intrinsically violent is rendered even more violent.

But to a young boy it all seems natural. Little does he know that the extreme violence he sees often grows more out of the owners' commercial interests than players' inclinations.

Some of this violence—such as brawls between teams—does not appear to be orchestrated by coaches or owners, however. In the case of collegiate sports it often causes embarrassment to school officials. The recent increase in brawls and fistfights may be due in part to the general escalation of violence in our society. Athletes with violent inclinations will tend to feel less social restraint on acting them out. Once they do, it becomes unmanly for their opponents not to respond in kind.

The prevalent view in the United States is that violent sports operate as a catharsis, allowing athletes and spectators to release hostile, aggressive energy in a relatively harmless way, thus cutting down crime, domestic violence, or warfare. Research reveals that the facts are actually quite the reverse.

An exhaustive study of heavyweight prizefights held between 1973 and 1978 and subsequent homicide statistics revealed that U.S. homicides increased by 12.46 percent directly after heavyweight championship prizefights. The increase was greatest after heavily publicized prizefights.[10]

A study of ten relatively warlike and ten relatively peaceful societies revealed that in most of the warlike societies young men engaged in combative sports. In the more peaceful societies such sports were rare.[11] (Boxing and football are examples of combative sports in our society.)

As we shall see in the next chapter, these negative findings with respect to the catharsis hypothesis receive considerable confirmation from TV and film research. Watching violence on the screen encourages violent behavior.

A boy who watches acts of violence committed by thieves, murderers, or sadists in films or on TV knows that society disapproves of these acts. The boy who watches sports knows that athletes' acts of violence are approved of. It makes sense that sports violence would serve as an important role model for boys who tend to be well adjusted socially, while illegal violence on the screen would tend to have a greater influence on the behavior of boys who are more psychologically damaged and/or feel more alienated from society.

Because of the respectability of sport, its language and values permeate other areas of legitimate male endeavor.

When New York University professor Martin Hoffman analyzed studies comparing the moral attitudes and behavior of
men and women, he found that the women (who as children
participate in contact sports far less than do men and watch less
sports both as children and adults) were more concerned with
fairness, honesty, and helping others than the men.[12]

There are causes other than sports participation that may
explain this discrepancy. Hoffman focuses on the fact that boys
more than girls are socialized for egoistic achievement and success. But sports play a major role in reinforcing the concern with
success, winning, and dominance. On the sports field these
goals *alone* justify illegal and violent acts.

What can we do to change this situation, to curtail the violence
in college and professional sports that boys grow up watching?

When it comes to borderline violence, a bill written by Minnesota State Senator Todd Otis, a former college hockey player,
points us in the right direction. The bill would have required a
hockey team owner to pay a ten-thousand-dollar fine for each
fighting penalty imposed by the referee on a player from that
team. A law of this kind would lead to the elimination from the
game of that small group of individuals who cannot or do not
want to control their violent behavior.

Hockey is by no means the only sport in need of such regulation.

Brawls and fistfights occur frequently in many contact sports,
including baseball, basketball, and football, both professional
and collegiate. Typical was the fight I saw recently on TV sports
news: After the pitcher intentionally hit the batter, subsequent
to a collision at home plate, baseball players from the University
of Oklahoma and Oklahoma State got into a huge brawl.

There is no reason why colleges should be excluded from
state fines. In the case of state universities, the withdrawal of
some state funds might coerce universities who make money off
big-time sports to exercise the moral and social responsibility
that one expects of them but sees too rarely.

In the spring of 1988 the National Collegiate Athletic Association Basketball Rules Committee toughened its penalties for
fighting. This is a step in the right direction. The formation of
the NCAA Presidents' Commission in order to provide some

direction from college presidents to intercollegiate athletics is another. But so far the Commission has done little if anything about college sports violence.

Representative Otis withdrew the bill described above before it came up for a vote in the Minnesota State Senate. He substituted a softer bill requiring only that owners make an effort to stop the violence. He withdrew the original bill not because he thought there was anything wrong with it, but because he knew that it had no chance of passing. He told me that if the present bill has no effect, he plans to reintroduce the stronger bill at a later date.

Violence is still so acceptable within the sports culture that antiviolence bills have very little chance of passing at any governmental level. When Boston's Mayor Ray Flynn, a former college basketball player, wanted to prosecute violent hockey players for assault, he was voted down by the Boston City Council.

At present these kinds of bills serve mainly as consciousness raisers. But as more men begin to take steps away from the values of the masculine mystique, concerned and courageous political leaders will stand a much better chance of getting legislation enacted.

Legislation represents our best hope of curtailing borderline violence. This would change the atmosphere of sports; quasi-criminal and criminal violence would become less frequent. In light of athletes short-lived careers, and the fierce competition to get on professional teams, it seems unlikely that professional sports associations will be able to get owners to agree to curtail the violence.

But what about intrinsic violence, what Smith calls brutal body contact?

The two sports which cause the most concern in the respect are football and boxing.

The American Medical Association, the American Neurological Association, and the American Academy for Neurology are a few of the medical groups in the United States that have joined with the World Medical Association and medical associations in other countries to call for the banning of boxing, both professional and amateur. As physicians dedicated to preserving life, they reject boxing as being dedicated to destroying the opponent's brain. They point to the prevalence of "punch-drunken-ness" and other neurological disturbances among boxers. In a 1986 article George D. Lundberg, M.D., states that it is the "high frequency of chronic brain damage (60% to 87%) among boxers who have had many fights that sets boxing apart medically."[13]

From the perspective of societal violence, the problem with boxing is the legitimizing of clear-cut physical assault.

Imagine a young boy watching boxing matches. The message is clear: punching someone and knocking him unconscious are acceptable, even admirable goals under certain circumstances. The men who are exceptionally good at it are national heroes like Muhammed Ali or Mike Tyson.

The argument that boxing should be permitted because it gives poor minority males, who represent a large percentage of boxers, a chance to move up in the world is a very weak one. Rates of violence in our inner-city ghettos are extraordinarily high. Boxers as role models further legitimize the use of violence. Besides, as New York University professor Jeffrey Sammons, an African-American historian and boxing expert, points out, the idea that boxing is a way out of the ghetto is false for a vast majority of boxers. Only a tiny percent derive any long-term profit from boxing; many are injured. (The odds of any amateur athlete making it to the professional level are one in twelve thousand.)

Given present-day alternatives, a young boy's involvement in a Police Athletic League boxing program certainly seems more desirable than his involvement in crime and drugs. But even here Sammons has serious doubts. He says, "Those who argue that boxing keeps young men off the street, out of crime, and away from drugs—a questionable argument at best—are not praising a sport but signaling a dismal failure of the American dream for many. For there is little difference between what boxing supposedly helps them to avoid and the tragic option the sport represents."[14]

Boxing, as we know it, should be banned. George Lundberg points out that we no longer allow dueling with sharp swords and with intent to injure or kill, but we do permit fencing as a sport in which dexterity is developed and measured electronically. The same could be done with boxing, which requires considerable dexterity, agility, and other skills. But without the violence, boxing would undoubtedly die out as a spectator sport. That is as it should be.

What about football? If the idea of banning boxing is invariably met with cries of dismay in some quarters, the idea of banning football would in many parts of this country be seen as nothing short of sacrilegious.

When CBS's "60 Minutes" sent Morley Safer to Texas to do a program on junior high and high school football (aired on January 11, 1981), he was told by seventh-grade coach Don Clapp that football is "almost like going to church . . . you do that on Sunday, you play football on Friday nights. It's always been here, and it's been big and it's getting bigger."

Safer concluded that "in this part of Texas and a half a dozen other states, junior high school football is the standard by which both man and boy are judged," and "one thing is certain, football in these parts is much more than football. It ranks up there with academics and is really much closer to a kind of theology."

The major focus of Safer's investigation was the "holdback" phenomenon. "Holdbacks" are boys who are held back in eighth grade at their parents' request so that they will be bigger and better at football by the time they get to high school. The motivating fantasy is often getting a college football scholarship and then making it to the professional leagues.

While football may be akin to religion in some states, throughout the United States it is deeply tied to nationalism, patriotism, and zeal about sending our boys to war.

In his book *Sports in America*, James Michener reminisces about a football game he attended in 1972 "at which a squad of marines, assisted by an army band, raised the flag at the start," and together with Boy Scouts, National Guardsmen and clergymen "assembled at midfield during half time . . . to honor America's participation in the Vietnam war."[15]

Michener also points out that football is the only sport in which players are often led in prayer and blessed by clergymen before games. Many NFL teams carry their own chaplain.

This connection between football, religion, and patriotism, as well as the enormous financial interest of colleges, team owners, and connected enterprises in its continued existence, make the notion of banning football politically unthinkable in any near future.

The growing insurance problems that surround the game offer some hope. Harry E. Figgie, Jr., is the chairman of the company that owns Rawlings Sporting Goods. In an October 9, 1988, *New York Times* op-ed piece he warns that "football may be an endangered American sport." It could be "gaveled into extinction" by injured players' lawsuits. By 1986 the cost of insuring his company against helmet-related lawsuits had rendered the production of football helmets unprofitable. In 1988 the company announced that it would no longer manufacture them. Figgie tells us that school systems, universities, coaches, and medical personnel are also increasingly being sued. As a result some school districts are no longer offering football programs.

Unless economic pressures force the abandonment of large numbers of football programs, I can only see the sport dwindling or withering away as a result of the kinds of changes recommended in this book. As the concept of masculinity moves away from obsessive competitiveness, dominance, and toughness, and comes to include empathy, nurturant fathering, and willingness to expose one's vulnerabilities, football will become less and less attractive to young boys and their parents. Some regulations which would help this happen will be discussed in the section below on youth and high school sports.

Until we as a nation outgrow football, the best we can do is to pass legislation banning borderline violence in all sports.

VIOLENCE IN THE STANDS

Physical violence and the use of foul or abusive language have become so common among spectators in all contact sports that some adults are reluctant to take children to games.

Sports Illustrated took an "unscientific poll of fans" and reported in its August 8, 1988 issue that *"everyone* who had ever been a spectator at a sporting event of any kind had, at one time or another, experienced the bellowing of obscenities, racial or religious epithets . . . abusive sexual remarks to women in the vicinity, fistfights between strangers and fistfights between friends."[16]

Increased spectator violence is one more manifestation of the escalation of violence which has taken place in American society in the last twenty-odd years. Violence between athletes can only serve to encourage it.

Another factor contributing to this behavior, according to experts, is beer. In that same issue of *Sports Illustrated* the cover story was devoted to problems resulting from the fact that "beer and sport have come to be as inseparable in the American lexicon as mom and apple pie."[17] The article describes how a few months earlier "baseball fans produced one of the sport's most memorable mass temper tantrums,"[18] turning Riverfront Stadium in Cincinnati into a garbage dump and forcing an umpire to flee the field. At least part of the blame is placed on enormous beer consumption.

The traditional connection between sports and beer has grown considerably stronger as beer companies have become some of the largest advertisers on TV sports events. A study carried out under the auspices of the American Automobile Association revealed that from the age of two to eighteen, when social learning is most pronounced, American children see approximately 100,000 television beer commercials.

Banning beer commercials from TV, just as cigarette commercials have been banned, would be one way to decrease the connection between sport events and beer.

In an effort to curtail verbal and physical violence some stadiums have set aside small areas, usually 5 percent, for nondrinkers. Some stadiums try to regulate beer drinking by stopping sales after a certain point in the game, limiting the number of beers bought by each customer, or using smaller cups. Richard Lapchick and Keith Lee both of Northeastern's Center for the Study of Sport in Society, are convinced that such measures are insufficient to deal with the problem. They favor total bans on beer drinking at sports events.

Besides restrictions on beer, some stadiums have enforced a behavior code. The Milwaukee County Stadium has such a code. "People from Milwaukee know that if they're out of order they'll be caught and ejected promptly," explains manager Bill Hanrahan. As a result "they act better here than at some other stadiums."[19]

YOUTH AND HIGH SCHOOL SPORTS:
"JUST LIKE THE GAME OF LIFE"

Thirty million school-age children are involved in youth sports in the United States. They play twenty-five different sports under the direction of 4.5 million coaches and 1.5 million administrators.[20] Four-year-olds play in Midget Hockey leagues. There are national mini-bike championships for six-year-olds.

Among the most popular youth leagues are Pop Warner Junior League Football for boys eight years and up, and Little League Baseball for boys six years and up. As the result of a successful lawsuit, girls have been allowed to play Little League Baseball since 1974, but most teams are still exclusively male.

Little League is the largest youth sports organization. It was created in 1939 by Carl Stotz, a Pennsylvania lumber company employee. By 1955, Stotz, who did not want the organization turned into a large corporation, was removed from his post as commissioner. He has since described Little League as a "Frankenstein" monster because of its commercialism.

Sociology professor Gary Alan Fine, in *With the Boys,* a study of Little League Baseball, tells us that private, community youth leagues came into being in part because professional recreation directors and educators in the 1930s were convinced that highly competitive sports were harmful to preadolescent development. They refrained from developing professionally directed programs.

There is nothing intrinsically wrong with adult-organized sports programs for young boys. At a time when so many parents both work outside the home, and there are so many single mothers, a seemingly healthy supervised outdoor activity must seem like a blessing to many parents.

It is only when these programs place inordinate emphasis on competition and winning that they become detrimental.* There

* Former athletes are often particularly critical of youth sports. Dave Meggyesy told me that Pop Warner football is "too dangerous; their [boys'] bones haven't grown yet; they're just teaching boys to smack into each other with equipment." In his book *Baseball and Your Boy,* former Cleveland Indians player Al Rosen deplores the fact that some Little League coaches risk serious injury to youngsters' arms by encouraging them to throw curveballs. In *Sports in America,* James Michener reports that many professional athletes

are undoubtedly youth sports programs across the country that emphasize fun and sportsmanship under the guidance of qualified coaches. But, as recreation and education professionals feared in the 1930s, the creation of private sports leagues has often led to extremely competitive programs for very young children.

Richard Lapchick warns that "most youth sport coaches lack even rudimentary knowledge of the emotional, psychological, social and physical needs of children."[21]

A theme that many athletes get back to again and again is the enormous importance of the coach for a young boy. Meggyesy writes about "the father-son relationship that is football's cornerstone."[22] Michael Oriard tells us, "From the fourth grade into my first year as a professional, I was to look to my coaches as figures of wisdom and authority whose pronouncements were gospel and whose expectations of me were to be met at whatever cost."[23] In a study of elite youth hockey and soccer programs, researcher Gai Berlage found that coaches were universally accepted as authority figures. This deep emotional relationship and respect for the coach's authority facilitates players' transference of moral responsibility from themselves to the coach.

The enormous influence of the coach is not limited to the sports field. "Character building" is commonly given as an important positive effect of playing contact sports. In discussing his high school football experience, Meggyesy tells us that "football represents the core values of the status quo, and coaches and school administrators want players to win adherents to these values, not only on the football field but also in their private lives."[24]

David Blankenhorn, the director of the Institute for American Values, played football for his high school in Jackson, Mississippi. In an interview with the author, he expressed his conviction that a core idea transmitted by football coaches and fathers is that "playing the game is just like the game of life. The rules you learn will stand you in good stead for the rest of your life."

Some of the rules that are emphasized sound good—team-

---

have told him they would not allow their sons to enter Little League until relatively late childhood.

work, sacrifice for the common good, never giving up, giving 110 percent of yourself—and in the hands of sensitive, knowledgeable, well-trained coaches they can be used to teach boys valuable habits. But such coaches are far from the rule. Michael Oriard provides us with vignettes of high school coaches whose understanding of what football is all about is, to put it mildly, problematic. There is the Texas coach who had students listen to "hypnotic tape recordings" that whispered, "when you're playing on that football field you have such aggressiveness it's absolutely unreal." There is the Wisconsin coach who after each game would give a "Hit of the Week" award for the most vicious hit he could find on the game film. An Iowa coach "spray-painted a chicken gold to represent the 'Golden Eagles' of a rival team, then threw it onto the field to be kicked around by his players. 'Get the eagle' was the name of the game."[25]

These are extreme examples. The following anecdotes are no doubt more typical. Fred Engh, the founder and president of the National Youth Sports Coach Association, describes his nine-year-old son coming home from playing baseball on a very hot July day in Indiana "looking in the dumps." When Engh asked what the matter was, the boy told him that the coach had decided that "nobody gets a drink of water until we score a run." "We didn't score a run until the fifth inning," his son explained. The boys were all thirsty and mad and "it just wasn't any fun even when we won."[26]

When "60 Minutes" did a program on youth football they found that the emphasis was very much on winning. The boys on one Hollywood, Florida, team analyzed game films; coaches sent plays in to the boys via headset communication. Detailed statistics were kept on each play. When Mike Wallace asked one of the boys whether he was ever scared when he went into a ball game, he replied yes. "Scared of losing." At the end of the season each player on the team was presented with a scroll containing some thoughts of that renowned coach, the late Vince Lombardi. "There is no room for second place," he states. "I have finished second twice in my time at Green Bay, and I don't ever want to finish second again. There is a second-place bowl game, but it's a game for losers played by losers. It is and always has been an American zeal to be first in anything we do, and to win and to win and to win."

The findings of academic researchers and writers like James Michener indicate that the obsession with winning is far from infrequent in youth and high school sports. After describing and deploring the extreme competitiveness of many junior football leagues, Michener quotes from some of their badges, which contain yells for the rooters. They include: Massacre the Braves, Mangle the Matadors, Destroy the Blue Devils, Slay the Aces. He comments that "after a steady diet of this from age eight through sixteen, it would seem that the boys could only escalate to machine-gunning the opposition high school, atom-bombing Notre Dame and hydrogen-bombing the Dallas Cowboys."[27]

Gary Fine points out that in Little League Baseball, at the beginning of the season coaches often play down the importance of their team's win-loss record and emphasize moral factors. But these statements are often very different from the conduct of the coaches. Eventually, "integrity takes a backseat to the pragmatic concern of *winning* baseball games. Players learn that integrity is a rhetorical strategy one should raise only in certain times and places. The adults involved with Little League tend to be oriented toward winning, losing, and competition."[28]

In keeping with this major emphasis on being number one, Fine describes the "rhetoric of toughness" that some of the boys use. He attributes their attitude at least in part to learning from adult athletes. One boy was depicted by his teammates, with some pride, as "a real kamikaze on the basepaths" because he specialized in "taking out" opposing fielders, even when this was not entirely necessary. Another boy yelled out to a teammate who had just been hit by a pitch, "Do what Rod Carew [of the Minnesota Twins] did." When Fine asked him what that was, he replied, "When he got beaned in the back, he smacked the pitcher."[29]

Fine assures us that the boys' behavior does not usually reflect this callous talk. Their interest in the game goes far beyond winning at any cost. For example, a coach insisted in an important game that players not swing at pitches, hoping that the opposing pitcher would tire and become wild. The team won the game and the league championship, but the players were annoyed. They "were unhappy and were unanimous in telling me that they wanted to swing, even though they had just won the game."[30]

This anecdote captures one of the major gripes that many boys have with organized sports both at the youth and high school levels. The emphasis on winning deprives them of the pleasure of playing the game. Instead of giving everyone the opportunity to play, coaches leave perfectly decent players sitting on the bench watching top players win games for the team. It is not surprising that American children are among the least physically fit of those in any industrialized democracy. Instead of focusing on enjoying sports, reaping physical benefits, and instilling a lifelong involvement in athletics, too many of our sports programs are geared exclusively toward winning.

Sociology professor Jonathan Brower spent ten months following twenty-eight teams in playground baseball leagues. He found it to be a pressure-packed environment, especially difficult for the boys who were not good athletes and were trying to please their managers and parents. Brower describes one father who proudly told a friend, "My kid doesn't care about sportsmanship. He says winning is what's important."[31]

This obsession with competitiveness and winning was far more pronounced among managers and coaches than players. When kids wanted to help other teams, adult leaders dissuaded them from assisting boys who might later be their opponents for the league championship.

Reluctant boys are often pressured to play by fathers who won't hear of the boys' quitting, and expect them to excel. In an article on the emotional repercussions of childhood sports, Bill Bruns and Tom Tutko of San Jose State University report being told by boys "that they purposely played poorly because they wanted to be thrown off the team; they couldn't take the conflict with their fathers any longer."[32]

Richard Lapchick told me about the first time he went to see his twelve-year-old son play ice hockey. The boy's team lost the game by five to four. After the game, in the locker room, one of the fathers came in, picked his son off the bench in front of his contemporaries and screamed at him: "You fucking son of a bitch; if you'd hit that guy against the wall you wouldn't have lost this game."

While youth sports do not involve much borderline violence, the language and attitudes developed serve as preludes to high school contact sports. There, especially in football, borderline violence is often encouraged.

In an interview, University of New Haven sociology professor Allen Sack reminisced about his experience playing high school football: "The coaches thought it was correct to use techniques of pushing, yelling, dehumanizing" the opposing team. "The way I was coached was destroy the bastards . . . punish people, take people out."[33]

To play the game as violently as this, boys must learn to repress empathy. They work hard at it.

Dave Meggyesy tells us that already in high school "the business of setting up a dividing line between us and our opponents went on the whole week before a game. [Coach] Vogt would call Chagrin Falls, our big rival, 'the boys from across the river,' and Mayfield was a team of 'dumb but tough Wops.' . . . We were really fired up and felt we were going to annihilate 'them.' I particularly didn't want to see their faces, because the more anonymous they were the better it was for me . . . They were a faceless enemy we had to meet."[34]

Sociology professor Michael Messner reports on an interview with former Oakland Raiders football player Jack Tatum, whose fierce, violent "hits"—one of which broke Darryl Stingley's neck and left him a paraplegic—led to his being known as "The Assassin." Tatum told Messner, "When I first started playing, if I would hit a guy hard and he wouldn't get up, it would bother me. [But] when I was a sophomore in high school, first game, I knocked out two quarterbacks, and people loved it. The coach loved it. Everybody loved it . . ."[35]

By the time they play college and professional football, players have received so much reinforcement for concerns with dominance, for playing as violently as they can, that empathy has been largely conquered. Michael Oriard provides us with a perceptive description of playing at Notre Dame. "On play after play I rammed my shoulder and forearm into the shoulders and headgear of the man trying to block me . . . I wanted him to feel an ache at ten o'clock that night and think, 'That sonuva-bitch Oriard.' . . . I wanted physically to dominate the offensive players attempting to block me. I wanted to feel contempt for their inability to do so, and satisfaction in knowing I was tougher than they were." He then comments, "I could not have continued to maul someone I had come to *know*—even if only a little. But I did not know them."[36]

Former Canadian Football League player John McMurtry, now a professor of philosophy, writes that "the truly professional attitude is not to think of the opponent as a human being at all—he is a 'position' to be removed as efficiently as possible in order to benefit the team's corporate enterprise of gaining points."[37]

It seems that many of the men who succeed in repressing empathy on the football field do so by "doubling"—a psychological process that psychiatrist Robert J. Lifton describes as compartmentalizing the self. They split up into a "personal life self" and a "football self."

In 1983 Ron Rivera, then a linebacker with the University of California at Berkeley, described the difference in these terms: While the off-field Ron is soft-spoken, considerate, and friendly, the on-field Ron is "totally opposite from me . . . He's a madman . . . No matter what happens, he hits people . . . I'm mean and nasty then . . . I have a total disrespect for the guy I'm going to hit."[38]

In interviewing three former football players—two professional and one collegiate—I could not help being struck by their decency, helpfulness, friendliness. Clearly when these men had been on the field, they had become different; they had doubled.

Doubling is facilitated by the legitimacy of the game and the undisputed authority of the coach. Players are just doing what is expected of them by the coach and the public. The moral responsibility for their actions is transferred to the coach and other authority figures.

Learning to endure pain and play with it without complaining, learning to conquer and hide fear, are further conditions of playing football. In his autobiography, Meggyesy tells of being shot up with novocaine for a high school game after he had injured his neck so badly during a drill that he couldn't move his head. Oriard describes his experiences in a game played when he was in fifth grade. When confronted with "repeatedly having to tackle one of the biggest kids in the school . . . I was afraid of him, but my greater fear was to show my fear . . . By not quitting and not flinching from contact I proved my 'courage' to myself . . ."[39]

Keith Lee, who is now associate director of Northeastern University's Center for the Study of Sport in Society, started playing junior league football at age nine and went on to play in high school, in college, and with the New England Patriots. He puts it this way: "You're afraid of getting hit in the knees, of having the wind knocked out of you, but you don't tell your buddies, only you know. You come through the crisis . . . and you feel good about yourself, that you conquered your own fear."[40]

Life is filled with difficulty, danger, and suffering. The reader may wonder what is wrong with teaching boys and men to overcome their fears, to be courageous, to withstand pain.

There is nothing wrong with it. But when a high school football player is shot up with novocaine in order to play, when he plays with injuries that if aggravated could lead to permanent damage, he is learning much more than to withstand pain. *He is learning to sacrifice his body unnecessarily and to hide all feelings of fear and vulnerability, however warranted they may be. He is also being taught to sacrifice the bodies of others.* For if he is willing to risk serious injury to himself, then why shouldn't he be willing to risk injuring others seriously? If he is not allowed to feel sympathy for himself when he is injured or justifiably frightened, why should he feel empathy for anyone else?

When boys have to hide all feelings of fear and vulnerability in order to be accepted as "real men," they are learning to take unnecessary risks that will endanger their and others' health and lives. These lessons learned at an early age can lead to driving cars at ninety miles an hour, enthusiastically going off to unnecessary wars, or sending others off to war.

Males from ages fifteen to twenty-four experience 96.7 accidental deaths per 100,000. Females in that age group experience 26.1 accidental deaths per 100,000. Eighty percent of all spinal cord injuries in the United States occur in males.[41]

Aristotle, in his theory of the golden mean, argued that human dispositions can suffer from excess or lack. A person who is unwilling to risk life or injury even when that sacrifice is justified is a coward. A person who is willing to risk life or injury when that sacrifice is not justified is foolhardy. True courage involves taking risks at the right time, in the right place, for the right reason.

The sacrifice of young boys to the gods of football, car racing, or military adventurism represents foolhardiness, not courage. Their willingness to sacrifice themselves has everything to do with proving manhood.

Dave Meggyesy describes how on one occasion his coach accused him of being afraid and told him that he had looked "almost feminine" in making a tackle. Meggyesy comments that "this sort of attack on a player's manhood is a coach's doomsday weapon. And it almost always works, for the players have wrapped up their identity in their masculinity, which is eternally precarious for it not only depends on not exhibiting fear of any kind on the playing field, but is also something that can be given and withdrawn by a coach at his pleasure."[42]

The language of sport is filled with insults suggesting that a boy who is not tough enough, who does not live up to the masculine mystique, is really a girl or homosexual.

Football player David Kopay writes of his high school coach that "like many other coaches, Dillingham [fictitious name] used sexual slurs —'fag,' 'queer,' 'sissy,' 'pussy'—to motivate (or intimidate) his young athletes."[43]

Gary Fine reports on the frequent use of this kind of language in Little League. Boys use expressions like "You're a faggot" or "God, he's gay." One eleven-year-old says of another that he "takes birth [control] pills" (i.e., he is a girl). The term "wuss"— a combination of "woman" and "pussy"—is also used as an insult. Fine tells us that *each insult means that the target has not lived up to expectations of appropriate male behavior,* and is being sanctioned [my emphasis]."[44]

In a May 16, 1988, *New York Times* article, Ira Berkow reports that Indiana University basketball coach Bobby Knight was known to "put a box of sanitary napkins in the locker of one of his players so that the player would get the point that Knight considered him less than masculine."

The significance and influence of this type of thinking, talking, and acting on the psyche of young boys can perhaps be best understood if one imagines a reversal. Imagine girls from age six on involved in a communal activity so highly respected that the President of our country plays a role in launching it each year. Those women who are most proficient at this activity are regularly invited to the White House for celebrations and serve as important role models for girls. When they are involved in this activity, little girls and later women constantly use terms and expressions like "boy," "mock" (combination of "man" and "cock"), "dyke," or "You wear a jockstrap," to embarrass and insult each other. Imagine a respected and admired female leader of these activities putting a jockstrap in a girl's closet or locker in order to insult her.

We are so accustomed to women and homosexuals being denigrated that we must do this reversal in order to appreciate fully how much such attitudes encourage disrespect and contempt for women and homosexual men. How many fathers would stand for their daughters' talking like this? But many mothers accept their sons' denigration of women as part of being a "real boy." Surely it is no accident that Bobby Knight, who puts sanitary napkins in basketball players' lockers in order to insult them, has also commented on TV that if a woman can't do anything about rape, she may as well lie back and enjoy it.

As we have seen, it starts much earlier, but from high school on, the concern with dominance, winning, and manhood rather than just enjoying the sport becomes close to all-pervasive. Football in particular affords boys a legitimate opportunity to deal with the self-doubts and insecurities of adolescence by asserting their physical dominance over others. "I loved to dominate my opponents physically in a public arena. Such dominance was a salve for the many wounds my adolescent ego received during my high school years," writes Michael Oriard.[45] If one combines this early reinforcement of physical dominance with the ongoing expression of contempt for girls and women, one can see how the end product, for some of the more angry or disturbed players, may be rape. Some preliminary studies indicate that athletes may well be overrepresented in college sexual assaults. In a study of twenty-four cases of campus gang rape, discussed in her forthcoming book *Nice Boys, Dirty Deeds*, psychologist Chris O'Sullivan found that nine of them were by athletes. *Philadelphia Daily News* sportswriter Rich Hoffman carried out an investigation of sexual assaults on college campuses which included interviewing over 150 campus police departments. In a March 17, 1986, article, he informs us that in the fifty reported incidences brought to his attention, football and basketball players were overrepresented by 38 percent.

Concealing rapes committed by football players has been one of the traditional tasks of many university sports departments, a task that has become more difficult as a result of the women's movement.

In 1976 James Michener wrote: "Many big-time schools designate one coach or faculty member to protect the young athlete from the law . . . Not surprisingly, several of our most famous universities have found themselves involved in ugly scandals when whole segments of a team have engaged in gang-rape, a jovial collegiate version of *jus primae noctis* in which the football hero expects to be accorded seignorial rights while the local sheriff stands guard."[46]

FOOTBALL, SOCIAL STRATIFICATION, FOREIGN POLICY, AND WAR

Professor Allen Sack grew up in a working-class South Philadelphia neighborhood where he played high school football. His son now attends a prep school where he also plays football. In an interview, Sack contrasted his experience with that of his son to illustrate the social stratification of sports in America. His son is not taught to "sacrifice his body," "to take people out," as he was. His son's coach doesn't shout, berate, or abuse the boys as his coach did. He doesn't encourage them to push, yell, and dehumanize members of opposing teams.

Lower-class boys, Sack explains, are expected to "sacrifice their bodies" more than upper-class boys. At the college level there are two different types of sport. There is the "Ivy League model," which is a tough game but is devoid of most excessive violence. Such violence is taken for granted at Midwestern and other colleges where football is highly commercialized. Boxing, which demands the most obvious sacrificing of one's body, has traditionally been limited almost entirely to very poor boys. Michael Smith tells us that "the most violent brand of hockey . . . recruits the greatest proportion . . . of working- and lower-class players."[47]

It is not only in sports that lower-class men are more likely to "sacrifice their bodies" than upper-class men: there is a tendency for them to be overrepresented on the battlefield as well. This was true in the Vietnam and Korean wars, in which large numbers of college students received deferments. But even in the Revolutionary War, we are informed, "the human clay of combat was fairly modest stuff . . . drawn mainly from the poorest class of whites . . . Slave owners never lacked for substitutes to send to the Militia."[48]

For men of all social classes, involvement in war is proof of manhood. The fearlessness, the toughness, the concern with dominance that were reinforced in the sports arena in both players and spectators find further expression in the military.* The abdication of personal moral responsibility in favor of obedience to superiors is particularly valuable.

But many upper-class men are able to achieve dominance through wealth and prestigious positions. Their money and power win them respect and desirable women. They do not have as great a need to sacrifice their own bodies or those of their sons, whether in war or in sport, in order to prove their manhood.

For men at the bottom of the social hierarchy it is far more difficult to achieve dominance and win respect. At work they are usually subordinate to others. Regardless of how essential their work may be to society, it does not win them widespread admiration, respect, or large salaries. These men are more likely to prove their manhood through physical dominance. Dominance over other men can be achieved in war, through gang warfare or other forms of more random fighting, or in competitive and often violent sports. Dominance over women and children can be assured through wife- and child-battering. While rape, and child- and wife-battering, are serious problems among all social classes, they are more pronounced among the lower classes.

For upper-class men, sports experience both as players and as spectators often translates into a tough, unempathic win/lose, us/them outlook that includes the willingness to sacrifice *other*

* The reinforcement works in both directions. Oriard tells us that at Notre Dame "on Friday nights before games, the entire team convened . . . for a . . . John Wayne movie. Usually the Duke himself was in the film, but even if he was not, it was still always a 'John Wayne movie.' . . . We invariably spent the nights before games watching good guys killing bad guys . . . What better psychic preparation for facing the hated Boilermakers—or even Illini—the next day."[49]

men's bodies and lives in wars. As we saw in Chapter 2, sports language and analogies are frequently used in the areas of military and foreign policy.

In foreign policy, as in football, anything that smacks of empathy, concern with moral issues, or aversion to violence is rejected as feminine. In terms of underlying attitude, President Johnson's dismissal of an advisor who was opposed to escalating the war in Vietnam with the comment "Hell, he has to squat to piss," is not that different from Bobby Knight's putting sanitary napkins in a player's locker to let him know he's a wimp.

Athletes in contact sports, especially football players, are expected to fight in response to any act on the part of the opposing team that could possibly be interpreted as aggressive. Allen Sack remembers instances both in high school and at Notre Dame of being hit a little late, after the whistle had blown, and knowing that the hit was unintentional: the opposing player couldn't control his momentum. But since the coach and players had seen it happen, he had to hit back and get into a fight.

This enormous concern with appearing strong, with proving a readiness to fight regardless of the cost and regardless of whether it is really necessary, is reminiscent of the attitude of American leaders described in the *New York Times* article entitled "War: Bush's Presidential Rite of Passage" discussed in Chapter 2. The article points out that American leaders since World War II have "felt a need to demonstrate their willingness to shed blood." They all believed that American political culture necessitated their showing the world that "they carried big sticks."

Dave Meggyesy says that in pro football the coaches' message is: "If you're going to make a mistake, make an aggressive one."[50] He tells how he "went crazy" with aggression in a game against Green Bay, but also made some big mistakes. Nevertheless, the Cardinals were so impressed with his aggressiveness that they started him as left linebacker in the next four games.

This resembles Richard Barnet's descriptions of generals and politicians who make horrendous errors and are rewarded as long as the errors consist of using excessive violence. But military men and politicians, however correct they may be, jeopardize their careers if they harbor moral scruples and show any reluctance to use violence.

There is much to be concerned about when many boys' most

admired and socially approved role models are dedicated to an ethic of "winning is the only thing" and "anything goes" in the game. There is further reason for concern when boys participating in youth and high school sports are frequently encouraged to emulate these values.

But the greatest concern of all is when boys become adult men and bring the language, attitudes, and values of sports to the governance of our nation. In 1973 then Vice President Spiro Agnew was the speaker at the annual Pop Warner Junior League Football national banquet. He praised the lessons learned in Junior League Football: "Football as we know it is a uniquely American game, emphasizing some of the finest aspects of our national character. We are a competitive people, and it is the spirit of competition which has made our economic system the envy of the world. It's the competitive spirit among the young that causes excellence in adult life . . ."[51]

It is the competitive spirit tempered by empathy, moral concern, and a sense of social responsibility that causes long-lasting excellence and brings benefits to the community at large. Shortly after giving this speech, Agnew was forced to resign the vice presidency because it was revealed that as governor of Maryland he had accepted bribes.

CREATING SPORTS PROGRAMS
THAT *REALLY* TEACH PRO-SOCIAL VALUES

Football was introduced to the United States in the second half of the nineteenth century. By 1905 football violence had reached such crisis proportions that President Theodore Roosevelt ordered representatives from thirteen colleges to the White House to deal with the killing of batches of young college men each season. The meeting led to changes in rules—the flying wedge was outlawed, the forward pass legalized—as well as the formation of the National Collegiate Athletic Association.[52]

We have reached another crisis point today.* What can we do

---

* Contributing to this crisis is TV, which introduces violent athletes as role models to very young boys and often focuses attention on the violence in sports. Also, as we have seen, the commercialization of youth sports introduces boys to inappropriately competitive sports at an early age. Both as players and as spectators, boys are learning all the wrong lessons.

in youth and high school sports to curtail violence, excessive concerns with winning and dominance, and the denigration of women and homosexuals?

Day care centers and nursery schools are licensed by states and cities. It is time for youth sports organizations, which involve thirty million school-age children and affect their physical and mental health, to be licensed as well. High school sports programs should be subjected to many of the same regulations as youth programs. The best way to do this would be through state legislation. Regulations of the type suggested below would begin to move youth and high school sports away from their current violence-oriented direction:*

- All coaches should have training in child development and physiology. While Michigan is alone in having a state-based coach training program, there are already private programs scattered around the country. For example, for the last twelve years the Sports Medicine and Fitness Institute of Adelphi University in Garden City, New York, has offered workshops to Little League Baseball coaches.
- All teams should have certified trainers, or someone with equivalent skills or training, available for assistance during games. At present only one percent of high schools have certified trainers.
- Boys should not be allowed to play with an injury that could permanently jeopardize their well-being if it were aggravated. A certified trainer or equivalent would make the final decision.
- Novocaine, or other drugs, should not be used in order to enable a boy to continue to play, or to enhance his performance.
- All attempts at injuring other players in order to "take them out" of the game and all borderline violence should be forbidden. Any attempt by a coach to encourage boys to behave in this way should be met with a severe penalty and eventual removal if repeated.
- All violent, insulting language on the part of the coach and the players, including slurs against women and homosexuals, should be forbidden.

* I am indebted to Richard Lapchick, whose comments on my recommendations led to revisions and improvements. However, I alone am responsible for these recommendations.

- Friendly, civil relations between teams should be encouraged. All games should start and end with handshakes.
- No financial benefits or gifts should be given to a boy or his parents to induce him to play on a particular junior high or high school team.
- In light of very high injury rates in football, all parents whose sons wish to play either youth league or high school football should be called to a meeting and informed of the number and nature of injuries incurred by the team's players for the last several years. They should be required to give written permission for their sons to play.

The following rules pertain to junior high and high school athletes only:

- Students who do not have at least a C average should not be allowed to play on a team. Laws of this type already exist in several states, including Hawaii, California, and Mississippi. No grade inflation for athletes should be allowed.
- Boys should not be allowed to repeat a grade in order to increase their size and football prowess.
- When recruiting football players, colleges should be required to inform them of their injury rates so that boys and their parents can take these into account in deciding which college the boy will play for. (This suggestion is analogous to the 1989 bill sponsored by Senator Bill Bradley and Congressmen Ed Towns and Tom McMillen, which includes the requirement that universities inform all high school athletes they are recruiting of graduation rates for students on athletic scholarships.)
- TV coverage of high school football should not be permitted. Cable networks have already begun such coverage, which further intensifies the already fierce emphasis on competitiveness and introduces all the problems of college sports at a high school level.

A major justification for our nation's enormous investment in competitive contact sports for young boys is that sports build character, teach team effort, and encourage sportsmanship and fair play.

In a 1978 article, professor George Sage discusses six studies of the effect of organized youth sports on sportsmanship. Three of the studies indicate that boys involved in organized sports show less sportsmanship than those who are not involved. One study found that as the children grew older they moved away from placing high value on fairness and fun in participation and began to emphasize skill and victory as the major goals of sport. In several other studies it was found that adolescent boys who participated in organized sports valued victory more than non-participants, who placed more emphasis on fairness.

Instead of learning fair play and teamwork, too many of our young boys are learning that winning is everything.

It is time to regulate children's sports so that boys will *really* learn the pro-social attitudes and values that they are supposed to learn from sports, instead of the obsessive competitiveness, emotional callousness, and disdain for moral scruples that are so often precursors to violence.

12

TV: The Babysitter That Teaches Violence

"He likes to watch wrestling on TV with his dad," Mrs. Glover explained matter-of-factly when her two-year-old son, Jayjay, grabbed a student's leg in the parenting class she had brought him to. It was obvious to her that Jayjay was imitating what he saw on TV. When author Marc Gerzon interviewed Vietnam veterans, he found many of them pointing to John Wayne movies in the course of explaining why they had volunteered for Vietnam. Over twenty-five hundred articles and books have been written by psychologists, sociologists, and other professionals examining scientific evidence of connection between TV and film viewing and individual behavior. Many Americans think the connection is obvious.

Unlike ads, TV programs are not designed to influence people. Their intent is to attract large audiences by entertaining them. Nevertheless the fact that companies spend billions of dollars a year on TV ads gives further credence to the view that TV does influence people. Certainly the families of the victims of "copycat" acts need no persuading.

Among them are the parents of Olivia Niemi, who was "raped" by a fifteen-year-old boy and three teenage girls using an empty beer bottle. Four days earlier a scene in a TV film entitled *Born Innocent* showed four teenage girls using the long wooden handle of a mop in a sexual assault on another girl.

Six-year-old Jeremy Nezworski watched an episode of "The Scooby Doo Show" in which a character covered his head with a pillowcase and put a rope around his neck in a mock hanging. Jeremy immediately imitated the stunt. He died.

In a 1987 article, Professor Juliet Lushbough Dee reviews fifteen court decisions on cases in which it was alleged that a child or a young adult was the victim of violence induced by television, films, or rock music. The Niemi and Nezworski cases are among them. The Niemi family lost their case because they could not prove that NBC had "incited" the teenagers who raped their daughter. "Incitement" requires the *intent* to stimulate illegal action and an immediate and likely danger of lawless action. ABC settled out of court with the Nezworski family.

In a 1982 Gallup poll 66 percent of those interviewed thought that there was "a relationship between violence on television and the rising crime rate in the United States." This belief is reflected in the formation since the late 1960s of numerous public interest groups concerned with the impact of TV violence. Action for Children's Television (ACT) was started in 1968 by Peggy Charren, a Boston housewife and mother, and is perhaps the best known. One of its major goals was to rid children's TV of excessive violence.

I asked Evelyn Kaye, ACT's first president, why ACT had been able to achieve so little over a period of twenty years, in spite of valiant efforts and considerable public support. She replied: "I think ACT was twenty years too late." She went on to explain that there should have been a real commitment to quality *non-*

commercial children's programming when TV first came into existence. Instead, children became part of the TV marketplace, and financial interests in keeping them there were too strong for ACT or any other organization to handle.

What happened in the United States was the reverse of what happened in European countries and in most of the world, where government- and citizen-funded public television was created first and commercial TV allowed much later. And so in much of the world children's TV is noncommercial or much more regulated than ours.

No country comes near us with respect to TV violence. This remains true even though European TV has grown more violent recently as a result of increased privatization. On American TV, children's weekend daytime programs averaged 15.5 violent acts per hour in 1988. Evening prime-time programs averaged 6.2. On all three networks children's weekend programs have long been and continue to be three to six times more violent than evening prime-time programs.[1]

"The Transformers," a very popular cartoon in the mid to late 1980s, contained an average of eighty-three violent acts per hour. Typical was a show I watched in which the good guys assert, "We'll trash every Decepticon [bad guy] in the galaxy," and from then on it was almost nonstop intergalactic chases, violence, and mayhem carried on with futuristic weapons.

"Teenage Mutant Ninja Turtles" seems to have fewer violent acts per hour, but it is still about violent conflict. The sword-wielding turtles fight mad scientists, evil extraterrestrials, and other enemies.

After watching hours of violent cartoons, it struck me that it probably matters very little whether a show has twenty or eighty violent acts per hour. In either case, the boy is drawn into a world of endless conflicts settled with fistfights, swords, guns, and hi-tech weapons of destruction.

In the mid 1980s the World Wrestling Federation decided to market professional wrestling to young children by introducing a Saturday morning wrestling show on TV. Even toddlers now have the opportunity to watch wrestlers shove, push, and punch each other, pull hair, and toss each other out of the ring.

Insults and ethnic slurs are *de rigueur* in the world of wrestling. On one show a bad guy named "The Ultimate Warrior" looked like an insane American Indian. A French Canadian manager, "Frenchie," carried a sign saying "U.S.A. is not O.K." The response was "Come on America, let's show 'em our pride. Tell 'em to get out of the country." On another show a wrestler wore tights with the image of his opponent's wife on the crotch.

Children also watch hours of adult programs, which include violent police shows and films, and more recently crime tabloids that often depict gruesome real-life crimes in great detail.

Outsiders' most cynical interpretations of what motivates broadcasters to present so much violence are confirmed by former insider Arthur Taylor who was president of CBS from 1972 to 1976. When I interviewed him in 1989, Taylor pointed out that while Peggy Charren and other reformers were deeply concerned with the quality of programming, this was not a significant concern for broadcasters. For them "the most important part of broadcasting is the size of the audience . . . It really had to do with 'Did it sell? Did the sponsor like it? Did it produce the size and definition of audience that was required?" Taylor does not deny that some people in broadcasting are concerned about TV violence, but he adds they are not concerned enough to risk losing six-figure salaries. Taylor is convinced that his attempts at curtailing violence on CBS and other major networks eventually led to his being fired.

None of this is to deny that there are some good, nonviolent programs for children on commercial TV. At present these include "Pee-wee's Playhouse" and "Garfield and Friends." But commercial stations cannot be counted on to continue offering even these few better quality or less violent shows, because the goal of TV networks and stations is not good programming for children but profit maximization. If at any point it looks as if ratings can be brought up by replacing a nonviolent program with a violent one, the pressure to do so will be enormous.

Fundamental structural change is necessary in order to protect our children.

The value of the profit motive as a spur to economic development is being recognized increasingly worldwide. But when it comes to the socialization of children, it is a different story. The reinforcement of responsible, pro-social, nonviolent behavior becomes highly problematic when a major source of that socialization lies in the hands of commercial interests.

American children watch TV an average of twenty-four hours a week. This is more time than they spend in school. By the time they are eighteen years old our children have viewed approximately twenty-six thousand murders on the screen.[2]

TV executives will point out again and again that TV is entertainment and nothing more. They give the public what the public wants to see. Programs reflect the values of our society. Violent cartoons are a reflection of what boys want to see.

Certainly TV does reflect our societal values. For starters, if we didn't value business interests more than our children's well-being, it would be unthinkable to have the programs our children watch determined by marketplace factors. The rejection of moral responsibility and the "looking out for number one" attitude of the 1970s and 1980s further facilitated the exploitation of some boys' basest tendencies.

But TV is a major if not the major component of American popular culture. By reflecting and magnifying our worst aspects it significantly aggravates these tendencies, especially in children, whose values and attitudes are in the process of being formed. We know from past and present history that human beings have the potential to commit the most violent and cruel acts conceivable. We saw in Chapter 3 that some boys seem to have a particularly strong potential for such behavior. In light of this it should come as no surprise that many boys are particularly attracted to very violent programs. It is precisely because the potential for violence is so great that we must take every precaution not to reinforce it.

None of this is to say that TV violence is *the* cause of societal violence. There is no one area of socialization that is *the* cause of violent behavior; there are many significant contributors. Television is one of them.

If television has the power to amplify our children's worst tendencies, it also has the power to encourage the development of their best qualities.

In the latter part of this chapter I outline some of the measures we must take if television is to help rather than hinder parents in raising caring, responsible, nonviolent children. The first part of the chapter leads readers through some of the roads I traveled before arriving at my conclusions so that they can better judge the problems and the solutions.

WHAT DOES WATCHING VIOLENCE ON TV
AND IN FILMS DO TO OUR CHILDREN?

In the last forty years over 235 studies on the effects of TV violence have been carried out. They have included laboratory experiments, surveys, and longitudinal studies. As mentioned above, this scientific evidence has been analyzed and discussed in over twenty-five hundred articles, books, and reports.[3]

In 1988, George Comstock, professor of public communication at Syracuse University and one of the leading authorities in the field of TV and film violence research, surveyed the research literature in the field and analyzed these studies. He concluded that the catharsis hypothesis is disproven: A large majority of studies show that viewing television and film violence does not help children get rid of antisocial, violent inclinations. Quite the contrary, it leads to increases in aggressive and antisocial behavior, and this is true for all ages.

Comstock's conclusions support those of the 1982 National Institute of Mental Health (NIMH) report entitled *Television and Behavior: Ten Years of Scientific Progress and Implications for the Eighties,* which asserted:

> The consensus among most of the research community is that violence on television does lead to aggressive behavior by children and teenagers who watch the programs . . . *In magnitude, television violence is as strongly correlated with aggressive behavior as any other behavioral variable that has been measured. The research question has moved from asking whether or not there is an effect to seeking explanation for the effect* [my emphasis].[4]

Comstock's survey and analysis further confirm that of the NIMH in that they both find that when children view constructive, altruistic behavior on the screen, antisocial violent behavior diminishes and pro-social behavior increases.

Research on the effects of TV focuses on specific observed correlations between TV or film watching and behavior. When it is carried out properly, its value lies in the precision and accuracy of its findings, which can be tested by replicable experiments. But long before the social sciences developed methods for establishing precise correlations between specific variables, thinkers like Alexis de Tocqueville were analyzing the interaction between socioeconomic and cultural conditions and the attitudes and behavior of people in a given society. Their insights, while more speculative, were of a much broader nature than the knowledge attained by social scientists who do effects research.

Since American children spend more time watching television than in any other activity, it is impossible to understand their values, attitudes, and behavior—including violent behavior—without taking into account TV's long-range cumulative effects. Neil Postman, professor of media ecology, at New York University, is operating within this broader sociological tradition when he analyzes the fundamental changes that childhood has undergone in recent years as a result of TV. He argues that with the advent of TV we have entered an era in which the dividing line between childhood and adulthood becomes blurred. Because of the electronic media, children and adults now live in the same symbolic world and share cultural information. As long as we lived in a print culture, children were to a large extent protected from most information about sex, violence, death, and human aberration. All of these are now revealed to children from the earliest age. TV has forced "the entire culture out of the closet."*

Even when news reports, documentaries, or programs dealing with adult emotional and/or sexual problems are of a high quality, they are inappropriate for children. A five-year-old or an eight-year-old is not ready to tune in to every aspect of the adult world. To do so can be frightening, anxiety provoking, confusing, and disorienting.

But the problem is aggravated by the fact that the picture of the adult world imparted by TV is often highly inaccurate, antisocial, and devoid of any moral or conceptual framework.

According to the 1982 NIMH report, approximately 70 percent of references to sex on television are to prostitution or extramarital sex. Men on television are not usually interested in marriage or family. Sex is commonly linked with violence. Just those stereotypes of the masculine mystique that tend to in-

---

* Postman is by no means alone in being concerned with the effect of the media on childhood. Author Marie Winn and psychiatrist David Elkind are among those who have also addressed the problem.

crease male violence are perpetuated. Males are often powerful, dominant, and violent. The report confirms that heavy TV viewing tends to perpetuate sex stereotyping. (On the other hand, when counterstereotypes are presented to children they are readily accepted, testifying again to the enormous power of TV images.)

George Gerbner, dean of the Annenberg School of Communications at the University of Pennsylvania, believes that the TV portrayal of men as dominant, powerful, and violent lets women know who is in charge: although in real life the most frequent victims of violence are men, on TV women are the most frequent victims. "What men want to do is to get their way," Gerbner told me in a 1988 interview. "The quickest demonstration of power is violence."

The fact that during prime time approximately half of all dramatic characters are involved in some kind of violence and about 10 percent in killing plays an important role in developing what Gerbner calls a "mean world" syndrome. "In such a mean and dangerous world, most people 'cannot be trusted' and . . . most people are 'just looking out for themselves.' "[5] The 1982 NIMH report confirms that "children who watch a lot of violence on television may come to accept violence as normal behavior."[6]

In 1950, when TV was in its infancy, in the entire United States only 170 persons under the age of fifteen were arrested for serious crimes such as murder, rape, robbery, and aggravated assault. By 1979 the rate of serious crime committed by children under fifteen had increased by 11,000 percent. The rate of nonserious crimes such as burglary, larceny, and auto theft increased 8,300 percent for children.[7]

While there are undoubtedly other significant contributing factors, it is difficult to escape the conclusion that the enormous increases in crime by very young boys and in teenage pregnancy that have taken place in the last forty years, have something to do with our children's spending an average of four hours a day watching TV, much of it adult TV. The highest rates of teenage pregnancy occur among that segment of the population—poor, uneducated minorities—who, according to the 1982 NIMH study, watch the most TV. A recent study indicates that in 1989,

African Americans watched 54 percent more TV than did other Americans.[8]

Faye Wattleton, the president of Planned Parenthood Federation of America, points out that "the United States has the dubious distinction of leading the industrialized world in its rates of teenage pregnancy, teenage childbirth, and teenage abortion." In the course of analyzing the reasons for this she argues that the mass media, especially television, exacerbate the problem. "Many teenagers spend more time in front of the television than they do in the classroom, and their sexual behavior in part reflects what they have learned from this thoroughly unreliable teacher . . . One study indicates that in a single year, television airs 20,000 sexual messages. Yet rarely is there any reference to contraception or to the consequences of sexual activity."[9]

As we saw in the chapter on child-rearing, boys without fathers or with inadequate fathers are more likely to become violent and to commit criminal acts. Most of today's teenage mothers do not have husbands. Because their sons grow up without fathers, they are particularly likely to be influenced by the domineering, violent male role models that they see on TV. The fact that "marriage and family are not important to television's men"[10] just helps perpetuate the cycle of absentee fathers.

But upper-class children also watch TV.

In June 1988 five boys who had just graduated from Fordham Preparatory School, a Catholic high school in New York City, went on an armed robbery crime spree in order to raise the nine hundred dollars one of them needed to repair his father's car (which he had damaged during a joy ride). The boys were all from solid upper-middle- and middle-class families. One of them was killed by an off-duty police officer whom the boys tried to rob.

Fordham Prep headmaster Dr. Neil McCarthy commented: "I do not want to say it's television that gave them ideas, but who knows?"[11]

Without being familiar with their personal histories, it is impossible to know what motivated these five young boys. But it is difficult to avoid the conclusion that growing up in TV's "mean world," in which violence is "normal," facilitates committing acts of violence.

When boys need some quick money, going on a robbery spree is no longer as unthinkable as it was forty years ago. When a boy is furious at his parents, killing them is no longer as unthinkable as it was forty years ago. When a girlfriend or a wife breaks up a relationship, killing her is no longer as unthinkable as it was forty years ago.

TWENTY YEARS OF TRYING TO CURB TV VIOLENCE

During these years of intensive research and study of the broad social effects of TV, many professional, religious, and citizens' groups such as the American Medical Association, the National Parent-Teacher Association, and the National Council of the Churches of Christ became actively involved in efforts to decrease TV violence. Several organizations were formed with the sole purpose of improving the quality of American television. Some were dedicated entirely or to a great extent to the elimination of gratuitous violence.

One of the main goals of Action for Children's Television (ACT) was to rid children's programming of violence by banning commercials. The underlying assumption was that the only reason for producing violent, antisocial programs aimed at children's worst potentialities was the money motive. Remove that motive and the violence would dissipate. This assumption is borne out by the fact that none of the PBS children's programs —such as "Sesame Street," "Mister Rogers' Neighborhood," and the now defunct "Electric Company"—contains gratuitous violence.

It was the deep commitment of ACT's founders to what they considered to be First Amendment rights that led them to choose this indirect route for getting rid of violence. Advertisements have not been viewed by the courts or the Fair Trade Commission as subject to the same First Amendment protections as other forms of speech. Ads that are unfair, deceptive, or injurious can be banned.

ACT's position is that the First Amendment applies equally to programming directed at children and at adults. Therefore any attempt at regulating the hours when violent TV programs may be shown in order to protect children, or any attempt at prohibiting gratuitous violence from programs made for children, is considered an infringement on the First Amendment rights of broadcasters.

This position is typical of all the groups concerned with TV violence. They have not wanted the Federal Communications Commission to interfere directly with the content of programming, but to bring about structural changes which would lead to improved content. One of ACT's first petitions to the FCC was characteristic of the kind of structural change these groups find acceptable. The petition requested that "each station be required to carry fourteen hours of commercial-free, child-oriented programs each week."[12]

The National Citizens' Committee for Broadcasting (NCCB) was started in Washington and issued public denunciations to pressure companies to withdraw their advertising from violent programs. Nicholas Johnson, one of the most outspoken and critical men ever to serve on the Federal Communications Commission, became the head of this committee after leaving that agency.

More recently Dr. Thomas Radecki, an Illinois psychiatrist, started the National Coalition on Television Violence (NCTV), which also is opposed to censorship. Among other goals, the organization works for legislation to put warnings on children's TV about the bad effects of viewing violence.

One of the major targets of these groups' efforts has been the FCC, an agency established by Congress in 1934. The 1934 Communications Act forbids censorship but gives the FCC the power to license TV and radio stations and make rules affecting them. This power is based on the fact that there are a limited number of airwaves which belong to the public. The agency is directed to favor those applicants most likely to serve "the public interest, convenience, or necessity."

These two seemingly contradictory directives have been interpreted as meaning that the FCC may not directly censor radio or TV content, but may do so indirectly by not renewing, or threatening not to renew, the license of a station that does not fulfill its obligation to the public interest. The anti-censorship clause is further weakened, some might say nullified, by a federal obscenity law forbidding the use of "obscene, indecent, or profane language" in broadcasting.

Despite their tireless efforts to influence the FCC to use its rule-making and licensing power to decrease TV violence, the public interest groups have had little effect.* Their deep commitment to a strict interpretation of the First Amendment leads them to propose rules that can in no way be construed as censorship. An ever growing body of research supports their contention that to decrease TV violence would be in the public interest. Strong public support was demonstrated from the beginning by the more than a hundred thousand supporting letters sent to the FCC when Act first petitioned to eliminate commercials on children's television. By 1982 a majority of Americans favored much stronger measures. A Gallup poll indicated that 67 percent of the population favored scheduling TV shows with violence after 10 P.M.

In spite of all this there has been no significant decrease in the level of TV violence since 1967. According to Gerbner's September 1986 "Violence Profile," the 1984–85 season was the highest and the 1985–86 season the fourth highest on record.

The inability of the consumer groups over a period of more than twenty years to influence significantly the FCC and Congress grows mainly out of the enormous disparity between their resources and those of the broadcasters.

Richard Labunski, a broadcast journalist and author of *The First Amendment Under Siege: The Politics of Broadcast Regulation,* says that the National Association of Broadcasters, which represents one of the wealthiest industries in the country (in 1979 commercial broadcasting *profits* came to a total of $1.9 billion), has an annual budget in excess of $5 million. Its staff has only one mission: to help the industry maximize its profits. It works out of a $2.6-million building a few blocks from the FCC.

As a result of this proximity and abundance of funds, the NAB keeps its people in constant contact with FCC commissioners and staff. The NAB is the major source of information and guidance for the commissioners. Commissioners frequently attend industry parties and conventions. As with the Pentagon,

---

* NCTV, which is probably the most active organization at present, does boast a recent victory. Mainly by applying pressure on advertisers, it succeeded in getting two programs, "Freddy's Nightmares" and "Friday the 13th" to stop production of new shows. "Freddy's Nightmares," in which the psychopathic narrator delights in the suffering and deaths of victims (including graphic mutilations and decapitations) is not being shown in the United States at present. Some channels are still showing reruns of "Friday the 13th," which has featured graphic human sacrifices, electrocutions, and torture.

there is a "revolving door" problem at the FCC. In a 1988 interview, former FCC commissioner Nicholas Johnson told me quite simply that the FCC commissioners conceive their role as being advocates for the broadcasting system.

The FCC is funded by and works closely with Congress. Since the birth of TV nearly every session of Congress has had hearings and legislative debate on some aspect of the medium, with TV violence at the forefront. But very little ever gets done. Why hasn't Congress made the FCC take a more balanced treatment of broadcasters and the public? Why is it so reluctant to play an effective role in regulating TV in the public interest?

There appears to be a broad consensus among experts on this point: Few members of Congress are willing to offend broadcasters, because most of them regularly use free time given to them by stations back home. Besides their concern that they might be denied free time, politicians are also concerned with how radio and TV stations would depict them if they voted for strong measures.[13]

But Congress is not impervious to *intense* public pressure. By 1974 the outpouring of complaints from individual citizens and network affiliates was unprecedented. After NBC showed *Born Innocent* during prime time in the fall of 1974 (this is the film mentioned earlier in which a young woman is raped with a long wooden mop handle) the complaints came in from both conservatives concerned with sex and liberals concerned with violence. While neither group was strong enough to influence programming by itself, when they got together they were a force that Congress and the industry had to contend with.

In November 1974, under intense pressure from the House Appropriations Committee (which controls the FCC's funding) FCC Chairman Wiley called the heads of the three major networks to his Washington office and convinced them that the FCC would take action if they didn't. These threats led to the "Family Hour." At the instigation of CBS president Arthur Taylor, the major networks agreed to have the NAB create a rule that only programs suitable for family viewing would be shown during prime time.

The agreement did not last long. The Writers Guild, representing a group of well-known TV writers (including Norman Lear) successfully sued the networks to abolish the family hour on First Amendment grounds. (ACT, NCCB, and the Communications Office of the United Church of Christ were among the groups that filed suits supporting the Writers Guild. They considered the family hour to be an infringement on the First Amendment rights of broadcasters.)

The decision in favor of the writers was overturned in the fall of 1976 by a higher court. By then it was much too late. George Gerbner's Violence Index showed that by that season TV violence had reached the highest level in ten years and the level of violence had increased the most during the family hour.

In 1977 some members of Congress again stood up to the broadcast industry. The House Communications Subcommittee, headed by California Congressman Lionel Van Deerlin, published a very cautious report that made clear its unwillingness to pursue strong criticism or strong measures against the broadcasting industry, but a very strongly worded minority dissent was signed by seven of the fifteen committee members. One sentence in particular gets to the heart of what disturbed them about the majority report: "We believe this report is biased in favor of the networks."[14]

Only a few years later, these members of Congress, as well as members of public interest groups concerned about TV violence, were to experience their greatest frustration yet. Under the Reagan presidency the country moved in the direction of complete deregulation of the broadcast media. Reagan appointee FCC commissioner Mark Fowler announced that "the open marketplace would determine what was best for children."[15] The trade paper *Variety* captured the reaction of many skeptics when it headlined its story about the FCC's 1984 vote to remove all requirements for children's programming, "Fowler's FCC tells kids to get lost."[16]

The open marketplace quickly determined that "thirty-minute commercials" were best for children. Toy manufacturers and broadcasters joined together to develop toys that could be marketed through children's programs featuring the toy and its accoutrements. He-Man, Shira, Transformers, and Ninja Turtles are examples of this kind of toy and program. In some cases broadcasters agreed to schedule "thirty-minute toy commercials" in exchange for a part of the toy companies' profits from the product.

In the fall of 1988, a bill that represented a small step in the direction of reintroducing some minimal regulation of children's TV was passed by Congress. It put a limit of twelve minutes of advertising per hour on children's TV during weekdays and ten and a half minutes on weekends. (In fact the average total of children's commercials on most stations is eight and a half minutes per hour.) It barred "thirty-minute commercials," and required that television stations "serve the educational and informational needs of children" to get their licenses renewed. President Reagan vetoed the bill on the grounds that it represented an infringement of First Amendment rights. In the fall of 1990, a similar bill was passed by Congress. President Bush reluctantly decided to let it stand.

Many recommendations have been made over the years for changes that would lead to greater protection for the public interest both at the FCC and at other agencies. Ralph Nader's Public Citizen and other public interest groups have proposed that a consumer agency be created at the federal level to represent consumers before other federal agencies, making sure that these agencies were doing their job in terms of enforcing consumer laws. A Rand Corporation study recommended that in order to encourage more citizen participation in FCC proceedings, groups representing the public should receive financial assistance from the government when they appear before the FCC.[17]

When I asked Nicholas Johnson which of these alternatives he would favor, he answered, "I think I would tend to check all of the above." It is difficult to argue with his view that the public needs all the protection it can get.

For reasons that should be obvious by now, nothing has ever been done about these recommendations.

GIVING UP: FROM CHANGING TV TO EDUCATING PARENTS AND CHILDREN

With this history, it is not difficult to see why many of those involved in ridding children's TV of violence have given up on any hope of significant change through pressure on the Federal Communications Commission, the Federal Trade Commission, or Congress. Many of the reformers have now shifted from

trying to improve programming to educating parents and introducing TV education into the schools. For example, Leonard
Eron and Rowell Huesmann, both professors of psychology and
leading researchers in the area of TV violence, conclude that the
situation with respect to TV violence now represents "a massive
public health problem." They point out that many democratic
countries, such as England, Finland, and the Netherlands, restrict the amount of violence shown on television without this
being perceived as a threat to the rights of citizens.

After deploring broadcast executives' past refusal even to
acknowledge that a problem exists, they ask, "But what can we
do until the networks show some restraint or restraint is imposed on them by some government agency?"[18]

Their answer lies in urging professionals to educate parents.
Eron and Huesmann also recommend intervention in the
schools to teach children first that "television is an unrealistic
portrayal of the real world; second, that aggressive behaviors are
not as universal and acceptable in the real world as they would
appear on television; and third, that it is just not good to behave
like the aggressive characters on television."

On one level, it is difficult to take issue with Eron and Huesmann's recommendations that parents be educated about the
consequences of TV violence and that the schools try to eradi-
cate some of what children learn from TV. But, as they acknowledge, this is not a solution.

To begin with, there is an absurdity and unfairness to it.
Television programs that encourage violence and other antisocial behavior in children are permitted (as are commercials
which encourage them to eat unhealthy foods). Parents are then
told that it is entirely *their* responsibility to undo all this. They
are expected to monitor and discuss TV programs with their
children. Even when there is a full-time parent at home this is an
absurd imposition. Are parents who have worked hard all week
supposed to get up at 6 A.M. every Saturday to make sure their
children don't watch the wrong programs? What about the millions of latchkey children who come home to an empty house?
Who will discuss and supervise their TV watching?

What about parents of older children? It is an enormous relief
for most parents when they can finally take a nap, run out to the
market, or chat with a neighbor without having to worry about

their child's safety. Is it fair to expect these parents to spend this precious time monitoring what their children are watching on TV? Making sure they don't switch channels?

Another problem with these recommendations is the message about societal values that children would learn from them. Special programs would be set up in schools to teach children *not* to believe what advertisements tell them, *not* to accept the values and attitudes depicted in much of children's programming, *not* to imitate aggressive characters. Most young children are inquisitive and thoughtful enough to ask themselves why ads and programs which are so bad for children that they require special school programs to countermand them, are on television to begin with. What answer can a child come up with except that the people who run TV are more interested in money than in the welfare of children? Instead of being stopped from harming children these people are very handsomely rewarded. They are rich, powerful, and respected. They are beyond the control of parents, teachers, and political leaders. Parents and teachers can only issue warnings.

This is not a pro-social message. It shows children that society values money more than the well-being of people. We are back to the values of the masculine mystique. The split between the TV set and the school reflects the dichotomy between "masculine" and "feminine" values. On the one hand there are the powerful, wealthy broadcasters and advertisers—mostly male— who care primarily about making money and are rewarded with prestige and admiration. On the other hand there are the nice, caring teachers—mostly female—who look out for the welfare of children and enjoy low salaries and low prestige. Boys will know where their future lies. (And so will an increasing number of girls who identify with "masculine" goals and a "masculine" marketplace.)

WHAT ABOUT NICKELODEON, THE DISNEY CHANNEL, AND VCR'S?

One of the recurrent arguments for complete deregulation of the broadcasting media has been that with the advent of cable and its proliferation of stations, market factors will lead to programming to suit the needs of all groups. The availability of VCRs also provides diversity and individual control.

Nickelodeon, a cable station for children, is often pointed to as an example of the marketplace taking care of the needs of special groups. Nickelodeon's programming is superior to that of the networks and independents. David Horowitz, one of the Warner-Amex executives involved in getting the station started, told me that its founders wanted a station with pro-social, commercial-free programming for children. This is reflected in its programs: they contain less violence than children's programs on VHF channels. Nevertheless, when the National Coalition on Television Violence monitored the station's early evening programs in 1987, it found that 21 percent of the content was violent.

For a while Nickelodeon had no ads. It has ads now. They include commercials for violent toys and unhealthy foods. In spite of its founders' and producers' good intentions, the network's primary dedication is not to the well-being of children.

Nickelodeon is a money-making venture that is free at any time to increase its violent programming, to increase its ads, or to go off the air.

In analyzing Nickelodeon's chances for survival, Edward L. Palmer, author of *Television and America's Children: A Crisis of Neglect,* is pessimistic. The channel loses money. He points out that as cable reaches more and more homes, the need for a "loss leader" to entice people to subscribe to cable or to help the company obtain lucrative franchises will decrease. Revenues from advertisers will be difficult to come by, just as it is difficult to find sponsors for children's programming on the networks because children's buying power, while considerable, is significantly less than that of adults.

Horowitz confirms that the station originally did not make money, but says that it now does. He is more optimistic than Palmer about its chances of survival.

Even if Nickelodeon were to survive, it would be limited to cable, which is not available in many parts of the country and is based on a monthly fee. About 56 percent of American homes have cable at present, and while cable owners would like to see this rise eventually to 60 or possibly 70 percent of the population, it is doubtful that it will ever go much higher than that, or even get that high. Some rural areas will never receive cable. Many Americans cannot afford it.

The Disney Channel is a pay cable channel with very little violent programming (only 5 percent, according to NCTV's 1987 monitoring). It is not yet available in many parts of the country. Both its cost and the fact that it is on cable will make it permanently unavailable to many American children. Like Nickelodeon, it is a commercial venture driven by market forces. Its owners can at any point decide to cease operating if they think their capital can be better invested elsewhere.

What about videotapes? For financially secure and concerned parents they represent a way of exerting some control over what their children watch, especially when the children are little and parents choose tapes for them.

Good videotapes for children are a welcome substitute or supplement to TV programming, but they are very unlikely ever to replace it, just as video rentals or subscribing to HBO will not replace the need for regular TV channels.

It is impossible to predict the kinds of technological changes in TV that will take place in the future. The rapidity with which changes take place in television can be seen in the fact that the introduction of cable has caused the major networks' share of prime-time audience to plummet from 92 to 68 percent in ten years. But whatever changes the future brings, there is one near-certainty: *as long as children's television is left in the hands of commercial interests, in the long run the primary factor in determining its content will be the financial advancement of broadcasters and sponsors, not the well-being of our children or our nation.*

WHY A CHILDREN'S PUBLIC BROADCASTING SYSTEM IS OUR BEST BET

Television is a major cultural influence on our children. It can continue to be used in such a way as to increase violence or it can be changed and used to decrease violence and promote pro-social behavior. My conviction that the most effective way to produce the second result is through the creation of public children's television grows out of both theoretical and practical reasons.

On the practical side, twenty years of frustrated attempts at minimal regulation by public interest groups suggest that the enormous power of the commercial media will continue to prevent efforts to significantly influence commercial television.

Another practical reason grows out of contemporary interpretations of the First Amendment. While a Children's Public Broadcasting Service (CPBS) combined with mandatory lock boxes poses no serious First Amendment problems, any attempt to regulate commercial TV content with respect to violence is fraught with them.

There is in the case of violence, no long legal history of censorship, as there is with respect to pornography. The present legal situation reflects our very divergent attitudes toward the two. There are very few individuals or groups in this country who would argue that broadcasters have the First Amendment right to show pornographic films on TV any time of day.

Yet this is precisely what is asserted with respect to violent films. Even those groups who want to decrease TV violence are opposed not only to censorship but also to regulating the hours when violent programs can be shown.

The source of this double standard lies in our long-standing tradition of keeping children innocent of sex. The idea of a three-year-old or an eight-year-old watching people enjoy intercourse or cunnilingus or fellatio is genuinely repugnant. There is no comparable repugnancy toward allowing our children to see people being shot, stabbed, or beaten.

Violence is fun. Violence is a sport. Top-notch prizefighters can make millions of dollars in a few minutes or even a few seconds. Boys soon learn that the willingness to fight, in the school yard or in war, is part of being a real man. For many people there is no repulsion at all to letting children see violence, or, in the case of boys, participate in it.

And so we have a double standard. On the one hand there is overwhelming documentation that viewing violence is socially harmful, yet it goes unregulated. Broadcasters can show people all the shooting, killing, and maiming they want during hours when children are awake. But, on the other hand, they cannot show pornographic films even though there has never been a study done on the effects on young children of watching pornography.

Studies of the effects of pornography on adult men suggest

that what is most harmful about pornography is the violence and debasement of women that is often part of it. It is not as clear that nonviolent pornography which is not debasing to women has socially negative effects. Yet even this kind of pornography is banned from TV, except for late-night shows, and even then there are limits on what can be shown.

I am not proposing that we allow nonviolent erotic films to be shown on Saturday morning. I am suggesting that at some future point when we begin to find violence genuinely repulsive, when it is no longer part of the definition of manhood, then the idea of letting children watch violent programs will be as repugnant as the idea of letting them watch pornographic programs.

At that time we will become consistent. The courts may decide that violent speech, like obscene speech, is unprotected by the First Amendment: In the 1957 case of *Roth v. U.S.*, the Supreme Court took a two-level approach to free speech, arguing that some speech is beneath the protection of the First Amendment. Obscenity, considered to be "utterly without redeeming social importance," fell into this category.

Or the courts may decide that violent speech, like indecent speech, can be regulated for the protection of children. In the 1973 *Carlin v. FCC* case, the Supreme Court held that a radio station did not have the right to broadcast indecent speech including sexual and excretory words such as "cocksucker," "fuck," "cunt," and "shit," which are not considered obscene and are protected by the First Amendment—during hours when children were likely to be part of the audience.

The latter ruling would permit the kind of regulation that exists in some countries, including England, where violent programming is not permitted until after 9 P.M.

Research and interviews with First Amendment law specialists have convinced me that the opposition to treating violence the way we treat obscenity is so strong within the legal world that consistency is a long way off.

Research and interviews with Peggy Charren, Nicholas Johnson, Thomas Radecki, Rev. Everett Parker, and other leading figures in the movement to decrease TV violence have convinced me that most critics of TV violence will continue to oppose any attempt to regulate the airing of violent programs.

Because they make no distinction between children and adults with respect to the First Amendment, they cannot go much further than to demand that commercial channels be required to have one or two hours a day of noncommercial children's programming, or to demand that commercial TV stations carry warnings about the dangers of children's watching violent programming.

While such measures—were they ever to be enacted—would constitute improvements, they would not be enough. For, apart from these concessions, stations would still be free to show all the violence they wanted, both on children and adult programming.

My *TV Guide* informs me that on weekdays children can watch "Hawaii Five-O," at three, and "Hunter" at four. Both are violence-packed series. Programs such as "A Current Affair" and "Unsolved Mysteries" give detailed, graphic accounts of some of the bloodiest and most vicious murders ever committed. They can be seen at 7:30 and 8:00 P.M.

In addition, many programs for adults may not be suitable for children, especially children under the age of about fourteen, *regardless of their quality or intent.* A PBS documentary that focused on genocide during World War II comes to mind. Programs about concentration camps, comedies or dramas dealing with adult emotional and sexual problems, many aspects of the evening news, are not appropriate for children. We are back to Neil Postman's well-taken argument that the advent of TV has signaled the end of childhood and the early initiation into all areas of adult life.

Even if we could pass a law prohibiting gratuitous violence on commercial TV before 9 or 10 P.M., we would still have the problem of children viewing otherwise inappropriate programs. Children would continue to be subjected to advertisements.

The creation of noncommercial stations with pro-social programming for children, combined with an easy-to-use mandatory lock box permitting parents to scramble all adult channels, would create an entirely separate TV world for children. It would help parents to regain control over the moral education of their children. A parental control device that locks out cable channels such as the Playboy Channel or HBO is already available. The technology for building one that would scramble VHF and UHF as well as cable exists.

As matters stand now, conscientious parents are swimming

against the tide. Instead of receiving outside support when they undertake one of the most difficult tasks—raising children—they must deal with the fact that by the age of two or three their children will be initiated into the adult world, as *misrepresented* on TV. They must deal with their children's wanting to watch programs parents do not approve of. They must deal with their wanting the unhealthy foods and the often violent or otherwise inappropriate or too expensive toys they see advertised.

No wonder many parents give up! And not just in terms of controlling what their children watch on TV. I suspect that for many parents the inability to control what their children learn from the TV set in their home plays an important role in their giving up, to a large extent, on influencing their children's values and restraining their behavior.

The channels I am advocating would be dedicated to helping, not hindering, good parenting.

At present many parents who have themselves grown up surrounded by TV and film violence have become so desensitized to violence that they do not realize that there is anything wrong with exposing their children to it.

Mandatory lock boxes would have to be accompanied by a major publicity and educational campaign geared at making parents aware of the important role that television plays in the formation of their children's values and encouraging parents of young children to keep all adult channels locked except when they are home and watching TV themselves.

I am aware that a certain percentage of parents—hopefully it will be small—will not use, or rarely will use, the parental control device. As children get older, the fact that they have been kept away from adult TV will no doubt make it particularly intriguing. There is likely to be a transition period during which preadolescents will increasingly watch adult TV. There is no way to completely put the genie back into the bottle once it is out. CPBS, combined with mandatory lock boxes and education, is the closest we can get to protecting our children from inappropriate TV programming.

Parents and children often watch TV together in the evening and on the weekend. The educational program accompanying the creation of CPBS would lead parents to be much more careful in what they let their children watch with them. About 70 percent of American homes have more than one TV set. With a lock box on each set, parents would have the option of watching an adult program while their children watch the children's channel.

In a number of countries a white dot is placed in the top corner of programs that are inappropriate for children. Such a dot could be made mandatory for American commercial TV in cases of unacceptable sexual or violent content. Parents would then know immediately whether an adult program is acceptable for watching with children. This would also have the advantage of alerting adults who do not want to watch gratuitously violent or sexually explicit programs.

For both parents and children, the creation of a children's public television network would be a sign of deep societal concern for the well-being of children and the curbing of violence. Parents, and children who will one day become parents, would receive the message that children do matter, that money-making is not life's overarching value. The very existence of CPBS would constitute a reinforcement of pro-social values.

THE CHILDREN'S PUBLIC BROADCASTING SYSTEM

We need two public television channels dedicated to top quality, nonviolent, pro-social programming—one for young children, roughly aged two to nine; another for preadolescents aged ten to thirteen.

The specific form that the Children's Public Broadcasting System (CPBS) should take will have to be determined by a blue-ribbon committee made up of experienced experts in media, child development, and other relevant fields.

The creation of a viable CPBS will require a long-range congressional commitment to ongoing funding so that attention and time can be focused on high-quality programming. At present, PBS and the 258 independent stations that are part of public television spend huge amounts of time and money on fund-raising, often competing with each other.

The New York State tax form permits citizens to make a direct contribution to the Wildlife Conservation Fund. A similar provision on federal taxes for CPBS would be an excellent source of additional funds.

Foundations and corporations could also be solicited for contributions. But it is essential that CPBS not be reduced to PBS's position of constantly scrounging for money in order to survive. We are not even close to other industrialized nations, such as Japan and England, in what we spend on public television. Our 1985 per capita expenditures for public TV came to $4.58. Japan's came to $11.83. Britain's came to $16.14.

In terms of programming, the model of collaboration between researchers, subject specialists, and television production specialists that has characterized Children's Television Workshop—the creators of "Sesame Street," "The Electric Company," "3-2-1 Contact," and "Square One TV"—is probably highly desirable.

It is of utmost importance that CPBS appeal to lower-class and ghetto children. These are the children who watch the most TV and who are most in need of the educational and socializing benefits that can be reaped from good programming. Poor minority boys are also the most likely to commit acts of violence or to become victims of acts of violence.

Robert Coles, author of the Pulitzer-Prize-winning series "Children of Crisis," points out that in spite of the very high quality of "Sesame Street" and a concerted effort on the part of its producers to include and reach ghetto children, for many underprivileged children the show represents "an island of promise, a ray of hope . . . but for them, the real clouds are always there, and the thunder and lightning . . . 'Sesame Street' cannot provide the needed intellectual or emotional nourishment to children all too familiar with the consequences of drugs and alcoholism, children exposed to a dispirited, melancholy adult world."[19]

Coles's point is well taken. The problems of our ghettos are so devastating that nonviolent, pro-social TV programming runs the risk of being little more than a mirage in a desert of despair.

Such programming, as well as child-rearing and conflict resolution classes starting in elementary school, would, however, be important ingredients in any program geared toward dealing with the sociocultural aspects of ghetto problems.

Some readers may still be skeptical about the ability of CPBS's pro-social programming to hold the attention of underprivileged children or even to reach middle- and upper-class boys after a certain age.

We are in the midst of such a strong cultural bias in favor of the lurid, grotesque, violent, decadent, and terrifying, that it is difficult to imagine children—especially boys—over the age of ten or eleven enjoying anything with "soft" or pro-social content. But preadolescent and teenage boys watch "The Cosby Show" and "Family Ties." They used to watch "The Partridge Family" and "The Brady Bunch." They loved movies like *Big, Stand by Me,* and *Breaking Away.*

People, including children, tend to develop a taste for what they are conditioned to. There is no indication that in the 1950s boys enjoyed TV less because it was less violent. There is no inherent need to view extremely violent programs. It is an acquired taste that the media have played an important role in developing.

In the days of gladiatorial fights and public executions there were undoubtedly those who argued that people had an irrepressible need to view these spectacles.

The taste for violence is one that teenagers and adults are less likely to acquire if they become accustomed in early childhood to high-quality TV programming. A child accustomed to TV dramas, comedies, and adventure shows that are uninterrupted by commercials, that have a real story line and character development, that deal in a realistic way with life's problems, and that offer life-affirming, pro-social attitudes, might well be bored by the endless blood-and-guts, special effects, and car chases that characterize so many of today's films and TV programs.

Violence, conflict, and anger are facts of life. There is no reason to exclude them from programming, as long as they are dealt with in a non-exploitative, constructive way. The kinds of problems that children of different social classes encounter with siblings, with friends, with teachers, with parents, with bullies, with street violence, with drugs, can be dealt with in either fictionalized or direct form appropriate for differing ages.

Nor is there any reason to exclude adventure films and programs with suspense, danger, fast action, and excitement as long as they are appropriate and do not dominate programming.

Instead of adventures consisting again and again of shootouts between cops and gangs, or GI Joe and his enemies, or He-

Man and his enemies, many adventure movies and series could be based on dangerous and exciting rescue missions or escapes from danger. There is no reason to believe that stories of rescuing victims of tornados, floods, accidents, and so on under perilous conditions are less exciting than adventure films based on armed conflict between enemies.

CPBS: IS IT AN IMPOSSIBLE DREAM?

By now the reader may be thinking that CPBS may not be such a bad idea, just an unrealistic one.

Start-up costs would be high—although not nearly so high as they were for PBS (which had to start from scratch). A patchwork of existing cable channels and UHF channels could be used in most of the country, with VHF channels used where they are still available.

Even if some programs were acquired from other sources— old films, Nickelodeon, foreign TV—even if a backlog of reusable programs were developed, two children's channels would still cost hundreds of millions per year to run.

With our national debt in the trillions, how can we possibly expect Congress to add hundreds of millions to it by voting into existence two public children's TV channels?

"As a theoretical ideal it's very hard to argue with," Nicholas Johnson commented when I sought his reaction to the idea of CPBS. But then he went on to point out that "we don't do that kind of stuff on the other side of the river."

In Washington, D.C., among government people, "the river" refers to the Potomac, which separates the Capitol from the Pentagon. Johnson was telling me that while it was perfectly acceptable for the Pentagon to spend billions on highly controversial weapons systems—*one* stealth bomber runs over half a billion—it was not acceptable for Congress to spend half a billion or so a year on public children's television. Driving his point home, he added: "We spend more on military bands than the totality spent on public TV in this country."*

---

* The double standard with respect to military and pro-social spending that Johnson emphasized has gained a high level of implicit acceptance in our society. For example, in December 1988, a Pentagon commission recommended that eighty-six unnecessary military bases be closed down at a savings of $694 million dollars a year and $5.6 billion

Besides the financial barriers, there would be political problems.

When I mentioned CPBS to George Comstock, he thought it was "an excellent idea." Then came the warnings: Hollywood companies that produce children's programs for commercial TV, such as Hanna-Barbera, would fight it. Advertising agencies would fight it; the networks would fight it (while weekday children's TV is not profitable, Saturday mornings are).

On the positive side, those opposed to the creation of CPBS would not be able to hide their financial concerns behind a First Amendment smoke screen—the creation of CPBS can in no way be construed to interfere with their First Amendment rights. Nor would members of Congress fearful of commercial broadcasters' power be able to conceal their fears in First Amendment rhetoric.

It is impossible not to be pessimistic about *any* improvement in children's TV when one is aware of the power and finances of the opposing forces, and the depth of the resistance to federal funding for pro-social programs.

One might argue that with the cards being so stacked against *any* change it becomes more rather than less reasonable to recommend an ideal solution. If twenty years of modest, "reasonable," accommodating demands have produced so few results with respect to commercial TV, why not go for the best? Why not ask for what our children and our country *really* need?

Operating in favor of CPBS would be the support that it would be likely to get from both conservatives and liberals. We have seen that one of the few times when Congress pressured the FCC to do something about TV violence was when both liberals concerned with violence and conservatives concerned with sex were outraged by NBC's show "Born Innocent."

With a lock box device, CPBS would give conservative parents the ability to protect their children from the excessive and explicit sex that they find particularly offensive on commercial TV. At the same time it would raise their awareness of the nefarious

---

over twenty years. That evening on the NBC News, anchor Connie Chung stated that the "savings are minuscule." My guess is that if an anchorperson were to announce that Congress had decided to spend $694 million dollars a year for the next twenty years on two pro-social public television channels for children, this would not be described as a minuscule amount.

effects of children's watching violent programming. It would give liberal parents concerned about TV violence the ability to protect their children from it, and it would raise their consciousness about the inappropriateness of adult programming for children.

CPBS would radically change the nature of children's television viewing. It would make TV the ally rather than the enemy of good child-rearing. It would protect children from an adult world they are not ready for. It is an idea that can be rallied around and supported with enthusiasm by all segments of the population.

CPBS's major selling point in terms of winning congressional approval would probably be its educational potential.

In the 1950s, after the Russians launched Sputnik, Congress appropriated considerable amounts of money for programs intended to help us catch up with the Russians' space program. We are now flagrantly lagging behind countries like West Germany and Japan in educational and economic achievement.

In a 1988 Gallup poll survey of nine countries, our young people—ages eighteen to twenty four—ranked the lowest in knowledge of geography of any country. Their knowledge of history is so poor that some think we fought alongside the Germans in World War II.

In a study of science and math performances of thirteen-year-olds in the United States and eleven other countries and Canadian provinces, the United States came out at the bottom. South Korean children scored highest.[20]

There is fear that the abysmal ignorance and the shocking level of illiteracy and "innumeracy" among our people threaten our economy, our political system, and our national security.

Public children's television could play an important role in remedying this situation, both through some of its entertainment programming and through educational material produced for classroom use or for home use in conjunction with schoolwork.

In Japan some 85 percent of classrooms have TV sets. Since the 1970s the Koreans have made extensive use of television and radio programming to help teach math and science skills.

In the United States the older children's channel could be used for educational purposes during school hours.

It is just possible that the combination of an epidemic of violence and the proliferation of illiteracy and ignorance among our young will lead Congress and the President to turn to the enormous educational and socializing potential of public children's television.

13
Films and Videos: When Blood and Guts Is Fun

When the problem of violence in films is brought up there are invariably those who argue that things haven't changed much: There have always been violent plays and stories, such as Homer's *Iliad,* Shakespeare's *Macbeth,* or Melville's *Moby Dick.* Generations of children have been terrified by gruesome fairy tales like "Hansel and Gretel." Through the centuries a few disturbed individuals have been tilted toward acts of violence by what they have seen or read. Only hysterics would propose that we suddenly begin censoring the arts.

This argument is based on two mistaken assumptions. The first is that it makes sense to use past customs and traditions with respect to children in order to justify present practices. The second is that there is no significant quantitative and qualitative difference between the past and the present with respect to violent entertainment.

Throughout most of Western history children have been the victims of cruel and often violent practices. In *The History of Childhood: The Untold Story of Child Abuse,* Lloyd deMause advises us that "the history of childhood is a nightmare from which we have only recently begun to awaken. The further back in history one goes, the lower the level of child care, and the more likely children are to be killed, abandoned, beaten, terrorized, and sexually abused."[1]

To adopt uncritically past traditions with respect to child-rearing is akin to accepting unquestioningly that placing leeches on people in order to draw out "bad blood" is a good medical practice.

For example, it should not be *assumed* that all classic fairy tales or epic tales of violence are good for children and do not encourage violence. They need to be carefully and thoroughly assessed in light of contemporary knowledge of child development and psychology.

As for the assumption that there is no quantitative or qualitative difference between the past and the present with respect to violent entertainment, it ignores the fact that technological advances have led to our children's being enveloped in audio-visual entertainment from morning to night. How can we even begin to compare a child who watches TV twenty-four hours a week, listens to rock music for as much as four hours a day, attends movies and rents videos regularly, and owns boxes and shelves full of toys, with a child of a hundred years ago who might occasionally read or be read a violent story or fairy tale, or be bought a toy soldier? Fifty years ago a child might have listened to a few radio shows containing some verbal descriptions of violent acts, or watched some violent films at a movie house. Unlike that in earlier films, so much of today's violence is depicted at length and in graphic detail. Blood and guts are often presented from the perspective of sadistic perpetrators who view it as great fun and never get caught. As for the assumption that only a few disturbed individuals will be influenced by any of this, as we saw in Chapter 3, there are millions of boys and men who are at risk for violent behavior.

I strongly suspect that those who cling to the assumption that things haven't changed that much have had very little firsthand acquaintance with the culture in which American children grow up.

When I began to question friends, acquaintances, and people attending my lectures, I discovered that many had never even heard of slasher films, one of the most popular genres among adolescents. They had heard of Rambo films but had not seen any. Nor had they seen any of Chuck Norris's or Arnold Schwarzenegger's violence-packed "adventure" films.

This "culture gap" extends far beyond films. How many educated Americans watch twenty-eight hours of TV a week, much of it violent cartoons and police shows? How many listen to heavy metal rock and rap music or watch MTV, where violent and rapist lyrics or images are by no means an occasional aberration? How many are familiar with the military arsenals that make up a major part of the boys' aisles at many toy stores?

This culture gap permits many highly educated and often politically active and influential Americans to blind themselves to the fact that there is a qualitative difference between writers of the past describing violence in the course of their art, and the contemporary violence *industry* that surrounds children often as young as two or three with *gratuitous* violence not only in films but *in almost all areas of play and entertainment.*

When I watched several popular slasher films, including *Texas Chainsaw Massacre 2,* on my VCR I was at times so nauseated by seeing people being skinned, burned alive, cut up, dismembered, turned into meat for chili con carne or eyeball pâté that in spite of my commitment to seeing it all, I ended up pushing the fast-forward button several times. When my husband and I went to see the slasher film *Nightmare on Elm Street 4* at a movie complex in a small-town shopping mall (the culture gap is so great that some people assume these films are confined to "sleazy" theaters that specialize in X-rated films), he walked out of the theater, revolted, after about ten minutes. I stayed, occasionally closing my eyes.

The producers of slasher films assure us that their films are not really violent. They are all tongue-in-cheek, humorous, lots of fun.

Perhaps my husband and I are lacking in a sense of humor? Too old? Just not getting it? Perhaps not. When I asked some nine-year-olds how they felt about slasher/horror films, the responses included: "I watch a horror movie, I get a nightmare" and "I watched a few and I got nightmares."

I use the term "slasher film" to include slasher/horror films. Before the unprecedented violence of slasher films was introduced, horror films were not especially violent. They were spooky and scary. Since the mid-1970s the two genres have been mixed, reaching unprecedented heights of horror and gore in films like the Nightmare on Elm Street series. Some science fiction/horror films can also be terrifying to children: A seventeen-year-old told me that when she was six she happened to see a preview of *Invasion of the Body Snatchers.* She was so disturbed by it that for about five years thereafter when going to the movies, she would wait outside until the previews were over, before entering.

A study reported in *The Journal of Personality and Social Psychology* informs us that "teenage men who can watch horror movies like the 'Friday the Thirteenth' series without showing signs of distress are seen by their dates as more attractive because of their bravado."[2] The research on which this article is based corroborates what I was told at my local video store: slasher films are taken out mostly by teenage boys, frequently to watch them with dates.

It is the qualities of the masculine mystique—toughness, fearlessness, emotional detachment, insensitivity—that these young men are demonstrating to their dates, not their sense of humor. It seems that we adults are not alone in "misunderstanding" these films. Many young people do not grasp their tongue-in-cheek quality either. Girls are often disgusted and terrified by them. Boys often prove their manhood by staying cool.

In a book entitled *The Question of Pornography,* psychologists Edward Donnerstein, Daniel Linz, and Steven Penrod point out that desensitization therapy has proven to be the most effective technique for getting people to engage in behavior that was previously too anxiety provoking. A major component of the technique involves combining stimuli that provoke anxiety with stimuli that promote relaxation. Slasher films frequently combine stimuli in this fashion. Extremely violent scenes are often followed by relaxing music or mildly erotic scenes. Many of the films are set in nice, "normal" suburban environments.

Donnerstein and his coauthors describe a research study in which they sought to test the desensitizing qualities of slasher films. Fifty-two men were chosen out of a larger group because they seemed *"least likely to become desensitized."* They were then shown one slasher film a day for five days. The results of the experiments lent support to earlier studies that had shown an increase in the acceptance of violent behavior as a result of viewing violent films. Changes occurred in the men's evaluation of how violent, degrading, and offensive scenes were. Material that the men had earlier found anxiety provoking and depressing became less so. After being exposed to large doses of filmed violence against women, they judged that female victims of assault and rape were less injured than did men in a control group. They were less able to empathize with *real-life* rape victims.

It seems that many of the young men who show off their "masculinity" to their dates by remaining cool at slasher films may simply have become desensitized to grotesque, extreme violence through long-term exposure.

Millions of Americans, teenagers especially but also many younger children, have been watching slasher films in movie theaters and on VCRs for the last fourteen years or so.

The *NCTV News* tells us that "It is now a standard part of American culture to view numerous extremely graphic and brutal horror films before the age of 12. In one central Illinois High school studied by NCTV [the National Coalition on Television Violence], virtually every student had seen *Friday the 13th* and *Halloween* and 20% had seen the *Texas Chainsaw Massacre.*"[3] The article goes on to point out that "the current generation of Americans [are] being raised on the most sadistic material ever conceived by humans . . ."

Slasher films appear to be very popular in our ghettos. My informal survey of films shown at some inner-city New York movie theaters over a period of several years leaves me with the impression that approximately 70 percent of them (including many slasher and adventure films) are violent.

Why do so many young people see these films?

There is not one answer. For relatively healthy kids they may represent a form of adolescent rebellion: the facts that the films are so grotesquely violent, revolting, without any social or other redeeming value, and are disliked by most parents (or would be if the parents saw them) may all be pluses in their eyes. Then there is peer pressure. Many young people see them so that they can say that they saw them, so that they can be "in." For boys there is the opportunity to prove one's toughness. There is the search for intense experiences, thrills, excitement—motivations similar to those attracting people to roller coaster rides. But for disturbed young men, the interest can have a very different and far more intense quality, involving a fascination, in some cases an obsession, with the morbid, the violent. The violence against women can no doubt serve as an added attraction. For some, the films serve as detailed gruesome blueprints for acting out their rage and frustration.

Just before Halloween 1988, in the small town of Greenfield, Massachusetts, twenty-year-old Sharon Gregory's mutilated body was found by her twin sister in the bathtub of their parents' home. She had been murdered by eighteen-year-old Mark Branch, a young man of limited intelligence, who hanged himself shortly afterward. In a 1989 interview, Greenfield Police Captain Joseph La Chance told me that in searching Branch's home the police had found more than one hundred slasher films. Branch had a fascination with Jason, the hero of the very popular *Friday the 13th* movie series. Jason stabs, slashes, mutilates, and kills teenagers, but can't be killed. La Chance also told me that in his home Branch "had a lot of the Jason paraphernalia —the hockey mask, combat boots, and some of his apparel would match the clothes that would be worn by Jason in the film."

A few years ago three high school students—including the student body president—from Carl Junction, Missouri, bludgeoned a fellow student to death with about seventy blows from their baseball bats. They did it just for "fun," they later explained. Perhaps to bolster their courage—they had lost their nerve when they set out to kill the boy a week earlier—two of the boys watched *Texas Chainsaw Massacre 2* the night before the killing.[4]

In slasher films as in the endlessly violent "adventure" films featuring such actors as Sylvester Stallone, Chuck Norris, or Arnold Schwarzenegger, the perpetrators of violence are almost invariably men. It is young boys in particular who are being reinforced to commit acts of rape, murder, and sadism. Girls are also being influenced to commit acts of violence—studies show that girls more frequently identify with male heroes than boys do with heroines—but even more so to accept victimization. In slasher films women are constantly depicted as victims of the most extreme violence.

A recent survey of seventeen hundred students in the sixth to ninth grades revealed that 65 percent of the boys and 57 percent of the girls said it was acceptable for a man to force a woman to have sex if they had been dating for more than six months. And 51 percent of the boys and 41 percent of the girls said a man had a right to force a woman to kiss him if he had spent "a lot of money" on her. That amount was defined as ten to fifteen dollars.[5]

REGULATING FOR THE PROTECTION OF CHILDREN

There is no reason why future generations of Americans must continue to be raised on entertainment that encourages them to act violently and to accept violence as a natural and inevitable part of their lives. There is a long tradition in the American judicial system of special laws for the protection of children. These include labor, liquor, child pornography, and child welfare laws. As we saw earlier, in the First Amendment area, laws protecting children from pornography and "indecent" language have been upheld in recent years. The 1973 *Carlin v. FCC* Supreme Court decision held that children must be protected from "indecent" language on the radio. In 1968, in the case of *Ginzberg v. New York,* the Supreme Court held that the state had the right to forbid children under seventeen to buy sexually explicit magazines that adults could legally purchase.

Our double standard with respect to sex and violence has led to a dearth of precedents for protecting children from violent entertainment. But First Amendment specialists assure me that laws designed for that purpose would stand a very good chance of being upheld in the courts as long as they did not interfere with adults' viewing whatever they chose. Films and videotapes, unlike television, can easily be regulated for children without interfering with adult activities.

The problems involved in establishing such regulations, as well as the other regulations recommended in this chapter, are mainly those that are common to any regulatory process. They include financial costs both to government and to the regulated industries, difficult and sometimes arbitrary or erroneous decisions in borderline cases, problems in enforcing regulations, establishment of yet another government bureaucracy intruding into the private sector, the risk of co-option of the agency by the industry, and danger that the bureaucracy will exceed its proper limitations.

In spite of these kinds of difficulties, there are few of us who would like to see the Federal Drug Administration or the Consumer Safety Protection Agency abolished simply because they sometimes make mistakes and cost a lot of money. The pertinent question is whether a particular area needs regulation in order to protect the interests of citizens. If the answer is yes, then the imperfections of the regulatory system are something that must be dealt with.

We need a rating system for films and video films based on violent content. Children and adolescents* should not be admitted into movie theaters showing inappropriately violent films; nor should they be allowed to rent or buy violent videotapes. In video stores these tapes should be kept in an inaccessible area. (At present there is no rating or regulation of video films in most states. A child of any age can rent any film.)

Consultations with specialists in the field of government regulation have led me to envisage a system combining federal and state regulation. The process might begin with the appointment by Congress or the President of a blue-ribbon Commission for Standards in Children's Entertainment. Its mission would be to set up a viable film violence rating system. Congress would then

---

* Here, and in following chapters, when I advocate regulations limiting children's access to violent entertainment, I leave open the question at what age regulations should cease to be enforced. It can best be answered by the blue-ribbon Commissions for Standards in Children's Entertainment described below. There would no doubt be variations in age restrictions. For example, some films may be acceptable at age thirteen; others not before age seventeen or eighteen.

pass legislation requiring disclosure by the motion picture and video industry of violence in films in accordance with this rating system. A Bureau for Standards in Children's Entertainment, which might be housed in the Department of Health and Human Services or in the Consumer Product Safety Commission, would make sure that the industry complies with disclosure standards. States would pass laws prohibiting children under a certain age from seeing films with high violence ratings. These laws would be enforced through routine inspections and significant penalties imposed on movie houses and video stores that do not comply.

The blue-ribbon commission should include some of the most distinguished social scientists in the field of media violence research, representatives of film companies, filmmakers, communications experts, representatives of professional associations such as the American Academy of Child Psychologists, representatives from major parent groups such as the PTA, and representatives from each of the major religious denominations.

Under the guidance of the research knowledge brought to bear by the social scientists, this group would develop a rating system. There is no reason to believe that the difficulties in establishing such a system are insuperable.

George Comstock, on the basis of his survey and analysis of 235 TV and film studies, has compiled a list of characteristics that make films particularly likely to influence young people to violence. These characteristics include the graphic depiction of violence, the absence of punishment for violent acts, and the absence of serious emotional or physical consequences. This kind of information and analysis would be invaluable in establishing viable criteria to distinguish between acceptable and unacceptable violence. A rating system created with the help of social science experts, professionals concerned with the wellbeing of children, representatives of children's and parents' interests groups, and so forth would be more likely to come up with viable criteria for rating children's films than a filmmakers' association such as the MPAA, which has been rating films' sexual content since 1968. The MPAA's main concern is still with helping filmmakers maximize profit.

In current MPAA ratings, films deemed appropriate for adults only are rated NC-17. Children under seventeen are not allowed in. Slasher films are rated R: those under seventeen are allowed in if accompanied by an adult. However, *the enforcement of these ratings is entirely voluntary.* A random, informal survey of young people from a variety of states across the country reveals that the R ratings are rarely enforced.

The National Coalition on Television Violence has developed a rating system for both violence and inappropriate sex. (Film ratings appear in its newsletter.)

The NCTV ratings include R-13, which allows adolescents to see a movie without parent or guide even though it may promote "minor amounts of inappropriate violence" or "contains antisocial themes that parents should discourage." A PGV rating informs parents that a film has violence that "may frighten some young children, but probably does not teach violence." An XV rating stands for "high levels of intense violence of a very harmful nature."

In some films the graphic depiction of violence may serve an educational or other meaningful purpose. For example, the NCTV describes *Hope and Glory,* a film about a little boy's experience of World War II in London, as being highly violent, yet gives it an R-13 rating. *Platoon* is an extremely violent film but by contrast with *Rambo* would be very unlikely to encourage violence or unrealistic fantasies about war.

Borrowing the MPAA terminology, it is important that films with the highest ratings of gratuitous graphic violence—slasher and Rambo films would be a prime example—be rated NC-17 rather than R. Some parents are so desensitized to violence that they take their young children to see the most violent films imaginable. The movie theater where I saw *Nightmare on Elm Street 4* was filled with young children. In front of me, clinging to her mother—or perhaps it was a sister or babysitter—sat a little girl who could not have been more than two or three years old. It is difficult to imagine many experiences more terrifying to young children than watching Freddy Krueger, the monster-hero of the series, use the immense knives that are attached to his fingers to slice up teenagers, or to see Freddy crack open a girl's body at the joints and have blood and muscle oozing out.

We do not allow adults to take children to see pornographic films; they should not be allowed to take them to see violence-ridden films either.

I am well aware that parents could still rent films rated NC-17 for violence and allow their children to see them at home. Here, as with TV viewing, there is no perfect system, no way to completely protect children from inappropriate violence. An ongoing educational campaign and child-rearing classes would help enormously.

If there were regulations protecting children from gratuitously violent films, eventually it would become as unthinkable for parents to rent such films for their children as it is now to rent pornographic films for one's children.

14
Music and Wrestling: The "Joys" of Rape, Satanism, and Bigotry

In November 1985 the city of San Antonio, Texas, passed an ordinance forbidding any child under the age of thirteen from attending violent and lewd rock concerts unless accompanied by a parent or guardian. I suspect that many if not most Americans are unaware that children as young as nine or ten attend rock concerts. Nor are they aware of what goes on at some of these concerts.

Most rock musicians are responsible, concerned performers and people. Many have donated their talents to raise money for victims of starvation, AIDS, and other worthy causes; some have taken strong positions against the abuse of drugs and alcohol.

But there are some who seem neither responsible nor concerned, at least when it comes to the effect of their music on young people. Almost all of them belong to that subgroup of rock known as heavy metal. The full impact of their lyrics of violence, satanism, and suicide can only be appreciated in the context of the harsh, angry music and demeanor of the men performing. The reader will have to make do with the lyrics, in most cases highly truncated.*

A youngster at a heavy metal concert might hear the popular group Motley Crue sing a song that describes fantasies of assaulting a woman and then states: "Get my ways at will. / Go for the throat, . . . / Going in for the kill."[1]

Kids at a Ted Nugent concert might hear the following lyrics from a song entitled "Violent Love": "Took her in the room with the mirrors on the walls, / Showed her my brand new whip . . . / Screamed as she started to slip. Give me a dose / Of your violent love."

Young people's sex education might continue with Judas Priest singing about a "chick" "squealing in passion as the rod of steel injects" ("Eat Me Alive"); or the Great White singing "Gonna drive my love inside you / Gonna nail your ass to the floor" ("On Your Knees").

When it comes to satanism, a song entitled "Sacrifice" by Venom begins by describing candles and altar aglow, prepared for a sacrifice to the master Lucifer. Some of the other lyrics include, "Virgin's death is needed there . . . raise the knife . . . Plunge the dagger in her breast."

Lest the reader think I have dragged out a few obscure titles, let me make it clear that while heavy metal fans represent only one segment of young rock music fans, their numbers are by no means insignificant. Albums containing violent lyrics are often on the Billboard pop chart, and millions have been sold.

For example, included in *Girls, Girls, Girls,* a 1987 Motley Crue album that reached #2 on the Billboard pop chart and sold over

* In spite of repeated written requests over a period of three months, most of the publishers who hold the copyrights to these songs have failed to send me permission to quote from them. (Their fervent commitment to the First Amendment rights of their performers does not seem to extend to my rights as an author.) As a result, most excerpts are limited to very short passages which may be quoted without permission. The four companies that granted me permission are listed in the acknowledgments at the beginning of the book.

two million copies, is a song that goes, "Those last few nights it ['the blade of my knife'] turned and sliced you apart / Laid out cold, now we're both alone . . . / But killing you helped me keep you home."

In 1989 Guns N' Roses came out with an album called *G'N'R Lies* which was number five among the year's top sellers and sold over four million copies. It featured a hatemongering song that includes the following lyrics: "Police and niggers—that's right—get outta my way . . . / Immigrants and faggots, they make no sense to me . . . / Think they can do what they please . . ."

Besides these kinds of lyrics, kids are sometimes treated to "entertainment" that reinforces the music's messages of violence.

Ozzy Osbourne, the lead vocalist for the heavy metal band Black Sabbath, once bit off the head of a live bat at a concert.

Blackie Lawless of W.A.S.P. (which stands for We Are Sexual Perverts) has drunk "blood" out of a human skull. Past performances of W.A.S.P. have included simulating violent attacks against half-nude women involving torture racks, attacks with knives and circular saw blades, and fake blood.

After listening to the music and hearing about the "entertainment," one is not surprised to hear about violence at or after concerts. For example, at a concert in Los Angeles featuring the group X, a girl of seventeen was raped at knife point. In Tacoma, Washington, a nineteen-year-old man was killed and a sixteen-year-old girl stabbed at a Judas Priest Concert.

Teenage suicide rates have soared since 1960. Rates are highest among white males, who are also the greatest fans of heavy metal rock.[2] There have been several lawsuits by parents whose sons committed suicide after spending hours listening to groups like Suicidal Tendencies sing songs like the following: "Sick of people—no one real; / Sick of chicks—they're all bitches; / Sick of you—you're too hip; / Sick of life—it sucks . . . / Sick of life —it sucks; / Sick and tired—and no one cares; / Sick of myself—don't wanna live; / Sick of living—gonna die."

Heavy drinking and drugs play an important part in many acts of violence. Children and teenagers get the message on "drinking and doing drugs" not just from songs but from the lifestyle and concert behavior of some musicians.

Mick Mars of Motley Crue advises the boys: "After you're

done relaxing you can drink a lot. Drink and bone massive amounts of women. In that order, because some girls look a little better when you're high."[3]

Black Sabbath has a song about "drinking whiskey and tequila while cruising down the road at 105 miles an hour."

Kids are aware that the use of drugs is rampant among rock stars, but musicians could get arrested for snorting coke or shooting heroin at a concert and so they don't. There is no such concern with liquor.

Dr. Carl Taylor teaches criminal justice at Michigan State University and is president of a company that provides security services at rock concerts. He tells us that sometimes a performer "goes right into the crowd. A singer will pull out his bottle of Jack Daniel's, and the kids will pull out theirs."[4] More generally he is convinced that rock stars are "dictating a lifestyle to the kids, who say, 'If this guy drinks Jack Daniel's, I'll drink Jack Daniel's.' " He concludes: "Yes, the band members *do* influence the kids, very much so." One area in which they are no doubt influenced is driving. These plugs for alcohol can only serve to increase drunk driving, which is the leading cause of death among white males aged fifteen to twenty-four.

Serious concern with violent rock music lyrics is often dismissed on the grounds that very few young people listen to this music. A recent survey of 694 junior and high school students casts doubt on this assumption. Researchers found that 9 percent of the junior high school students, 17 percent of the rural and 25 percent of the urban high school students were fans of HSS (homicide, satanism, suicide) rock music. Slightly over 72 percent of the HSS fans were male, and about 96 percent were white.

Another common assumption is that young people are unable to decipher the lyrics of these songs. This study revealed that HSS fans spent considerably more time listening to rock music than the rest of the rock fans surveyed and a far higher proportion of them knew the lyrics of their favorite songs.[5]

Our attention until now has been focused on heavy metal rock music, but rap music has also become extremely popular with many young people. Many rappers, almost all of whom are African-Americans, are committed to helping young people move away from drugs and violence. Some even started a "Stop the Violence" movement. However, too many rap lyrics still encourage violent behavior, or center on the denigration and subjugation of women. There is a frequent boastfulness in the lyrics that makes it unthinkable that a woman could or should resist a man's advances. Here, as with rock music, young boys are encouraged to connect sex with dominance and rape. 2 Live Crew is a particularly offensive group. The following lyrics are excerpted from one of its songs entitled "We Want Some Pussy." It describes a group of young men involved in a game called "train" or "Amtrack" in which they take turns "waxin' girls' behinds." The penis of one of the young men gets stuck. The song continues: "The girls would say 'Stop,' I'd say 'I'm not' " and then "With my dick in my hands, as you fall to your knees . . . Just nibble on my dick like a rat does cheese."

The lyrics of another piece, entitled "Dick Almighty," describe a young woman's enormous desire and efforts to have oral sex with "this big black cock." It goes on to say "He'll tear the pussy open, 'cause it's satisfaction . . . Dick's so proudful, she'll kneel and pray . . . Suck my dick, bitch, it'll make you puke."*

Rapper Eazy-E goes beyond penis worship in the following piece: "I creeped on my bitch with my / Uzi machine / Went to the house and kicked / down the door / Unloaded like hell . . ."

Eazy-E is a member of a rap group that calls itself NWA (Niggas With Attitude). NWA has been widely criticized for glamorizing gang violence. At a time when the major cause of death among young African-American males is homicide, lyrics like the following are particularly disturbing. They are from a song on NWA's very popular album entitled *Straight Outta Compton.*

Since I was a youth, I'd smoke weed out
Now I'm the motherfucker that you read about

* "Dick Almighty" is from an album entitled *As Nasty as They Wanna Be.* In October 1990, a Fort Lauderdale, Florida, record-store owner was convicted for selling a copy of the album, which was deemed to be obscene. Shortly thereafter members of the group went on trial for performing the same material at a Fort Lauderdale concert. They were acquitted. Besides my reservations about censorship aimed at adults, I am disturbed that an African-American group was singled out for prosecution when the lyrics of some white heavy metal performers are just as offensive.

> Takin' a life or two, that's what the hell I do
> You don't like how I'm livin', well fuck you
> This is a gang and I'm in it . . .
> I got a shotgun and here's the plot
> Takin' niggers out with a flurry of buckshot
> Boom boom boom, yeah I was gunnin'
> And then you look all you see is niggers runnin
> And fallin and yellin and pushin and screamin and cussin . . .

When a popular group like NWA sings lyrics like these, when they fail to deplore the violence or point to other ways of being, they are obviously doing much more than just depicting ghetto reality. They are reinforcing it.

By the late 1980s rap music had become very popular among young white Americans. An April 10, 1990, *New York Times* article reported that some upper-middle-class white boys were forming gangs of their own or joining African-American or Hispanic gangs like the Crips and Bloods. It may well be that the glamorization of gang violence by NWA and groups like them is playing a role in this new trend.

Another song by NWA on the *Straight Outta Compton* album is entitled "Fuck the Police." It includes a line about "taking out a cop or two" and has led to protests from the FBI and police groups.

A rap group called Public Enemy has achieved some notoriety because of the anti-Semitic pronouncements of one of its members, Richard Griffin (known as Professor Griff). Griffin has cited the forged *Protocols of the Elders of Zion* as evidence of an international Jewish conspiracy and has blamed Jews for "the majority of wickedness that goes on across the globe."[6] Jewish organizations have denounced some of the lyrics in Public Enemy's song "Welcome to the Terrordome" as being anti-Semitic. They have become increasingly concerned, as one Anti-Defamation League official put it, that "hatred is becoming hip" in popular music.

Like heavy metal concerts, rap concerts have their share of violence. When a Run-DMC concert in Long Beach, California, led to forty-two injuries, *Rolling Stone* reported that this was the fifth time in a period of months that a concert of theirs had been marred by serious injuries and arrests. After a Run-DMC concert in Pittsburgh, twenty-five people were arrested and twenty-two were treated at hospitals. Eight store windows were broken, and some looting took place.

When the wives of several government officials, among them Tipper Gore, the wife of Tennessee Senator Albert Gore, started listening to some of the tapes and records their children were bringing home, they decided to do something about violence and pornography in rock music.

In 1985 they formed a nonprofit organization, Parents Music Resource Center (PMRC). In 1987 Tipper Gore published *Raising PG Children in an X-rated Society*. PMRC's goals include publicizing the excesses in song lyrics and videos and creating a consumer movement to put pressure on the industry. They want industry leaders to take corporate responsibility for their products. One of their demands has been that recording companies publish lyric sheets attached to record albums and/or place warning labels on explicit or violent albums, so that parents can know what their children want to buy or have bought.

PMRC, and in particular Tipper Gore, have been virulently attacked by some industry members, performers, and civil libertarians, who contend that these proposals amount to an infringement of First Amendment rights.

Gore's efforts to protect children and adolescents from violent, rape-glorifying lyrics have led to her repeatedly being called a prude and suffering a variety of personal insults. A rap song called "Freedom of Speech" by Ice-T includes the following lines: "Think I give a fuck about some silly bitch named Gore / Yo PMRC, here we go, roar / Yo Tip, what's the matter with you, ain't get no dick."

When I visited a Tower Records store in the summer of 1988, I found neither printed lyrics, nor warnings, nor much corporate responsibility in titles such as "Final Genocide," "Eat Shit Get Away," "Chainsaw Slaughter," and "Fuck Off," by Dissection. The jacket of this particular album showed a man with a chainsaw cutting up another man. The address of the "Chainsaw Slaughter Fan Club" was included for those interested. A record by The Dehumanizers included titles like: "Chemical Death," "Grandma, I'm a Drug Fiend," and "Mow 'Em Down."

Around the same time, when I spoke to Jennifer Norwood, the

Executive Director of PMRC, she expressed her disappointment at the response of most record companies. Few of the twenty-two companies that had agreed to label their albums actually did so. Some of those who did used minuscule labels, some of them hardly visible. Some companies printed lyrics for a while and then discontinued the practice.

By March 1990, things had begun to change. Norwood told me that the PMRC now anticipated that voluntary standardized labeling would become the norm throughout the industry within six months. She attributed this change in large part to the fear of mandatory regulation: eighteen states were considering legislation and the Missouri legislature had already introduced a bill mandating warning labels. Norwood's prediction was borne out in May 1990 when the industry announced that it would voluntarily apply standardized labels to all albums, tapes, and discs.

REGULATIONS, NOT CENSORSHIP

PMRC's work and Gore's book have been of great value in making parents more aware of the content of some contemporary music, but, like every group concerned with violence in the media, PMRC is firmly opposed to any "censorship." They are even opposed to states' mandating warning labels.

I share these groups' concern about the dangers of censorship. But as we have seen *censorship must be distinguished from regulations that protect children and do not interfere with the First Amendment rights of adults.* (The distinction between forbidding something and regulating it is captured by the difference between the 1920s Prohibition laws and current laws *regulating* the sale of liquor to minors.)

The kinds of regulations I advocate in this chapter would do much more to enhance the personal freedom of Americans than continuing to allow children to be raised in a culture that encourages them to commit acts of violence that threaten not only the freedom but the very lives of others and themselves.

With respect to live concerts, I would go further than the San Antonio statute described at the beginning of this chapter. Minors are not allowed in bars or pornographic shows. I would favor similar state bans with respect to concert performances in which violence, racism, anti-Semitism, bigotry, drinking, or taking drugs, is promoted. We also need state laws regulating the sale of tapes, compact discs, and records to children and adolescents.*

As with films, a blue-ribbon Commission for Standards in Children's Entertainment would establish guidelines. A disclosure law enacted by Congress would require that the industry rate all tapes, discs, and records in accordance with these guidelines.

Much has been made of the difficulty of rating rock music because some of the violent and pro-drug messages are hidden behind symbolism. Such difficulties are not insurmountable. The commission might decide to stick to clear-cut statements— of the kind quoted in this chapter—and let symbolic messages pass, since they are more difficult to deal with. This would still represent enormous improvement over the current situation. And if one considers the alternative of continuing to let our children be exposed to rapist, satanic, suicidal, bigoted lyrics, the difficulties of regulation are well worth dealing with.

I can hear voices of dissent questioning the regulation of violent rock and rap music when, unlike TV and films, there are no definitive studies showing that listening to violent lyrics leads young people to act violently. It is true that so far there are few studies on the effects of listening to violent rock or rap music. But do we need such studies?

There is considerable evidence from the field of child development that children learn by emulating those they admire. From the field of anthropology we know that the elements that compose a culture are rarely disconnected from each other. Lyrics that describe violence and drug taking in a positive way both reflect a society which is violent and drug-ridden and help to perpetuate violence and drug abuse.

In addition, there is considerable clinical and anecdotal evidence that young people are influenced by music. Dr. Paul King is a clinical professor of child and adolescent psychiatry at the University of Tennessee's medical school in Memphis. He is also

---

* At present, in most states there is no rating or regulation of VCR films whatsoever, so that a child of any age can rent any film. The Motion Picture Association of America (MPAA) is actively lobbying against bills pending in several states which mandate severe penalties for renting R-rated or NC-17–rated films to minors. A minority of video store owners voluntarily refuse to rent such films to young people.

director of adolescent services at Lakeside Hospital, where he carried out a study of 470 adolescents admitted for drug or psychiatric treatment. Of 203 chemically dependent adolescents, 59 percent were "into" heavy metal music and 79 percent had problems with violence.

He writes: "Heavy metal music has been cited by parents of drug-addicted teenagers as aggravating their children's problem. Police and social agency workers from New Jersey to California have implicated it as a contributing factor in a number of highly publicized murder and suicide cases."[7] His own conclusion is that "a teenager already saturated with negative feelings about self and the future can draw inspiration from heavy metal music that affirms antisocial, drug-addictive behavior. The attraction of heavy metal music is its message that a higher power controls the world, and that that power is hate—often personified by Satan. Hopeless, troubled youngsters can sink their teeth into this philosophy . . ."[8]

In treatment, young patients at Dr. King's hospital are "demetalized" : no music or paraphernalia is allowed. This practice is typical of a good number of treatment centers around the country where the connection between violent behavior and heavy metal, satanism, and chemical dependence has been observed.

This connection is documented in numerous issues of the National Coalition on Television Violence's newsletter, the *NCTV News.* The January–February 1988 issue tells us that "Richard Ramirez, a serial murderer, was deeply into heavy metal music and was an AC/DC fan. When arrested he was wearing an AC/DC T-shirt and told the investigating officer, 'I love to kill people, I love to see them die.' He was humming the AC/DC song 'Night Prowler' at the time of the arrest. The heavy satanic themes of AC/DC were noted. In another AC/DC-linked satanic death Ricky Kaso of Riverhead, New Jersey, in 1984 stabbed a friend seventeen times and plucked out the friend's eye while killing him. Kaso and his friends were into heavy metal and satanism."

The Carl Junction, Missouri, high school students mentioned earlier who bludgeoned a fellow student to death just for "fun" after watching *Texas Chainsaw Massacre 2* the night before were also heavy metal rock fans, and involved in satanism.

When it comes to the physical health of Americans, the Federal Drug Administration takes no chances. New drugs may not be sold until they have been thoroughly tested and shown to be safe. I would recommend a similar attitude with respect to the mental health and moral well-being of our children.

The only practical justification I see for having further studies done before enacting regulations with respect to violent rock or rap music would be that such studies are necessary in order to get popular support for the regulations.

Professor of public administration, Alan Rosenbloom has suggested to me that because my proposals with respect to regulating children's entertainment go "against deeply ingrained values which support violence," it may be necessary in order to develop a public consciousness of the problems to start out with some kind of advisory presidential commission similar to the Council on Environmental Quality or an independent commission like the Commission on Civil Rights.[9] A commission of this type could provide a form of consciousness-raising preliminary to the kinds of regulations that I am advocating, and could develop support for child-oriented protective regulations.

If Professor Rosenbloom is right and we are not as a nation ready for the regulation of children's entertainment, then perhaps studies on the effects of violent rock and rap music would be part of that consciousness-raising process.

As we have seen, there are more than enough studies of TV and film violence. Their results need to be more widely publicized.

PROFESSIONAL WRESTLING: FIGHTING AND ETHNIC SLURS AS FAMILY FUN

Professional wrestling is a form of entertainment in which wrestling is simulated. It shares several characteristics with violent heavy metal concerts. They both attract large numbers of children and teenagers. They are both saturated with violence. Attendance at both has been increased through TV programming; MTV increases interest in rock concerts; Saturday morning TV wrestling aimed at young children increases interest in live wrestling, especially among young boys.

Heavy metal rock musicians and professional wrestlers have

been known to pool their talents. They have joined forces for mud-wrestling performances in which scantily clad female wrestlers go at each other to the accompaniment of heavy metal music.

While heavy metal concerts attract children as young as nine or ten, wrestling exhibitions are filled with *very* young children—more boys than girls—who are brought there by their parents. Some of them are only two or three years old, although most of them seem to be in the six to twelve range. About one third of the audience at the Madison Square Garden exhibition I attended on a school night was made up of children. This seems to be fairly average, judging by the composition of the audience in televised performances.

When professional wrestling groups first decided to market wrestling to children, they hired rock star Cyndi Lauper, who was extremely popular with young teens, to make appearances at live and televised wrestling matches.

While the performers' violence at rock concerts is mostly verbal, the violence at wrestling exhibitions is physical. Most adults know that the wrestlers' acts of violence are simulated. I suspect that most children do not know. To them when the wrestlers kick and punch each other, pull each other's hair, throw each other down to the mat and sometimes out of the wrestling ring, it is real. The reality of the punches, the groans, the bodies falling to the ground, is amplified through the loudspeakers hidden under the wrestling ring.

In spite of this heightened reality no one ever gets hurt. There are no concussions, no broken legs, almost no blood.

Children are being completely misled as to the effects of physically attacking others.

They are also being reinforced in the most perverse xenophobia and simplistic good-guys-versus-bad-guys thinking.

Every wrestling exhibition has its good guys to root for and its bad guys to boo. And a lot of the time, the bad guy is a foreigner or a member of a minority group.* Combining both of these characteristics was a late 1980's tag team called the Bolsheviks—

---

* At the wrestling match I attended at New York City's Madison Square Garden, the bad guys were all Canadians. Apparently the city is so filled with ethnic minorities that Canadians are the only safe group to hate.

evil Commies who will do anything to win—managed by Slick, an African-American man who looked like a pimp.

All this may seem very funny to some adults, but the six- and eight-year-olds are not laughing. They are taking it all very seriously. They are learning.

But surely some of the children—especially the older ones—must know that it is all a show, that these people aren't really hurting each other, or not as badly as they seem to be. What if they do? How much difference does that make?

We have overwhelming evidence from TV and film research that viewing simulated violence on the screen encourages violent behavior. Why would simulated violence in the form of wrestling be exempt? And why would live wrestling have less influence on boys than wrestling viewed on TV?

I would favor regulations prohibiting children from attending professional wrestling exhibitions, whether accompanied by an adult or not. Since wrestling exhibitions are not covered by the First Amendment, there would be no legal impediment to passing state regulations to this effect.

15
When the Toy Store Looks Like a Military Arsenal

As we saw earlier, it cannot be assumed that what children were allowed or even encouraged, to do in the past was good for them or for society. When we are told not to worry, that boys have always played with toy soldiers, guns, tanks, and bows and arrows, we must not forget that many of those same boys, when they became men, enthusiastically went off to or supported wars they knew little about, got into barroom brawls, and battered their wives and children. Today the situation with respect to violence toys* is very seriously aggravated in several ways:

* In order to capture the quality of today's toys more accurately, I use the term "violence toys," instead of the usual "war toys." The reasons for this usage will be discussed below.

1. Not only are boys encouraged to play with violence toys, but TV, films, and VCRs provide them with an endless series of violent heroes and scenarios to emulate.

In addition, as we saw in Chapter 12, since the early 1980s TV programs centered around a particular toy have been created by toy manufacturers with no other goal than to advertise that product. A boy who plays with Transformers, He-Man, or Ninja Turtles, or some of the numerous accoutrements that come with these toys, has a specific violent story line to imitate in his play. When the show is eventually taken off the air, it is still available at the video store.

2. Toy manufacturers now often provide a violent story line or characterization that goes along with their toy. The story line sometimes has political content.

The Rambo 81mm Mortar Thunder–Tube Assault, which is recommended for age five and up, comes with a detailed scenario: "The S.A.V.A.G.E. Army will stop at nothing in their attempt to control the world!" the box cover explains. "Their weapons, mostly stolen from the free world's ammo dumps, see a lot of action against Rambo and The Force of Freedom." Boys are also provided with factual information about the real weapon that the toy is based on: "The 81mm mortar is used to lob ammo over hills and fortifications, and is effective because of its large bursting radius. It is currently used by the U.S. Forces, Australia, Austria, and Italy."

The GI Joe series of war toys make it clear that the enemy consists of "jungle-dwelling guerrillas dedicated to totalitarian world takeover."

Transformers are extremely popular futuristic, militaristic toys. Each toy can be transformed from a metal robot warrior into a plane or helicopter or other military object. In addition to having been for many years the subject of one of the most violent cartoon shows on TV (now available on video), every Transformer comes with a motto, a characterization, and a function.

The motto for the "Rampage" Transformer is "those who conquer act; those who are conquered think!" Its characterization includes: "Barrels through life with an uncontrolled fury. Has difficulty talking coherently for more than a few seconds before violently lashing out at anything near him, friend or foe." Its function is: "Gunner."

The "Horri-Bull" Transformer is described as "a snorting, belching bully with a nasty temper . . . Enjoys destroying anything that stands in his way . . ."

The Slugslinger Transformer likes "sneaking up and shooting enemies in the back . . ." These and other Transformer toys are recommended for children age five or six and up.

3. Video games represent a new area of toy violence. They were first introduced in video arcades in 1979, expanding later into the home market. According to Terri Toles, professor of communications studies at Muhlenberg and Cedar Crest colleges, approximately 90 percent of video game players are male. Women rarely appear in the games and when they do it is usually in a traditional passive "damsel in distress" role. Out of a hundred games sampled by Toles, sixty-six revolved around outright destruction.

Some games offer historic simulations; the most popular are based on battles of World War II. In some cases a boy can choose which side of the battle to take—Rommel's or Patton's. Also offered are games called "hotspots," in which a boy can simulate bombing Tripoli, or fight those smuggling arms to Nicaragua.

Sometimes political conflicts and attitudes are combined with fantasy, as in a game called "Communist Mutants from Space," in which "swarms of Marxists from the planet Rooskie attack the Earth, [and] the player is enjoined to keep the planet safe for democracy and the free enterprise system."[1]

While it is sometimes possible to attain the game's goal while avoiding violent acts, far more points are awarded when the player acts violently and aggressively. Toles also points out that since "players *must* follow the demands of the microchip that runs the game in order to play,"[2] winning involves following orders. Video games reinforce the idea of destroying "evil enemies" without asking any questions or taking any personal responsibility.

Perhaps the most common setting where obedience leads to aggression is the military. Toles informs us that the Pentagon has spent between two and three million dollars to develop training devices resembling video games. In light of the similarities between the games and combat, the army has set up video games in dayrooms and snack bars so that soldiers can sharpen their skills in their leisure time.

By 1988, the Nintendo home video game had become the most popular boys' toy in the United States, accounting for 70 percent of the two billion-dollar video game market. By February 1990 20 percent of American homes had a Nintendo video game. Rick Anguilla, editor of *Toy and Business World,* an industry trade journal, states that "for boys in this country between the ages of eight and fifteen, not having a Nintendo is like not having a baseball bat."[3] A survey conducted by the National Coalition on Television Violence revealed that 71 percent of Nintendo video games are high in violence.

Even many of Nintendo's sports games are violent. "Blades of Steel," a very popular hockey game, is described as follows: "With sharpened blades and a lethal stick you slash into a rink . . . Your opponent viciously checks you from behind, making an incredible steal. You charge after him, crushing him against the board. Suddenly tempers flare, off come the gloves, and you're swinging fists like a prizefighter."

A game of tennis is turned into something closely akin to warfare. The name "Racket Attack" is suggestive of the game's description: "Racket Attack has made you a pro, the toughest, most awesome champ ever to hit center court . . . You're fearsome at the net and in the back court. On clay or grass you attack . . . Your service, you launch it like a rocket . . ."

Nintendo's "action-adventure" games include the very popular "Super Mario 2," now a TV cartoon, which features "fierce action-packed battle to free the land of Subcon from the curse of the Evil Wart"; and "Contra," in which the universe teeters on the brink of total annihilation at the hands of a vile alien warmonger.

Among the company's more recent releases are "Nightmare on Elm Street" and "Friday the 13th" games.

4. Many men who reminisce about their own childhood war play will talk about playing cowboys and Indians, or cops and robbers, or some other version of the triumph of good over evil. Many of these games reinforced xenophobia, racial prejudices, and a narrow American perspective on the sociopolitical world. They did, however, reflect the view that right and wrong exist and that the boy will identify with what is morally right. Many of today's toys no longer make that assumption.

In the "Gunfight at O.K. Corral Game" two boys are depicted facing each other with pistols over a board game. There is no good or bad guy here; it's just plain violent fun: "It's six-shootin,' gunslingin' action two cowboys duel in an old west town." In another game the boys are encouraged to take the bad-guy role and have an "infra-red shoot-out" with the good guy Laser-Fire Marshall BraveStarr. The City Connection Nintendo game directs the boys to "Drive For Your Life! Your mission: Race your speed demon car from New York to Tokyo in record time . . . With the cops and the enemy on your tail."

Besides encouraging boys to identify with characters who are running away from the police, this Nintendo game also turns them on to speed driving. (When I observed boys playing video games in a suburban movie complex, I found that out of nine video games, seven were violent and two involved car races. As previously noted, car accidents are the most common cause of death for young white males, homicide for young African-American males.)

5. Today's toy manufacturers are not content to exploit traditional forms of violence in boy's toys—soldiers, military weapons, cowboy and Indian outfits. They have widened their horizons considerably. A large number of toys involve interplanetary violence that often has a military quality, but as can be seen from the characterizations of the Transformers the meaning of "military" is expanded to include repellent characters who kill for fun or are natural bullies. A game called Lasercommand features characters dressed in outer-space garb. Without any military or law enforcement context, the boy is told that "Mules Mayhem is constantly bringing evil into the World. But Matt Trakker will always be there to stop him with 'Laser technology.' "

The expansion of violence is not limited to outer space. Many aspects of life on earth have become violence-ridden in toyland. Dino-Riders features heavily armed dinosaurs who are used in wars between humans. Turtles become "Ninja Turtles" constantly involved in violent conflict. The toys accompany the Ninja Turtles TV cartoon. In the spring of 1990 the very violent film *Teenage Mutant Ninja Turtles* was released in movie theaters and was number one at the box office.

Building on the Transformers model, some toys feature everyday objects (like tow trucks) that change to "vertical fighting" machines. Gas stations turn into armed bunkers.

In the tradition of slasher films, a "mad scientist" set called Dissect-An-Alien permits a boy to "yank out Alien Organs Dripping in Glowing ALIEN BLOOD." A set called Monster Lab enables him to "Make Disgusting, Gross Monsters . . . Then Sizzle the Flesh Off Their Bones." These sets are for ages seven and up. Author Letty Cottin Pogrebin tells us that in the early 1970s "a toy manufacturer introduced a series of torture kits for boys called Monster Scenes. In one, a semi-nude female figure could be assembled and then strapped to a platform with a razor-sharp pendulum guillotine at her throat. For bigger and better thrills, a boy could imprison his 'girl victim' in a 'hanging cage' or 'pain parlor' equipped with blood-flecked spikes or 'hot' coals to force her to stand on."[4] After selling eight hundred thousand torture kits the company discontinued them, apparently because of protests and boycotts.

Aliens, with no one around to stand up for their rights, are a wonderful substitute for women as victims of sadism. Their organs can be yanked out; their flesh can be sizzled without protest.

Most writers still refer to today's toys of violence as "war toys." But as we have just seen, these toys go far beyond traditional toy soldiers, tanks, and guns. In today's toy world, war toys represent *one type* of violence toy. The new *violence* toys multiply the opportunities for boys to engage in violent play, and teach boys that violence is fun, an acceptable option in a large variety of situations and not a last resort. They set up patterns for expressing anger, rage, and frustration. They encourage the need for enemies by constantly focusing play on conflict between "them" and "us." The frequent portrayal in video games of women as passive and in distress, combined with the premium on toughness and readiness to fight in men, can only encourage attitudes of dominance toward women.

There is reason to believe that these toys encourage assault, murder, racial violence, and rape as well as a militaristic attitude.

Boys who are not given violence toys to play with may nevertheless use sticks as pretend guns or pretend spears or arrows. They can make believe that snowballs are hand grenades. A truck can serve as a tank. There is an important distinction between this kind of play and violent play with violence toys.

Many parents who are concerned about reinforcing violent behavior in their sons do not buy them violence toys, but allow them to engage in some violent play. They usually set limits on it and express their negative feelings. That is a far cry from going out and buying boys a military arsenal or an alien torture kit. They have made clear their moral repugnance to violence. Many parents who do not want to buy these toys for their sons are under intense pressure to do so. Some eventually break down and buy them. This is a perfect example of how caring parents who want to raise decent, nonviolent sons are hindered by a commercially created culture of violence.

Our concern in this section is with violence toys which encourage and direct violent play.

In a 1987 book entitled *The War Play Dilemma,* education professors Nancy Carlsson-Paige and Diane Levin report that the escalation of "war play" has many parents and teachers deeply concerned. In fact, the primary focus of the book is not on war play but on play with violence toys. In order to treat their work accurately, and also that of Bruno Bettelheim and Brian Sutton-Smith, I use their terminology, although I remain convinced that "violence toys" and "violent play" are more accurate terms.

Carlsson-Paige and Levin sent questionnaires to parents of three-to-five-year-old children attending four socioeconomically diverse day-care centers. Almost all the parents of boys reported that their sons engaged in war play.

> Three-quarters of the parents allowed toy guns and weapons and/or action figures in the home; those who did not often mentioned "child-made" weapons as acceptable. With respect to the sources and content of the play, two-thirds of the parents described television and/or commercial war toy themes as present in their sons' war play . . . Parents who could remember when the play first began indicated its onset from as early as eighteen months to as late as three years of age.[5]

Many parents of three-to-five-year-old boys reported that they felt somewhat out of control in terms of regulating their sons' war toys. Carlsson-Paige and Levin tell us that for parents of older boys war play is a constant source of friction. Many feel out of control or have a sense of resignation concerning their ability to influence and/or set limits on their sons' involvement in it. When parents were asked why war play had become such a problem, they often mentioned changes in society, television, and toys. "They said that they could not turn on the television, visit other children, or go to a supermarket, toy store, or playground with their children without encountering some reminder of war and weapons play."[6]

Parents' descriptions of their boys' play as influenced by TV and their feelings of having little control over it are supported by teachers. Many of them, especially those who have been teaching for a long time, have noticed significant changes in the content of play, including war play. Today's war play tends to be repetitive. Boys often assume the roles of characters they have seen on television and play out scenes that resemble television scripts. There is "a lot of aimless running around combined with aggressive 'macho' and stylized actions."[7]

Typical of many educators' complaints is that of a teacher of three-year-olds who does not permit war play in the classroom, but finds that it is there anyway. "Some of the kids find ways to bring it into anything. One boy got red paint on his hands and went around threatening the other children with 'blood from where he was shot.' Another child, with no warning, started crashing into children [who were] playing ball, saying he was 'Rambo.' In the house area recently, three children tore the head off of the teddy bear. All they could tell me was that the bear was the 'bad guy.' They can't seem to get war play out of their minds."[8]

The authors conclude from their interviews with educators that "children seem to be increasingly obsessed with . . . [war] play; that it is harder to allow and manage, or ban; and that it is invading the curriculum in a way that is eroding the teachers' sense of control."[9]

A school director who is also a father and grandfather sums up the change: "When I was the parent of a young child and first started teaching, I didn't permit war or weapons play at home or school. Most children accepted this easily. Now, my son shares my political attitudes. He has been trying to prevent war play in his home with his six-year-old son. He tells me that it's a constant struggle. All of his child's environment—his friends, the toys they play with, television programs, and ads—is permeated with aggression and violence which keeps erupting in his play. The teachers and many of the parents at my school tell me the same thing. They don't know what to do in or out of the classroom to stop the play."[10]

In a book entitled *Who's Calling the Shots,* published in 1990, Carlsson-Paige and Levin tell us that they have continued to talk to hundreds of teachers and parents, many of them increasingly frustrated and concerned about boys' war play. They find that almost every adult "mentions the influence of television on the play—the characters, actions, and scripts all originate in T.V. cartoons."[11]

DO WE REALLY WANT TO GO BACK TO THE "GOOD OLD DAYS"?

Teachers who believe that war toys imbue boys with violent, militaristic ways of thinking are not the only ones who are deeply troubled by the changes that have taken place in recent years. Some educators and psychologists, Carlsson-Paige and Levin among them, believe that playing creatively with war toys can be helpful to boys, rendering them less violent in the long run by helping them work out their aggressive feelings. But they are convinced that much of the current play no longer fulfills developmental needs, because instead of the origins and themes of play coming from the boys themselves they come from the media. They would like to go back to "the good old days" when boys played creatively with guns and tanks, when they did not have TV shows, Rambo movies, or scripts on box covers to guide them. If that is not possible, they want to find ways to encourage boys to use war toys creatively within the present-day context.

The arguments of proponents of "creative war play" ultimately rest on a belief in the erroneous catharsis theory. A few of the major developmental arguments are summarized and analyzed below.

. . . .

Some, like psychoanalyst Bruno Bettelheim, believe that creative war play helps boys gain control over their impulses. As Bettelheim sees it, war play permits a cathartic "discharge of aggression," which is necessary if the superego is to gain control of the irrational forces of the id. This enables the ego to function again. On this view, forbidding war toys is similar to repressing sexual feelings in children and creating guilt in them. Sexual urges will then tend to be expressed in unhealthy or even perverted ways. Psychological difficulties will ensue.

Following this line of thought, education and folklore professor Brian Sutton-Smith tells us that "banning war toys and war play parallels what we did with sexuality in children's literature during the Victorian period . . . to ban war toys or war play only takes away a child's healthy response to his universe."* He draws an analogy to today's children's literature, which, "thanks to people like Judy Blume," is "dealing with issues that children really have to deal with instead of looking the other way."[12]

The proper parallel to Victorian sexual prudery with respect to violence is not banning war toys and war play. It is forbidding children to express any feelings of anger and rage at all, and making them feel very guilty about any kind of aggressive play. Buying boys Transformers, GI Joes, and Nintendo games is not akin to buying them Judy Blume books, which deal in a sensitive, healthy, realistic way with the sexual and other concerns of children. It is akin to buying them pornographic magazines designed especially for children. During the Victorian era, young children who masturbated were often told that this could lead to insanity. Today's enlightened parents wouldn't dream of saying such a thing to their children. But on the other hand they don't go out and buy them toy dildos and sex magazines either. If they find children of opposite sexes playing a racy game of doctor

---

* Unlike most advocates of war toys, Sutton-Smith likes many of the new products, in particular Transformers, of which he writes: "These toys are marvelous. They stimulate a child's imagination; through them, a child certainly gets the idea that what a thing is is not necessarily what a thing can be. It's true that many of these creatures are violent. But they're more akin to characters in Disneyland than Soldiers of Fortune." I wonder if Sutton-Smith has read the characterizations and mottoes of the Transformers. Horri-Bull and Slugslinger are not exactly Disneyland characters. How can toys that come with an explicit function, a motto, a detailed characterization, and a TV program stimulate imagination?

they do not buy them toy condoms and vaginal jelly to help them act out and work through their juvenile sexual impulses.

The intense jealousy and anger that young children feel toward their siblings is so common that it has been given a specific name in the psychoanalytic literature—sibling rivalry. It is something that most parents who have more than one child have to deal with. I did.

"Alisa is so cute, so cute, I'd like to chop her little head off," my older daughter at the age of five commented about her little sister.

Following Bettelheim's and Sutton-Smith's line of thought, I should have run out and bought her a toy guillotine to help her express her violent impulses and eventually gain control of them.

In fact I acknowledged her feelings, permitting her to express them verbally as much as she wanted. I recognized that it is hard when you have had your mommy and daddy all to yourself for many years to have to share their attention. I pointed out to her that while she sometimes hated her sister she also loved her very much and would in fact be very upset if she died. Perhaps my daughter acted out her violent feelings in some physical way, although I don't remember finding any headless dolls around the house. I certainly would not have punished her and made her feel guilty if I had, but rather would have used this for further discussion of her feelings. In any case, I doubt very much that giving her a toy guillotine would have helped her achieve a healthy "discharge of aggression." It seems to me that it would have helped her think that chopping people's heads off is an acceptable way of dealing with intense jealousy and anger.

When it comes to violence, there is a fundamental distinction between feeling and acting. *Most of us have had the impulse at times to kill or hurt someone who enraged us, but most of us don't act on it.*

In an interview with the author, professor of clinical psychology Robert R. Holt pointed out that not being allowed to express one's *feelings of anger* can lead to psychosomatic illness or other psychological and behavioral problems. Not being allowed to *act violently* teaches a child that violent behavior is not socially acceptable and that he or she must learn to control impulses to act violently.

Girls don't play with guns and yet they are able to control their impulses better than boys. Even if we allow for some biologically based differences in the propensity to act violently, *girls and women are often filled with intense rage and anger but act on it far less frequently than do men.* As we saw earlier, compared to men, very few women kill spouses or lovers who have left them.

If the acting out of violent impulses in childhood were really an important factor in the later ability to control impulses, then women should have much higher rates of violence. The fact that they don't suggests that other factors are much more important in controlling violent impulses. The rejection of violence by parents and society as an appropriate response to conflict on the part of girls is one of them. Girls are not usually given guns, rifles, or Transformers to play with. They don't learn from the earliest age that it is appropriate to express one's anger by shooting people. What is true of girls is equally true of boys who are raised in nonviolent societies such as the Amish or the Hutterites, where violence toys are forbidden. These boys are far less violent than boys in our mainstream society.

But apart from their own violent impulses, what about the fact that children need to deal emotionally with living in a very violent society and world?

Sutton-Smith argues that "playing with war toys gives a child a chance to react to the constant portrayal of violence on TV and in the news. If kids play war it's because they need to come to terms with the meaning of it. They need to feel some sense of control."[13] Along the same lines, Carlsson-Paige and Levin tell us that "the sense of power and competence that is experienced in war play—as children pretend to be superheroes with superpowers, for instance—can help children feel like strong and separate people who can take care of themselves."[14]

This can be a very dangerous and misleading sense of power and competence.

For some men the feelings of power, glory, and superiority they experienced as children in war play are something they want to replicate in adult life. This seems to be at least part of what is motivating them when they enlist or eagerly go off to wars they know next to nothing about. John Floyd is a former Marine Corps pilot who served in Vietnam, dropping an average of fifteen thousand pounds of explosives per mission on civilians and soldiers. "I loved the excitement of it, the feeling of power, of control," Floyd told me more than twenty years later.[15] It was a trip to Hiroshima (on his way back from Vietnam) that changed his life. His victims went from being inconsequential "Commie enemies" to becoming hauntingly real people. In *Born on the Fourth of July,* Ron Kovic comments that when his foot was injured (in the battle that was to leave him paraplegic), instead of giving up in a hopeless situation he continued to fight just as he would have when he was a little boy playing war in the woods near his home in Massapequa, New York.

Both Floyd and Kovic went to Vietnam feeling powerful and competent. Kovic came back crippled for life. Floyd came back having to live the rest of his life with feelings of guilt and horror. Letting boys act out the violence they hear, see, or read about, and control it in their war play, gives many of them the impression of invincibility. But, as Ron Kovic learned the hard way, in real war even the most intelligent, talented, and courageous soldier has only the most limited control over his fate.

It may well be that when political leaders wage unnecessary wars in order to aggrandize their own or their nation's power and glory, part of what they are doing is replicating the grandiosity and invincibility they experienced in childhood war play.

Noted historian Johan Huizinga considered the role of play in human society so important that he devoted a book, *Homo Ludens* (Man at Play), to the topic. In a chapter entitled "Play and War," he points out that "ever since words existed for fighting and playing, men have been wont to call war a game."[16] Huizinga argues that this is not a metaphorical use of the word "game." His analysis reveals that through much of human history wars between equals have to a large extent been played as contests or games. He notes that "a custom that stems from the idea of war as noble game of honour and still lingers even in the dehumanized wars of today is the exchanging of civilities with the enemy."[17] In World War I enemy officers often treated each other with courtesy and respect when they met or had occasion for any contact. In earlier times opposing forces would sometimes go through elaborate opening ceremonies before starting to fight and kill each other.

But the connection between war and play is not limited to formal external characteristics. Huizinga argues that in a majority of cases "pride and vainglory, the desire for prestige and all the pomps of superiority" are major motives for war.[18]

As we saw earlier, boys' groups are much more concerned with ranking, with hierarchy, with superiority and prestige, than are girls' groups. By buying boys violence toys that reinforce the connection between warfare and achieving superiority over others, we are both encouraging their interest in war play as a way of attaining power and permitting them to develop highly unrealistic, romanticized notions of what real war is like. As Huizinga points out, there is not much connection between the "grimness and bitterness" of war and the "exhilarating game of courage and honour" that it is cracked up to be.[19] There is not much connection either between, on the one hand, the sense of excitement and adventure that boys get from emulating film and TV violence with their toy rifles and guns, or playing violent video adventure games, and, on the other hand, the reality of going on a robbery spree, a racial attack, or a mugging. Whether the perpetrators are Fordham Preppies, Bensonhurst or Howard Beach white middle-class boys, or African-American ghetto boys, the reality of jail and death is neither exciting nor adventurous.

It is true that the level of national and international violence can be frightening to children. I would suggest encouraging them to express their fears about international and criminal violence. Discussing with children why there is so much violence and what they can do to protect themselves—learn to avoid fights, become streetwise, perhaps learn karate or some other self-defense techniques—helps. Also, discussing how they can contribute to decreasing violence in their immediate environment and in the world at large and getting involved in that endeavor gives children a feeling of empowerment.

One of the most common reasons given for dismissing criticism of war toys is that for most children war play is "just pretend" unconnected in their minds to real-world violence. One reason for this is that young children do not think of death as a permanent and irreversible condition. Another is that their thinking is egocentric: "they can pretend to kill someone else without thinking about it from the point of view of the person killed."[20]

In seeming contradiction to this view that war play is just

pretend and completely unconnected to "real world" violence, it is also argued that "war play can help [boys] to confront and understand different points of view."[21] Along these lines, Bettelheim thinks that war play helps boys become more objective and moral. It helps them go from an "unstructured free-for-all shooting match . . . to a more structured game setting in which not mere discharge of aggression but a higher integration —the ascendancy of good over evil—is the goal. So *we* destroy *them:* the Greeks defeat the knavish Trojan wrongdoers, the Christian knights destroy the infidels, the cops corner the robbers, the cowboys crush the savage Indians."[22]

Bettelheim points out that while "as objective adults, we may know . . . that the case of the Indian was at least as strong as that of the cowboy . . . for the child such objectivity is not yet possible, because emotions, not intellect, are in control during the early years. Our children *want* to believe that good wins out, and they *need* to believe it . . . It serves their developing humanity to repeat the eternal conflict of good and evil in a primitive form understandable to them, and to see that good triumphs in the end."[23]

Through the evolution of his war play, the boy learns that "to fight evil is not enough; one must do so in honor of a higher cause and with knightly valor—that is according to the rules of the game, the highest of which is to act with virtue."[24]

Bettelheim is assuring us that if we let boys repeat the eternal conflict of good and evil in a primitive form, we can look forward to their someday becoming "objective adults" whose intellect controls their actions, who understand the Indians' side as well as the cowboys.

Where are these mature, objective, empathic adults?

They are not among the Cossacks, whose pogroms against Jews terrorized my father and his family when he was a child. They believed that they had God and virtue on their side and were ridding Russia and Poland of despicable infidels. They are not among the Germans who threw my aunts and uncles and cousins—some of them babies—into gas chambers. They believed that they were serving the higher cause of purifying the Aryan race of Jewish vermin. They are not among the well-intentioned young Americans who volunteered for Vietnam because like John Floyd or Ron Kovic they believed we were the

John Wayne-type good guys and the Commies were the bad guys.

Bettelheim's description of boys' development through war play toward objectivity, rationality, and virtue reads to me like a blueprint for training future soldiers. *Instead of turning boys into mature, empathic men, childhood involvement in war toys and war play contributes to adult men acting like insensitive, immature, egocentric boys.*

If boys were encouraged to think of war realistically, to look at issues from different perspectives, and to be empathic, then as adults they would not so readily go to wars, or send their sons to war. They would be more reluctant to vote for or support belligerent leaders.

Bettelheim states that children have a need to believe that there is good and evil and that good always triumphs. As Robert Holt sees it, "we indoctrinate children into a very dichotomous view of the world and then laboriously later on try to teach them that this is not the way things are."[25] Perhaps our children need to be taught that whether one succeeds or not, standing up courageously for what one believes is right is one of the highest moral values, typified by such figures as Christ, Gandhi, Elizabeth Cady Stanton, Rosa Parks, Martin Luther King. In conjunction with this, perhaps they need to be taught that there are many situations in which what is good and what is bad, who is right and who is wrong, is not so easy to figure out. Too often we encourage children to think in simplistic, egocentric, selfish ways and then claim that this is natural.

It is difficult to escape the conclusion that the war play that Bettelheim is writing about is the war play he experienced as a young boy seventy years ago. While his article was published in 1987, there is no indication that Bettelheim ever bothered to go to a toy store and see what boys are playing with today. Had he done so he would have known that many of the toys have nothing to do with morality and virtue. He would have seen that violence has been injected into almost every type of toy sold to boys. More than ever before, today's violence toys in conjunction with TV and film violence encourage violence at all levels— domestic, criminal, and international.

Studies show that children from the youngest age are capable of empathic, caring behavior. It is the reinforcement of this behavior and not the supposed "catharsis" and "maturational effects" of war play that will make boys more empathic and less violent.

We need to encourage boys to play with toys that reinforce nurturing, caring, fathering—not killing.

NO MORE VIOLENCE TOYS

Since toys are not a form of speech, they are not covered by the First Amendment. This would make regulation relatively easy from a legal point of view. But the political problems would remain. Strong opposition from toy manufacturers could be overcome only by the development of intense public consciousness about the problem and strong widespread support for regulations to protect children from violence toys.

When I asked public administration professors Alan Rosenbloom and Fred Thayer how toys could best be regulated—whether by the states or by the federal government—they agreed that it would have to be done by the federal government. If states regulated toys, there would inevitably be inconsistencies in regulations from state to state. This could lead toy companies to file legal suits on the grounds of interference with interstate commerce.

They also agreed that at the cost of some bottlenecks, toys would require premarket approval. While a particular kind of lawn dart can be shown to be dangerous by statistics of deaths and injuries sustained, and therefore removed from the market, there is no simple analogous cause-effect relationship between a toy and violent behavior. Toys would have to be evaluated beforehand in terms of how antisocial they are judged to be. Here, as in the case of wrestling and violent music, if the public outcry against violent toys were strong enough there would be no need for "definitive studies" prior to regulation.

Given the powers of the states and the federal government to regulate for the protection of children, a strong community conviction that certain toys are antisocial would be enough— just as the community conviction that viewing pornography is detrimental to children is enough.

In fact, there are several studies that lend support to the view that playing with violent toys increases violent behavior. In one study, observers found that when four- and five-year-old children (mostly boys) were given toy guns to play with, the number of inappropriate antisocial acts increased significantly compared to when the same children played with non-violent toys. Antisocial acts that were part of the toy gun play—such as pointing and shooting the gun and saying "bang bang"—were not counted since they were considered appropriate. Increases in fighting, pushing, shoving, grabbing objects, damaging property, making insulting remarks, threatening violence, and so on were counted. This study corroborated earlier research findings.[26]

If there were not enough popular support for regulating violence toys, more such studies might have to be done prior to regulation. Here, as in other areas of children's entertainment, a presidential or independent commission might play a consciousness-raising role.

In any case, regulating toys would involve the same initial steps as the other forms of regulation discussed earlier—legislation mandating regulation, a blue-ribbon commission charged with arriving at a viable definition of what constitutes a violent toy, and recommendations as to how these toys should be regulated.* A bureau dealing with the regulation of toys would be part of a larger Office for Standards in Children's Entertainment and Toys.

WHAT WILL THE BOYS PLAY WITH IF WE TAKE AWAY THE VIOLENCE TOYS?

As boys grow older, the pressure to conform to the masculine mystique becomes more intense. Educator Raphaela Best, in her study of a suburban public school, stated that boys in first grade were still willing to play house, but were shamed out of it by second grade. Teachers say that the pressure now starts earlier than ever. By age four the boys are out of the dollhouse and into the trenches.

If violence toys were regulated, and if parents realized that

* Such a commission would have much to learn from the experiences of those European countries—Sweden, Finland, West Germany—that have regulated the sale of war toys. Their laws prohibit the sale of toys based on wars from 1900 to the present. This has apparently been interpreted by some toy store owners as permitting the sale of "future war toys" such as Transformers.

playing with toys that rehearse fatherhood, encourage empathy, and celebrate nurturance would not turn their sons into homosexuals, many boys would spontaneously move toward more gentle play.

While boys' desires for adventure, excitement, and danger are exaggerated by the masculine mystique, some of these interests would in all likelihood remain under any conditions. Can we satisfy them without violence toys?

The regulation of violence toys should be accompanied by research and development of toys that fulfill these interests while encouraging pro-social values. Such research could be done through federal grants to researchers at universities or at the National Institute of Mental Health. It could also be done by manufacturers who would be given tax credits for researching and developing such toys. Private foundations might want to contribute as well.

Here, as in other areas of entertainment, there appears to be no reason why adventure, excitement, and danger cannot to a significant extent grow out of missions to rescue people from airplane crashes, fires, tornadoes, earthquakes, and other natural disasters.

Boys can contend with the elements and a variety of other physical obstacles as they climb Mount Everest, track through the Himalayas, pilot glider planes, explore outer space or the ocean floor.

If they crave competition, it can be introduced in the form of who saves more earthquake victims or who gets to the top of Mount Everest first.

16
Taking Children Out of the Commercial Market

When I asked Monroe Price, dean of Yeshiva University's Cardozo Law School and an authority on First Amendment law, about the legality of regulating children's entertainment, he confirmed what Stanford Law professor Marc Franklin had previously told me: With respect to films, videos, and rock music, as long as my recommendations did not interfere with adults' rights they seemed to be within the realm of what is acceptable from a First Amendment perspective. With respect to toys, sports, and wrestling, the First Amendment does not apply.

At the same time Price expressed distaste for the kind of solution I was seeking. "The enforcement of the standards would lead to such a different society from what we have now that I'd have a hard time dealing with it," he told me.

I must admit that I do not share Price's apprehensions. As I see it, the society we have now is a violence-ridden one that treats children as a commercial market instead of a treasured national resource. It allows the exploitation of children's worst potentials without any regard for their well-being or societal consequences. In the preceding chapters I have tried to capture the extraordinary levels of violence that exist in distinct areas of sports and entertainment. *But to appreciate fully the gravity of the problem, it is essential to focus on the cumulative effect on boys of being surrounded by so much violence.* Whether it be on the TV or in films, at wrestling matches, heavy metal or rap concerts, hockey and football games, or in toys—the message far too often is that violence is acceptable; violence is fun.*

Unlike Monroe Price, Peggy Charren, Tipper Gore, and others who are genuinely concerned with preserving what they take to be First Amendment freedoms, those reponsible for creating our extraordinarily violent popular culture often use the First Amendment as a smoke screen for unmitigated greed.

Laws enacted to protect children from commercial exploitation would be much closer in their purpose to child product safety laws enacted and enforced by the United States Consumer Product Safety Commission than to laws genuinely infringing on First Amendment rights. While the CPSC is concerned with regulating products that can be dangerous to our physical health, the purpose of laws regulating the media and sports with respect to children would be to protect children from activities and products that can be dangerous to their mental health and moral development.

The use of the word "product" is not accidental. It is difficult after examining the contemporary world of children's entertainment to escape the conclusion that it has much more to do with making money than with making art.

Rock musician Frank Zappa tells us that "teenagers are the

---

* This message is apparently also being conveyed in comic books. In its June/July 1988 Newsletter, the NCTV reports on its analysis of eighty popular comic book series. The review revealed that violent themes including cannibalism, satanism, and rape are becoming increasingly common.

most sought-after consumers. The whole idea of merchandising the prepubescent masturbational fantasy is not necessarily the work of the songwriter or the singer, but the work of the merchandiser who has elevated rock 'n' roll to the commercial enterprise it is . . . Today rock 'n' roll is about getting a contract with a major company, and pretty much doing what the company tells you to do."[1]

Rev. Everett Parker is the former head of the United Church of Christ's Communications Office. He has devoted a good part of his life to trying to improve the quality of the media. There was frustration and bitterness in his voice as he described to me the inaccessibility and indifference to moral issues of TV executives, who Parker said are "the most arrogant people in the world . . . [and] have the power to protect themselves from contact with the public." They put on TV "whatever makes the most money."[2]

There is little doubt in my mind that if they were ever put under *intense* public pressure and *seriously* threatened with regulation of the kind I am proposing, entertainment producers would make changes, would clean up their act to a significant extent.

If this should ever happen it would be tragic to stop and claim victory. For as long as the protection of children from commercial entertainment exploitation is not guaranteed by law, it will crop up again. Whether it takes two years or twenty years, when the heat is off, when the struggle is forgotten, the alien torture kits, the slasher films, the rapist rock lyrics—or some futuristic version of them—will be back.

Since children's formative years are so important and of such short duration, we cannot afford the kinds of pendulum swings that would be the best we could hope for if we had no laws forbidding the commercial exploitation of children.

In one of his letters, Thomas Jefferson writes:

I am certainly not an advocate for frequent and untried changes in laws and constitutions. I think moderate imperfections had better be borne with . . . But I know also, that laws and institutions must go hand in hand with the progress of the human mind. As that becomes more developed, more enlightened, as new discoveries are made, new truths disclosed, and manners and opinions change with the change of circumstances, institutions must advance also, and keep pace with the times . . . Let us provide in our constitution for its revision at stated periods.[3]

Present-day technology permits a mass culture that promotes assault, murder, sadism, drugs, alcohol, satanism, early and sadistic sex to young children. There is little doubt in my mind that this is the kind of "change of circumstances" that Jefferson thought required "changes in laws and constitutions." We have gone far beyond Jefferson's category of "moderate imperfections [that] had better be borne with."

First Amendment historian Leonard W. Levy tells us that "no one can say for certain what the Framers had in mind" when they introduced the free speech and free press clause into the Bill of Rights.[4] Jefferson is telling us that regardless of precisely what *they* had in mind, *our* legal system must be responsive to changing historical conditions.

The problem of the commercial exploitation of American children is so serious that it might warrant a constitutional amendment to protect them. It is because they are so vulnerable and malleable, because their values, attitudes, and behavior are in the process of being formed, that children require special protection from commercial exploitation.

In our legal history the most commonly accepted interpretation of the First Amendment emphasizes the importance in a democracy of citizens and the press being free to express political opinions without government censorship or reprisal. This freedom enables well-informed citizens to make informed, rational political decisions.[5]

Many media experts feel that this freedom is threatened today by the inadequacy of antitrust regulations that permit an increasingly small and wealthy group of people to control a large percentage of the media.* Fears about media concentration are further increased by the recent elimination of the "Fairness Doctrine," which required broadcasters to provide contrasting viewpoints on controversial issues of public importance.

If there exists a *real* threat to our First Amendment rights, I

---

* Professor Ben Bagdikian, author of *The Media Monopoly*, points out in a 1987 article that while the United States has twenty-five thousand media outlets, most magazines, daily newspapers, books, television, and motion pictures are controlled by 29 corporations. Some experts in media acquisitions believe that by the year 2000 six conglomerates may control all U.S. media.

suspect it lies in the concentration of the means of communication in powerful and wealthy hands, not in the regulation of the mass media in order to protect our children from being exposed to antisocial, violent messages from the earliest age.

In fact, if we allow the unfettered commercialization of children's culture to continue, our democratic institutions and constitutional rights may be in serious danger. The stated purpose of our Constitution is to "establish justice, insure domestic tranquility, provide for the common defense, promote the general welfare, and secure the blessings of liberty." The Declaration of Independence proclaims life, liberty, and the pursuit of happiness as the goals for which our nation was created.

When children grow up watching tens of thousands of hours of TV shows and films in which people are assaulted, shot, stabbed, disemboweled, chopped up, skinned, or dismembered, when children grow up listening to music which glorifies rape, suicide, drugs, alcohol, and bigotry, they are not likely to become the kind of concerned, educated, responsible citizens who can help us maintain those values and goals.

John Stuart Mill pointed out that in order to have a viable society—one that is dedicated to principles of the kind expressed in our Constitution—it is necessary to educate people so that "a direct impulse to promote the general good may be in every individual one of the habitual motives of action . . ."[6]

Consideration for others, honesty, and empathy must be instilled so profoundly that they become second nature. Our country is composed of numerous religious and ethnic groups who disagree on a variety of moral issues. *But there can be no disagreement with respect to these basic moral qualities—they form the characterological foundation upon which the continued adherence to this nation's values rests.*

We have allowed the creation of a culture that discourages these qualities and instills extreme competitiveness, selfishness, greed, and violence.

Our extraordinarily high rates of violent crime, as well as the presence of close to sixty thousand nuclear warheads globally, are a constant threat to life, liberty, domestic tranquility, and the general welfare.

As long as we allow our children, in particular our boys, to be raised in a culture of violence, we will never be able to build enough prisons, hire enough police officers, build enough drug and alcohol rehabilitation centers.

It is as if we had no regulations whatsoever with respect to the pollution of our drinking water, and then had to deal with the problem of detoxifying highly poisonous water on a national scale. Present measures with respect to water pollution may be inadequate, but one shudders to think what it would be like without them. *There is no regulation whatsoever of violence pollution with respect to our children.*

There is also the danger that future generations will to a significant extent be desensitized to the problem. Will people raised on violent entertainment and violent sports in a violent society realize that it doesn't have to be this way, that there is something deeply wrong with its being this way? Or will Americans eventually become fully habituated to a greedy, selfish, violent society, and take it for granted, much as people in countries with long histories of intense corruption, bribe-taking, political repression, and military coups tend to take their societies' ways for granted?

Another possibility is that of the pendulum swinging in the opposite direction. If those groups who have a deep concern with preserving the principles of our Constitution and the First Amendment do not act, then those who do not have that concern, or for whom that concern is overridden by fundamentalist religious beliefs, might.

Already, in 1990, several steps were taken in this direction. While the *regulations* proposed here are aimed exclusively at the protection of children, the 2 Live Crew and Robert Mapplethorpe prosecutions represent *censorship* aimed at adults as well as children. The imposition of content restrictions on artists funded by the National Endowment for the Arts—currently being debated by Washington lawmakers—is also aimed at adults. Many Americans are deeply concerned about the influence that the mass media is having on their children.* If we do not address

---

* Until recently the preoccupation has been almost entirely with protecting children from obscenity, but many parents are becoming increasingly concerned with their children's exposure to both sex and violence. Typical is the young mother who told me that in the course of playing with her Barbie dolls her three-and-a-half-year-old daughter placed Ken on top of Barbie. "Ken is showing Barbie how much he loves her," the child explained. When the mother inquired about another Barbie doll that was lying nearby with bent and distorted limbs, the little girl said, "Ken got mad at Barbie and killed her."

their concerns, if we do nothing to protect children from violent, rapist, and sadistic entertainment, then the messages of extremists and bigots may seem increasingly attractive to large segments of our population.

Conclusion:
Beyond
the Masculine
Mystique

More than four years have gone by since I began to work on this book. During that period, there has been an increase of over 19 percent in the rate of violent crime.* The violence has become increasingly haphazard and senseless. Between late July and mid-October 1990, eight children fourteen years old or younger were killed by random gunfire in New York City. "Your Sneakers or Your Life" is the title of the cover story on the May 13, 1990, issue of *Sports Illustrated.* The article describes how an increasing number of boys mug or murder their peers in order to get a pair of expensive sneakers or a coveted jacket bearing sports insignia. In Dallas, Texas, when ten current and former high school athletes were sentenced to prison for armed robbery, it turned out that their motives included "extra money for prom night" and "trips to an amusement park, food and athletic shoes."[1]

One would think that in light of this further escalation, every effort would be made to socialize boys so as to decrease violence. But this is not the case.

The atavistic values of the masculine mystique continue to be reinforced in most areas of entertainment, as well as in some sports.

---

* While the increase in violent crime is due in part to the epidemic of drug use and drug dealing in recent years, the tendency, on the part of some, to see violent crime as *primarily* related to our current drug problem is misguided. Our violent crime rates were already extremely high in the early eighties, before the widespread introduction of crack.

Not only are fathers not being encouraged to play a major role in nurturant child-rearing, thus denying their sons nonviolent, caring masculine role models, but many boys are being deprived of adequate mothering. Most working mothers must conform to a marketplace designed for men with homemaker wives. This leaves millions of children unattended and emotionally deprived—a good breeding ground for anger and violence. Inadequate day care compounds the situation. Divorce leaves many women impoverished and makes child-rearing even more difficult for them. In the last forty years there has been a sixfold increase in the percentage of women giving birth who are unmarried. Very little is being done to change this or to encourage divorced or unmarried fathers to remain involved with and financially responsible for their children. With all due respect to "The Cosby Show" and a few other exceptions, the primary images of manhood projected by the media and reinforced by toy manufacturers have nothing to do with being a loving, nurturant father.

The increase in children deprived of fathering, the crisis in child care, and the creation of a culture of violence have gone hand in hand with a breakdown of moral values that emphasized personal and social responsibility, caring for and respecting others. While these values were seen as operating mainly in the personal realm—women guarded them and transmitted them to children while men went out into the "dog eat dog" world to earn a living—they did have some tempering effect on the world of men. Bribery and money scandals are nothing new, but they have reached new heights in recent years both on Wall Street and in government.

Prep school boys and high school football players who go on robbery sprees when they need some extra money are a recent phenomenon, as are high school boys who kill a classmate to see what it feels like.

Men who value money and power above all think nothing of hiring six-year-olds to help them sell drugs, or machine-gunning their rivals in drug wars that often take the lives of innocent bystanders as well.

The situation is aggravated by the ready availability of almost any weapon imaginable to boys and men who are raised to be violent. With two hundred million guns and seventy million gun owners in the United States, our current situation is analogous to making matches easily available to known pyromaniacs. This availability of weapons is facilitated by many men who seem to experience any form of gun control as emasculating.

Our government continues to misappropriate billions in taxpayers' money for military use. According to Robert Costello, the Pentagon's top procurement official in the late 1980s, 20 to 30 percent of defense expenditures for procurement of weapons and armed forces operations and purchasing "could be saved through the application of fundamental changes in procurement practices and . . . quality management principles."[2] In 1989, former Secretary of Defense Robert McNamara estimated that our annual military budget could be cut in half without any threat to our national security. At the same time, our national security is *genuinely* threatened by internal violence, drug use, and illiteracy. Programs geared toward helping children are regularly rejected for lack of funds, yet a small fraction of our close to three-hundred-billion-dollar annual military budget would help us begin to raise physically and mentally healthy, well-educated children who would genuinely be able to say no to drugs and to violence. This neglect goes hand in hand with the lack of recognition of the enormous importance of child-rearing as reflected in the $4.55 an hour earned by day-care center employees in 1987. Child-care workers earn less than parking-lot attendants or animal caretakers.

Everywhere there is homophobia, the fear that if we don't raise boys who are tough and tearless, they will be gay or at the very least wimpish. There is an abysmal failure of the imagination here, as if our choice were between John Wayne and Mr. Milquetoast. It is as if we cannot imagine boys and men who are strong, courageous, curious, and adventurous without being violent and obsessed with domination and power.

Instead of moving beyond an outdated and dangerous concept of masculinity, our society has encouraged the escalation of the masculine mystique's violent content. We have come a long way from the 1950s when the pressure to prove manhood tended to take the form of going to a hooker at age sixteen or seventeen, bragging about "scoring" with girls, making the football team, or "borrowing" mom or dad's car for a joy ride. In Harlem, according to Claude Brown's autobiography,

Manchild in the Promised Land, it often meant more, perhaps stealing and conning, but not the random, senseless assault or murder of the 1970s and 80s.

More than any other group, African-American males are negatively affected by the values of the masculine mystique. As we saw in Chapter 11, men at the bottom of the social hierarchy, without other outlets for achieving dominance and power, are the most likely to prove manhood through violence. This tendency has been exacerbated in the last few decades by the enormous increase in African-American teenage girls having babies. Our inner cities are now filled with millions of fatherless boys who are extremely susceptible to "hypermasculinity" and the values of the masculine mystique. Since the mid to late eighties, an increasing number of teenage girls and women in ghetto areas have become addicted to cheap and readily available drugs. Their sons, often born addicted and then emotionally and physically neglected or battered, are at an even greater risk for violence than the other boys. The mass media furnish them with endless images of violent males.

While poor, fatherless boys are especially likely to be affected, these images influence boys of all races and social classes who are entertained by sociopathic and sadistic role models such as slasher film "heroes" Freddy Krueger and Jason, as well as Rambo. Freddy Krueger even has a fan club; children proudly wear T-shirts portraying their favorite sadistic sociopath. Behavior that would have been unthinkably repugnant twenty-five years ago is now seen over and over again on the screen.

A teacher at a good junior high school in a middle- to upper-middle-class suburb recently told me how disturbed she was by her students' reaction to a social studies classroom discussion about alleged cannibalism in Jamestown, Virginia, in the early seventeenth century; a few students had seen a film on TV that depicted it as having taken place during a time of intense starvation. "They—especially the boys—weren't horrified or repelled at all, they were excited by it and wanted to get all the details. Were the people cooked or raw? How did they cut them up?"

I was not surprised by her story. It makes sense that boys who grow up surrounded by the gore of slasher films, the xenophobia of professional wrestling, the rapist lyrics of some heavy metal and rap groups, not to mention the endless violence on

TV and in toys, will become so desensitized that nothing becomes unthinkable in terms of gore and violence.

Is there really something unmanly about a boy or young man who is repelled by luridly violent films, who does not enjoy breaking bones and rupturing muscles—his own or others'—whether it be in the school yard, on the street, or on the football field? Is there really something unmanly in choosing to seek adventure by biking cross-country, going white water rafting, fighting forest fires, or volunteering for the Peace Corps in South America or Africa? We desperately need new heroes and new myths for our boys—heroes whose sense of adventure, courage, and strength are linked with caring, empathy, and altruism.

Women have much to gain from such a change. The present definition of masculinity leads many of them to admire and reinforce just those traits that are conducive to rape, wife abuse, child abuse, and murder.

There is the fear that if boys and girls are raised more alike, if boys are encouraged to play house and push baby carriages and make believe they are daddies, then we will obliterate all but the obvious physiological differences between men and women. As we have seen, such fears were expressed in the nineteenth century when women began to enter universities and wanted the vote. Today's women are not just like men, nor is there any reason to believe that if we cease raising boys by the values of the masculine mystique they will become just like girls. In fact, recent brain research, as well as some of the studies discussed in Chapter 3, suggests that there may well be differences in the male and female brain which will ensure some emotional, cognitive, and behavioral variance between males and females as a group, under any conditions.

As we approach the twenty-first century, we face a choice. We can begin to control violent behavior, both on a national and international level, or we can continue to let it control and perhaps ultimately destroy us. We have enough knowledge to be able to significantly decrease violence, which is not to say that our knowledge is definitive or that we don't have much to learn. Just as the work of research physicians ensures progress in the control of physical diseases, continued research in the social and biological sciences could ensure progress in the control of the social disease of violence.*

As of now we can, with some assurance, make the following assertions:

1. *The traditional "either/or" debate between nature and nurture with respect to violence is simple-minded and obsolete.* Human behavior grows out of a complex interaction between a biologically given potential and environmental factors. If human beings had no biological potential for violence, it could never develop regardless of external conditions. On the other hand, the environment plays an all-important role in encouraging or discouraging this potential.

Equally simplistic is the notion that any *one* factor will *necessarily* cause an individual to act violently. Any serious study of violence—or of any other aspect of human conduct—is limited to researching and analyzing significant, *not universal,* correlations between behaviors.

2. *The behavior of human beings is extremely malleable.* Anthropological studies reveal the enormous variability of human behavior and values in different cultures. Studies in psychology and sociology show us how early childhood experiences, family, peer groups, and culture mold the individual. History reveals that radical changes have taken place within a given culture in a very short period of time: extremely violent groups have become peaceful, and vice versa.

We have the clearest example of the malleability of human beings within our own country. Boys raised in Hutterite communities start out just the same as other American boys. They have their conflicts and brawls. The community has its share of boys who suffer from attention deficit disorder and/or learning disabilities, and they are especially difficult to deal with. But Hutterite boys are raised to value community, charity, love, and nonviolence. Parents and teachers are intent on helping them resolve their quarrels nonviolently. Toy guns are not allowed. Play with make-believe guns is discouraged. Hutterite children's TV viewing is limited to carefully chosen videocassettes. Child-

---

* The present separation of academic disciplines with very little interdisciplinary contact is an impediment to progress. Researchers often seem unaware of data relevant to their work but arising in other fields.

rearing is a focal point of community life. Fathers spend large amounts of time with their children.

Ian Winter, who is the principal at the Hutterian Brethren community school in Rifton, New York, tells me that physical fights do very rarely break out among thirteen- or fourteen-year-old boys. But by the time they are sixteen, the boys have learned to resolve their conflicts nonviolently. Domestic violence and criminal behavior are unheard of.

Benjamin Zablocki, professor of sociology at Rutgers and author of *The Joyful Community*, a study of the Hutterite Brethren, confirmed, in an interview, that violence is virtually unheard of among them.

3. *Human beings, especially men, have a significant potential for violent behavior.* A few of the twentieth-century manifestations of this potential have been two world wars that took tens of millions of lives, genocides of Armenians and Jews, the slaughter by their fellow countrymen of millions of Russian peasants and Cambodians. As I write, human beings all over the world are being beaten, tortured, and killed. This suggests that *if we are to significantly and lastingly decrease violence, it can only be done through an ongoing relentless effort. For short of widespread genetic mutations, the potential for violence, bigotry, and xenophobia will always be with us.*

We must acknowledge fully that many normal, otherwise decent people are capable of committing, either directly or indirectly, the most cruel and violent acts. Only if we do so will we be able to recognize and act on the enormous importance of encouraging empathy and discouraging xenophobia and bigotry in our children, and of teaching them the true courage and integrity of standing up for humane, altruistic, moral convictions and feelings regardless of external pressures or monetary rewards.

If we take these steps, if they become an integral part of early child-rearing, and a mandatory part of our educational system, then we may begin to move away from what political philosopher Hannah Arendt refers to as "the banality of evil."

In her book *Eichmann in Jerusalem*, Arendt concluded that Nazi henchman Adolf Eichmann, who shared responsibility for the deaths of millions of Jews, was "normal." Again and again Eichmann explained to the Israeli court that put him on trial that he was only doing his duty. Arendt writes that Eichmann suffered from a "lack of imagination." He *"never realized what he was doing . . . It was sheer thoughtlessness . . . that predisposed him to* become one of the greatest criminals of that period."[3] She comments that "such remoteness from reality and such thoughtlessness can wreak more havoc than all the evil instincts taken together . . ."[4]

In a study of Greek military policemen who served as torturers during the period from 1967 to 1974, when Greece was ruled by a right-wing military regime, researchers found no evidence of any abusiveness, sadism, or authoritarianism in these men's previous histories. When interviewed, the men were all leading normal lives. The researchers are convinced that certain kinds of training can lead "decent people to commit acts, often over long periods of time, that otherwise would be unthinkable for them. Similar techniques can be found in military training all over the world."[5]

These findings and Arendt's analysis of Eichmann are borne out by Stanley Milgram's study on obedience. As we have seen, a majority of Milgram's subjects continued to give what they thought were increasingly high electric shocks to a "victim" even after the victim screamed in pain, and in spite of the fact that they were free to disobey the psychologist's orders. Many more subjects disobeyed when the victim was in the same room than when the victim could only be heard but not seen.

We do not need to look at laboratory studies, or at studies of torturers or people like Adolf Eichmann, to become aware of any of this.

John Floyd is a friend of mine, a perfectly decent, nice guy. Yet when he served in Vietnam, John enjoyed the excitement and feeling of power of dropping bombs on Vietnamese and Laotians whom he thought of as "Commie enemies" and could not see from the height of his plane. It was only after his trip to Hiroshima that he began to realize what he had done.

When I interviewed former Secretary of Defense Robert McNamara I found him to be a thoughtful, appealing man, deeply concerned about the danger of nuclear destruction, and about the plight of poor African-Americans. Several former friends of McNamara's have corroborated my positive impression. Some of them are still shocked at the thought that Robert McNamara shares major responsibility for the *unnecessary* deaths of over a million Americans and Vietnamese.

Neither Floyd nor McNamara seems to have thought of the

people whose lives they took as anything but abstractions. As a result, they were devoid of empathy or, as Hannah Arendt put it, they suffered from a "lack of imagination."

The enormous human potential for emotional detachment, denial, and lack of empathy is increased further by modern technology. Millions can now be killed without any direct contact between perpetrators and victims. This makes it even easier for decent men raised on the values of the masculine mystique to commit horrendous acts of violence.

Boys suffering from the kinds of physical conditions described in Chapter 3 will always require special attention and services, since many of them are even more prone than the rest of the population to engage in violent behavior. We must develop techniques for discouraging violence in them from the earliest age. The demise of the masculine mystique would ensure that the tendency on the part of some of them to reckless and violent behavior would in no way be admired and emulated by their peers. Instead it would be viewed as immature and problematic.

While many normal men can be recruited to participate in mass murder, it is nevertheless worth investigating whether inordinate numbers of men belonging to groups such as the Nazi brownshirts, the Haitian Tonton Macoute death squads, and the Ku Klux Klan suffered from some of these disabilities as children. More generally we need more research to determine the psychological profiles and backgrounds of the men who start and seek out these groups. Understanding will help us in taking the proper preventive measures.

4. *Human beings, male and female, have a significant potential for empathy and altruism.* According to recent studies, shortly after they have reached the age of one, virtually all children begin to have some level of understanding of other people's experiences and attempt to help or comfort the person who is in distress. From age one and a half to age two, there is a great increase in altruistic behavior. As children get older there is more variation in their behavior. Researchers have found that in older children the degree of empathy and altruism is linked to maternal and paternal behavior. As we saw in Chapter 4, nurturant involvement in child-rearing on the part of fathers is linked to increased and enduring empathy in their children. Studies of mothers and children indicate that when mothers are themselves empathic, when they make their children aware emotionally of how hurtful behavior affects others, when they establish principled moral prohibitions against hurting others, then children will tend to be empathic and alruistic.[6]

Among adults, these empathic, altruistic tendencies manifest themselves in a variety of ways.

During World War II, in Le Chambon, a small French town near Switzerland, villagers, led by their Protestant minister and his wife, risked their lives to hide Jews from the Nazis. As a result, thousands of people were saved.

In the United States, Americans with low incomes, for whom the tax deduction incentive is not a factor, give a larger percentage of their hard-earned incomes to charity than do wealthy Americans.

It is not at all unusual for human beings to spontaneously jump into a river or in front of a car to save the life of a complete stranger, often at great personal risk.

The upshot of all this is that we can, if we want to, decrease violence. Human beings are born with a vast array of often conflicting potential behaviors. The environment they grow up in determines which of these behaviors will become dominant in their lives. It is nothing short of tragic that while the results of research findings are used regularly to prevent physical illness, the findings of the social sciences are rarely used in preventive programs. Changes in hygiene, the creation of vaccines, and more recently recommendations for dietary changes play a major role in preventing illness and saving lives. But *there are analogous measures that could be taken to prevent the social disease of violence.*

American boys must be protected from a culture of violence that exploits their worst tendencies by reinforcing and amplifying the atavistic values of the masculine mystique. Our country was not created so that future generations could maximize profit at any cost. It was created with humanistic, egalitarian, altruistic goals. We must put our enormous resources and talents to the task of creating a children's culture that is consistent with these goals.

Notes

See bibliography for more detailed references.

Chapter 1   When Male Behavior Is the Norm . . .

1. For sources of male/female violent crime statistics, see Statistics section. Information about women assaulted by husbands or boyfriends is based on the author's 1987 interview with David Finkelhor, associate director of the Family Research Laboratory at the University of New Hampshire.

2. Aristotle, *Politics* 1254 b. 7, Tr. B. Jowett.

3. Thomas Aquinas, *Summa Theologica*, Q. 70, Art. 3, vol. 38, Marcus Léfébure, trans.

4. "Some Psychical Consequences of the Anatomical Distinction Between the Sexes" (1925) in The Standard Edition of the *Complete Psychological Works of Sigmund Freud,* edited by James Strachey, pp. 257–58.

5. Lorenz, *On Aggression,* p. 280.

6. Arendt, *On Violence,* p. 8.

7. James, "The Moral Equivalent of War" in *Essays on Faith and Morals* by William James, p. 325.

8. Klass and Wallis, "Macho Medicine," in *Lear's,* October 1989.

9. Rothenberg, "Out on a Limb," in *Fortune News,* Spring 1983.

10. Ibid.

11. Both sayings are quoted by Helen Caldicott in *Missile Envy*, p. 299.

12. Friedan, *The Feminine Mystique*, p. 325.

Chapter 2 "Real Men," "Wimps," and Our National Security

1. *Abraham Lincoln A Press Portrait*, edited by: Herbert Mitgang, p. 55.

2. Warnke, interview with the author, 1987.

3. Gerzon, *A Choice of Heroes*, p. 52.

4. Halberstam, *The Best and the Brightest*, p. 606.

5. Gerzon, op. cit., p. 93.

6. *New York Times*, December 21, 1989.

7. Barnet, *Roots of War*, p. 109.

8. Ibid., p. 109.

9. Ibid., p. 111.

10. Ibid., p. 112.

11. Ibid., p. 111.

12. See Cousins, *The Pathology of Power;* Rasor, *The Pentagon Underground;* Stubbing and Mendel, *The Defense Game;* Halloran, *To Arm a Nation;* Kotz, *Wild Blue Yonder;* and Smith, *The Power Game.*

13. Barnet, op. cit., p. 59.

14. Ibid., p. 60.

15. Fisher and Ury, *Getting to Yes*, pp. 23–24, 30, and 19.

16. Ibid., p. 58.

17. Kovic, *Born on the Fourth of July*, pp. 166–67.

18. Barnet, op. cit., p. 16.

19. All quotes and comments by Evans are from a 1987 interview with the author.

20. Mark Hertsgaard, *On Bended Knee*, p. 289.

21. Kull, *Minds at War*, p. 224.

22. Cohn, "Sex and Death in the Rational World of Defense Intellectuals," privately published by the Center for Psychological Studies in the Nuclear Age, p. 4. Somewhat different versions of this paper were published in *The Bulletin of Atomic Scientists*, June 1987 and in *Signs*, Summer 1987.

23. Cohn, op. cit., p. 27.

24. Gerzon, op. cit., p. 53.

25. Gerzon, op. cit., p. 32. The following quote is from p. 34.

26. Manchester, "The Bloodiest Battle of All," *New York Times Magazine*, June 14, 1987, p. 84.

Chapter 3 "Boys Will Be Boys"

1. Erhardt, "The Psychobiology of Gender," in *Gender and the Life Course*, edited by A. S. Rossi, 1985, pp. 81–95; and "Gender Differences: A Biosocial Perspective," in Nebraska Symposium on Motivation 1984: *Psychology and Gender*, 1985, pp. 37–57. In both these articles Erhardt argues that a "dynamic interactional model," one that does not assume that one factor is the determining or predominant influence on behavior, must be used in the study of gender-related behavior.

2. Olweus, "Development of Stable Aggressive Reaction Patterns in Males," in *Advances in the Study of Aggression*, Volume I, edited by R. J. Blanchard and C. L. Blanchard, pp. 131–34. See also his "Aggression and Hormones: Behavioral Relationship with Testosterone and Adrenaline," in *The Development of Antisocial and Prosocial Behavior*, edited by D. Olweus, J. Block, and M. Radke-Yarrow, pp. 53–59.

3. Maccoby stated this in a 1989 interview with me. She referred to several studies summarized in her book *Social Development*, and to a study by Dutch psychologist Cornelius Van Lieshout in which he found that already by the age of two, boys are more easily frustrated and irritated than girls.

4. Wilson, *On Human Nature*, p. 102. (Some of the material paraphrased in this section is taken from *Sociobiology: The New Synthesis*.)

5. Wilson, *On Human Nature*, p. 108.

6. Ibid., p. 123.

7. Ibid., p. 175.

8. Freud, "Why War?" *Standard Edition of the Complete Psychological Works of Sigmund Freud*, Vol. 22, edited by James Strachey, p. 211. See also *Civilization and Its Discontents*, pp. 85, 86.

9. For example, see Charles Brenner, *An Elementary Textbook of Psychoanalysis*, p. 18.

10. Freud, *Civilization and Its Discontents*, pp. 101–2.

11. Wilson, op. cit., p. 108.

12. Bateson, "Is Aggression Instinctive?" in *Aggression and War*, edited by Jo Groebel and Robert A. Hinde, p. 41.

13. Holt, "Converting the War System to a Peace System," a paper prepared for a conference of the Exploratory Project on the Conditions of Peace, May 1987, p. 6.

For further critical analysis of Freud's death instinct, see Holt's "Drive or Wish? A Reconsideration of the Psychoanalytic Theory of Motivation," in *Psychological Issues*, Volume 9, Monograph No. 36, as well as the writings of psychoanalyst and social philosopher Erich Fromm and Freudian psychoanalyst Lawrence Kubie. They, among others, argue that this concept of an aggressive instinct or drive is not founded in any clinical evidence but is an outgrowth of nineteenth-century mechanistic psychology, which attempted to mimic the physical sciences. In *The Anatomy of Human Destructiveness*, Fromm tells us that Freud's teachers "looked on man as a machine driven by chemical processes" (p. 449). Just as physicists used the concept of quanta of physical energy, Freud wrote about psychic energy and argued that quanta of this energy (referred to as cathexes) were attached to mental representations of people or things. Analogously to engineers who worked with hydraulic pressures, psychoanalysts perceived themselves as working with pressures and tensions exerted by internal psychic forces seeking to express themselves emotionally and behaviorally.

Lawrence Kubie explains that the Freudian emphasis on psychological explanations in terms of variations in instinctual energy is "buttressed by a conviction that a science is not mature until it can count. Consequently to talk even of hypothetical and unmeasured quantitative variations gives us a feeling of scientific maturity which may in fact be premature and illusory" ("Symbol and Neurosis," *Selected Papers of Lawrence S. Kubie,* edited by Herbert J. Schlesinger, p. 44).

14. Freud, *Civilization and Its Discontents,* p. 91. There are repeated statements in the book to this effect. For example: "men clearly do not find it easy to do without satisfaction of this tendency to aggression that is in them; when deprived of satisfaction they are ill at ease" (p. 90). Freud states that with respect to happiness primitive man was better off—as long as he was not attacked by others—for "he knew nothing of any restrictions on his instincts" (p. 91).

Those familiar with psychoanalytic theory may protest that my analysis ignores the "neutralization" of aggressive drive energy which is analogous to the "sublimation" of sexual drive energy. Neutralization makes aggressive energy available to the ego and permits the latter to find gratification in activities and behaviors that bear little resemblance to the original drive. But while Freud first introduced the concept of neutralization in 1923, the passages quoted above in which he suggests that holding back aggression can lead to unhappiness were written much later. It seems that neutralization is not enough to take care of all that aggressive energy.

The concept of neutralization is itself highly problematic. First the concept of an aggressive drive, which is not warranted by empirical data, is introduced. Since it is impossible to explain much of human behavior directly in terms of this drive (or in terms of a sex drive), it is then postulated that this drive is "neutralized" (and the sex drive sublimated) into all the various motives and behaviors that make up human existence!

15. Robert R. Holt, Lawrence S. Kubie, Benjamin B. Rubinstein, and E. Peterfreund are among the psychoanalytic theorists who argue that the concept of an aggressive drive as psychic energy which fuels motives and behavior has no explanatory value whatsoever.

16. Brittain, *Testament of Youth,* p. 129.

17. Ibid., p. 172.

18. Freud, "The Economic Problem of Masochism," in *Complete Psychological Works,* Vol. 19, p. 163.

Discussing this passage in *The Anatomy of Human Destructiveness,* Erich Fromm points out that "Freud combines here three very different tendencies. The instinct to destroy is basically different from the will for power: in the first case I want to destroy the object; in the second I want to keep and control it, and both are entirely different from the drive for mastery, whose aim it is to create and produce, which in fact is the precise opposite of the will to destroy" (p. 444).

19. Blanck and Blanck, *Ego Psychology II: Psychoanalytic Developmental Psychology,* p. 39.

The authors also state that "over and over again, in early development, libido will seek connection while aggression will seek and maintain separation and individuation" (p. 39). They quote René Spitz, who wrote that "the aggressive drive is not limited to hostility. Indeed, by far the largest and most important part of the aggressive drive serves as the motor of every movement, of all activity, big and small, and ultimately of life itself" (p. 106).

In *An Elementary Textbook of Psychoanalysis*, Charles Brenner furnishes us with another example of the broad use of "aggression." He tells us that during the anal stage of development soiling or retention of feces are important outlets for the aggressive drive (p. 30). What does this mean? Fromm explains that "for Freud and his pupils the essential aspect of anality lies in the tendency to control and possess . . ." (*The Anatomy of Human Destructiveness*, p. 461). But as Fromm points out, "possession" and "control" are not intrinsically connected with destructiveness, with the wish to destroy or kill.

Brenner goes on to expound his view that during the phallic phase, the aggressive drive manifests itself in a boy's playing with spears, arrows, guns, etc., which represent the penis: "In his fantasies he is unconsciously destroying his enemies with his powerful and dangerous penis" (p. 30). Here he is writing about "aggressive energy" which fuels violent behavior, or at least violent play behavior.

20. Fromm, op. cit., p. 298.

21. Heinz Kohut, "Thoughts on Narcissism and Narcissistic Rage," in *The Search for the Self*, edited by Paul Ornstein, pp. 637–38.

22. Id, p. 617

23. The survey is reported by James Q. Wilson and Richard J. Herrnstein in *Crime and Human Nature*, pp. 104–5.

24. See also Nancy Chodorow, *The Reproduction of Mothering;* Lillian Rubin, *Intimate Strangers;* and Jessica Benjamin, *The Bonds of Love.*

25. See Dan Olweus, in Blanchard and Blanchard, op. cit., p. 126. Olweus discusses the results of his own research and lists other studies that also point to permissiveness and parental modeling as causal factors. Rejection on the part of the mother was also found to be a causal factor. Olweus discovered that the mother's rejection was often correlated with a poor emotional relationship between her and the boy's father. This point will be discussed at length in Chapter 4. See also K. A. Dodge, J. E. Bates, and G. S. Pettit, "Mechanisms in the Cycle of Violence" in *Science*, December 21, 1990, pp. 1678–83. In reporting on a study of 309 children the authors state that "this prospective study provides stronger evidence than ever before to support the hypothesis that physical abuse leads to a cycle of violence." (p. 1682) Because the children studied have only reached kindergarten age, the researchers refrain from any conclusions with respect to long range effects. They plan further longitudinal follow-ups.

26. See Dorothy Otnow Lewis et al., "Psychomotor Epilepsy and Violence in a Group of Incarcerated Adolescent Boys" in the *American Journal of Psychiatry*, July 1982, pp. 882–87, and Dorothy Otnow Lewis et al., "Intrinsic and Environmental Characteristics of Juvenile Murderers" in the *Journal of the American Academy of Child and Adolescent Psychiatry*, 1988, pp. 582–87.

27. Descriptions of Seth Maxell's behavior are based on 1988 and 1989 interviews with his mother.

28. My estimates are based on information and statistics that appear in the *Diagnostic and Statistical Manual of Mental Disorders—Revised;* in *Learning Disabili-*

ties: Proceedings of the National Conference, 1988; in *Learning Disabilities, A Report to the U.S. Congress,* 1987; and in the 1989 issue of *Their World,* a publication of the National Center for Learning Disabilities. These works are also a major source of the descriptive material that appears in this chapter. I am indebted to Dr. James F. Kavanagh, Associate Director of the Center for Research for Mothers and Children of the National Institute of Child Health and Human Development, and coeditor of *Learning Disabilities: Proceedings of the National Conference,* for his help and guidance. However, I alone am responsible for the material presented here.

29. The interaction is described in the *Proceedings of the 1987 National Conference on Learning Disabilities,* p. 473. The following passage captures it succinctly (the term "attention deficit disorder" (ADD) as used there refers both to children with ADDH and children who suffer from attention deficit disorder without hyperactivity): "A child's genetic endowment provides the biologic basis for particular behaviors. However, the clinical expression of these behaviors is influenced considerably by the child's environment. Thus, given a heavy loading of biologically determined behaviors for ADD, we might expect to see ADD expressed under most environmental conditions. Conversely, given a moderate loading for biologically determined behaviors consistent with ADD, we might expect to see the symptoms only in stressful environments. Finally, a particularly damaging environment may provoke symptoms even in children with very little biologically determined loading."

30. See U.S. Department of Justice, National Institute of Corrections, *Programming for Mentally Retarded and Learning Disabled Inmates: A Guide for Correctional Administrators;* and Senator Weinstein and Assemblyman Feldman's January 26, 1989, act to amend the correction law of New York State.

31. *Learning Disabilities: A Report to the U.S. Congress,* p. 221. There is at present some controversy concerning the correct definition of "learning disability." The definition used here has been endorsed by most professional and lay organizations in the field.

32. See U.S. Department of Justice, National Institute of Corrections, *Programming for Mentally Retarded and Learning Disabled Inmates: A Guide for Correctional Administrators,* p. 21, and "The Mentally Retarded Person in the Criminal Justice System," by Cecelia Ann Forget, in *Journal of Offender Counseling, Services and Rehabilitation,* Spring 1980, 285–95.

33. See "The Genetic Bases of Aggression," by University of Edinburgh zoologist Aubrey Manning, in *Aggression and War,* edited by Jo Groebel and Robert A. Hinde, p. 54.

34. Simon Baron-Cohen, "An Assessment of Violence in a Young Man with Asperger's Syndrome," *Journal of Child Psychology and Psychiatry,* 1988, p. 353. See also A. Mawson, A. Grounds, and D. Tantam, "Violence and Asperger's Syndrome: A Case Study," *British Journal of Psychiatry,* 147 1985, pp. 566–69.

35. See Joyce Sprafkin and Kenneth Gadow, "Television Viewing Habits of Emotionally Disturbed, Learning Disabled, and Mentally Retarded Children," *Journal of Applied Developmental Psychology,* Jan–Mar 1986, pp. 45–59.

36. Wilkens, "When War Becomes a Crime: The Case of My Lai," in *The Lessons of the Vietnam War,* p. 27.

37. "Crack's Toll Among Babies: A Joyless View, Even of Toys," *New York Times*, September 19, 1989.

38. See Sanday's *Female Power and Male Dominance: On the Origins of Sexual Inequality*. Holt's report is from an unpublished paper entitled "Converting the War System to a Peace System."

Chapter 4   Where Have All the Fathers Gone?

1. Richard Koestner, Carol Franz, and Joel Weinberger, "The Family Origins of Empathic Concern: A 26-Year Longitudinal Study," *Journal of Personality and Social Psychology*, 1990, pp. 709–17. For other studies on the relationship between involved, nurturant fathering and the development of empathy and altruism in sons, see Michael E. Lamb, "Fathers and Child Development: An Integrative Overview," in *The Role of the Father in Child Development*, edited by M. E. Lamb; A. Sagi, "Antecedents and Consequences of Various Degrees of Paternal Involvement in Child-rearing: The Israeli Project," in *Nontraditional Families*, edited by M. E. Lamb; Diane Ehrensaft, op. cit.

2. Mill, "On the Subjection of Women," *Essays on Sex Equality*, p. 218.

3. Best, *We've All Got Scars*, p. 78.

4. Ibid., pp. 72–73.

5. In an article entitled "Sex Differences in Aggression: A Rejoinder and Reprise," in *Child Development*, 1980, p. 974, Eleanor Maccoby and Carol Jacklin inform us that recent research reinforces fragmentary earlier evidence indicating that "fathers appear to be considerably more likely than mothers to put pressure on their children (particularly their sons) not to engage in cross-sex play."

6. Holt, interview with the author, 1989.

7. Willis, interview with the author, 1988.

8. Miller, "Lower Class Culture as a Generating Milieu of Gang Delinquency," in *The Sociology of Crime and Delinquency*, edited by M. E. Wolfgang, L. Savitz, and N. Johnston, p. 270.

9. Whiting discusses the correlation between lack of paternal involvement and violent behavior in an article entitled "Sex Identity Conflict and Physical Violence: A Comparative Study," in *Ethnography of Law* 67, pt. 2, Laura Nader, ed., pp. 123–40 (1965). It is based on *Six Cultures: Studies in Child Rearing*, edited by Beatrice Whiting. Other studies pointing to the correlation between the absence (or infrequent presence) of the father and violence include M. K. Bacon, I. L. Child, and H. Barry III, "A Cross-Cultural Study of Correlates of Crime," *Journal of Abnormal and Social Psychology* 66 1963, pp. 241–300; J. H. Rohrer and M. S. Edmondson, *The Eighth Generation;* R. V. Burton and J. W. M. Whiting, "The Absent Father and Cross-Sex Identity," in *Merrill-Palmer Quarterly*, 1961, p. 90. For further discussion, see also M. M. Katz and M. J. Konner, "The Role of the Father: An Anthropological Perspective," in *The Role of the Father in Child Development*, edited by M. E. Lamb.

10. Beatrice Whiting, "Sex Identity Conflict and Physical Violence: A Comparative Study," in *Ethnography of Law*, p. 137.

11. Burton and John Whiting, "The Absent Father and Cross-Sex Identity," in *Merrill-Palmer Quarterly*, 1961, p. 90.

12. Ibid.

13. Burton and Whiting, op. cit., p. 90.

14. Kakar, "Fathers and Sons: An Indian Experience," in *Father and Child*, edited by S. H. Cath, A. R. Gurwitt, and J. M. Ross, p. 420.

15. Best, op. cit. p. 79.

16. Diane Ehrensaft, *Parenting Together*, pp. 235, 236.

17. In one study seventy-one boys and girls ages two to six were brought into a playroom one by one. A six-to-eight-month-old baby was in the room. The boys and girls interacted with the baby equally. This experiment was carried out at Purdue University by Professors Gail F. Melson and Alan Fogel, and was reported in "Learning to Care," *Psychology Today*, January 1988, p. 42.

In another experiment, carried out by Phyllis Berman at the National Institute of Child Health and Human Development, two sets of children divided by age were asked to "take care" of a baby. In the 2½-to-5-year-old group, both the girls and the boys spent about the same amount of time playing with the baby. In the 5½-to-7½ age group the girls spent considerably more of their time playing with the baby than the boys. The older girls also talked to and touched the baby much more than did the older boys. This study was described in a 1989 interview with the author and in Melson and Fogel, op. cit., pp. 42 and 44.

18. Berman described the study in a 1989 interview.

19. See Norma Deitch Feshbach, "Sex Differences in Empathy," in *The Development of Prosocial Behavior*, edited by Nancy Eisenberg, p. 317.

20. Hoffman, interviews with the author, 1988, 1990.

21. Best, op. cit., p. 91.

22. Ibid., p. 92.

23. Ibid., p. 75.

24. Ibid., p. 135.

25. Pruett, *The Nurturing Father*, p. 138.

26. Ehrensaft, op. cit., p. 164.

27. Pruett, op. cit., p. 290.

28. Pruett, op. cit., pp. 300–1.

29. Broyles, Jr., "Why Men Love War," *Esquire*, November 1984, p. 61.

30. Cohn, *Sex and Death in the Rational World of Defense Intellectuals*, pp. 13, 14.

31. Pruett, op. cit., p. 210.

32. Gray, *The Warriors*, p. 238.

33. Pruett, op. cit., p. 127.

34. Willock, "Narcissistic Vulnerability in the Hyperaggressive Child: The Disregarded (Unloved, Uncared-for) Self," in *Psychoanalytic Psychology* 3, 1986, p. 65. For further discussion of the effects of the father's absence on mother's behavior, see also Martin Hoffman's article "The Role of the Father in Moral Internalization," in *The Role of the Father in Child Development*, edited by M. E. Lamb.

Chapter 5   "You Can't Trust Men with Kids" and Other Objections Answered

1. Information about child sexual abuse and battering is based on a 1987 interview with David Finkelhor, Associate Director of the Family Research Laboratory at the University of New Hampshire. Other statistics and estimates are cited in Hilda Parker and Seymour Parker, "Father-Daughter Sexual Abuse: An Emerging Perspective," *American Journal of Orthopsychiatry*, October 1986, pp. 531–49.

2. Pruett, The Nurturing Father, p. 122.

3. Ibid., p. 212.

4. See Parker and Parker, op. cit. The study revealed that "only 5.4% of the abusers and 37% of the nonabusers were involved frequently in performing three or more child-care and nurturant tasks."

5. Ibid., p. 547.

6. Best, *We've All Got Scars*, p. 60.

7. Socarides, "Abdicating Fathers, Homosexual Sons: Psychoanalytic Observations on the Contribution of the Father to the Development of Male Homosexuality," in *Father and Child*, edited by S. H. Cath, A. R. Gurwit, and J. M. Ross, p. 512.

8. Green, The *"Sissy Boy Syndrome,"* p. 377.

9. Isay, *Being Homosexual*, p. 32.

10. Biller, "The Father and Sex Role Development," in *The Role of the Father in Child Development*, edited by M. E. Lamb, p. 335.

11. See Green, op. cit., pp. 380–81; and M. E. Lamb, "Fathers and Child Development: An Integrative Overview," in *The Role of the Father in Child Development*.

12. Green, op. cit., pp. 297–98.

13. Dave Meggessey, interview with the author, 1988.

Chapter 7   Alternatives to Fistfights and Bullying

1. Educators for Social Responsibility is a national organization founded in 1982 by educators concerned primarily about the danger of nuclear war. The New York City chapter's work includes the teaching of conflict resolution, the development of multicultural education, and a project for combating racism.

2. Metis Associates: New York, N.Y., *The Resolving Conflict Creatively Program: A Summary of Significant Findings*, p. 16.

3. See Alfie Kohn, *No Contest: The Case Against Competition*.

Chapter 8   Taking the Glory Out of War and Unlearning Bigotry

1. Fitzgerald, *America Revised*, p. 47.

2. Ibid., p. 129.

3. Herbert J. Bass *et al.*, *America and the Americans*, p. 389.

4. Sidney Schwartz and John R. O'Connor, *Exploring Our Nation's History*, p. 123.

5. Ibid., p. 239.

6. Starr, interview with the author, 1989.

7. Quoted in M. S. Strom and W. S. Parsons, *Facing History and Ourselves, Holocaust and Human Behavior*, p. 281.

8. Ibid., p. 10.

9. The following descriptions are based on interviews with Moorehead Kennedy (1989), Colman McCarthy (1989), Lawrence Gibson (1988), and Alan Shapiro (1990). I observed classes taught by McCarthy and Gibson, watched videos of Kennedy and Martha Keys's hostage crisis simulations, and read about all the programs. Bob Veeck's course is described in Phyllis La Farge's *The Strangelove Legacy: Children, Parents, and Teachers in the Nuclear Age*.

10. See Phyllis La Farge, "Nuclear Teaching: Propaganda or Problem Solving?" *Bulletin of the Atomic Scientists*, July/August 1988, pp. 14–200.

Chapter 9   Changing the Male Mind-set

1. The remarks here are by Professor Christina Price of Troy State University, quoted in *Facing History and Ourselves News*, Winter 1988–89.

Chapter 10   The Culture of Violence

1. Benedict, *Patterns of Culture*, p. 18.

2. Ibid., p. 42.

3. Ibid., p. 43.

4. Ibid.

5. I owe this point to Letty Cottin Pogrebin in *Growing Up Free*.

Chapter 11   Sports: When Winning Is the Only Thing, Can Violence Be Far Away?

1. Smith, *Violence and Sport*, p. 10.

2. B. J. Bredemeier and D. L. Shields, "Values and Violence in Sports Today," *Psychology Today*, October 1985, p. 25.

3. Bredemeier, "Athletic Aggression: A Moral Concern," in *Sports Violence*, edited by J. H. Goldstein, p. 64.

4. Oriard, *The End of Autumn*, p. 11.

5. See J. Bryant and D. Zillman, "Sports Violence and the Media," in Goldstein, op. cit., p. 196.

6. Meggyesy, interview with the author, 1988.

7. See Richard E. Lapchick, editor, *Fractured Focus*, p. 220.

8. See Michael Messner, "When Bodies Are Weapons: Masculinity and Violence in Sport," *International Review of Sociology of Sport*. August 1990.

9. Meggyesy, *Out of Their League*, pp. 81–82.

10. See David Phillips, "The Impact of Mass Media Violence on U.S. Homicides," *American Sociological Review*, August 1983, pp. 560–68. Phillips's findings persisted after corrections for secular trends, seasonal factors, and other extraneous variables. Four alternative explanations for the findings were tested and

found wanting. His homicide statistics were taken from the National Center for Health Statistics.

11. See Richard G. Sipes, "War, Sports and Aggression: An Empirical Test of Two Rival Theories," *The American Anthropologist* 75, 1973, pp. 64–86.

12. See Hoffman, "The Role of the Father in Moral Internalization," in *The Role of the Father in Child Development*, edited by M. E. Lamb, pp. 373–74.

13. Lundberg, "Boxing Should Be Banned in Civilized Countries—Round 3," *Journal of the American Medical Association*, May 9, 1986, p. 2483.

14. Sammons, "Why Physicians Should Oppose Boxing: An Interdisciplinary History Perspective," *Journal of the American Medical Association*, March 10, 1989, p. 1484–86.

15. Michener, *Sports in America*, p. 469.

16. W. O. Johnson, "Sports and Suds," *Sports Illustrated*, August 8, 1988, p. 70.

17. Ibid.

18. Ibid.

19. Ibid., p. 81.

20. Lapchick, op. cit., p. 177.

21. Ibid., p. 178. Lapchick makes these comments in the course of summarizing Bennett J. Lombardo's article "The Behavior of Youth Sports Coaches: Crisis on the Bench," which appears in the same volume.

22. Meggyesy, op. cit., p. 20.

23. Oriard, op. cit., p. 13.

24. Meggyesy, op. cit., p. 23.

25. Oriard, op. cit., pp. 49–50.

26. See Fred Engh's introduction to Pat McInally's book *Moms and Dads and Kids and Sports*, p. xiii.

27. Michener, op. cit., p. 131.

28. Fine, *With the Boys*, p. 74.

29. Ibid., p. 83.

30. Ibid., p. 84.

31. Brower quoted in Michener, op. cit., pp. 137–38.

32. Bruns and Tutko, "Dealing with the Emotions of Childhood Sports," in Lapchick, op. cit., p. 216.

33. Sack, interview with the author, 1988.

34. Meggyesy, op. cit., p. 28.

35. Messner, op. cit., p. 7.

36. Oriard, op. cit., pp. 97–98.

37. McMurtry quoted in Michael Smith, *Violence and Sport*, p. 33.

38. Rivera, quoted in Bredemeier and Shields, op. cit., p. 24.

39. Oriard, op. cit., pp. 14–15.

40. Keith Lee, interview with the author, 1988.

41. The statistics on accidental deaths are from the National Safety Council. They were reported in a March 1, 1987, *New York Times* article by Janet Nelson. Spinal cord injury statistics are from Steve Lerch, "The Adjustment of Athletes to Career Ending Injuries," *Arena Review*, March 4, 1984, p. 62.

42. Meggyesy, op. cit., p. 181.

43. Kopay and Perry Deane Young, *The David Kopay Story*, p. 58.
44. Fine, op. cit., p. 114.
45. Oriard, op. cit., p. 28.
46. Michener, op. cit., pp. 470–71.
47. Smith, op. cit., p. 63.
48. Geoffrey Perret, *A Country Made by War*, p. 72.
49. Oriard, op. cit. pp. 113–14.
50. Meggyesy, op. cit., p. 171.
51. Agnew quoted in Michener, op. cit., p. 131.
52. See Michener, op. cit., p. 492.

Chapter 12   TV: The Babysitter That Teaches Violence

1. Statistics are from George Gerbner and Nancy Signorielli, *Violence Profile 1967 Through 1988–89: Enduring Patterns,* January 1990.

2. Nielsen ratings are the source for the number of hours children watch TV. The breakdown by age groups is as follows: ages two to five: 27 hours 49 minutes; ages six to eleven: 23 hours 39 minutes; ages twelve to seventeen: females: 21 hours 16 minutes, males: 22 hours 18 minutes.

The National Coalition on Television Violence is the source for the number of murders children see. It estimates that children living in homes with pay cable TV and/or a VCR will see about 32,000 murders and 40,000 attempted murders by age 18.

3. Laboratory experiments are usually carried out at universities on carefully selected subjects. Researchers start out with a very specific hypothesis and then construct an experiment to test it. For example, to test the catharsis hypothesis psychologist Leonard Berkowitz conducted three experiments in which college students were divided into two groups. One group was shown a "cathartic" boxing film. Berkowitz found that when the men who had seen the supposedly cathartic film were given an opportunity to act aggressively, they acted *more* rather than less aggressively than the men who had not seen the film. He concluded that the experiments cast considerable doubt on the view that watching filmed violence leads to a cathartic purge of anger. (See Berkowitz, "The Effects of Observing Violence," *Scientific American,* 1964, 210 pp. 35–61). Later studies by other researchers confirmed his findings and conclusions.

Surveys and longitudinal investigations involve the study of groups of people in their natural environment. For example, in the late 1950s psychologist Leonard Eron and colleagues conducted a study of 875 eight-year-old children living in a semirural county in New York State. The study included classroom testing, peer nomination for aggressive behavior, and interviews with parents. Ten years later the researchers were able to locate and interview 427 members of this group. They found that "the single best predictor of how aggressive a young man would be when he was 19 years old was the violence of the television programs he preferred when he was 8 years old." (See Eron, "Prescription for Reduction of Aggression," in *American Psychologist,* March 1980, p. 246.) Eron points out that a very careful analysis of the data made him and co-researchers confident that "there is a causal effect going from violence viewing to aggressive behavior" (Op. cit., p. 246). This direction of causation has been found in a number of subsequent studies done by other researchers.

By the late 1960s concern about TV violence had led to the formation of government-sponsored committees, which were to review research and make recommendations.

In 1969 the National Commission on the Causes and Prevention of Violence, headed by Dr. Milton S. Eisenhower, concluded on the basis of data from laboratory experiments that "violence on television encourages violent forms of behavior and fosters moral and social values about violence in daily life which are unacceptable in a civilized society" (quoted in "Violence and Sexual Violence in Film, Television, Cable and Home Video," National Council of the Churches of Christ in the U.S.A., p. 5). Its recommendations included an overall reduction in violent programming, elimination of violence from children's cartoons, and the scheduling of violent programs after 9 P.M.

In 1972 the Surgeon General's Scientific Advisory Committee reported on the results of two years of studies on violence commissioned by the government. The committee concluded that while there was evidence for short-run causation of aggression due to viewing violence on the screen, the evidence for long-term effects was insufficient to make any statement. But in testifying to the Senate, then Surgeon General Jesse L. Steinfeld took a much stronger position, stating: "It is clear to me that the causal relationship between televised violence and antisocial behavior is sufficient to warrant appropriate and immediate remedial action" (quoted in Tipper Gore, *Raising PG Kids in An X Rated Society*, p. 50). The discrepancy between the Surgeon General's statement and the committee's conclusions reflects his conviction, shared by numerous behavioral scientists, that the committee's conclusions were too cautious and tentative. They blamed this on the makeup of the committee: the television industry was asked to name members and had veto power over those considered for appointment.

By the time the National Institute of Mental Health published its 1982 report, the number of English-language publications on TV violence had gone up from about three hundred titles (in 1970) to twenty-five hundred titles.

4. 1982 NIMH report, p. 6.

5. George Gerbner, Michael Morgan, and Nancy Signorielli, "Living with Television: The Dynamics of the Cultivation Process," *Perspectives on Media Effects*, edited by J. Bryant and D. Zillman, p. 28.

6. N.I.M.H. report, p. 6.

7. These statistics are from Neil Postman, *The Disappearance of Childhood*, p. 134.

8. See Bozell Inc. *Media Insights, Television Viewing Among Blacks*, p. 1.

9. Wattleton, "The Case for National Action," *The Nation*, July 24–31, 1989, p. 140.

10. 1982 NIMH report, p. 55.

11. *New York Times*, August 9, 1988.

12. Geoffrey Cowan, *See No Evil*, p. 91.

13. See, for example, Harry J. Skornia's *Television and Society*. Skornia, who is

the former president of the National Association of Educational Broadcasters, explains, "Since industry controls most of the television and radio outlets which politicians need for reaching the people, few politicians will risk defying or offending them" (p. 27).

In *The First Amendment Under Siege* Richard Labunski tells us, "Many members of Congress would rather not offend broadcasters . . . An estimated 70 percent of the U.S. senators and 60 percent of the representatives regularly use free time offered by broadcasting stations back home" (p. 109).

In *See No Evil,* Geoffrey Cowan, a public interest attorney and author specializing in communications law, says, "It would be difficult to overstate the broadcasting industry's political muscle . . . Television lobbyists rely . . . on each politician's intense concern about the way he or she will be treated by the radio and television stations in his or her district" (p. 278–79).

For a detailed description and analysis of Congress's lack of action see *The Politics of T.V. Violence,* by Willard D. Rowland, Jr., dean of the University of Denver School of Communications.

14. Quoted in Rowland, op. cit., p. 285.

15. *New York Times,* June 8, 1988.

16. Quoted by Jeremy Tunstall, *Communications Deregulation,* p. 157.

17. John R. Bittner, *Broadcast Law and Regulation,* p. 57.

18. Eron and Huesmann, "Television Violence and Aggressive Behavior," *Advances in Clinical Child Psychology,* B. B. Lahey and A. E. Kazdin, eds., 1984, p. 54.

19. Cole, "Is 'Sesame Street' Really on the Right Track?" *New York Times,* November 13, 1988.

20. The study, conducted by the Educational Testing Service, is described by Albert Shanker, then president of the American Federation of Teachers, in a February 5, 1989, op-ed column in the *New York Times.*

Chapter 13   Films and Videos: When Blood and Guts Is Fun

1. DeMause, ed., *The History of Childhood,* p. 1.

2. Quoted in "Horror Films Boost Teens' Sex Appeal," a September 16, 1986, *New York Times* article that discusses the study.

3. *NCTV News,* June–October 1988, p. 3.

4. See Tamara Jones, " 'Fun' Killers Now Paying Devil's Dues," the *Los Angeles Times,* October 20, 1988.

5. Judy Mann, the *Washington Post,* May 6, 1988.

Chapter 14   Music and Wrestling: The "Joys" of Rape, Satanism, and Bigotry

1. I am indebted to the Parents Music Resource Center, which made available to me many of the lyrics quoted in this chapter. Tipper Gore's book, *Raising PG Children in an X Rated Society,* has been another valuable resource for both lyrics and other information pertaining to violence in rock music.

2. Among males age fifteen to twenty-four, suicide rates have gone from 8.6

per 100,000 in 1960 to 23.3 per 100,000 in 1986 (Statistical Abstract of the United States, 1973, 1990).

3. Quoted in Tipper Gore, *Raising PG Kids in an X Rated Society,* p. 95.

4. Carl Taylor quotes are from Gore, op. cit., p. 102.

5. See Hannelore Wass, "Adolescents' Interest in and Views of Destructive Themes in Rock Music," *Omega,* 1988–89, pp. 177–86. Wass's findings confirm an earlier study by H. Stipp, who reported that all the adolescents in his sample knew the lyrics of their favorite songs. See Stipp, "Children's Knowledge of and Taste in Popular Music," in *Popular Music and Society,* 1985, pp. 1–15. On the other hand, a study by Lorraine E. Prinsky and Jill Leslie Rosenbaum, " 'Leer-ics' or Lyrics: Teenage Impressions of Rock 'n' Roll" in *Youth and Society,* June 1987, pp. 384–97, found that most of the teenagers in their sample had a limited understanding of song lyrics. This study did not distinguish between HSS and other rock fans. It seems, at the very least, that those boys who have a deep fascination with violent, satanic, suicidal songs are especially likely to understand their lyrics.

6. Quoted in Eric Breindel, "Rapping to the Same Tune," the *Washington Times,* January 9, 1990.

7. King, "Heavy Metal Music and Drug Abuse in Adolescents," *Postgraduate Medicine,* April 1988, p. 295.

8. Ibid., p. 298.

9. Rosenbloom, interview with the author, 1989

Chapter 15   When the Toy Store Looks like a Military Arsenal

1. Toles, "Video Games and American Military Ideology," *Arena Review,* March 1985, pp. 61–62.

2. Ibid., p. 68.

3. Quoted in D. C. McGill, "Nintendo Scores Big," the *New York Times,* December 4, 1988.

4. Pogrebin, *Growing Up Free,* p. 376.

5. N. Carlsson-Paige and D. Levin, *The War Play Dilemma,* p. 80.

6. Ibid., p. 9.

7. Ibid., p. 11.

8. Ibid., p. 12.

9. Ibid.

10. Ibid., p. 8.

11. Carlsson-Paige and Levin, *Who's Calling the Shots,* pp. 12–13.

12. These quotes, and the passage quoted in the footnote to p. 270, are from "Do War Toys Make Sense?" edited by Emrika Padus, in *Good Toys,* Fall 1986, p. 28.

13. Ibid.

14. Carlsson-Paige and Levin, *War Play Dilemma,* p. 19.

15. Floyd, interview with the author, 1987.

16. Huizinga, *Homo Ludens,* p. 89.

17. Ibid., p. 98.

18. Ibid., p. 90.

19. Ibid., p. 101.

20. Carlsson-Paige and Levin, *War Play Dilemma*, p. 19.

21. Ibid., p. 18.

22. Bruno Bettelheim, "The Importance of Play," *The Atlantic*, March 1987, p. 46.

23. Ibid.

24. Ibid.

25. Holt, interview with the author, 1988.

26. The study described was carried out by Professor Charles Turner and Diane Goldsmith of the University of Utah. See their article, "Effects of Toy Guns and Airplanes on Children's Antisocial Free Play Behavior," *Journal of Experimental Child Psychology*, 1976, vol. 21 pp. 303–15. Their research corroborated findings of a 1956 study of sixty-one five-to-eight-year-old children done by UCLA professor Seymour Feshbach. See his article "The Catharsis Hypothesis and Some Consequences of Interaction with Aggressive and Neutral Play Objects," *Journal of Personality*, June 1956, pp. 449–62. Research done by A. Mendoza in a 1972 (University of Miami) doctoral dissertation comparing children playing with "war toys" and children playing with neutral toys also corroborates Turner and Goldsmith's study. (See Bibliography.)

Several studies with adults indicate that just the presence of guns increases the probability that frustrated and uninhibited persons will act aggressively. See for example Leonard Berkowitz and Anthony LePage, "Weapons as Aggression-Eliciting Stimuli," *Journal of Personality and Social Psychology* 1967, p. 202–7.

Chapter 16   Taking Children Out of the Commercial Market

1. Frank Zappa, "On Junk Food for the Soul," *New Perspectives Quarterly*, Winter 1988, p. 28.

2. Parker, 1988 interview with the author

3. Jefferson, letter to Kercheval, *Social and Political Philosophy*, ed. by John Somerville and Ronald E. Santoni, 1963, pp. 275–76.

4. Levy quoted in Marc A. Franklin, *The First Amendment and the Fourth Estate*, p. 24.

5. See, for example, the writings of legal theorist Alexander Meiklejohn, who states: "The primary purpose of the First Amendment is, then, that all the citizens shall, so far as possible, understand the issues which bear upon our common life." (Franklin, op. cit., p. 83).

6. Mill, *Utilitarianism*, p. 17.

Conclusion   Beyond the Masculine Mystique

1. The *New York Times*, September 24, 1989.

2. Costello, interview with the author, 1990.

3. Hannah Arendt, *Eichmann in Jerusalem*, pp. 287–88.

4. Ibid., p. 288

5. Janice T. Gibson and Mika Haritos-Fatouros, "The Education of a Torturer," *Psychology Today*, November 1986, p. 57.

6. See Carolyn Zahn-Waxler and Marian Radke-Yarrow, "The Development of Altruism: Alternative Research Strategies," in *The Development of Prosocial Behavior,* edited by Nancy Eisenberg. In the same volume, see Martin L. Hoffman, "Development of Prosocial Motivation: Empathy and Guilt." See also Radke-Yarrow and Zahn-Waxler, "The Role of Familial Factors in the Development of Prosocial Behavior: Research Findings and Questions," in *Development of Antisocial and Prosocial Behavior,* edited by D. Olweus, J. Block, and M. Radke-Yarrow.

Statistics

Sources
Uniform Crime Reports (UCR), Federal Bureau of Investigation, U.S. Department of Justice, 1990

Statistical Abstract of the United States (SA), U.S. Bureau of the Census, 1990

Children in Custody, 1975–1985, Bureau of Justice Statistics

The UCR defines violent crimes as offenses of murder, forcible rape, robbery, and aggravated assault. Burglary, larceny-theft, and motor vehicle theft are considered property crimes.

1990 Crime Statistics and Rates
source: UCR 1990

88.7% of persons arrested for violent crimes were male; 11.3 were females.

16.2% of those arrested for violent crimes were under eighteen; 4.6% were under fifteen.

53.7% of those arrested were white; 44.7% were African-American.

30% of female murder victims were killed by husbands or boyfriends.

4% of male victims were killed by wives or girlfriends.

1,820,127 Americans were the victims of a violent crime: 23,438 were murdered, 102,555 forcibly raped, 1,054,863 were victims of aggravated assault. The violent crime rate per 100,000 inhabitants was 731.8.

Increases in Violent Crime
sources: UCR 1990, SA 1990, Children in Custody, 1975–1985

Between 1986 and 1990, the number of males arrested for violent crimes increased by 33.1%, from 315,082 to 419,448. During the same period, the number of females arrested for violent crimes increased by 41% from 38,104 to 53,721 (UCR 1990).

In 1960, the homicide rate in the U.S. was 4.7 per 100,000. In 1990, it was 9.4 per 100,000 (SA 1990, UCR 1990).

Federal and state prisoners: In 1960, there were 212,953 prisoners. In 1988 there were 603,928. This represents an increase from 118.6 to 244.0 per 100,000 (SA 1990).

Between 1975 and 1985 there was a 30% increase per 100,000 in the number of juveniles in custody in public and private facilities (Children in Custody, 1975–85).

Homicide Victims by Race and Sex
source: SA 1990

Males are about 3 times as likely as females to be victims of homicide. African-American males are at highest risk. In 1987, there were 53.3 African-American male victims of homicide per 100,000. For African-American females the figure was 12.6. For white males, victimization rates were 7.9 per 100,000; for white females, 3.0.

Births to Unmarried Women
source: SA 1985, 1990

In 1950 4.0 of all births were to unmarried women. In 1960 5.3% of all births were to unmarried women. In 1970, the figure was 10.7%. By 1987, it was 24.5 percent. Racial breakdown: In 1970 5.7% of white women giving birth were unmarried; in 1987, the figure was 16.7%. In 1970 37.6% of all black women giving birth were unmarried; in 1987, the figure was 62.2%.

Cumulative Statistics
source: UCR 1990

From 1974 to 1990, 350,018 Americans were murdered.

Bibliography

ABC News, "Nightline." *Mock War Games*, September 1, 1987.

———. *Prejudice: The War Between the Classes*, January 19, 1987.

ABEL, JOHN D., and BENINSON, MAUREEN E. "Perceptions of TV Program Violence by Children and Mothers," *Journal of Broadcasting* 20 (Summer 1976), pp. 355–63.

ALBERT, JAMES A. "Constitutional Regulation of Televised Violence," *Virginia Law Review* 64 (December 1978) pp. 1299–1346.

American Psychiatric Association. *Diagnostic and Statistical Manual of Mental Disorders,* Third Revised Edition. Washington, D.C.: American Psychiatric Association, 1987.

APTER, STEVEN J., and GOLDSTEIN, P., eds. *Youth Violence: Programs & Prospects.* New York: Pergamon Press, 1986.

AQUINAS, THOMAS. *Summa Theologica,* Vol. 38., Marcus Lefebure, trans. O. P. Westminster: Blackfriars, 1975.

ARCANA, JUDITH. *Every Mother's Son: The Role of Mothers in the Making of Men.* Seattle: The Seal Press, 1986.

ARCHER, DANE. *Violence and Crime in Cross-National Perspective.* New Haven: Yale University Press, 1984.

ARDREY, ROBERT. *African Genesis.* New York: Dell Publishing Co., 1961.

ARENDT, HANNAH. *Eichmann in Jerusalem: A Report on the Banality of Evil.* New York: Penguin Books, 1977 (1963).

———. *On Violence.* San Diego: Harcourt Brace Jovanovich, 1969.

ARISTOPHANES. *Lysistrata,* Douglass Parker, trans. New York: New American Library, 1970.

ARISTOTLE. *Politics,* B. Jowett, trans. New York: Modern Library, 1943.

ASTRACHAN, ANTHONY. *How Men Feel: Their Responses to Women's Demands for Equality and Power.* Garden City, N.Y.: Anchor Press, 1986.

AUFDERHEIDE, PAT. "The Look of the Sound," *Watching Television*, Todd Gitlin, ed. New York: Pantheon Books, 1986.

AXELROD, ROBERT. *The Evolution of Cooperation.* New York: Basic Books, 1984.

BACON, M. K., CHILD, I. L., and BARRY, H. "A Cross-Cultural Study of Correlates of Crime," *Journal of Abnormal and Social Psychology* 66 (1963), pp. 241–300.

BAGDIKIAN, BEN. "The Media Brokers," *Multinational Monitor* 8 (September 1987), pp. 7–12.

BANDURA, ALBERT. *Aggression: A Social Learning Analysis.* Englewood Cliffs, N.J.: Prentice Hall, 1973.

BARASH, DAVID. *The Whispering Within.* New York: Penguin Books, 1985.

BARNET, RICHARD J., *Real Security.* New York: Simon and Schuster, 1981.

———. *Roots of War: The Men and Institutions Behind U.S. Foreign Policy.* New York: Penguin Books. 1973.

BARON-COHEN, SIMON. "An Assessment of Violence in a Young Man with Asperger's Syndrome," *Journal of Child Psychology and Psychiatry* 29 (1988), pp. 351–60.

BASS, HERBERT J., et al. *America and the Americans.* Morristown, N.J.: Silver, Burdett and Ginn, 1983.

BEAUVOIR, SIMONE DE. *The Second Sex,* trans. H. M. Parshley. New York: Bantam Books, 1961.

BELL, DONALD H. *Being a Man: The Paradox of Masculinity.* New York: Harcourt Brace Jovanovich, 1984.

BELSON, W. A. *Television Violence and the Adolescent Boy.* Lexington, Mass.: Lexington Books, 1978.

BEM, SANDRA L. "The Measurement of Psychological Androgyny," *Journal of Consulting and Clinical Psychology* 42 (1974), pp. 155–61.

BENEDICT, RUTH. *Patterns of Culture.* New York: Mentor Books, 1946 (1934).

BENEKE, TIMOTHY. *Men on Rape.* New York: St. Martin's Press, 1982.

BENJAMIN, JESSICA. *The Bonds of Love: Psychoanalysis, Feminism, and the Problem of Domination.* New York: Pantheon Books, 1988.

BENNETT, GEORGETTE. *Crimewarps.* Garden City, N.Y.: Anchor Press, 1987.

BERKOWITZ, LEONARD. "The Effects of Observing Violence," *Scientific American* 210 (1964), pp. 35–61.

BERKOWITZ, LEONARD, and LePAGE, ANTHONY. "Weapons as Aggression—Eliciting Stimuli," *Journal of Personality and Social Psychology* 7 (1967), pp. 202–7.

BERLAGE, GAI I. "Are Children's Competitive Sports Teaching Corporate Values?" *Fractured Focus,* Richard E. Lapchick, ed. Lexington, Mass.: D. C. Heath and Co., 1986.

BERMAN, PHYLLIS W. "Young Children's Responses to Babies: Do They Foreshadow Differences Between Maternal and Paternal Styles?" *The Origins of Nurturance,* Alan Fogel and Gail Melson, eds. Hillsdale, N.J.: L. Erlbaum, 1986.

BERMAN, PHYLLIS W., and GOODMAN, VICKIE. "Age and Sex Differences in Children's Responses to Babies: Effects of Adults' Caretaking Requests and Instructions," *Child Development* 55 (1984), pp. 1071–77.

BEST, RAPHAELA. *We've All Got Scars: What Boys and Girls Learn in Elementary School.* Bloomington: Indiana University Press, 1983.

BETTELHEIM, BRUNO. "The Importance of Play," *The Atlantic* (March 1987), pp. 35–46.

———. *The Uses of Enchantment: The Meaning and Importance of Fairy Tales.* New York: Vintage Books, 1989 (1975).

BITTNER, JOHN R. *Broadcast Law and Regulation.* Englewood Cliffs, N.J.: Prentice-Hall, 1982.

BLANCHARD, D. C., and BLANCHARD, R. J. "Ethoexperimental Approaches to the Biology of Emotion," *Annual Review of Psychology* 39 (1988), pp. 43–68.

BLANCHARD, ROBERT J., and BLANCHARD, CAROLINE D., eds. *Advances in the Study of Aggression,* vol. 1. Orlando: Academic Press, 1984.

BLANCK, GERTRUDE, and BLANCK, RUBIN. *Ego Psychology II: Psychoanalytic Developmental Psychology.* New York: Columbia University Press, 1979.

BLEIER, RUTH. *Science and Gender.* New York: Pergamon Press, 1984.

BLOCK, JEANNE HUMPHREY. "Conceptions of Sex Role," *American Psychologist* (June 1973), pp. 512–26.

BLY, ROBERT. *Iron John: A Book About Men.* Reading, Mass: Addison Wesley, 1990.

BOULDING, ELISE. "Two Cultures of Religion as Obstacles to Peace," *Zygon* 21 (December 1986), pp. 501–17.

BOWER, ROBERT T. *The Changing Television Audience in America.* New York: Columbia University Press, 1985.

Bozell Inc. Advertising. *Media Insights: Television Viewing Among Blacks.* Bozell Inc. (April 1990).

BRANTENBERG, GERD. *Egalia's Daughters: A Satire of the Sexes,* trans. Louis Mackay. Seattle: The Seal Press, 1985.

BREDEMEIER, BRENDA JO, and SHIELDS, DAVID L. "Values and Violence in Sports Today," *Psychology Today* (October 1985)

BRENNER, CHARLES. *An Elementary Textbook of Psychoanalysis.* Garden City, N.Y.: Anchor Press, 1957.

BRENNER, DANIEL L., and RIVERS, WILLIAM L. *Free but Regulated: Conflicting Traditions in Media Law.* Ames: Iowa State University Press, 1982.

BRITTAIN, VERA. *Testament of Youth* New York: Wideview Books, 1980 (1933).

BROAD, WILLIAM J. *Star Warriors.* New York: Simon and Schuster, 1985.

BROCK-UTNE, BIRGIT. *Educating for Peace.* New York: Pergamon Press, 1985.

BROD, HARRY, ed. *The Making of Masculinities.* Winchester, Mass.: Unwin Hyman, 1987.

BROWN, CLAUDE. *Manchild in The Promised Land.* New York: New American Library, 1965.

———. "Manchild in Harlem," *New York Times Magazine* (September 16, 1984)

BROWN, ELIZABETH F., and WILLIAM, HENDEE R. "Adolescents and Their Music: Insights into the Health of Adolescents," *Journal of the American Medical Association* 262 (September 22–29, 1989), pp. 1659–63.

BROWN, LES. *Television: The Business Behind the Box.* New York: Harcourt Brace Jovanovich, 1971.

———. *Keeping Your Eye on Television.* New York: The Pilgrim Press, 1979.

BROWNMILLER, SUSAN. *Against Our Will: Men, Women, and Rape.* New York: Bantam Books, 1976.

BROYLES, WILLIAM. "Why Men Love War," *Esquire* (November 1984).

BURSTYN, VARDA, ed. *Women Against Censorship.* Scranton, Pa.: Salem Publishing House, 1985.

BURTON, ROGER V., and WHITING, JOHN W. M. "The Absent Father and Cross-Sex Identity," *Merrill-Palmer Quarterly* 7 (1961), pp. 85–95.

CALDICOTT, HELEN. *Missile Envy: The Arms Race and Nuclear War.* New York: William Morrow and Co., 1984.

CAMERON, DEBORAH, and FRAZER, ELIZABETH. *The Lust to Kill.* New York: New York University Press, 1987.

CAPLAN, ARTHUR L., ed. *The Sociobiology Debate.* New York: Harper Torchbooks, 1985 (1978).

CAPLAN, PAULA J. *The Myth of Women's Masochism.* New York: New American Library, 1987.

CAPUTO, PHILIP. *A Rumor of War.* New York: Ballantine Books, 1977.

CARLSON, DON, and COMSTOCK, CRAIG, eds. *Securing Our Planet.* Los Angeles: Jeremy P. Archer, Inc., distributed by St. Martin's Press, 1986.

CARLSSON-PAIGE, NANCY, and LEVIN, DIANE E. *The War Play Dilemma: Balancing Needs and Values in the Early Childhood Classroom.* New York: Teachers College Press, 1987.

———. *Who's Calling the Shots? How to Respond Effectively to Children's Fascination with War Play and War Toys.* Philadelphia: New Society Publishers, 1990.

CASE, ROBERT W., and BOUCHER, ROBERT L. "Spectator Violence in Sport: A Selected Review," *Journal of Sport and Social Issues* 5 (1981), pp. 1–14.

CATH, STANLEY H., GURWITT, ALAN R., and ROSS, JOHN MUNDER, eds. *Father and Child: Developmental and Clinical Perspectives.* Boston: Little, Brown and Co., 1982.

Center for Social Studies Education. *The Lessons of the Vietnam War,* Pittsburgh, Pa.: Center for Social Studies Education, 1988.

CHESLER, PHYLLIS. *About Men.* New York: Simon and Schuster, 1978.

CHODOROW, NANCY. *The Reproduction of Mothering: Psychoanalysis and the Sociology of Gender.* Berkeley: University of California Press, 1978.

COHN, CAROL. "Nuclear Language," *Bulletin of the Atomic Scientists* (June 1987), pp. 17–24.

———. *Sex and Death in the Rational World of Defense Intellectuals,* privately published by the Center for Psychological Studies in the Nuclear Age (Cambridge, Mass.: 1987).

COLE, HOWARD J. "Patterns of Gender-Role Behaviour in Children Attending Traditional and Non-Traditional Day-Care Centres," *Canadian Journal of Psychiatry* 27 (August 1982), pp. 410–14.

COLES, ROBERT. "Harvard Diary." *New Oxford Review* (April 1988), pp. 25–28.

COMSTOCK, GEORGE, "Television Violence and Antisocial and Aggressive Behavior." Paper prepared for *Television and Teens: Health Implications,* a conference sponsored by the Kaiser Foundation, Los Angeles. (June 22–24, 1988).

COUSINS, NORMAN. *The Pathology of Power.* New York: W. W. Norton and Co., 1987.

COWAN, GEOFFREY. *See No Evil: The Backstage Battle over Sex and Violence in Television.* New York: Simon and Schuster, 1979.

DALY, MARY. *Beyond God the Father: Towards a Philosophy of Women's Liberation.* Boston: Beacon Press, 1985 (1973).

————. *Gyn/Ecology: The Metaethics of Radical Feminism.* Boston: Beacon Press, 1978.

DAVIS, ELIZABETH GOULD. *The First Sex.* New York: Penguin Books, 1972.

DEE, JULIET LUSHBOUGH. "Media Accountability for Real-Life Violence: A Case of Negligence or Free Speech?" *Journal of Communications* 37 (Spring 1987), pp. 107–38.

DEMAUSE, LLOYD, ed. *The History of Childhood: The Untold Story of Child Abuse.* New York: Harper and Row, 1975.

DESMOND, ROGER JON, et al. "Gender Differences, Mediation, and Disciplinary Styles in Children's Responses to Television," *Sex Roles* 16 (1987), pp. 375–89.

DIAMOND, MILTON. "Sexual Identity, Monozygotic Twins Reared in Discordant Sex Roles and a B.B.C. Follow Up," *Archives of Sexual Behavior* 11 (1982), pp. 181–86.

DINNERSTEIN, DOROTHY. *The Mermaid and The Minotaur: Sexual Arrangements and Human Malaise.* New York: Harper and Row, 1977.

DODGE, KENNETH A., BATES, JOHN E., and PETTIT, GREGORY S. "Mechanisms in the Cycle of Violence," *Science* 250 (December 21, 1990), pp. 1678–83.

DONNERSTEIN, EDWARD, LINZ, DANIEL, and PENROD, STEVEN. *The Question of Pornography: Research Findings and Policy Implications.* New York: The Free Press, 1987.

DUNIVANT, NOEL. "The Relationship Between Learning Disabilities and Juvenile Delinquency: Executive Summary," a report of the National Center for State Courts. Williamsburg, Va.: 1982.

DWORKIN, RONALD. *Taking Rights Seriously.* London: Gerald Duckworth and Co., 1977.

EDMUNDS, LAVINIA. "Lessons in Fatherhood," *Johns Hopkins Magazine* (August 1988), pp. 41–49.

EHRENSAFT, DIANE. *Parenting Together: Men and Women Sharing the Care of Their Children.* New York: The Free Press, 1987.

EHRHARDT, ANKE A. "Gender Differences: A Biosocial Perspective," *Nebraska Symposium on Motivation 1984: Psychology and Gender* 32 (1985), pp. 37–57.

————. "The Psychobiology of Gender," *Gender in the Life Course,* A. S. Rossi, ed. Hawthorne, N.Y.: Aldine de Gruyter, 1985.

EIBL-EIBESFELDT, IRENAUS. *The Biology of Peace and War: Men, Animals, and Aggression,* Eric Mosbacher, trans. New York: Viking Press, 1979.

EISENBERG, NANCY, ed. *The Development of Prosocial Behavior.* New York: Academic Press, 1982.

EISENBERG, NANCY, and STRAYER, J., eds. *Empathy and Its Development.* Cambridge: Cambridge University Press, 1987.

ELKIND, DAVID. *The Hurried Child: Growing Up Too Fast Too Soon.* Reading, Mass.: Addison-Wesley, 1981.

ELSHTAIN, JEAN BETHKE. "A Cross-Cultural Perspective on Sex Differences,"

Handbook of Cross-Cultural Human Development, Ruth H. Munroe, Robert L. Munroe, and Beatrice B. Whiting, eds. New York: Garland Press, 1981.

———. "Reflections on War and Political Discourse," *Political Theory* 13 (February 1985), pp. 39–57.

———. *Women and War.* New York: Basic Books, 1987.

EMBER, CAROL R. "Feminine Task Assignment and the Social Behavior of Boys," *Ethos* 1 (Winter 1973), pp. 424–39.

———. "Men's Fear of Sex with Women: A Cross-Cultural Study," *Sex Roles* 4 (1978), pp. 657–77.

EMBER, CAROL R. and EMBER, MELVIN. "Cross-Cultural Tests of Ecological, Psychological, and Social Explanations of Warfare and Aggression." Prepared for delivery at the 1987 Annual Meeting of the American Political Science Association, the Palmer House, September 3–6.

ENGELHARDT, TOM. "The Shortcake Strategy," *Watching Television,* Todd Gitlin, ed. New York: Pantheon Books, 1986.

ERON, LEONARD D. "The Development of Aggressive Behavior from the Perspective of a Developing Behaviorism," *American Psychologist* 42 (May 1987) pp. 435–42.

———. "Prescription for Reduction of Aggression," *American Psychologist* 35 (March 1980), p. 244–52.

ERON, LEONARD D., and HUESMANN, ROWELL L. "Adolescent Aggression and Television," *Annals of the New York Academy of Sciences* 347 (June 20, 1980), p. 319–31.

———. "Parent-Child Interaction, Television Violence, and Aggression of Children," *American Psychologist* 37 (February 1982), pp. 197–211.

———. "Television Violence and Aggressive Behavior," *Advances in Clinical Child Psychology* Vol. 7, Benjamin B. Lahey and Alan E. Kazdin, eds. New York: Plenum, 1984.

ERON, LEONARD D., HUESMANN, ROWELL L., et al. "Aggression and Its Correlates over 22 Years," *Childhood Aggression and Violence,* David Crowell, Ian M. Evans, and Clifford R. O'Donnell, eds. New York: Plenum, 1987.

FARRELL, WARREN. *Why Men Are the Way They Are.* New York: McGraw-Hill, 1986.

FASTEAU, MARK FEIGEN. *The Male Machine.* New York: McGraw-Hill, 1974.

FAUSTO-STERLING, ANNE. *Myths of Gender: Biological Theories About Men and Women.* New York: Basic Books, 1985.

FEDDERS, CHARLOTTE, and ELLIOT, LAURA. *Rights, Justice, and the Bounds of Liberty.* Princeton: Princeton University Press, 1980.

———. *Shattered Dreams: The Story of Charlotte Fedders.* New York: Harper and Row, 1987.

Federal Bureau of Investigation, *Uniform Crime Reports, Crime in the United States 1989.* Washington, D.C.: U.S. Government Printing Office, 1990.

FESHBACH, SEYMOUR. "The Catharsis Hypothesis of Interaction with Aggressive and Neutral Play Objects," *Journal of Personality* 24 (June 1956), pp. 449–62.

———. "Dynamics and Morality of Violence and Aggression: Some Psychological Considerations," *American Psychologist* 26 (March 1971), pp. 281–92.

FINE, GARY ALAN. *With the Boys: Little League Baseball and Preadolescent Behavior.* Chicago: The University of Chicago Press, 1987.

FINEBERG, JOEL, ed. *Rights, Justice, and the Bounds of Liberty: Essays in Social Philosophy.* Princeton: Princeton University Press, 1980.

FINEBERG, JOEL, and GROSS, HYMAN, eds. *Philosophy of Law.* Encino, Calif.: Dickenson, 1975.

FISCHER, DIETRICH. *Preventing War in the Nuclear Age.* Totowa, N.J.: Roman and Allanheld, 1984.

FISHER, ROGER, and BROWN, SCOTT. *Getting Together: Building a Relationship That Gets to Yes.* Boston: Houghton Mifflin Co., 1988.

FISHER, ROGER, and URY, WILLIAM. *Getting to Yes: Negotiating Agreement Without Giving In.* New York: Penguin Books, 1983.

FITZGERALD, FRANCIS. *America Revised.* New York: Random House, 1979.

FOGEL, ALAN, and MELSON, GAIL, eds. *The Origins of Nurturance.* Hillsdale, N.J.: L. Erlbaum, 1986

FORGET, CECELIA ANN. "The Mentally Retarded Person in the Criminal Justice System," *Journal of Offender Counseling, Services and Rehabilitation* (Spring 1980), p. 285–95.

FRANCOIS, WILLIAM E. *Mass Media Law and Regulation,* 3d ed. Columbus, Ohio: Grid Publishing, 1982.

FRANK, JEROME D. *Sanity and Survival: Psychological Aspects of War and Peace.* New York: Random House, 1967.

FRANKLIN, MARC A. *The First Amendment and the Fourth Estate: Communication Law for Undergraduates.* Westbury, N.Y.: Foundation Press, 1981.

FRENCH, MARILYN. *Beyond Power: On Women, Men and Morals.* New York: Summit Books, 1985.

FREY, WILLIAM H., with LANGSETH, MURIEL. *Crying: The Mystery of Tears.* Minneapolis: Winston Press, 1985.

FRIEDAN, BETTY. *The Feminine Mystique.* New York: Dell Publishing Co., 1964.

FREUD, SIGMUND. *Civilization and Its Discontents,* Joan Riviere, trans. London: The Hogarth Press, 1955 (1930).

————. "The Economic Problem of Masochism," *Standard Edition of The Complete Psychological Works of Sigmund Freud,* Vol. 19, James Strachey, ed. London: Hogarth Press, 1961 (1924) pp. 159–70.

FREUD, SIGMUND, and EINSTEIN, ALBERT. "Why War?" *Standard Edition of the Complete Psychological Works of Sigmund Freud* Vol. 22, James Strachey, ed. London: Hogarth Press, 1961 (1924) pp. 199–215.

FROMM, ERICH. *The Anatomy of Human Destructiveness.* New York: Holt, Rinehart and Winston, 1973.

FULBRIGHT, WILLIAM J. *The Arrogance of Power.* New York: Vintage Books, 1966.

GAYLIN, WILLARD. *The Killing of Bonnie Garland.* New York: Simon and Schuster, 1982.

GELLES, RICHARD J., and PEDRICK, CLAIRE. *Intimate Violence in Families.* Beverly Hills: Sage Publications, 1983.

GERBNER, GEORGE, et al. "Television's Mean World: Violence Profile" No. 14–15, privately published by the Annenberg School of Communications (Philadelphia, September 1986).

GERBNER, GEORGE, MORGAN, MICHAEL, and SIGNORIELLI, NANCY. "Living with Television," *Perspectives on Media Effects,* Jennings Bryant and Dolf Zillman, eds. Hillsdale, N.J.: L. Erlbaum Associates, 1986, pp. 17–40.

GERBNER, GEORGE (University of Pennsylvania) and SIGNORIELLI, NANCY (University of Delaware). "Violence Profile 1967 Through 1988–89: Enduring Patterns," privately published (January, 1990).

GERZON, MARK. *A Choice of Heroes: The Changing Face of American Manhood.* Boston: Houghton Mifflin Co., 1982.

GIBSON, JANICE T., and HARITOS-FATOUROS, MIKA. "The Education of a Torturer," *Psychology Today* (November 1986).

GILDER, GEORGE F. *Sexual Suicide.* New York: Bantam Books, 1975.

GILLIGAN, CAROL. *In a Different Voice: Psychological Theory and Women's Development.* Cambridge: Harvard University Press, 1982.

GOLDBERG, HERB. *The Hazards of Being Male.* New York: New American Library, 1977.

———. *The New Male.* New York: New American Library, 1980.

GOLDING, WILLIAM. *Lord of the Flies.* New York: Perigee Books, 1954.

GOLDBERG, STEVEN. *The Inevitability of Patriarchy.* New York: William Morrow and Co., 1973.

GOLDSTEIN, ARNOLD P., et al. "Training Aggressive Adolescents in Prosocial Behavior," *Journal of Youth and Adolescence* 7 (1978), pp. 73–92.

GOLDSTEIN, JEFFREY H., ed. *Sports Violence.* New York: Springer-Verlag, 1983.

GORE, TIPPER [Mary Elizabeth]. *Raising PG Kids in an X-rated Society.* New York: Bantam Books, 1988.

GRAY, J. GLENN. *The Warriors.* New York: Harper and Row, 1970.

GREEN, RICHARD. *The "Sissy Boy Syndrome" and the Development of Homosexuality.* New Haven: Yale University Press, 1987.

GRIMSHAW, JEAN. *Philosophy and Feminist Thinking.* Minneapolis: University of Minnesota Press, 1986.

GROEBEL, JO, and HINDE, ROBERT A., eds. *Aggression and War: Their Biological and Social Bases.* Cambridge: Cambridge University Press, 1989.

HALBERSTAM, DAVID. *The Best and the Brightest.* New York: Penguin Books, 1983 (1969).

HALLIE, PHILIP P. *Lest Innocent Blood Be Shed: The Story of the Village of Le Chambon and How Goodness Happened There.* New York: Harper Colophon Books, 1980.

HALLORAN, RICHARD. *To Arm a Nation.* New York: Macmillan, 1986.

HANEY, CRAIG, BANKS, CURTIS, and ZIMBARDO, PHILIP. "Interpersonal Dynamics in a Simulated Prison," *International Journal of Criminology and Penology* 1 (1973), pp. 69–97.

HART, M. *Sport in the Sociocultural Process.* Dubuque, Iowa: W. C. Brown Co., 1976.

HARTOGS, RENATUS, and ARTZT, ERIC. *Violence: Causes and Solutions.* New York: Dell Publishing Co., 1970.

HEARN, JEFF. *The Gender of Oppression: Men, Masculinity, and the Critique of Women.* Brighton, England: John Spiers, 1987.

HEATH, HARRIET, SCATTERGOOD, SARA, and MEYER, SANDRA. *Learning About*

Parenting: Learning to Care (handbook). Philadelphia: Education for Parenting, 1983.

HERTSGAARD, MARK. *On Bended Knee*. New York: Farrar, Straus and Giroux, 1988.

HERZIG, ALISON C., and MALI, JANE L., *Oh Boy! Babies!* Boston: Little, Brown, 1980.

HOCHSCHILD, ARLIE, with MACHUNG, ANNE. *The Second Shift: Working Parents and the Revolution at Home*. New York: Viking Penguin, 1989.

HOFFMAN, MARTIN L. "Empathy, Its Development and Prosocial Implications," *Nebraska Symposium on Motivation* 25 (1978), pp. 169–218.

———. "Is Altruism Part of Human Nature?" *Journal of Personality and Social Psychology* 40 (1981), pp. 121–37.

———. "Sex Differences in Empathy and Related Behaviors," *Psychological Bulletin* 84 (1977), pp. 712–22.

HOLLANDER, HARRIET E., and TURNER, FLOYD D. "Characteristics of Incarcerated Delinquents: Relationship Between Developmental Disorders, Environmental and Family Factors, and Patterns of Offense and Recidivism," *Journal of Child Psychiatry* 24 (March 1985), pp. 221–26.

HOLT, ROBERT R. "Converting the War System to a Peace System." Paper prepared for a conference of the Exploratory Project on the Conditions of Peace, Cohasset, Mass., May 1987.

———. "Drive or Wish? A Reconsideration of the Psychoanalytical Theory of Motivation," *Psychological Issues* (*Psychology Versus Metapsychology*), Vol. 9., Monograph No. 36. M. M. Gill and P. S. Holzman, eds. New York: International Universities Press, 1976, pp. 158–197.

———. "Freud's Mechanistic and Humanistic Images of Man," *Psychoanalysis and Contemporary Science*, Vol. 1, R. R. Holt and E. Peterfreund, eds. New York: Macmillan, 1972, pp. 3–24.

———. "On the Interpersonal and Intrapersonal Consequences of Expressing or Not Expressing Anger," *Journal of Consulting and Clinical Psychology* 35 (1970), pp. 8–12.

HORNEY, KAREN. *Feminine Psychology*, Harold Kelman, ed. New York: The Norton Library, 1973.

HOSPERS, JOHN, ed. "Sociobiology and Philosophy," *The Monist* 67 (April 1984).

HOSTETLER, JOHN A. *Hutterite Society*. Baltimore: The Johns Hopkins Press, 1974.

HRDY, SARAH BLAFFER. *The Woman That Never Evolved*. Cambridge: Harvard University Press, 1981.

HUIZINGA, JOHAN. *Homo Ludens: A Study of the Play Element in Culture*. Boston: The Beacon Press, 1955.

HUMPHREYS, ANNE P., and SMITH, PETER K. "Rough and Tumble, Friendship, and Dominance in Schoolchildren: Evidence for Continuity and Change with Age," *Child Development* 58 (February 1987), pp. 201–12.

Institute for Economic and Policy Studies. *Programming for Mentally Retarded and Learning Disabled Inmates: A Guide for Correctional Administrators*. Prepared for the U.S. Department of Justice: National Institute of Corrections, Washington, D.C., January 1989.

Interagency Committee on Learning Disabilities. *Learning Disabilities: A Report to the U.S. Congress.* Washington, D.C.: Interagency Committee on Learning disabilities, 1987.

ISAY, RICHARD A. *Being Homosexual: Gay Men and Their Development.* New York: Farrar, Straus & Giroux, 1989.

JAMES, WILLIAM. "The Moral Equivalent of War," *Essays on Faith and Morals,* Ralph Barton Perry, ed. New York: New American Library, 1974.

JANOWITZ, MORRIS. *The Reconstruction of Patriotism.* Chicago: University of Chicago Press, 1983.

JEFFERSON, THOMAS. Letter to Kercheval, July 12, 1816, in *Social and Political Philosophy,* John Somerville and Ronald E. Santoni, eds. Garden City, N.Y.: Doubleday and Co., 1963.

JOHNSON, NICHOLAS, and DYSTEL, JOHN JAY. "A Day in the Life: The Federal Communications Commission," *The Yale Law Journal* 82 (July 1973), pp. 1675–1734.

JOHNSON, ROBERT A. *He: Understanding Masculine Psychology.* New York: Harper and Row, 1977.

JOHNSON, WILLIAM OSCAR. "Sports and Suds: The Beer Business and the Sports World Have Brewed Up a Potent Partnership," *Sports Illustrated* (August 8, 1988), pp. 70–82.

JOSEPH, PAUL, and ROSENBLUM, SIMON, eds. *Search for Sanity: The Politics of Nuclear Weapons and Disarmament.* Boston: South End Press, 1984.

KAPLAN, ALEXANDRA. "Human Sex-Hormone Abnormalities Viewed from an Androgynous Perspective: A Reconsideration of the Work of John Money," *The Psychology of Sex Differences and Sex Roles,* J. E. Parsons, ed. New York: Hemisphere Publishing, 1980.

KATZ, JACK. *Seductions of Crime: Moral and Sensual Attractions in Doing Evil.* New York: Basic Books, 1988.

KAVANAGH, JAMES F., and TRUSS, TOM J., eds. *Learning Disabilities: Proceedings of the National Conference.* Parkton, Md.: York Press, 1988.

KEEGAN, JOHN. *The Face of Battle.* New York: Penguin Books, 1983.

KELLER, EVELYN FOX. *Reflections on Gender and Science.* New Haven: Yale University Press, 1985.

KENNAN, GEORGE F. *The Nuclear Delusion: Soviet-American Relations in the Atomic Age.* New York: Pantheon Books, 1983.

KING, PAUL. "Heavy Metal Music and Drug Abuse in Adolescents," *Postgraduate Medicine* 83 (April 1988), pp. 295–304.

KITCHER, PHILIP. *Vaulting Ambition: Sociobiology and the Quest for Human Nature.* Cambridge: MIT Press, 1985.

KITTAY, EVA FEDER, and MEYERS, DIANA T., eds. *Women and Moral Theory.* Totowa, N.J.: Rowman & Littlefield, 1987.

KLASS, PERRI, and WALLIS, LILA. "Macho Medicine," *Lear's* (October 1989).

KLEIMAN, HOWARD M. "Indecent Programming on Cable Television: Legal and Social Dimensions," *Journal of Broadcasting and Electronic Media* 3 (Summer 1986), pp. 275–94.

KOESTNER, RICHARD, FRANZ, CAROL, and WEINBERGER, JOEL. "The Family Origins of Empathic Concern: A 26-Year Longitudinal Study," *Journal of Personality and Social Psychology* 58 (1990), pp. 709–17.

KOHN, ALFIE. *No Contest: The Case Against Competition.* Boston: Houghton Mifflin Co., 1986.

KOHN, HANS. *Nationalism: Its Meaning and History.* Melbourne, Fla.: R. E. Krieger, 1982.

KOHUT, HEINZ. *The Search for the Self: Selected Writings of Heinz Kohut,* Vol. 2, Paul Ornstein, ed. Madison, Conn.: International Universities Press, 1989.

KONNER, MELVIN. *The Tangled Wing: Biological Constraints on the Human Spirit.* New York: Harper and Row, 1983.

KOONZ, CLAUDIA. *Mothers in the Fatherland: Women, the Family, and Nazi Politics.* New York: St. Martin's Press, 1987.

KOPAY, DAVID, and YOUNG, PERRY DEANE. *The David Kopay Story.* New York: Donald I. Fine, 1980.

KOTZ, NICK. *Wild Blue Yonder: Money, Politics and the B-1 Bomber.* Princeton: Princeton University Press, 1988.

KOVIC, RON. *Born on the Fourth of July.* New York: Pocket Books, 1977.

KRATTENMAKER, THOMAS G., and POWE, L. A. "Televised Violence: First Amendment Principles and Social Science Theory," *Virginia Law Review* 64 (December 1978), pp. 1125–1297.

KREIDLER, WILLIAM J. *Creative Conflict Resolution.* Glenview, Ill.: Scott, Foresman and Co., 1984.

KUBIE, LAWRENCE S. "The Fallacious Use of Quantitative Concepts in Dynamic Psychology, *Psychological Issues" (Symbol and Neurosis, Selected Papers of Lawrence S. Kubie),* 11, Monograph No. 44 (1978), pp. 41–51.

KUHN, THOMAS S. *The Structure of Scientific Revolutions.* Chicago: The University of Chicago Press, 1962.

KULL, STEVEN. *Minds at War: Nuclear Reality and the Inner Conflicts of Defense Policy Makers.* New York: Basic Books, 1988.

———. "Nuclear Nonsense," *Foreign Policy* 58 (Spring 1985), pp. 28–52.

KUTASH, I. L., KUTASH, S. B., and Schlesinger and Associates, eds. *Violence: Perspectives on Murder and Aggression.* San Francisco: Josey-Bass, 1978.

LABUNSKI, RICHARD E. *The First Amendment Under Siege.* Westport, Conn.: Greenwood Press, 1981.

LAFARGE, PHYLLIS. "Nuclear Teaching: Propaganda or Problem Solving?" *Bulletin of the Atomic Scientists* (July/August 1988), pp. 14–20.

———. *The Strangelove Legacy: Children, Parents, and Teachers in the Nuclear Age.* New York: Harper and Row, 1987.

LAMB, MICHAEL E., ed. *The Father's Role: Cross Cultural Perspectives.* Hillsdale, N.J.: L. Erlbaum, 1987.

———. *Nontraditional Families.* Hillsdale, N.J.: L. Erlbaum, 1982.

———. *The Role of the Father in Child Development.* New York: John Wiley and Sons, 1981.

LAMB, MICHAEL E., PLECK, JOSEPH H., and LEVINE, JAMES A. "The Role of the Father in Child Development: The Effects of Increased Paternal Involve-

338   BIBLIOGRAPHY

ment," *Advances in Clinical Psychology* 8, B. Lahey and A. Kazdin, eds. New York: Plenum, 1985.

LAMB, MICHAEL E., and SAGI, ABRAHAM, eds. *Fatherhood and Family Policy.* Hillsdale, N.J.: L. Erlbaum, 1983.

LAPCHICK, RICHARD E. *Fractured Focus: Sport as a Reflection of Society.* Lexington, Mass.: D. C. Heath and Co., 1986.

LAZERE, DONALD, ed. *American Media and Mass Culture.* Berkeley: University of California Press, 1987.

LEE, PATRICK C., and STEWART, ROBERT SUSSMAN. *Sex Differences: Cultural and Developmental Dimensions.* New York: Urizen Books, 1976.

LERCH, STEVE. "The Adjustment of Athletes to Career Ending Injuries," *Arena Review* 8 (March 4, 1984), pp. 54–67.

LERNER, GERDA. *The Creation of Patriarchy.* Oxford: Oxford University Press, 1986.

LEVIN, JACK, and FOX, JAMES ALAN. *Mass Murder: America's Growing Menace.* New York: Plenum Press, 1984.

LEVINE, JAMES A. *Who Will Raise the Children? New Options for Fathers (and Mothers)* New York: Bantam Books, 1977.

LEWIS, DOROTHY OTNOW, et al. *"Intrinsic and Environmental Characteristics of Juvenile Murders,"* Journal of the American Academy of Child and Adolescent Psychiatry 27 (1988), pp. 582–87.

————. "Psychomotor Epilepsy and Violence in a Group of Incarcerated Adolescent Boys," *American Journal of Psychiatry* 139 (July 1982), pp. 882–87.

LEWIS, ROBERT A., ed. *Men in Difficult Times: Masculinity Today and Tomorrow.* Englewood Cliffs, N.J.: Prentice-Hall, 1981.

LIEBERT, ROBERT M., and SPRAFKIN, JOYCE. *The Early Window: Effects of Television on Children and Youth.* New York: Pergamon Press, 1988.

LIFTON, ROBERT JAY. *The Nazi Doctors: Medical Killing and the Psychology of Genocide.* New York: Basic Books, 1986.

LINZ, DANIEL, PENROD, STEVEN, and DONNERSTEIN, EDWARD. "Issues Bearing on the Legal Regulation of Violent and Sexually Violent Media," *Journal of Social Issues* 42 (Fall 1986), pp. 171–93.

LLOYD, GENEVIEVE. *The Man of Reason.* Minneapolis: University of Minnesota Press, 1984.

LORENZ, KONRAD. *Behind the Mirror: A Search for a Natural History of Human Knowledge,* Ronald Taylor, trans. San Diego, Calif.: Harcourt Brace Jovanovich, 1978.

————. *On Aggression.* New York: Bantam Books, 1971.

LUNDBERG, GEORGE D. "Boxing Should Be Banned in Civilized Countries— Round 3," *Journal of the American Medical Association* 255 (May 9, 1986), pp. 2483–85.

LUNDE, DONALD T. *Murder and Madness.* New York: W. W. Norton and Co., 1975.

LUDWIG, ROBERT. "Making Boxing Safer," *Journal of the American Medical Association* 255 (May 9, 1986). p. 2482.

LURCAT, LILIANE. *Violence à la télé: l'enfant fascine.* Paris: Editions Syros, 1989.

MACCOBY, ELEANOR. *Social Development: Psychological Growth and the Parent-Child Relationship.* New York: Harcourt Brace Jovanovich, 1980.

————, ed. *The Development of Sex Differences.* Stanford: Stanford University Press, 1966.

MACCOBY, ELEANOR, and JACKLIN, CAROL NAGY. *The Psychology of Sex Differences,* Vol. 1. Stanford: Stanford University Press, 1974.

————. "Sex Differences in Aggression: A Rejoinder and Reprise," *Child Development* 51 (1980), pp. 964–80.

MCALLISTER, PAM, ed. *Reweaving the Web of Life: Feminism and Nonviolence.* Philadelphia: New Society Publishers, 1982.

MCCARTHY, COLMAN. "Study War No More," *The Progressive* 50 (November 1986), pp. 26–29.

MCINALLY, PAT. *Moms and Dads and Kids and Sports.* New York: Ivy Books, 1989.

MACKINNON, CATHARINE A. *Feminism Unmodified.* Cambridge: Harvard University Press, 1987.

MCNAMARA, ROBERT S. *Blundering into Disaster: Surviving the First Century of the Nuclear Age.* New York: Pantheon Books, 1986.

MAGUIRE, JOSEPH I., and BENSON, WILLIAM E. "Retinal Injury and Detachment in Boxers," *Journal of the American Medical Association* 255 (May 9, 1986), pp. 2451–53.

MANCHESTER, WILLIAM. "The Bloodiest Battle of All," *New York Times Magazine* (June 14, 1987).

MANSFIELD, SUE. *The Gestalts of War: An Inquiry into Its Origins and Meanings as a Social Institution.* New York: The Dial Press, 1982.

MAREK, ELIZABETH. "The Lives of Teenage Mothers," *Harper's* (April 1989), pp. 56–62.

MAWSON, A., GROUNDS, A., and TANTAM, D. "Violence and Asperger's Syndrome: A Case Study," *British Journal of Psychiatry* 147 (1985), pp. 566–69.

MAY, ERNEST R. *"Lessons" of the Past: The Use and Misuse of History in American Foreign Policy.* Oxford: Oxford University Press, 1973.

MAY, ROBERT. *Sex and Fantasy: Patterns of Male and Female Development.* New York: W. W. Norton and Co., 1980.

MEAD, MARGARET. *Male and Female: A Study of the Sexes in a Changing World.* New York: New American Library, 1962.

————. *Sex and Temperament in Three Primitive Societies.* New York: Dell Publishing Co., 1969 (1935).

MEGGYESY, DAVE. *Out of Their League.* Berkeley: Ramparts Press, 1970.

MELMAN, SEYMOUR. *Pentagon Capitalism: The Political Economy of War.* New York: McGraw-Hill, 1970.

MELSON, GAIL F., and FOGEL, ALAN. "Learning to Care," *Psychology Today* (January 1988).

MENDOZA, A. *The Effects of Exposure to Toys Conducive to Violence.* Unpublished doctoral dissertation. University of Miami, 1972.

MESSNER, MICHAEL. "When Bodies Are Weapons: Masculinity and Violence in Sport," *International Review of Sociology of Sport* (August 1990).

Metis Associates. *The Resolving Conflict Creatively Program: A Summary of Significant Findings,* New York: Metis Associates (November 1988).

MICHENER, JAMES A. *Sports in America*. Greenwich, Conn.: Fawcett Publications, 1976.

MIDGLEY, MARY. *Beast and Man: The Roots of Human Nature*. Ithaca: Cornell University Press, 1978.

MILGRAM, STANLEY. *Obedience to Authority*. New York: Harper Torchbooks, 1974.

MILGRAM, STANLEY, and SHOTLAND, R. LANCE. *Television and Antisocial Behavior*. New York: Academic Press, 1973.

MILL, JOHN STUART. *On Liberty*. New York: The Liberal Arts Press, 1956.

————. "The Subjection of Women," *Essays on Sex Equality* by John Stuart Mill and Harriet Taylor Mill. Alice S. Rossi, ed. Chicago: The University of Chicago Press, 1970.

————. *Utilitarianism*. Indianapolis: Hackett Publishing Company, 1979.

MILLER, ALICE. *For Your Own Good: Hidden Cruelty in Childrearing and the Roots of Violence*, Hildegarde and Hunter Hannum, trans. New York: Farrar, Straus and Giroux, 1983.

MILLER, JEAN BAKER. *Toward a New Psychology of Woman*. Boston: Beacon Press, 1976.

MILLER, WALTER B. "Lower Class Culture as a Generating Milieu of Gang Delinquency," *The Sociology of Crime and Delinquency*, Marvin E. Wolfgang, Leonard Savitz, and Norman Johnston, eds. New York: John Wiley and Sons, 1962.

MITGANG, HERBERT, ed. *Abraham Lincoln: A Press Portrait*. Chicago: Quadrangle Books, 1971.

MITSCHERLICH, MARGARETE. *The Peaceable Sex: On Aggression in Women and Men*, Craig Tomlinson, trans. New York: Fromm International Publishing Corp., 1987.

Model Peace Education Program. *Resolving Conflict Creatively: A Draft Teaching Guide for Grades Kindergarten–Six*. New York: Educators for Social Responsibility and New York City Board of Education, 1987.

MONEY, JOHN, and EHRHARDT, ANKE. *Man and Woman, Boy and Girl*. Baltimore: The Johns Hopkins University Press, 1972.

MONTAGU, ASHLEY, ed. *Man and Aggression*. Oxford: Oxford University Press, 1973.

————. *Sociobiology Examined*. New York: Oxford University Press, 1980.

MOORE, SHEILA, and FROST, ROON. *The Little Boy Book: A Guide to the First Eight Years*. New York: Clarkson N. Potter, 1986.

MORRIS, DESMOND. *The Naked Ape*. New York: Dell Publishing Co., 1967.

MORRIS, RICHARD. *Evolution and Human Nature*. New York: Seaview/Putnam, 1983.

MORRISON, ROBERT GLENN. "Medical and Public Health Aspects of Boxing," *Journal of the American Medical Association* 255 (May 9, 1986), pp. 2475–80.

MOSHER, DONALD L., and TOMKINS, SILVAN S. "Scripting the Macho Man: Hypermasculine Socialization and Enculturation," *The Journal of Sex Research* 25 (February 1988), pp. 60–84.

MUMFORD, LEWIS. *The Pentagon of Power: The Myth of the Machine*. Vol. 2. New York: Harcourt Brace Jovanovich, 1964.

NADER, RALPH, and RILEY, CLAIRE. "Oh, Say Can You See: A Broadcast Network for the Audience," *The Journal of Law and Politics* (Fall 1988).

National Center for Learning Disabilities. *Their World.* New York: National Center for Learning Disabilities, 1989.

National Coalition on Television Violence. *NCTV News.* P.O. Box 2157, Champaign, Illinois 61825.

National Institute of Mental Health. *Television and Behavior: Ten Years of Scientific Progress and Implications for the Eighties.* Rockville, Md.: National Institute of Mental Health, 1982.

NICHOLS, JACK. *Men's Liberation: A New Definition of Masculinity.* New York: Penguin Books, 1975.

NICHOLSON, JACK. *Men and Women: How Different Are They?* Oxford: Oxford University Press, 1984.

NOVAK, MICHAEL. *The Joy of Sports.* New York: Basic Books, 1976.

OATES, JOYCE CAROL. *On Boxing.* Garden City, N.Y.: Dolphin/Doubleday, 1987.

OATES, JOYCE CAROL, and HALPERN, DANIEL, eds. *Reading the Fights.* New York: Henry Holt and Co., 1988.

OGILVIE, BRUCE C., and TUTKO, THOMAS A. "Sport: If You Want to Build Character, Try Something Else," *Psychology Today* (October 1971).

OLWEUS, DAN. "Bully/Victim Problems Among Schoolchildren: Basic Facts and Effects of a School-Based Intervention Program," *The Development and Treatment of Childhood Aggression,* K. Rubin and D. Pepler, eds. Hillsdale, N.J.: L. Erlbaum, 1989.

OLWEUS, DAN, BLOCK, JACK, and RADKE-YARROW, MARIAN, eds. *The Development of Antisocial and Prosocial Behavior.* New York: Academic Press, 1986.

ORIARD, MICHAEL. *The End of Autumn.* Garden City, N.Y.: Doubleday and Co., 1982.

OSHERSON, SAMUEL. *Finding Our Fathers.* New York: Fawcett Book Group, 1987.

PADUS, EMRIKA. "Do War Toys Make Sense? Two Top Experts Debate," *Good Toys* (Fall 1986), pp. 26–28.

PALMER, EDWARD L. *Television and America's Children: A Crisis of Neglect.* Oxford: Oxford University Press, 1988.

PARKER, HILDA, and PARKER, SEYMOUR. "Father-Daughter Sexual Abuse: An Emerging Perspective," *American Journal of Orthopsychiatry* 56 (October 1986), pp. 531–49.

PARSONS, JACQUELINE E. "Psycho-Sex Neutrality: Is Anatomy Destiny?" *The Psychology of Sex Differences and Sex Roles,* J. E. Parsons, ed. New York: Hemisphere Publishing Corp., 1980.

PATTERSON, G. R., LITTMAN, R. A., and BRICKER, W. "Assertive Behavior in Children: A Step Toward a Theory of Aggression," *Monographs of the Society for Research in Child Development* 32 (1967), pp. 1–41.

PATTERSON, RUSSEL H. "On Boxing and Liberty," *Journal of the American Medical Association* 255 (May 9, 1986), p. 2481–82.

PERRET, GEOFFREY. *A Country Made by War: A Story of America's Rise to Power.* New York: Random House, 1989.

PHILLIPS, DAVID P. "The Impact of Mass Media Violence on U.S. Homicides," *American Sociological Review* 48 (August 1983), pp. 560–68.

342 BIBLIOGRAPHY

PLECK, JOSEPH H. *The Myth of Masculinity*. Cambridge: The MIT Press, 1983.

PLECK, JOSEPH H., and SAWYER, JACK. *Men and Masculinity*. Englewood Cliffs, N.J.: Prentice-Hall, 1974.

POGREBIN, LETTY COTTIN. *Growing Up Free: Raising Your Child in the 80's*. New York: Bantam Books, 1981.

POSTMAN, NEIL. "The Blurring of Childhood and the Media," *Religious Education* 82 (Spring 1987), pp. 293–97.

———. *The Disappearance of Childhood*. New York: Delacorte Press, 1982.

PRESCOTT, JAMES W. "Body Pleasure and the Origins of Violence," *Bulletin of the Atomic Scientists* (November 1975), pp. 10–20.

PRINSKY, LORRAINE E., and ROSENBAUM, JILL L. " 'Leer-ics' or Lyrics: Teenage Impressions of Rock 'n' Roll," *Youth and Society* 18 (1987), pp. 384–96.

PRUETT, KYLE D. *The Nurturing Father*. New York: Warner Books, 1987.

RANELAGH, E. L. *Men on Women*. London: Quartet Books, 1985.

RASOR, DINA. *The Pentagon Underground*. New York: Times Books, 1985.

REARDON, BETTY A. *Sexism and the War System*. New York: Teachers College Press, 1985.

ROCHLIN, GREGORY. *Man's Aggression*. New York: Dell Publishing Co., 1973.

ROSENBLOOM, DAVID H. *Public Administration*. New York: Random House, 1986.

ROWLAND, WILLARD D., Jr. *The Politics of TV Violence*. Beverly Hills: Sage Publications, 1983.

RUBIN, JEFFREY Z., PROVENZANO, FRANK J., and LURIA, ZELLA. "The Eye of the Beholder: Parents' Views on Sex of Newborns," *American Journal of Orthopsychiatry* 44 (July 1974), pp. 512–19.

RUBIN, LILLIAN B. *Intimate Strangers: Men and Women Together*. New York: Harper and Row, 1983.

RUBINSTEIN, ELI A. "The TV Violence Report: What's Next?" *Journal of Communication* 24 (Winter 1974) pp. 266–71.

RUDDICK, SARA. *Maternal Thinking: Towards a Politics of Peace*. Boston: Beacon Press, 1989.

RUITENBEEK, HENDRIK M., ed. *Psychoanalysis and Male Sexuality*. New Haven: College and University Press, 1966.

RYERSON, ANDRÉ. "The Scandal of 'Peace Education,' " *Commentary* (April 1985), pp. 37–46.

SAGAN, ELI. *The Lust to Annihilate: A Psychoanalytic Study of Violence in Ancient Greek Culture*. New York: Psychohistory Press, 1979.

SAGE, GEORGE H. "Blaming the Victim" : NCAA Responses to Calls for Reform in Major College Sports," *Arena Review* 11 (November 1987), pp. 1–11.

———. "Psychosocial Implications of Youth Sports Programs," *Arena Review* 2 (Winter 1978), p. 18–22.

SAHLINS, MARSHALL, *The Use and Abuse of Biology*. Ann Arbor: The University of Michigan Press, 1977.

SAMMONS, JEFFREY. *Beyond the Ris: The Role of Boxing in American Society*. Champaign: University of Illinois Press, 1988.

———. "Why Physicians Should Oppose Boxing: An Interdisciplinary History Perspective," *Journal of the American Medical Association* 261 (March 10, 1989), pp. 1484–86.

SAMPSON, RONALD V. *The Psychology of Power*. New York: Vintage Books, 1968.

SANDAY, PEGGY REEVES. *Female Power and Male Dominance: On the Origins of Sexual Inequality*. Cambridge: Cambridge University Press, 1981.

SANDMAN, PETER M., RUBIN, DAVID M., and SACHSMAN, DAVID B. *Media: An Introductory Analysis of American Mass Communications*. Englewood Cliffs, N.J.: Prentice-Hall, 1982.

SCHILLER, HERBERT I. "Corporate Speech, Power Politics, and the First Amendment," *The Independent* (July 1988), pp. 10–13.

SCHULMAN, MICHAEL, and MEKLER, EVA. *Bringing Up a Moral Child*. Reading, Mass.: Addison-Wesley, 1985.

SCHWARTZ, SIDNEY, and O'CONNOR, JOHN R. *Exploring Our Nation's History*. Englewood Cliffs, N.J.: Globe Publishers, 1984.

SHARP, GENE. *Social Power and Political Freedom*. Boston: Porter Sargent, 1980.

SHATAN, CHAIM F. "Bogus Manhood, Bogus Honor: Surrender and Transfiguration in the United States Marine Corps," *Psychoanalytic Review* 64 (Winter 1977), pp. 585–610.

SHORT, JAMES F., and WOLFGANG, MARVIN E. *Collective Violence*. Chicago: Aldine Artheron, 1972.

SIANN, GERDA. *Accounting for Aggression*. Boston: Allen and Unwin, 1985.

SINGER, DOROTHY G. "Does Violent Television Produce Aggressive Children?" *Pediatric Annals* 14 (December 1985), pp. 804, 807–810.

SINGER, DOROTHY G., and SINGER, JEROME L. "Family Experiences and Television Viewing as Predictors of Children's Imagination, Restlessness, and Aggression," *Journal of Social Issues* 42 (1986), pp. 107–124.

———. "Raising Boys Who Know How To Love," *Parents* (December 1977). *Popular Magazine*

———. "Some Hazards of Growing Up in a Television Environment: Children's Aggression and Restlessness," *Applied Social Psychology Annual* 8, Stuart Oskamp, ed. Beverly Hills: Sage Publications, 1988.

———. "Television Viewing and Aggressive Behavior in Preschool Children: A Field Study," *Annals of the New York Academy of Sciences* 347 (1980), pp. 289–303.

SIPES, RICHARD G. "War, Sports and Aggression: An Empirical Test of Two Rival Theories," *American Anthropologist* 75 (1973), pp. 64–86.

SKORNIA, HARRY J. *Television and Society*. New York: McGraw-Hill, 1965.

SMITH, HEDRICK. *The Power Game: How Washington Works*. New York: Random House, 1988.

SMITH, MICHAEL D. *Violence and Sport*. Toronto: Butterworth and Co., 1983.

SONKIN, DANIEL JAY, and DURPHY, MICHAEL. *Learning to Live Without Violence: A Handbook for Men*. San Francisco: Volcano Press, 1982.

SPENCER, MIRANDA. "What Are We Teaching Our Kids?" *Nuclear Times* (September/October 1988), pp. 17–20.

SPRAFKIN, JOYCE, and GADOW, KENNETH, "Television Viewing Habits of Emotionally Disturbed, Learning Disabled, and Mentally Retarded Children," *Journal of Applied Developmental Psychology* 7 (Jan–March 1986), pp. 45–59.

STARK-ADAMEC, C. ed., *Sex Roles*. Montreal: Eden Press Women's Publications, 1980.

344   BIBLIOGRAPHY

STEINFELD, JESSE L. "TV Violence Is Harmful," *Readers Digest,* April 1973.

STIPP, H. "Children's Knowledge of and Taste in Popular Music," *Popular Music and Society* 10 (1985), pp. 1–15.

STORR, ANTHONY. *Human Aggression.* New York: Bantam Books, 1970.

STROM, MARGOT STERN, and PARSONS, WILLIAM S. *Facing History and Ourselves: Holocaust and Human Behavior.* Watertown, Mass.: Intentional Educations, 1982.

STUBBING, RICHARD A., and MENDEL, RICHARD A. *The Defense Game: An Insider Explores the Astonishing Realities of America's Defense Establishment.* New York: Harper and Row, 1986.

SUTTON-SMITH, BRIAN. *Toys as Culture.* New York: Gardner Press, 1986.

SYMONS, DONALD. *The Evolution of Human Sexuality.* Oxford: Oxford University Press, 1979.

TAVRIS, CAROL, and WADE, CAROL. *The Longest War: Sex Differences in Perspective.* San Diego: Harcourt Brace Jovanovich, 1977.

TEC, NECHAMA. *When Light Pierced the Darkness: Christian Rescue of Jews in Nazi-Occupied Poland.* Oxford: Oxford University Press, 1986.

TERKEL, STUDS. *The Good War: An Oral History of World War II.* New York: Ballantine Books, 1985.

THAYER, FREDERICK C. *An End to Hierarchy and Competition.* New York: Franklin Watts, 1981.

THELIN, BENGT. "What to Do About War Toys: The Swedish Experience," *Prospects* 16 (1986), pp. 505–11.

THEWELEIT, KLAUS. *Male Fantasies, Vol. 1,* Stephen Conway, trans. Minneapolis: University of Minnesota Press, 1987.

THOMPSON, KEITH. "What Men Really Want: A New Age Interview with Robert Bly," *New Age* (May 1982), pp. 30–51.

TIEGER, TODD. "On the Biological Basis of Sex Differences," *Child Development* 51 (1980), pp. 943–63.

TIGER, LIONEL. *Men in Groups.* New York: Marion Boyars, 1984.

TOCH, H. *Violent Men: An Inquiry into the Psychology of Violence.* Harmondsworth: Penguin, 1972.

TOLES, TERRI. "Video Games and American Military Ideology," *Arena Review* 9 (March 1985), pp. 58–73.

TUNSTALL, JEREMY. *Communications Deregulation.* New York: Basil Blackwell, 1986.

TURNER, CHARLES W., and GOLDSMITH, DIANE. "Effects of Toy Guns and Airplanes on Children's Antisocial Free Play Behavior," *Journal of Experimental Child Psychology* 21 (1976), pp. 303–15.

TWITCHELL, JAMES B. *Preposterous Violence: Fables of Aggression in Modern Culture.* Oxford: Oxford University Press, 1989.

National Council of Churches. *Violence and Sexual Violence in Film, Television, Cable and Home Video.* New York: National Council of Churches (September 19, 1985).

U.S. Bureau of the Census. *Statistical Abstract of the United States:* Washington, D.C.: U.S. Bureau of the Census, 1990.

U.S. Department of Justice, Bureau of Justice Statistics. *Children in Custody,*

1975–85: Census of Public and Private Juvenile Detention, Correctional, and Shelter Facilities. Washington, D.C.: U.S. Department of Justice, 1989.

WASS, HANNELORE, et al. "Adolescents' Interest in and Views of Destructive Themes in Rock Music," *Omega* 19 (1988–89), pp. 177–86.

WATTLETON, FAYE, "The Case for National Action," *The Nation* (July 24–31, 1989), pp. 138–41.

WEIL, SIMONE. *Iliad; or, The Poem of Force,* Mary McCarthy, trans. Wallingford, Pa.: Pendle Hill, 1945.

WHITING, BEATRICE B. "Sex Identity Conflict and Physical Violence: A Comparative Study," *The Ethnography of Law* 67, pt. 2, Laura Nader, ed. Menasha, Wis.: American Anthropological Association, 1965, pp. 123–40.

WHITING, BEATRICE B., and EDWARDS, CAROLYN POPE. *Children of Different Worlds.* Cambridge: Harvard University Press, 1988.

WHITING, BEATRICE B., and WHITING, JOHN W. M. *Children of Six Cultures: A Psycho-cultural Analysis.* Cambridge: Harvard University Press, 1975.

WHITING, JOHN, KLUCKHOHN, RICHARD, and ANTHONY ALBERT. "The Function of Male Initiation Ceremonies at Puberty," *Readings in Social Psychology,* E. E. Maccoby, T. M. Newcomb, and E. L. Hartley, eds. New York: Holt, 1958.

WILLOCK, BRENT. "The Devalued (Unloved, Repugnant) Self—A Second Facet of Narcissistic Vulnerability in the Aggressive, Conduct-Disordered Child," *Psychoanalytic Psychology* 4 (1987), pp. 219–40.

———. "Narcissistic Vulnerability in the Hyperaggressive Child: The Disregarded (Unloved, Uncared-for) Self," *Psychoanalytic Psychology* 3 (1986), pp. 59–80.

WILSON, EDWARD O. *On Human Nature.* New York: Bantam Books, 1982.

———. *Sociobiology: The New Synthesis.* Cambridge: Harvard University Press, 1975.

WILSON, JAMES Q., and HERRNSTEIN, RICHARD J. *Crime and Human Nature.* New York: Simon and Schuster, 1985.

———. *The Politics of Regulation.* New York: Basic Books, 1980, pp. 357–95.

WINN, MARIE. *Children Without Childhood.* New York: Pantheon, 1981.

YEAGER, R. C. *Seasons of Shame: The New Violence in Sports.* New York: McGraw-Hill, 1979.

ZABLOCKI, BENJAMIN. *The Joyful Community: An Account of the Bruderhof, a Communal Movement Now in Its Third Generation.* Harmondsworth: Penguin Books, 1971.

ZAPPA, FRANK. "On Junk Food for the Soul," *New Perspectives Quarterly* (Winter 1988), pp. 26–29.

ZUCKERMAN, DIANA M., SINGER, DOROTHY G., and SINGER, JEROME L. "Children's Television Viewing, Racial and Sex-Role Attitudes," *Journal of Applied Social Psychology* 10 (1980), pp. 281–94.

Index

ABOUT THE AUTHOR

Myriam Miedzian holds a Ph.D. in philosophy from Columbia University and a Master's in Clinical Social Work from Hunter College, City University of New York. Both her degrees and her publications—in the popular and academic press—reflect her interest in applying critical thinking and research findings to issues of public concern. Dr. Miedzian has been a professor of philosophy at a number of universities, including Rutgers and the City University of New York.